THE

Fly

THE *Fly*

ANDREW HERD

THE MEDLAR PRESS LTD
ELLESMERE

Published by The Medlar Press Limited,
The Grange, Ellesmere, Shropshire.
www.medlarpress.com

ISBN 1899 600 297

First published as a limited edition hardback in 2001

This paperback edition published 2003

Designed and typeset in 10 on 11½pt Bembo Roman by Jonathan Ward-Allen.
Chapter line illustrations by Paul Cook.
Produced in England by The Medlar Press Limited, Ellesmere.

For every man who wishes
to know all about fishing,
there are a dozen
willing to tell him.

Dedication and Acknowledgements

This book is dedicated to fly fishing historians everywhere, and to my fishing partner Patrick Annesley, who should really have written this, but between the jigs and the reels, never got round to putting pen to paper. We talked so much about fly fishing history in the fishing room at Anne's Grove that the subject seeped into my soul.

My thanks also go to David Beazley and to Fred Buller, for taking time out to read the manuscript, and for giving me their usual patient and sound advice. The book would have been far less than it is without them. Much of the section on early Spanish fly fishing history could not have been completed without the generous help of Tino Corderas i Pol, and Dr Goran Grubic deserves special mention for all the time he spent advising me on traditional fly fishing in former Yugoslavia, at a time when he should have been editing a book on ruminant nutrition.

I am also in special debt to Gary Tanner, Ken Cameron, Paul Schmookler and Professor Richard Hoffmann, for all their ideas and contributions.

Paul Schullery deserves special mention because his writing made me look beyond the conventional hagiography of fly fishing. *American Fly Fishing* is probably the most entertaining and authoritative work ever published on the history of fly fishing in North America. It was the book that inspired me to write *The Fly* and if you enjoy the pages which follow, I suggest you put it next on your list.

I think that John Betts put it in a nutshell when he wrote to me and said that 'the level of dedication assigned to creating and sharing the knowledge [of fly fishing history] obtained is still as high as it ever was'. Never was a truer word said; I have received help everywhere I have turned, from people only too delighted to be of assistance. John in particular has been pure gold. I only hope that I can do the same for someone else when the time comes.

Finally, I would like to make a special mention of Hector Yamasaki, who runs my web site at *www.flyfishinghistory.com,* on a server located many thousands of miles from where I live, in Mexico. I have never met Hector, and maybe I never will, but his endless generosity and tireless enthusiasm are typical of the spirit of the Internet.

Maybe there is hope for the human race after all.

Contents

Chapter 4 : The Early Nineteenth Century
163

Chapter 5 : The Late Nineteenth Century
213

Chapter 6 : The Dry Fly
269

Chapter 7 : The Twentieth Century
305

Foreword

Fred Buller

English readers who are interested in the history of angling are fortunate indeed because there are quite a few excellent books on the subject, the most famous and the most informative being William Radcliffe's *Fishing from the Earliest Times* (1921).[1] The authority and scholarship of Radcliffe's work has been equalled only by one other author - Richard Hoffmann, whose book *Fishers' Craft and Lettered Art: Tracts on Fishing from the End of the Middle Ages*[2] has been steadily impacting on angling historians since 1997.

If we select just one aspect of history, namely fly fishing, then without doubt John Waller Hills in *A History of Fly Fishing for Trout* (1921)[3] deserves an accolade for fine writing and for giving us the model of an unmuddled coherent account of the subject. However, I suspect that the next book to receive high acclaim is the one that you are about to read. Those who have already studied Hoffmann's closely argued case, set out in his essay *Fishing for sport in Medieval Europe: New Evidence* (1985),[4] will have a problem with their former loyalty to the John Waller Hills concept that 'the history of fly fishing begins at the close of the fifteenth century' and may want to bestow faith on Hoffmann as Andrew here has done. 'There is hard evidence,' he says, 'that fly fishing was widely practised in Europe as early as the beginning of the thirteenth century.'

From the above it is transparently obvious that we have come to a great divide and as a consequence Herd's book will be the first European angling book to carry Hoffmann's most important message that despite our invention of cricket, football, rugby and tennis, the British did not invent angling as a sport. Perhaps it is truer to say that Herd's book is the first to be published post divide for the benefit of fishermen who are interested in a comprehensive up-to-date history of all aspects of fly fishing, whereas Hoffmann's writings heretofore have mainly been for the benefit of the serious students of angling history.

Andrew Herd's text bristles with facts but the facts are usually blended with fresh and often colourful comments on the valuable and sometimes bizarre background material that has somehow eluded other authors. For instance, when dealing with fly fishing in classical times Herd runs through what is known of Martial's (as he does with ÆLian's) contribution to the history of fly fishing, but he also proffers some personal detail about these ancient authors. Not only are we told that Martial's real name is Marcus Valerius Martialis but we also discover that he was a poet and the author of no less than one thousand five hundred and sixty-one clever and occasionally obscene epigrams about life in ancient Rome.

As we leap from the ancients to the Middle Ages we sense that Herd won't be satisfied just to remind us that in 1496 Wynkyn de Worde added a fishing tract to the second edition of the Book of St Albans; embellishingly he writes:

> He squeezed into the same covers an unknown work which just happened to catch his eye, a manuscript called *A Treatyse of Fysshynge wyth an Angle.* Wynkyn didn't know at the time, but not only would the Treatyse become one of the most important books on fishing ever published; it would immortalise him.

Not content with a description of the activities of the first two English printers i.e. Caxton and de Worde, Herd gives us a run-down on early printing that turns out to be an immensely interesting diversion. I don't think that I shall ever forget this bald statistic - from 1455 when the printing press was invented until 1500, more than nine million books were printed. It's a lot of books in an age when only one in five could read.

Herd's grasp of all aspects of history seems to me to be quite astonishing for while he is tracing the spread of fly fishing, fly tying and tackle making through the ages, he takes account of what was happening to the people who were living at the time. So what we are treated to is all sorts of interesting aspects of British, European and world history.

Herd reports that when G. E. M. Skues returned from a fishing trip to Bosnia in 1897 he admitted that he had been out-fished by the natives despite the fact that the latter tightlined (without a reel) with four hackled flies attached to a horse-hair line cast out with a shortish homemade rod. This single report was and still is a monument to our ignorance of Balkan trouting and even more shaming when we remember that the first-ever indisputable notice of fly fishing - was Ælian's description of it in the Balkans (Macedonia) nearly two thousand years ago. Now our shame will be alleviated because Andrew Herd has been to the former Yugoslavia with the sole purpose of discovering what he could (with the help of Dr Grubic) of the methods used by the native fly fishermen who have passed the know-how of fly fishing and fly tying down from generation to generation, apparently without the support of documentation or tackle shops.

Herd's account is fascinating and one remark in a letter from Grubic is worth noting; in defence of the native persistence in using an ancient method, he observed, 'They are uniquely adapted to the rivers they know.'

Herd's tracing of the developments of rods, reels, lines, hooks, flies, and methods has not been done on the basis of chapters devoted to each subject. Rather his plan has been to travel chronologically from the earliest times, noticing and commenting on new trends and improving techniques.

He takes the opportunity to quote from the writers of the day to support or question new technology or changes in fashion. Now and again our author documents both sides of the inevitable classic controversies that were enacted in the letter columns of the angling press. One of the most famous clashes - the one between William C. Stewart and Harry Cholmondeley-Pennell - was about the relative wisdom of casting a fly upstream or downstream with the inevitable result that Stewart won hands-down.

Long before the reader nears the end of this book he may well be thinking, as I did, how can an author collect, understand, handle, and organise so much on the history of fly fishing? Andrew Herd has managed it. I take my hat off to him.

Preface

John Betts

There is probably more material published in the English language on fly fishing than in all of the other languages combined. This wealth of documentation has provided us with an extraordinary record of the progress of the sport.

Since the mid 1600s the flow of that work has increased and shows no sign of abating. A good deal of it includes historical reporting through the mention of previous writers. In early books credit was either declared or undeclared. If the latter, then verbatim or near verbatim usage would quickly identify the source to anyone familiar with the literature. At that time, within limits, this was a perfectly acceptable way to include other people's ideas. Footnotes and bibliographies, as we know them, were still a long way off. Of the thousands of books printed on fly fishing only a handful have been devoted to a discussion of the sport's history. The bulk of these have been of limited literary value.

For historical works, one of two formats can be used. The first is a separate chapter on each subject, beginning and ending with chosen dates. Using this method, one could find a section on lines; followed by something on leaders, and still another on knots. The second arrangement involves including a number of different subjects, say lines, leaders, and knots, in a single chapter in the nineteenth century. Regardless of which system was used, previous authors seldom showed the reader the past, present and possibly future relationship that one subject has had, has, or may have to another. Further, when these relationships are stated, the connection is often an assumption rather than one of evidence accumulated by thought and research. Only rarely are various subjects connected in such a way as to illustrate a cause and effect or coincidental association.

Developing links among subjects is often hard to do. The events which have been, are, and will be part of our lives are simultaneously in constant motion, multidimensional, and related to one another. However, any phenomena being considered must be reported on and limited by a two dimensional piece of paper. This condition is complicated by the linear arrangement of one word coming after another, even though what they describe may be occurring at the same time. When we encounter lists of events, our background has taught us to make some automatic adjustments in order to be able to bridge the differences between realities and their presentation. Going a step further we find that considerable amounts of time and tedious effort are necessary to show how one subject might be related to another. Describing the equipment and physics of casting a fly is simple, showing the relationship of these pieces during each moment of this single unified event is not easy.

In its early stages this book was set out in the first of the two formats; i.e. each subject having its own complete history in its own section. It didn't take long for Dr Herd to discover that the history of fly fishing is very different in character from that of other areas. The development of most industries, such as steel, is fairly straightforward since nearly all of the advances are made by the industry's own momentum. Even apparently remote and spontaneous events may later be shown to have been closely related to the original scheme.

Fly fishing has never been essential to our survival, and, for that reason, has never been the subject of, nor had the need for, the discipline of a self-advancing force. Because nearly everything used in fly fishing was initially garnered from the leavings of others, it has been pushed and pulled back and forth and from side to side in fits and starts along its path by forces completely unrelated to it. If it has a tradition it is one of unanticipated and unforeseeable change. That kind of input often leaves behind it a confusing and discontinuous path made up of dead ends, incomprehensible thoughts, inaccurate reporting and occasionally superior deductive reasoning - virtually every word of which has been put down by passionate amateurs.

It is said that there is nothing new in fly fishing. It is a concept that I believe is incorrect. Granted, the natural forces we employ are the same as they always have been. However, combining these properties in new ways must produce something new. As all fields of interest are finite there is a finite number of questions that can be asked about them. For these questions there is a finite number of answers. As a result, two people working thousands of miles and sometimes centuries apart can come up with the same result in the same subject area even if they have been working with different tools. For each of them their result will be 'new' provided they did not have prior knowledge of each other.

There are many new ideas in this book. One of the most notable is the section on false casting. It is the first time it has been fully appreciated for its real importance. The author relates that it did not come about on a certain day. As with most changes it started in blurred beginnings, just as something people did, and gradually enhanced a mature successful practice that had been in existence for centuries, and could not have developed much farther. Any major shifts here could only have come from changes in technology - which is just what happened in an unrelated field. The addition of a new function to the false cast and what it represents is the beginning of modern fly fishing.

Because the writer's work is well organised and comprehensive, the reader may go from one point of interest to others of that era or beyond, and never lose hold of the fact that they and their developments are related. There is no sense anywhere in this book that unfounded theories will be allowed to stand simply because that has been the practice in the past. The relationships here are created from a combination of insight and extensive references that include both standard and unsual citations. Disagreement with these conclusions will have to be well defended in order to stand up.

Dr Herd has approached the history of fly fishing along two parallel courses. One considers the events and their evolution, and the other looks at their relationship to one another as they evolved. A smooth, imaginative, and beautifully written text fully supports the synthesis of these two themes, and creates a seamless piece that evinces none of the difficulties encountered in producing it.

Although many will be familiar with the sources for this book, they will be pleasantly surprised by the setting of the information in its proper surroundings. This is done by weaving a history of the people concerned and that of the society they lived in. This addition is essential if the developments in fly fishing are to be seen as symptoms of their time and characteristic of the field. The result of Andrew Herd's design is one of the best pieces of writing and thought in fly fishing literature.

Introduction

We take things for granted these days, so much so that I met an angler recently who had no idea that fly fishing was practised in the nineteenth century, let alone two thousand years ago. We sat on the bank and watched the antics of a dipper, while I explained to him that his Zulu was the product of three hundred years of experimentation, and how our arcane terminology and peculiar customs date back to the late Middle Ages, if not before. He looked sceptical, and I don't blame him, but when all is said and done, we are all as much a part of history as Walton and Cotton. When our day is done, another generation will look back at us, and wonder at our strange passions.

Strange passions are one of the dominant themes I can detect in the history of fly fishing, the other being a particularly stubborn brand of conservatism. The two characteristics have alternately pushed and pulled the development of fly fishing through the ages, and if at times it seems incredible that people made the choices they did, you are in good company. But don't laugh too much; we are probably making exactly the same kind of mistakes, did we but know it.

So before you read this book, I want you to rig up a rod and line, and cast a fly. I'm perfectly sure that you have done far too many times before for it to have any novelty, but this time my request is that you fix in your mind the exact feeling the rod gives when it loads under the first strain of the forward cast and the line curls lazily out before it hisses through the rings and delivers your fly to the target. I don't know what rod you are likely to be fishing with; perhaps I can't even imagine the type of rod you are fishing with, because you are far in my future, and I am dead and gone. Maybe your time is so far removed from mine that this book is old and foxed and you have just found it languishing at the bottom of an old packing case.[1] In any event, time doesn't really matter, because I am certain that whatever type of equipment you do have, it has to be orders of magnitude better than the fly rods, reels and lines I am going to tell you about. The reason I want you to make a cast now is because if you don't drink in the quality of modern equipment one more time, you will not even begin to appreciate the skill of the fishermen that you are going to read about, and if that is the case, you will miss half the point of this book.

Our ancestors managed to catch fish, and to harbour a great love for their sport, whilst using the sort of tackle that you and I would absolutely refuse to use, were we offered it new today. They were a tough breed. Despite all the hardships they endured – unreliable reels, rotting lines, smashed rods, and wet wading in icy rivers – they built fly fishing into the pleasurable recreation that it is today. This book pays homage to those anglers: to the author of the Treatyse, to Cotton, to Blacker, Gordon, Ronalds, Scrope, Kelson, Halford, Norris, Skues, Wood, Wulff and to the many others whose work it has been my pleasure to read over the last few years.

I have one request; if you enjoy this book, don't just put it on the shelf and forget about it, go out and find the books written by men like Grey, Kingsmill-Moore, Farson, and Plunket-Greene. If those names mean nothing to you now, then there is a whole world out there that you never suspected existed.

Andrew Herd, 2001

When I was asked to write a note to the paperback edition of The Fly, *my thoughts turned immediately to Vladimir Markov. Shortly after the limited edition was published, a large parcel arrived bearing a return address of Irkutsk, Siberia. Unwrapped, it revealed a small box containing a single fly - Vladimir's modern interpretation of the Francis Francis bee pattern that appeared on the cover of the first edition. Since Vladimir is one of today's most talented fly dressers, there was little discussion when it came to the cover of the paperback. Vladimir's bee captures the essence of my approach to history - understanding and learning from the past is the key to a better future.*

Andrew Herd, 2003

Beginnings

Detail of Beni Hasan tomb painting

CHAPTER ONE

Beginnings

THE HISTORY of fly fishing is so long that we will never know who first had the inspired idea of tying feathers around a hook. That doesn't mean that we can't speculate about what drove him to do it (I'm assuming it was a he); but the notion most probably came to him the hundredth time he lost the live insect he had so carefully impaled. I expect his friends thought he was completely mad to go to the trouble of winding stuff around a hook when bugs were flying around for free and he probably went to the river with abuse ringing in his ears, but I can imagine his grin of triumph when a fish rose and he proved them all wrong. More than likely the same group of sceptics heard him cussing and swearing ten minutes later when another fish smashed him.

The question which this book tries to answer is: what did it feel like to be that man? When our ancestor lost that first fly, did he throw his rod in the river and scream abuse at the gods? Or did he sit down and patiently tie another fly? And if he did tie another pattern, was it the same as the first, or did he try to improve on it? Your guess is as good as mine, but if he was anything like the fly tyers I know, he didn't just tie another pattern, he sat down and tied another ten, so starting on the slippery slope which nowadays ends in large credit card statements and long-running domestic disputes.

Despite the great gulf of time which separates us, I can see our first fly tyer quite clearly, totally absorbed, as he settles down comfortably with his back against the evening-lit wall of his hut, inhaling the sweet smell of the wood-smoke while he works out how to grip the hook and learns how to fix the unwilling materials to its unforgiving shank. I can imagine people trekking from far away to check out the rumours about this madman who had learnt how to deceive fish with his feathered lure. I can see the visitors squatting down next to him, craning their necks to see, while he ties his flies, and I can see their slow head-shakes of disbelief as he takes another fish. So are great obsessions born.

Sadly, imagination does not make history, though it can help us to understand it. The questions of when and where that first fly fisherman lived are just as difficult to answer as knowing who he was. We know so little about the early history of fly fishing that it is more than possible that it was the invention of a civilisation not normally connected with the sport, such as the Chinese. It is also a possibility, perhaps a probability, that fly fishing was invented by many civilisations at different times, resulting in quite separate lines of development, some of which have survived, while others were lost to plague, famine or war. To make matters worse, early fly fishing traditions were far less homogeneous than they are now and it is possible to discern the echoes of different regional and sub-regional traditions within separate countries, which make it hard to pick up the threads of development and to paint a picture of a coherent whole with any confidence.

The truth is that it is hard to even hazard a guess at the origins of fly fishing and the major problem with any exploration of the early development is that few pieces of ancient fishing tackle survive. For example, I am not aware of the survival of any flies tied prior to the eighteenth century and the earliest fly patterns we have date to the end of the Middle Ages, so archaeology isn't going to help us much. On the other hand, there are many collections of ancient hooks, some of which contain examples which could have been used to tie flies imitating larger insects like sedges, wasps and mayflies, and we know that threads which were fine enough to fix materials on a small hook started to emerge around 3000 BC. Any time after that is fair game for the invention of the fly, although to be fair, the first painted angling scene dates to 2000 BC and nothing was written down until much later. But with every passing year bringing discoveries of new material, it is dangerous to speculate any further and while it seems to me that the history of fly fishing can be as long as we care to make it, there is no doubt that the fly has a pedigree which stretches back at least two millennia.

If art and archaeology aren't much help to us, then we will have to rely on the written word and fortunately fly fishing has always been interesting enough to catch literary imaginations. There is a mention of gold hooks and dressings of kingfisher feathers in a Chinese manuscript written several centuries before Christ, though the passage isn't clear and the feathers could have ornamented the line rather than the fly, but the first fly fishermen we can definitely identify lived in the long shadow cast by the Roman empire. The earliest possible reference to the sport was made by one Marcus Valerius Martialis; a gentleman known to generations of reluctant young Latin scholars as Martial. Contrary to the popular belief that the Devil invented him in order to devise subtle and fiendish ways of torturing the schoolboy mind, Martial was a popular poet in his day and authored no less than 1,561 clever and occasionally obscene epigrams about life in ancient Rome. He lived between AD 41 and AD 104 and was born on the banks of the river Salo in Spain, though he moved to Rome early on and spent much of his life there. Martial sometimes fished for sport and it sounds as if he learned the hard way, because he left us at least one poem about the bad luck he had as a fisherman, but he also wrote this:

> Namque quis nescit
> Avidum vorata decipi scarum musca
> (Who has not seen the scarus rise
> Decoyed and killed by fraudful flies!) [2]

If you give Martial the benefit of the doubt, his words do make it sound as if fly fishing was pretty routine in his day, but the snag is that the Scarus is a sea fish and that it browses on seaweed and coral. So Martial's quote isn't universally accepted as the first description of fly fishing, not least because there is disagreement among academics about whether the final word should be translated *musco* (moss) or *musca* (fly). One school of thought even holds that Martial used the word musco to mean seaweed, which pretty much kicks the fly fishing argument into touch. However, if we take it that Martial was talking about a fly, then those two lines of his are potentially quite significant. An interesting side issue remains about whether he was talking about a live insect impaled on a hook, or about a truly artificial fly. On the face of it, it seems pretty unlikely that anyone would angle for a salt water fish by dapping, but I wouldn't completely rule it out, given, as I hope you will concede by the time you have finished this book, that logic has little to do with the way fly fishing has developed. William Radcliffe,[3] from whose text the above paragraphs are summarised, comes down firmly in favour of an artificial fly, but who can say for sure? So many centuries after the event, there is no one left to disagree with him and so it is possible that fly fishing has its roots in salt water lures.

Macedonia

The next author to set pen to paper on the subject was a Roman called Claudius Aelianus (more commonly known as Ælian,) in a book called *On the Nature of Animals*. This magnum opus was, as far as we know, written in about AD 200; at least a hundred years after Martial penned his epigram.

Ælian was born in about AD 170 at Praeneste, where he later held a religious post, dying in about AD 230. At some point he became a pupil of Pausanias of Caesarea, who taught him rhetoric, and as a good student Ælian also learnt excellent Attic Greek. He later studied history under the patronage of the empress Julia Domna, and moving within her circle would have allowed him to meet not only Galen, but Oppian. Despite his interest in the exotic, Ælian was not a traveller and he spent the vast majority of his life in Rome, which gave him easy access to the libraries he needed; he once boasted that he had never been outside Italy, had never been aboard a ship, and knew nothing of the sea; a statement which I find quite easy to believe having read his works. Ælian put his knowledge of Greek to good use when he wrote, and he drew from a vast range of reference works: his main source has been identified as being Pamphilus of Alexandria; but he also accessed a wealth of other writers including Democritus, Herodotus, Plutarch and Aristophanes.

In the seventeenth volume, *On the Nature of Animals,* Ælian mixes personal observation with fact, legend and fancy drawn from earlier authors, pouncing on passing ideas like a thirsty man upon flagons of ale, with the result that there is little order in the work. *On the Nature of Animals* intentionally lacked structure and it contains frequent errors many of which Ælian could have eliminated with very little effort. However, the book is pure entertainment which is why the author saw no reason why he should not discuss elephants in one breath and dragons in the next. We should be glad of this, because in the course of his frantic rush through all of nature Ælian chanced to write these immortal lines:

> I have heard of a Macedonian way of catching fish, and it is this: between Borœa and Thessalonica runs a river called the Astræus, and in it there are fish with speckled skins; what the natives of the country call them you had better ask the Macedonians. These fish feed upon a fly peculiar to the country, which hovers on the river. It is not like the flies found elsewhere, nor does it resemble a wasp in appearance, nor in shape would one justly describe it as a midge or a bee, yet it has something of each of these. In boldness it is like a fly, in size you might call it a midge, it imitates the colour of a wasp, and it hums like a bee. The natives generally call it the Hippouros.
>
> These flies seek their food over the river, but do not escape the observation of the fish swimming below. When then the fish observes a fly on the surface, it swims quietly up, afraid to stir the water above, lest it should scare away its prey; then coming up by its shadow, it opens its mouth gently and gulps down the fly, like a wolf carrying off a sheep from the fold or an eagle a goose from the farmyard; having done this it goes below the rippling water.
>
> Now though the fishermen know this, they do not use these flies at all for bait for fish; for if a man's hand touch them, they lose their natural colour, their wings wither, and they become unfit food for the fish. For this reason they have nothing to do with them, hating them for their bad character; but they have planned a snare for the fish, and get the better of them by their fisherman's craft.
>
> They fasten red (crimson red) wool around a hook, and fix onto the wool two feathers which grow under a cock's wattles, and which in colour are like wax. Their rod is six feet long, and their line is the same length. Then they throw their snare, and the fish, attracted and maddened by the colour, comes straight at it, thinking from the pretty sight to gain a dainty mouthful; when, however, it opens its jaws, it is caught by the hook, and enjoys a bitter repast, a captive.[4]

Now this is the real McCoy, since Ælian's turn of phrase doesn't leave room for the slightest doubt that he is talking about fly fishing. If there is a problem, it is the sad and certain fact that the author never went to Macedonia. While it is disappointing that we aren't reading a first hand account, it is probably reliable, since Ælian would have had plenty of opportunity to meet people who had been to the Balkans, given that a Roman army first entered Macedonia in the winter of 200-199 BC and that the unfortunate country was annexed as a province by the Senate only a few decades later. So we can take the phrase 'I have heard,' quite literally and it is probable that Ælian never saw anyone fish a fly, despite having immortalised it in words. None the less, his third hand report is the first conclusive reference to fly fishing and it proves beyond any shadow of a doubt that it is a very ancient art indeed.

It is difficult to pinpoint the location of the Astræus with complete certainty because the Macedonia that Ælian knew has known its share of the flames of war, with the result that today it is divided between Greece, Bulgaria and the Republic of Macedonia. To make matters worse, the ancient geography is confusing, with many redundant place names, and the chequered political history of this area means that maps are not always what they seem. Of all the attempts to locate the Astræus, the best is presented in a very erudite paper by Professor N. G. L. Hammond, an acknowledged expert on Macedonian History.[5] Hammond pointed out that a considerable drainage project took place in the region in the early twentieth century and that the river which Heroditus and Ælian knew was probably subsumed into a regional channel which carried the water from the western foothills of the plain of Beroea into the river Haliacmon. This would place the Astræus in modern day Greece, and on-going research by Dr Grubic and myself suggests the modern day river Arapitsa to be the most likely candidate.

We can only hope that the fish in Macedonian waters have not changed, as fortunately for us, the only speckled freshwater fish species found there today is the trout, of which *Salmo trutta macedonicus* Karaman is the only species seen in the Strumica. This particular sub-species differs from other Balkan trout in that (at least today) the majority of its spots are black, with red ones being almost entirely absent.[6]

Trout would certainly have been plentiful in Macedonia in Ælian's time, although not in the low lying areas near the sea, where the rivers generally have too lazy a flow to support salmonids. But it wouldn't have been necessary to travel very far from the beaten path to reach the foothills and see fishermen plying the sparkling streams as they rushed down from the mountains. The fly fishermen he wrote about may well have been reported by a merchant, a soldier or an administrator travelling along the Via Egnatia to Thessalonika. Beyond that town lay the frontiers of the empire: the Persian Royal Road and the Silk Road. Perhaps Ælian's source had escorted bales of silk through Beroea on their way to Rome and the fishers had bartered their catch with him. Of course, we can never know the exact circumstances, but it may well have been from this same person that Ælian obtained a list of materials considered necessary for angling in those far off times. Unlike many passages in *On the Nature of Animals*, this one has the ring of truth, not least because it is pure shopping list, and I find it easy to imagine our scribe furiously scribbling on his wax tablet:

> 'natural horsehair, white, and black, and flame-coloured, and half-grey; but of dyed hair, they select only those that are grey, or of true sea-purple, for the rest, they say, are pretty poor. They use, too, the straight bristles of the swine, and thread, and much copper and lead, and cords and feathers, chiefly white, or black, or various. They use two wools, red and blue.'[7]

Now this list argues for a fair bit of sophistication among Roman fishermen, particularly the use of copper and lead, which were probably used for sea fishing, to which Ælian devoted a good deal of space. Much of his writing about the sea was plagiarised directly from writers like Oppian, but there are one or two jewels of knowledge embedded in the reams of regurgitated text. For example, Ælian describes how sea fishermen caught fish on hooks wrapped with wool of Laconian red, hackled with a sea mew's feather.[8] But there was more, some of it just a little outrageous by our standards:

> ...corks, and wood, and iron, and of the things they need, are reeds well-grown, and nets, and soaked rushes, a shaved wand, and a dog-wood rod, and the horns and hide of a she-goat.[9]

And you thought history was dull? Corks and nets are fair enough and the shaved wand would be a real conversation piece, but quite what anglers would have done with the horns and hide of a she-goat was beyond me at first, though I imagine they would have cut quite a dash worn off the shoulder. Fortunately a friend rescued me here and pointed out that the horns may have been used for keeping live baits and the hide of the she-goat was in all likelihood used to make a sack for keeping fish as Macedonian shepherds did until recently. The detail about the sex of the animal is particularly important because billy goat skins have a peculiarly unwelcome smell all of their own, especially when they get wet.

The Macedonian Fly

The Macedonian fly must be the most interesting fly of all time, but imagining what it looked like is very difficult, not least because of what Ælian leaves unsaid. It pays to be just a little bit sceptical of his writing, in my opinion, as I don't think we should accept uncritically the words of a man who thought goats could breathe through their ears. My own reading of his description of the Hippouros is that:

- the fly probably didn't occur in the country we now know as Italy.
- it hovered.
- it was approximately midge-sized.
- it was coloured like a wasp (yellow and black), but with a body shape unlike one.
- it made a humming noise.
- and it landed on the water and floated there for long enough for fish to take it (though maybe he has this back to front and was actually describing hatching duns - easy mistake to make).

But, and this is the crucial bit, Ælian makes it clear that the fishermen did not use this fly to fish with, so, surprising though it may seem, the description of the Hippouros is interesting but is nothing to do with the fly pattern which he goes on to describe. Neither do I think we can call this dressing 'The Hippouros Fly' because if you read the text very critically, Ælian seems to be telling us that fishermen did not imitate the Hippouros, either:

> Now though the fishermen know this, they do not use these flies at all for bait for fish; for if a man's hand touch them, they lose their natural colour, their wings wither, and they become unfit food for the fish. For this reason they have nothing to do with them, hating them for their bad character . . .

So you could read the next quote as a description of an artificial which had nothing to do with the Hippouros. This would have the force of logic behind it, because the imitation is brown and red, while the Hippouros is yellow and black. According to our man in Rome:

> . . . but they have planned a snare for the fish, and get the better of them by their fisherman's craft. They fasten red (crimson red) wool around a hook, and fix onto the wool two feathers which grow under a cock's wattles, and which in colour are like wax.

If, on the other hand, we do think that the Macedonian fly is a Hippouros imitation, then we have to square the difficult circle of reconciling a pattern with a red body with a natural fly which had a yellow, or a yellow and black body. The only way I can think of doing this is if there is a fly which changes its body colour from yellow to red, but if we believe that the Hippouros is being imitated here, we also have to consider Ælian's 'hovering.'

The biggest problem of all is that Ælian was describing all this third hand. It might be that he was actually describing the ascent of duns - *Ephemera danica* duns and most spinners look as if they are hovering. To be fair, it might be that he was describing a truly hovering fly; but I can't think of any patterns anywhere which imitate this sort of insect, chiefly because they are hardly of any importance to fish in their diet. Bear these arguments in mind as you read on.

There has been an immense amount of speculation about what the Macedonian fly looked like and which insect the word Hippouros describes. The best essay I know on the subject was written by Fred Buller in *The American Fly Fisher* a few years ago and it repays a careful read.[10] This was a challenging piece of research. It is extremely difficult to look back two millennia and imagine what fishermen might have imitated then, but after extensive investigation, Fred decided that it was possible that the artificial represents either a horse fly, *Therioplectes tricolor* Kirchbergi or a drone fly, *Episyrphus balteatus* De geer. The article gives some speculative dressings for the fly, tied respectively by David Beazley and Kenneth Robson of the Flyfisher's Club.

Dressings of the Hippouros fly (courtesy of Fred Buller)

Both horse and drone fly naturals are used by modern fishermen from the area as live bait for summer chub fishing, though drone flies are not very much favoured. The only problem with Fred's theory is that horse and drone flies are robust creatures and Ælian implied an insubstantial insect when he wrote 'if a man's hand touch them, they lose their natural colour, their wings wither, and they become unfit food for the fish.' This doesn't sound much like a horse fly, given that they are so tough it is difficult to kill them without a well aimed and exceedingly brisk swat. The additional fact that horse flies are skilled fliers and rarely fall on the water might tip the balance toward the large and delicate *Siphlonurus* species of mayfly seen in southern European summers, the sub-imago of which has a rather appealing cherry-red body.

There things might have lain, but for a chance contact I had with Dr Goran Grubic at the Faculty of Agriculture, Zemun in Yugoslavia. Dr Grubic wrote to me about an expedition his father, a geologist, made to Macedonia many years ago, where he spent time watching a friend fly fishing in a traditional style. His father's friend subsequently sent the two flies he considered the best trout takers to Dr Grubic, who wrote in his letter:

> ...several years ago I received as a gift a fly that is as close to the Hippouros fly as a modern fly can be: the body is gold ribbed crimson red floss, the hackle is drab brown-red cock, and the hook size is 12. Please note: the natural beeswax colour of the hackles is not exactly blue dun, it is actually brownish. This fly was tied by the late Mr Dusan Pendzerkovski of Bitola, Macedonia. My father accompanied him while he was fishing rivers in the south-eastern part of what is today known as the Republic of Macedonia, some 10 years ago. He was also using the Ælian method: he used to cut his hazel rod on the river bank, attach some 10 ft of mono to the tip, and one or two flies on the end of the line. He was a very successful fisherman. Unfortunately I had no opportunity to meet him. As far as I know there are no such 'old time masters' in Macedonia anymore. Spinning tackle is now widely used to catch trout there.[11]

Mr Pendzerkovski's fly

It is too much to hope that this might be the original Macedonian fly pattern, handed down by word of mouth, although my heart would like to believe otherwise. For a start, Ælian makes no mention of a rib, gold or otherwise, but this fly might be something else. I doubt that the fauna of Macedonia has changed so much over the last two millennia and Mr Pendzerkovski's pattern might just be the spirit of an ancient fly, calling down to us across the centuries. Whatever the truth may be, we will never know for sure, because within a short space of time the old world was plunged into the Middle Ages and nothing more is known to have been written on the subject for a millennium.

Fishing in Medieval Europe

Until quite recently, almost nothing was known about fly fishing in medieval Europe and it was assumed that a book known as the *Treatyse of Fishing with an Angle* was the first work written about fly fishing. Much of the responsibility for the insular view that the English invented fly fishing can be laid at the door of the great John Waller Hills, who started *A History of Fly Fishing for Trout* with the words:

> The history of fly fishing begins at the close of the fifteenth century. It is true that there is one isolated record long before this; for the curious can carry its story back to the second century of our era and read in a Roman author an account of fly fishing for a fish, apparently the trout, in a river in Macedonia. But while there is no reason to doubt the truth of this, the fact is interesting rather than important, and for this reason. It had no influence on subsequent development: it stands by itself, and was unknown until a modern writer quoted it as a curiosity. And as such we can leave it.[12]

That wasn't an unreasonable statement to make in the 1920s, although it is hard to understand why Hills chose to discard the passage from *On the Nature of Animals* so absolutely, apart than the irritating fact that it didn't fit into his scheme of things. The trouble was that Hills was so influential that his words were accepted as holy writ until a few decades ago. The expression 'fog in channel, continent cut off' comes to mind, but Hill's decision illustrates to perfection one of the classic traps that lie in wait for historians: it isn't safe to assume that the surviving texts record everything that went on in times past. In fact, the opposite is more usually true, and until recent times the written record has barely scratched the surface, so that instead of a complete story it illuminates tiny cameos from which, if we are lucky, we can extrapolate to the bigger picture.

To be fair, there isn't much evidence that Ælian's passage isn't a curiosity, a solitary reference suspended out of time, but common sense dictates that Hills took one step too far in consigning it to the dustbin of history purely on the basis that nothing else was written about it. Given what we know about the sophistication of fly fishing in Roman times, it would be very surprising if the method had been completely abandoned during the Middle Ages and as John Betts quite rightly points out, there weren't many books on making wheels either and yet no one has tried to deny the existence of the chariot. Fish have always been an intensely valuable food for man and it is frankly incredible that a simple and useful technique like fly fishing would have been forgotten the moment Alaric and his motley crew of Visigoths swept out of the East and came hammering on the gates of Rome with such evil intent in AD 410.

Many other authors have interpreted the lack of any written record on the subject between Roman times and the late Middle Ages as evidence that fly fishing wasn't practised at all, but the truth is that records of any sort from that period are scanty and it wasn't known as the 'Dark Ages' for nothing. The vast majority of people were illiterate, with the result that, as Bloch points out in *Feudal Society*, 'whole aspects of social life were only very imperfectly covered by texts, and often not at all . . .'[13] So there are very few references to any kind of fishing during this time, but the manuscripts which have survived, like the *Aelfric's Colloquy,*[14] which was written near the end of the tenth century, show that bait fishing was alive and well and there is no conceivable reason why fly fishing did not flourish unrecorded. For a start, fish were even more important in the average diet than they are now, not least because, by the late Middle Ages, there were no fewer than one hundred and forty-five days of the year when the Church dictated that only fish or fruit could be eaten; a prejudice incidentally, which it reinforced with the occasional execution for non-compliance, for example that of the unfortunate Claude Guillon, who had the bad luck to be beheaded in 1629 for eating horse meat on the wrong day. The Peasant's Revolt, led by Wat Tyler, offers another insight into the importance fish assumed in a medieval diet – one of the men's minor demands was the right to fish the River Ver.

My own view is that fly fishing went on undisturbed, but unrecorded, for a thousand years. If fly fishing did originate in the Balkans, it is possible that during this period the technique spread across Europe and perhaps to the Far East and beyond. So who spread the word? To some extent, the sheer effectiveness of the method must have been its greatest recommendation, but one vehicle for the dispersion of fly fishing across such a wide area might have been the occupying Roman army and the administrators who followed in its wake. Sadly, while the vision of footsore legionaries tramping across Europe carrying fly lines in their dusty baggage is an appealing one, the two centuries that elapsed between Ælian's publication and the sack of Rome provide hardly enough time for the theory to be correct, unless of course, fly fishing was discovered long before *On the Nature of Animals* was written. Another option is that fly fishing was spread by the merchants who travelled in caravan type groups all over the Balkan peninsula during this period, and for long after. As part of their legacy, camels were kept in Macedonia until shortly before the beginning of the Second World War.[15] Nomadic shepherds are a third possibility, because they travelled far and wide through this ancient land in search of quality pasture. The sites they favoured were usually above 1500-1800 feet, which is the same area where trout live in southern Europe, and one of the very striking things about Macedonia is that even today shepherds are very often traditional fly fishermen.[16] During the day they move with their sheep, but since the dogs really do the work, they have plenty of time to cast a fly. The Stara Planina area was a centre of this way of life and the nomads are still fishing there today.

However the method spread from one country to another, there is little reason to doubt that fly fishing was widely practised during this period and it may well explain why the accounts written during the late Middle Ages and early Renaissance feature such comparatively rich lists of fly patterns. These artificials didn't spring into their authors' minds like rabbits out of conjuror's hats; instead they were the product of many centuries of patient experiment and refinement, passed down by word of mouth for thirty generations or more.

I'll go so far as to say that far from falling out of fashion after the sack of Rome, fly fishing continued to grow, to expand and to become more sophisticated. This seems to fly in the face of the evidence, but I'll defend my hypothesis on the basis that, by and large, fly fishing wasn't practised by the few sporting nobles who might have had the leisure and ability to put pen to paper; it was the work of illiterate peasants who desperately needed food in order to survive. Although there appear to have been some high-born sport fishermen in medieval Europe, on the whole nobles looked to hunting and hawking for sport and their only contact with fishermen was as employees. Otherwise fishermen were part of a subsistence economy and they didn't have any more opportunity to write down what they knew about their trades than did farmers or dyers.

You might ask how a sport could be practised on such a wide scale without leaving the slightest trace of its existence, but rods, lines and flies are ephemeral things and very few eighteenth century rods have survived, let alone eighth century ones. The one medium which we might expect to have recorded fly fishing, in the absence of the survival of artefacts or the written word, is art, and I have to concede that it is strange that there aren't more pictures of fly fishermen; but for one fact. I am fairly convinced that early fly fishers either dapped their flies or 'whipped' them on short, fixed lines using very quick wrist movements, and the visually appealing false casting which draws the artist's eye to the modern sport simply didn't occur that much. So pictures of fly fishermen executed prior to the early nineteenth century don't have any features to distinguish them from bait fishing, given that all fishermen adopted much the same pose, with a rod held at a low angle.

The other circumstance which has conspired to conceal the early history of fly fishing is that with few exceptions, fly fishing historians are a small and select club of amateurs who have tended to treat the literature which has survived as the only record - understandable, I suppose, given our common love of books; but it completely ignores the contribution of folk traditions which we know to have been a powerful influence. Even given the unlikely chance that books and magazines were the only route by which all knowledge of fly fishing was handed down, the literature is notoriously fickle, rarely records a complete picture and often misses major developments. In the light of recent discoveries some sacred cows are going to have to be sacrificed and we can't straight-facedly assume that the history of fly fishing during the Middle Ages chanced to be recorded in its entirety in the few fragments of text which have happened to be preserved. This revelation broadens our horizons at a stroke and the new and difficult problem we face is that envisaging the entire picture is like trying to guess the subject of a three-dimensional, ten thousand piece jigsaw from a collection of half a dozen unrelated bits.

If I am confident that there is much more to find out, then I am also frustrated to think what we must have lost. Eleven centuries is time enough for civilisations to flower and fade, let alone for a sport to find its feet. Who knows what knowledge was painfully gained, only to be snatched away by plague, war or famine? And who knows what remains to be discovered, locked in the recesses of the great libraries, like those of the Vatican? I don't think we command anywhere near a complete perspective on the subject and if, as we will shortly see, historians have been able to uncover several 'new' works on fly fishing in the space of the last thirty years, what else is left to find?

It would be neat if we could trace the growth of fly fishing from Macedonia as it matured and spread through Europe, and while we might do that one day, there are a few bits of the puzzle which don't seem to belong. For example, anecdotal evidence makes it seem probable that fly fishing was known in Japan as early as the late eighth and ninth centuries BC. This could be seen as weakening the theory that fly fishing began in the Balkans, because it isn't at all clear how fly fishing came to Japan, other than by people seeing and copying what their fellows did. Given the distance between Japan and Europe it may be that the Japanese mountain villagers discovered the technique for themselves, but it is also possible (and now we are into the realms of pure speculation) that the method could have been an import from Korea or even China. The Korean route carries some weight, because after the fall of Kudara in AD 660, many of that country's people emigrated to Japan bringing with them the ability to make steel hooks in the primitive blast furnaces which they busily set up along the sides of every stream in Kiso Fukusima district.

The Japanese method is known as 'Tenkara' although the origins of the name remain frustratingly obscure. In a country dogged by agricultural inefficiency it was a useful way of gathering food, rather than a sport, and perhaps because of this very little has ever been written about it. Fortunately for us, the oral tradition, saviour of so many ancient crafts, has ensured that Tenkara has survived to modern times and one can still see the odd fisherman using the ten foot rod, fixed line and hackled wet flies which are so characteristic of the technique. Interestingly, the flies have been tied since time immemorial with a cotton-like fibre taken from flowering ferns of the *Osmunda* family, which is spun into thread.[17]

Fly fishing became popular with Japanese peasants from the twelfth century onward, but during the Edo period, which spanned the early seventeenth to the late nineteenth century, fishing was promoted to a pastime worthy of *Bushi* (warriors), as part of an official policy to train the *Bushi's* mind during peacetime. This is very significant, because warriors were the highest ranking members of Japanese society at the time and it has obvious parallels with the increasing status of fishing in Spain and England during the same period. What we do not know is if there was any connection between the Eastern and Western traditions.[18-21]

Fortunately, we are on firmer ground from here on in. There is good evidence that fly fishing was popular in Europe as early as the beginning of the thirteenth century, a revelation which has simultaneously knocked the *Treatyse of Fishing with an Angle* off its pedestal and opened new vistas for those who believed that fly fishing started suddenly in the late fifteenth century.[22] In respect of this we owe a great deal to the ground breaking work carried out by two historians: Hoffmann and Braekman. Their patient study has shown that far from being a British secret, as was generally thought, during the Middle Ages there were three distinct streams of fly fishing development: British, central European and Spanish, to which we can now add Japanese, though at present we know a regrettably small amount about the development of fly fishing in the latter country. To what extent, if at all, the first three were inter-related is an open question and it may be that fly fishing developed quite separately in each area, although it seems unlikely, given that much of the western world was unified under Roman rule at the beginning of the period and trading routes were well developed. However, looking at the bare facts, we have no firm evidence that there was any cross-fertilisation of ideas between fly fishermen in different countries until the seventeenth century, although anglers could have travelled quite easily around Europe very much earlier than that.

German language texts mention the catching of trout and grayling using a 'feathered hook' (*vederangel*) from a very early date. Some of the evidence is gleaned from unlikely sources - the first reference we have is a metaphorical one in *Parzival*, a work written in about 1210 by Wolfram von Eschenbach. In *Parzival*, a heartless deceiver is compared to a fly in the brief, but biting epithet: 'You feathered hook, you adder's fang!' an insult which leaves no doubt that the audience must have known all about fly fishing. It is a clue, but not much, and fortunately we are treated to a more detailed reference in von Eschenbach's later romance, *Titurel*. Here the author describes the hero Schionatulander (who, incidentally, is cousin to King Arthur) wading in a stream while he fishes.

> Schionatulander caught grayling and trout with a vederangel . . . Schionatulander . . . caught fish with the hook as he stood barefoot in the cool, clear brook.

Putting the two quotes together, if fly fishing was common enough to be a source for literary allusion in the thirteenth century, then it seems safe to assume that it must have been a widespread activity. And so it proves to be, because other texts speak of fly fishing from 1360 onwards, across a vast area of running and inshore water reaching from the north-eastern Swiss plain to lower Austria. These early accounts of fly fishing in central Europe are complemented by at least a dozen manuscripts describing early sport fishing in Britain in the fourteenth and fifteenth centuries.

Now none of these early writers offer anything like a complete description of their subject and most only favour fishing with a passing reference, but they do show that fly fishing must have been practised on a wide scale and at a fair level of sophistication. Perhaps the most illuminating treatment of the subject is in a cryptic Bavarian manuscript volume, which dates from the early fifteenth century. Once again, we have Professor Richard Hoffmann to thank for bringing this work to our attention, and he includes a full translation of it in his book *Fisher's Craft and Lettered Art.*

The Bavarian manuscript, which was originally kept under the eagle eye of the dark-habited property manager at the abbey of Tegernsee, lists at least fifty different un-named flies, among which are patterns for catching carp, pike, catfish, burbot and salmon, as well as trout and grayling. The flies are sophisticated, and they use different colours of silk, and subtle shades of hackle. We have no idea how they were tied, and the translation of some of the terms eludes us, but the sheer variety of patterns and quarry listed argues for a long history of fly fishing in the Tegernsee area. Sadly, there is nothing in the manuscript about how the flies were fished, but I've given a few of the patterns below, to give some idea of their complexity:[23]

> The first hook should be tied after the 'carp flies' which there is called the 'wood fly,' and the feathering should be iron grey with dark brown speckled in it, [and] with black and yellow silk, and [around?] the 'heart' all yellow, and [around?] the stingel[24] black silk.
>
> The second hook should be tied after the 'grass fly' for the pike. The feathering should be of all different sorts mixed together, with lead coloured and light blackish and ash coloured [and] therein a black feather, with the silk pale coloured and around the 'heart' black light blue silk, around the stingel pinkish-coloured silk.
>
> The third hook should be tied after the little fly for the catfish. The feathering should be quail and that of a red-brown silk

> mixed together with red and lead-coloured silk, and around the 'heart' red silk, and around the stingel lead-coloured silk.
>
> The fourth hook should be tied after the knutter that is there called the spider for the bream. The feathering should be from a kingfisher [,namely,] the white which is on it, the feather that is multicoloured like a cuckoo, and [more of] the feathering light blackish with the silk lead coloured and white around the 'heart,' and around the stingel green silk.
>
> The fifth hook should be tied after the 'jumper'; the beetle is grey and pertains to the bream. The feathering should be partridge, of ash-coloured feather; [the silk?] blue green and brown and white, around the stingel brown.
>
> The sixth hook should be tied after the beetle called wengril for the chub in the water. The feathering should be black brown with the silks green and black and around the stingel green brown.

The Tegernsee manuscript is a perfect example of how dependent we are on the survival of manuscripts for our interpretation of history. If it had never been written, had been lost, then we would be unaware of the existence of Bavarian fly fishers and their entire tradition would be consigned, unknown, to history's gluttonous dustbin. As it is, we have another piece of our jigsaw, which forms part of an increasingly clear picture; there are several other German manuscripts written prior to the seventeenth century which mention fly fishing and either quote from the Tegernsee manuscript or have strong similarities to it, which indicates a common source, most likely an oral tradition.[25]

Now it is time to cross back over the channel, because there are a number of fifteenth century English treatises which mention fly fishing, all of which usually escape attention. This is reasonable enough, because there isn't much detail in them, just enough to whet our appetites perhaps, but they fill in a little more of our puzzle, and from now on we can increasingly start to fill in the facts, rather than deal in shadows and speculation. One is the British Library Harley 2389, which describes how to take 'trowte':

> ... in June, iuly an agust in the vpper part of the water with an artificiall flye, made vppon your hooke with sylke of dyverse coloures lyke vnto the flys which be on the waters in these monethes, and fethers be good & pecokes and popiniayes.

If peacocks and popinjays had to watch out, and the tyer needed silks of various colours, flies must have been pretty colourful to look at, even then. The second reference is *Medicina piscium* in the Bodleian Library, which not only describes flies for both trout and salmon, but which also calls for the imitation of natural insects:

> And iff ye fische for hym in the lapyng tyme ye must dubbe your hoke with the federys of a pertriche or with the federysse of a whyld doke and ye must loke what colowre that the fley is that the trowgth lepythe aftir and ye same colowre must the federisse be and the same colowre must the sylke be of for to bynde the federysse to your hoke.[26]

Again, only a fragment, but it discusses the need to imitate natural flies which the trout are seen to be taking, and gives us a very early mention of the use of silk in fly tying. From now on, the pieces of our jigsaw become much easier to collect, entirely because of an invention made by Johannes Gutenberg.

The Treatyse of Fishing with an Angle

The *Treatyse* is one of the works which has most profoundly influenced fly fishing, yet it was written at a time of complete international turmoil. The catastrophic second pandemic of Black Death of 1347 to 1351 had killed as much as one-third of the population of Europe, which would not return to its pre-1348 levels until the sixteenth century. So, at the time the author put pen to paper, England was a land of peasant farmers, many, but by no means all of whom were serfs. Landlords were struggling to cope with labour shortages by enclosing farmland in order to graze sheep. To make matters worse, the country was at war with France, in an interminable campaign that had dragged on since 1337. Despite this drain on the nation's resources, the lot of the peasant was improving, a developing land market enabling some to improve their status and become yeomen. The rise of the woollen and cloth trade industries had brought a new class of merchant adventurers into existence and it was a time of enormous development and change in the towns. Many schools and colleges were founded, not least Eton and King's College, Cambridge. Culturally, however, England was something of a backwater: monastic chronicles had come to an end, and the writing of history was in decline. But by the late Middle Ages, English prose had become a respected medium for writing, which was a significant development, since for most of the period, to be illiterate meant to be unable to read Latin, other languages being regarded as of little account. To put this into perspective, Edward II was the first English monarch who is known to have had more than a few words of the English language and before his reign there is no evidence of a king writing. The doyen of secular prose authors of this period was Sir Thomas Malory, who found a kind of immortality, thanks to his attribution as the author of the epic tale, *Le Morte Darthur*, which was completed in about 1470. However, Chaucer, the last distinguished poet England had known, had died in 1400, and no significant works of philosophy or theology were to be written during this time.

Perhaps none of this is too surprising, given the uncertainties of the period, not least the interminable conflict which characterised the Hundred Years War. After a faltering start in 1337, Edward III scored some early successes which led to a nine-year truce in 1360. War broke out again in 1369. By the mid-1380s, the English territorial gains had been reversed and internal power struggles in both countries led to a period of uncertain peace, fortunately in England's case, since the country needed time to recover from the Peasant's Revolt of 1381. War resumed in 1413 with Henry V's revival of his grandfather's claim to the French throne, and in the nine years that followed, Henry's leadership transformed England into the strongest nation in Europe, largely as the result of his inspired defeat of the French at Agincourt and again at the Battle of the Seine. But, sadly, the ascendancy was not to last. With the ill-timed deaths not only of Henry V, but also of Charles VI of France in 1422, Henry's infant son, Henry VI, was left as titular king of France. For a while, Henry's brother, the Duke of Bedford, struggled to defend English interests abroad against the campaigning Dauphin. It was a troubled time for the English peasantry, who found themselves pawns in a game which was well beyond their control. In the power vacuum left by Henry V's death, the country fell into the grip of warlords who levied arbitrary taxes and total lawlessness prevailed for at least another sixty years. If this was not enough, in 1429, Joan of Arc turned the tide of war decisively against England by raising the siege of Orleans. One by one, the French retook Henry's conquests, and by 1453, the port of Calais (later the cause of so much distress to Mary, Queen of Scots) was the only English possession left in France. Only a year later, the Earl of Warwick took advantage of the temporary insanity of Henry VI to install Richard, Duke of York as protector of the realm and the Wars of the Roses began, a conflict which would rage on for a further thirty years at an untold cost in human misery.

By contrast, in the calmer political climate which prevailed in the remainder of Europe, the mid-point of the fifteenth century marked the beginnings of one of the greatest periods of cultural development the world has ever known: the Renaissance. At one time regarded as a clean break away from medieval institutions and values, the Renaissance is now recognised as a broad watershed between medieval universalism and the sophisticated societies and systems that were to follow. Historians of the day pictured their era as a period when the cultural darkness of the Middle Ages was replaced by a revival of the classical world of Greece and Rome. One of the most significant features of the early Renaissance was the development of Humanism, a philosophy which looked forward to a rebirth of the human spirit, discarding the medieval ideal of a life of penance, replacing it instead with creative aspiration and a drive to master nature. Although Humanism penetrated English thinking much later than it did in the rest of Europe, the *Treatyse* has some claim to humanist credentials.

The Renaissance began in Italy, and it is convenient to anchor it to a seemingly trivial competition to design a pair of bronze doors for the baptistry of San Giovanni. The defeated parties, Filippo Brunelleschi and Donatello, left for Rome, where they threw their energies into the study of ancient sculpture and architecture. Their return fired a flowering of the arts in Florence, bankrolled by the Medici family, which became the powerhouse of a movement reaching its zenith in the work of three men: Leonardo da Vinci (1452-1519), Michelangelo (1475-1564), and Raphael (1483-1520). At the time that the *Treatyse* was written, England was virtually untouched by the cultural might of the Renaissance, but it would gain a late entrance in the 1480s, because the country stood on the threshold of a development that was to change the world for ever: printing.

Printing by movable type was invented by Johannes Gutenberg in about 1455, after a long period of experimentation that left him beset by lawsuits launched against him by the people who had lent him the money to develop his process. His system was a radical departure from anything that had previously been seen and it comprised a mould in which large quantities of type could be precisely cast in a special alloy, a press, and an oil based printing ink. He promptly used it to print the forty-two line Bible that ultimately inspired Martin Luther to print his ninety-five theses and trigger the Reformation, but that is another story.

Gutenberg's press was so well designed that it was used without major change until the twentieth century and it caught the eye of William

Caxton, who was engaged in the translation of Raoul Le Fèvre's *Recueil des histoires de Troye*, an exceptionally tedious task which he did not finish until September the nineteenth, 1471. At considerable personal expense, Caxton set up a press at Bruges and printed the *Recuyell*, the first book ever printed in English, four years later. After printing two or three other works, he returned to England, where he issued *Dictes and Sayenges of the Phylosophers*, in 1477, the first dated book to be printed in England.

It is very difficult to convey the impact that printing had on society in the fifteenth century, even by comparison with the changes wrought on modern day life by the Internet. But to give you some idea of the staggering change this new invention wrought on an unsuspecting society, before the invention of printing, the number of manuscript books in Europe could be counted in thousands, but by 1500, after only five decades of printing, there were more than nine million books, an absolutely phenomenal growth which gives an insight into just how vulnerable oral and written culture had been until then.[27]

Caxton was assisted from the very start by an Alsatian-born apprentice called Jan van Wynkyn, a man we know today as Wynkyn de Worde. Caxton printed about a hundred different books and pamphlets, and after his death in 1491, his assistant took over the operation of the press, moving it from Westminster to Fleet Street. For all that this was the 'Wild West' era of publishing, Wynkyn's output was quite startlingly prolific and it has been estimated that he published at least six hundred titles in his lifetime. In effect, he must have been the equivalent of an Internet entrepreneur, and it is easy to imagine him desperately searching for new manuscripts in order to feed the press which was making him so much money.

In the light of this, it is interesting that he published very little in the first few years of his operation of the press, contenting himself instead with a few reprints. In 1495, he released a translation of the *Vitae Sanctorum Patrum* of Jerome. The translation had been the work of Caxton and it was only finished on the last day of his life. Then de Worde published an English version of *Bartholomaeus de Proprietatibus Rerum*, to which he added a curious little epilogue containing some details about the beginning of Caxton's career as a printer, and the information that the book was the first to be printed on English made paper. In 1496, he published two new editions, one of which was *Dives and Pauper*. The other was the *Book of St Albans*, a popular sporting volume of the day.

I can imagine the prosperous de Worde looking very slightly nonplussed when he read the rather worthy text of the *Book of St Albans*, and wondering if he couldn't spice it up just a little with some kind of a tract on fishing. That is exactly what happened, because he squeezed into the same covers an unknown work which just happened to catch his eye, a manuscript called *A Treatyse of Fishing with an Angle*. Wynkyn didn't know it at the time, but not only would the *Treatyse* become one of the most important books on fishing ever published; it would immortalise him.

Frontispiece from the Treatyse

Although it was once regarded as the source from which all later works on fly fishing sprang, the *Treatyse* can now, more correctly, be regarded as a British text on fly fishing which happens to have survived, although its status as the earliest English printed book on fishing means that it remains hugely influential. The text comes from a manuscript thought to have been written in the early years of the fifteenth century, which is known to us from a copy held in the library at Yale and another fragment in Oxford; and there the certainties end. If ever there is a book which has been surrounded by controversy, the *Treatyse* is it - we are unsure even of the identity of the author. Some authorities believe that the *Treatyse* wasn't even the product of a single writer, and given the way I believe fly fishing developed over many centuries, this possibility can't be discounted. Rather than being the product of one person's experience, the text may represent a gradual crystallisation of many fishermen's ideas, collated by a single author. If this is true, then the *Treatyse* is a monument to an age-old process by which spoken knowledge was gradually distilled into isolated recipes, such as those found in the British and Bodleian library texts, before those recipes were themselves amalgamated into longer tracts. So the author of the *Treatyse* may have combined and edited the text from other sources into the work we know today, or he (or she) may have set them out *de novo*. What the writer did not do was to invent fly fishing.

The *Treatyse* did have an enormous influence on the subsequent development of fly fishing, largely as a result of its widespread distribution. We have absolutely no idea how many copies of the work were printed, although even a small print shop could have turned out between seven hundred and a thousand booklets a day. To begin with, the *Treatyse* couldn't have reached a wide audience. Readership would have been limited not only by its cost, but by the fact that at the time of its publication, fewer than one in five Britons could read. Most readers were male and the majority were members of the moneyed classes, professionals or the clergy. Ironically, Wynkyn de Worde tells us that he bound the *Treatyse* into his 1496 edition of the Book of St Albans in an attempt to limit the readership, for fear that the multitudes would descend and destroy all the good fishing:

> And in order that this present treatise should not come into the hands of every idle person who would desire it if it were printed alone by itself and put in a little pamphlet; I have therefore compiled it in a larger volume of various books pertaining to gentle and noble men, to the end that the aforesaid idle persons, who would have but little moderation in the sport of fishing should not by this means utterly destroy it.[28]

Much good it did him - every community could draw on the resources of a few readers and once its reputation had leaked out, the *Treatyse* became extremely popular. In retrospect, the book was Wynkyn's greatest success, enduring so long that in modified form it served as a basic textbook for fishers for almost two centuries.

Early Fishing Methods

Central though it is to the history of fly fishing, the striking thing about the *Treatyse* is that it tells us hardly anything about how anglers fished flies in the fifteenth century; though it is exceptionally thorough about bait fishing and lists almost every technique coarse fishers use today. Put in this light, the lack of detail about fly fishing methods is extremely odd, especially since the book goes into such abundant detail about patterns, and an unsettling explanation has been put forward that the list of flies might have been added to the *Treatyse* at a later date, perhaps by Wynkyn himself, a man who had already proved himself more than willing to 'improve' on other's work. And here we would be stuck, were it not for the surprising fact that we have modern examples of how similar tackle is used, which are very helpful when we try to look back across the centuries and attempt to work out how a fifteenth century fisher might have cast a fly.

The first comes from G.E.M. Skues, who pushed off on a fishing holiday in Bosnia in September 1897.[29] While he was there, he saw fishermen using gear which must have been well past its sell-by date even a hundred years ago. Skues wrote that they used rods about eight or nine feet long, with a horsehair line. The cast carried four silk-bodied soft-hackled flies, winged with soft hackle from wild goose, attached to lines a little longer than the rod, which the fishermen cast with great accuracy. When the fisher caught something, either it was flicked neatly out of the water and caught in the left hand, or it was hauled unceremoniously on to the bank. It sounds crude, but it wasn't and Skues was impressed because the natives out-fished him with tackle that, compared to his own, should have given him several hundred years' advantage; though it didn't impress him enough to make him give up on his beloved split-cane Leonard.

According to Dr Grubic, the technique Skues saw can still be seen in use in the western part of Bosnia today, particularly on the Una, Sana and Pliva rivers; interestingly enough, it seems to be quite distinct from the method used by 'traditional anglers' on faster flowing mountain streams elsewhere in former Yugoslavia, which is described below. The explanation may be that the Bosnian rivers are particularly clear, similar in many respects to the English chalk streams, and they have much larger trout. Present day Bosnian anglers who favour the traditional technique make their flies with floss, wool or flax bodies, and use soft, mobile game bird hackles, different patterns being used according to season. The patterns I have seen resemble traditional Spanish flies very much, with low wings and bodies which curve around the bend of the hook, giving them an appearance more like emergers than traditional wet or dry patterns; they are tied direct to nylon and generally fished in the low light of dawn or dusk using a downstream swing. From the sound of it, they don't differ very much from the flies Skues saw. Interestingly, a traditional Bosnian fly is listed in *Tying and Fishing the Sedge*, by Taff Price, 1994 on page 108.

Other similar accounts describe fishermen on the River Ain, near Lyon, early in the nineteenth century;[30] on the River Sesia, a tributary of the Po in Italy;[31] in the Asturias region of Spain;[32] as well as the 'Tenkara' technique, as practised in Japan and described earlier. Last, but not least, thanks once again to Dr Grubic, I can report that there are anglers in south-eastern Serbia, about thirty miles from the city of Pirot, who fish with a technique that Ælian's anglers might recognise, were they still alive to see it. The method was quite widespread until the fifties and was briefly described in *Fishing Rivers of Serbia*, published in 1962,[33] but there seem to be no other references to it. The fishermen are part of an age-old Balkan tradition which produced a self-sustaining society rooted in an agricultural system in perfect harmony with nature. The location where Dr Grubic witnessed the method is in the Stara Planina (it can be translated as 'Old Mountain') area of Serbia, in the heart of the Balkan Peninsula. Anglers using the method can occasionally be seen on the high tributaries of the Visocica river, near the villages of Dojkinci and Topli Do. Peasants from these villages are famous for their fly making skills, but it has always been a neglected corner of the country, which is why, perhaps, such an old method has survived. The best I can do is to quote Dr Grubic himself:

> During my fly fishing expeditions I discovered that this ancient form of fly fishing still exists in some places in Yugoslavia, Macedonia and Bosnia (former Yugoslav republics, now independent states). Possibly it is practised in Bulgaria, Greece and Rumania, but I'm not aware of that. It is usually practised by sheep keepers in far-away mountain regions. Today most of them use nylon mono instead of horse hair and cheap 10 ft long carbon rods (I believe that in England you call them 'roach poles'). But the technique is still the same and their selection of flies is usually small: 2-3 proven patterns are used throughout the season. Flies are of the spider type: usually black, yellow and red in sizes 12 and 14.
>
> I observed these men carefully and can tell you that what they lack in equipment they compensate with their skill. They are by no means inferior to modern fly fishermen, particularly on their river. This is first class fly fishing and I do not think that the fact that I use modern fly tackle makes me a better sportsman in any way. I know several exponents of this ancient art who are capable of catching over a hundred trout on a good day. It is important to note that this form of fishing remained in high mountain areas on small (less than 7-8 yards wide) and fast flowing rivers.
>
> There is a question that may arise: are these fellows just imitating modern fly fishers with less expensive tackle? I believe not. To the best of my knowledge they are genuine. The skill of fly making was passed from generation to generation. There are no written documents because most of them are illiterate, but there are stories. One thing is sure, they had no chance to see anyone using modern fly fishing tackle until recently... They don't want to waste money on tackle they don't need to catch trout.[34]

To this long list of countries which still have traditional fly fishers, we can tentatively add Bulgaria and possibly Russia; given a description of nineteenth century fishers near Novgorod,[35] raising the interesting prospect that the cradle of fly fishing stretched from the Atlantic coast of Spain to the Urals, a much wider area than originally thought.

Even without Dr Grubic's startling revelation, there is a surprising consistency between the accounts of present day traditional fishers and anglers could well have fished their flies the same way since time immemorial. But why have such archaic methods survived? At first glance, it seems surprising that anyone should persist in fishing with fixed lines on crude rods into modern times, when we all take carbon rods and aluminium alloy reels for granted, but all of the above are extremely effective techniques and every one of them is considerably cheaper than going out and buying the latest high modulus graphite fashion accessory.

In another letter, Dr Grubic gave an explanation which makes it clear not only how his anglers fished, but why they persisted in using such ancient methods – they are uniquely adapted to the rivers they know:

> First I must stress that these fishermen fish on rapid streams with numerous riffles and pockets behind boulders and very few large pools. Also these rivers have large populations of native brown trout. They usually have two flies – one on the end of the line and the other on a short dropper two feet from it. Flies are tied with cock's hackles but are not fished on the surface on purpose (as a normal dry fly). Today they prefer strong and heavy Mustad hooks. One fly is always a black one and the other is yellow, red or sometimes brown or grey. Bodies of flies are made from ordinary sewing thread and wool. They fish both upstream and downstream as their position and water dictates. It is clear that they do not fish 'across and downstream' or 'upstream wet fly' specifically. This method obviously precedes those clearly defined approaches. Mostly they cast slightly upstream and than drift flies into likely place (a pocket or run). Sometimes they even dap flies on the surface (and this is the closest they get to the dry fly). The important role in their approach is hiding from the fish, and they do all they can to hide successfully. They rarely wade – only when they have to cross the stream. They cast very often and very precisely. Average drift of their flies is maybe a yard or two. In this fast water flies never have a chance to sink deeply. So they usually see the fish attacking the fly in the clear water. Their line is always stretched tight so they also feel the fish as it hits. When a fish hits they strike in the wrist.[36]

The most interesting thing about all the examples above is that while a strong theme unifies them (which is a fly, or flies, fished on a fixed horsehair line in the very surface layers of the water, using the most economical of casting movements), they are all subtly different, reflecting the unique circumstances each group faces. Some use longer rods, some shorter, some use more flies, some less, each technique being tailored to the type of river the fishermen had to cope with; but the unifying feature of all these groups is that they don't fish upstream very much. At most they make an upstream quartering cast, letting the fly fish down below them, unless they are using such a short line that they can actually dangle the fly on the head of the fish in broken water. The reason for favouring an across or downstream cast is quite simple; it is very difficult to fish out an upstream cast with a line that is fixed to the top of the rod. The only way of shortening line in this circumstance is to raise the rod tip progressively as the fly nears the angler. Once the rod is nearly vertical, striking becomes impossible, and the line can only be cast out again with difficulty.

The long rod brings several advantages which are sacrificed by those using shorter ones: much better line control and the lack of any need to false cast being but two. An angler with a long rod can laugh at cross-currents, since he can lift the fly across them and with practice it is possible to drop the fly right on the head of the fish in a way which can't be managed with a shorter rod. As we shall see, though many early fly fishers used short rods, on more open waters the long trout rod was a clear favourite for many centuries; while it may look odd to our eyes, our forefathers had very good reasons for sticking with it.

If nothing else, I hope that the examples I have given of ancient fishing techniques persisting into modern times have made interesting reading, but in practice I believe that they illustrate the way medieval anglers would have fished. A fixed line limits the tactical options open to a fly fisherman, and the methods described in the accounts above are so strikingly similar, despite their temporal and geographical separation, that it is possible that they describe all the methods known at the end of the fifteenth century.

Origins of the Fish Hook

Hooks are so much a part of fishing that the very term 'angling' is derived from the ancient word for a hook. Nowadays we take hooks very much for granted, but before the invention of the hook, primitive man fished with bone gorges, which were made from slivers of bone, flint or turtle-shell, attached to a line which was knotted through a hole near the centre of the gorge. The idea was that the fish swallowed the gorge end first in a bait, and the fisherman hoped that a brisk pull on the line would lever the gorge across the fish's throat, trapping it in place. It isn't easy to catch fish using a gorge: they are hard to conceal, difficult to bait, tricky to hook large fish on, and prone to lose their hold when a fish is being played. Despite all these problems, in expert hands a gorge can prove highly effective and some eel fishermen still use them today, but in general the gorge is of historical interest only.

The search for something better led to the gorge being replaced by the hook, but we don't know exactly when this occurred. In my own view, it is quite probable that there was an intermediate stage between the gorge and the hook, as examples survive of spikes set obliquely in the end of pliant shafts, and fairly obviously, there was a long period of co-existence between the two technologies. The materials used to make early hooks varied a great deal depending on geography and circumstance. Neolithic man fashioned his hooks out of whichever happened to be nearest to hand, and so we have specimens of bone, shell, wood and thorn hooks. Although it seems an unpromising material at first sight, wooden hooks have seen widespread use over the centuries, and they are reliable enough for the African peoples to use them to catch crocodiles today. The Lapps used fire-hardened juniper hooks up to and beyond the end of the nineteenth century in their great cod fisheries, while the Canadian and Alaskan Indians caught huge halibut on enormous wooden hooks until comparatively recently. The Mohave people even used the recurved spines of certain species of cacti as hooks, but bone was undoubtedly the most popular material for making hooks during the late Palaeolithic period. Despite the low probability of bone surviving the elements, our oldest bone hooks date back nearly 20,000 years, and we have good specimens which were made at the end of the last ice age (about 9,000 years ago) and were found in Palestine.

Flies probably were not tied on bone or wood hooks, because they could not be made quite fine enough, but in about 4,000 BC, copper came into widespread use. From there it was only a short step to the discovery of bronze, and metal became the standard material for hook making. By 2000 BC the Egyptians were fishing with rods, lines and hooks, a level of sophistication that even the Chinese wouldn't match for a thousand years, and which other civilisations would wait even longer to attain. The early Egyptian hooks were made of copper and had uncomplicated shapes. There was no barb, and the head was made by doubling the end of the shank over, which leaves the possibility that these hooks may have had an eye.[37] The length of these hooks varied from 2 to 6 cm, and the gape was wide in proportion to the length of the shank.

Barbed hooks soon appeared and by 1500 BC, bronze barbed hooks predominated. These later hooks had the shank flattened to form a spade end, allowing the line to be attached to the shank below the spade. This design survived for centuries and if you look closely, it is the way the *Treatyse* hooks were made.

By Roman times, hooks were usually made of iron or bronze, although occasional bone hooks survive from this period. Bronze hooks either were more common, or have survived more frequently, though it must be noted that this was a quite different material to the bronze we know today. Ancient bronze contained much more copper than the metal we use, which makes the modern alloy too soft to manufacture hooks. Many bronze hooks were found in Pompeii and these are usually double-barbed; although it is worth noting that these appear to be sea-fishing hooks. However, examples of hooks suitable for fly fishing have survived: in 1915, during a clash between British and German troops in Macedonia, a stray shell exposed the most extraordinary find:

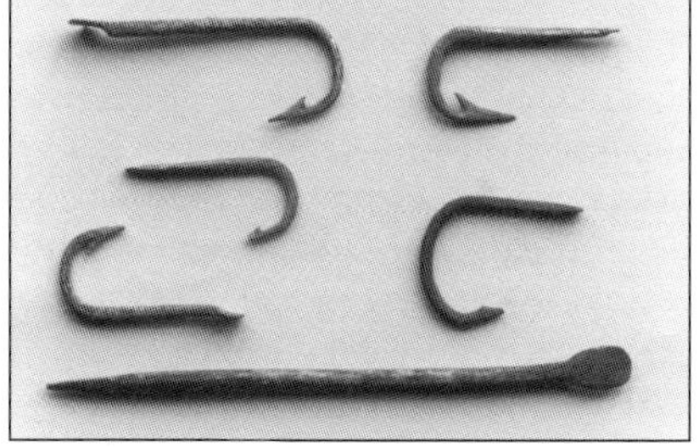

Roman hooks

> The front-line trenches occupied a causeway, bordered by the tombs of the ancient inhabitants of Amphipolis, which dates from 400 BC and was successively occupied by Greeks, Macedonians, and Romans. One day an enemy shell burst on one of these tombs, and when Dr Gardner and other officers examined the ruin out of curiosity they found the bones of a man dating from 200 BC holding in his hands a quantity of bronze fish-hooks. These ranged in size from about a No. 11 of our modern scale to No. 4 or No. 5. They were barbed and the ends of the shanks flattened with lines cut on the shanks below the flattened ends, to hold the whipping more securely.
>
> They were distributed among some of the officers and sergeants of the Expeditionary Force, who with them caught thousands of carp, the biggest weighing 14 lb; which formed a welcome change in the diet of the troops. One of these hooks was preserved and brought back to England, and is now in the R.A.M.C. section of the Imperial War Museum at South Kensington.[38]

These hooks could well have been in use even as Ælian wrote, and they may well have been made locally. There were small iron pits all over the area in Roman times which produced bar iron for use by local blacksmiths who produced swords and arrowheads, and for sale by merchants, who took it far abroad on their caravans.[39]

Little is known about the subsequent development of the hook in Europe, although fishing was widely practised and there was plenty of opportunity for experiment. The first instructions for making any kind of fly-fishing hook are given in the *Treatyse of Fishing with an Angle*, which illustrates a set of steel hooks. The interesting thing about this mention of steel is that it may well refer to metal made by a process which was quite new at the time.

Getting hold of reliable supplies of steel had been a problem since time immemorial. The ancients could make steel, but it was soft, due to a low carbon content. Although our ancestors had used the high carbon iron they found in meteorites for millennia, it was an incredibly rare and precious substance.

Very early steel was produced by heating iron up to about 900 degrees centigrade and then quenching it in water before heating it up again. This process is quite old and it has been established from analysis of implements that the Egyptians understood how to do it as early as 900 BC. However, at about the time the *Treatyse* was being written, at the beginning of the fifteenth century, some bright spark discovered how to use water power to blow air into the furnaces, with the result that temperatures could be increased to 1,200 degrees centigrade, producing a carbon-rich metal. The process was complicated and required huge kilns holding ten tons or more of metal mixed with two tons of charcoal and though it was expensive, the method produced a harder steel, with the result that it spread rapidly through Europe. Even then, it was a very poor substitute for the modern material, because these furnaces produced 'blooms', solid lumps of the metal which included generous amounts of impurities like slag and charcoal. Wrought iron was made by hammering the heated blooms into shape, but it was extremely difficult to control the composition of the metal produced this way and many of the early irons were annoyingly brittle because they contained far too much carbon.

There was another, more romantic source of steel, 'osmund', which was expensively imported from the Baltic in the form of very small rods or bars and was also used to make bell gear and arrow heads. Osmund steel seems to have been made from bog-iron ore in Sweden, where the name has been in use since early times.

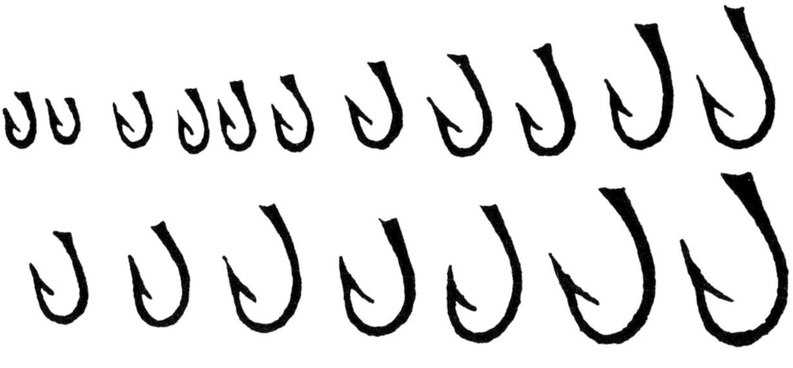

Hooks from the Treatyse

The woodcut of hooks shown above, was included in the *Treatyse* in order to help the readers, because in medieval times tackle-shops were unknown and there was no such thing as an 'authentic' pattern for a hook, since everything was more or less handmade. I am sure that the picture must have been useful then, but today it serves to highlight three of the greatest problems we face in understanding the history of the fly hook. First, we have lost the oral traditions by which fathers passed subtle instructions on hook making down to sons; second, we have no scale to determine the size of the hooks; and third,we have to accept the limitations of the wood-cut illustration. Fifteenth century wood engravings simply could not convey the fine detail of the smaller sizes of hooks. Readers can confirm this for themselves by examining the illustration of hooks in the *Treatyse*, which though it is crude manages to convey the major details of the hooks' design. Fortunately, the accompanying text clears some of the fog:

> You must understand that the subtlest and hardest art in making your tackle is to make your hooks, for the making of which you must have suitable files, thin and sharp and beaten small; a semi-clamp of iron; a bender; a pair of long and small tongs; a hard knife, somewhat thick; an anvil; and a little hammer. And for small fish, you must make your hooks in this manner, of the smallest square needles of steel that you can find. You must put the square needle in a red charcoal fire until it is of the same colour as the fire is. Then take it out and let it cool, and you will find it well tempered for filing. Then raise the barb with your knife and make the point sharp. Then temper it again, for otherwise it will break in the bending. Then bend it like the bend pictured hereafter as an example. And you must make greater

> hooks the same way out of larger needles, such as embroiderers' or tailors' or shoemakers' needles, or spear points; and of shoemakers' awls, especially, the best hooks are made for great fish. And the hooks should bend at the point when they are tested, otherwise they are not good. When the hook is bent, bend the hinder end out broad, and file it smooth to prevent fraying of your line. Then put it in the fire again, and give it an easy red heat. Then suddenly quench it in water, and it will be hard and strong.[40]

Don't take the word 'you' too seriously. Although there weren't any tackle dealers as such during the Middle Ages, it seems improbable that blacksmiths didn't make hooks for paying customers, since they would have had most of the tools and materials to hand. So although it is tempting to think of medieval fishermen making their own hooks, it is just as likely that they would have dropped in at the local forge and discussed what they needed.

Lawson's hooks

One has to be careful of drawing too many conclusions from the woodcut in the *Treatyse*, as it is quite likely that it only shows one fisherman's preference for hooks. A cut commissioned by Lawson a hundred and fifty years later shows a pair of hooks with markedly curved-in points, which may have been a new subtlety of hook design, but could equally likely have depicted a feature which had been in use for some time.[41] One thing that had definitely changed by the early seventeenth century was that Lawson could have bought his hooks, but despite this he preferred to make them out of Spanish and Milanese needles.

Artist's impression of a Tandy fly from the Treatise

Medieval Trout Flies

The *Treatyse of Fishing with an Angle* identifies twelve of the earliest trout flies we know, listing them month by month in a system which was faithfully used by many later authors. We are given two Dun flies, a Stone fly, a Yellow fly, the Black Leaper, the Dun Cut, the Maure fly, the Tandy fly, the Wasp fly, the Shell fly, the Drake fly and a twelfth unnamed fly. Things have moved on a bit from Ælian's scrap of crimson wool and ten materials are used: silk; various wools; hemp; feathers from partridge, mallard, jay and buzzard; cock and capon hackle; and peacock herl. The one disappointment about the *Treatyse* is that the instructions are so concise as to be almost unusable and worst of all, there is no illustration of the flies.

> *March*
>
> The dun fly: the body of dun wool and the wings of the partridge. Another dun fly: the body of black wool; the wings of the blackest drake mallard; and jay under the wing and under the tail.
>
> *April*
>
> The stone fly: the body of black wool, and yellow under the wing and under the tail; and the wings, of the drake. In the beginning of May, a good fly: the body of reddened wool and lapped about with black silk; the wings, of the drake and the red capon's hackle.

May

The yellow fly: the body of yellow wool; the wings of red cock hackle and of the drake dyed yellow. The black leaper, the body of black wool and lapped about with the herl of the peacock's tail: and the wings of the red capon with a blue head.

June

The dun cut: the body of black wool, and a yellow stripe after either side; the wings of the buzzard, bound on with barked hemp. The maure fly: the body of dusky wool, the wings of the blackest male of the wild drake. The tandy fly at St. William's Day: the body of tandy wool; and the wings contrary either against the other, of the whitest breast feathers of the wild drake.

July

The wasp fly: the body of black wool and lapped about with yellow thread: the wings of the buzzard. The shell fly at St. Thomas' Day : the body of green wool and lapped about with the herl of the peacock's tail: wings of the buzzard.

August

The drake fly: the body of black wool and lapped about with black silk: wings of the breast feathers of the black drake, with a black head.

Until the work of Braekman and Hoffmann and others pushed the frontier of fly fishing back, these twelve flies were thought to be the earliest known fly patterns and because of that they have puzzled scholars for hundreds of years. The fact that the interest hasn't yet faded can be accounted for by doubts about the origin of the flies and by our ignorance of what they might have looked like.

There are several reasons why the flies may not have been invented by the author; for a start, the *Treatyse* is written as if the subject is nothing new; promotes fishing in general, and the whole tone of the text assumes that the audience has some prior knowledge. In addition, the fly patterns are presented in a strikingly systematic way: the materials to be used for the body, then the wing, then the trimmings. Most early authors stuck to the same system, and since whoever wrote the *Treatyse* didn't take the trouble to explain how the flies should be tied, it is probable that a convention for tying flies was well established by the time he or she put pen to paper.

It would appear that none of the *Treatyse* flies were dressed with a wound hackle, which would give the patterns much in common with Cotton's flies, tied a century and a half later. But although the dressings are detailed enough to suggest in one case that materials be laid along the length of the body, rather than wrapped around it as is conventionally the case, we have no idea how the wings were attached. Since the attitude of the wings is one of the defining features of a fly, the lack of instructions is a serious handicap. We can speculate that the materials were tied on using the 'reversed-wing' method (a standard method from the seventeenth century onwards) but the Tandy fly pattern asks for opposed upwings; a technique which doesn't reappear until the nineteenth century, and this raises some uncomfortable questions about other conventions that may have been used. Another possibility is that the wings were tied using hackle fibre stripped off the stem and bunched together to form a downwing, but the patterns are so isolated in time and space that the best we can do is make an educated guess.

The intriguing thing about the flies is that the bodies are, without exception, tied from wool, whereas the flies in the contemporary Tegernsee manuscript use silk. I think this is significant because it may be the first sign of the English divergence from the custom elsewhere in Europe of tying the bodies of flies almost exclusively with silk; a tradition which was maintained until the late nineteenth century when the might of the British/American fly tying tradition began to wipe out other nations' fly tying heritages. The trouble is that we have very few medieval patterns to make a judgement on, but it is interesting that the flies described in the Bodleian and British Library manuscripts make no mention of wool at all.

The uncertainties left by the passage of so many centuries haven't dampened curiosity about what the flies looked like, perhaps the reverse. The difficulty of recreating the twelve flies is shown by the many attempts to tie them, resulting in some delightful patterns which have nothing in common beside the materials they use, and sometimes not even that. Perhaps the best known interpretation is shown in McDonald's excellent book, The *Origins of Angling,*[42] which pictures a series of flies bearing an acute resemblance to Doug Swisher and Carl Richards' 'No-hackle' duns.[43] Another series, tied by the late Jack Heddon, is shown in Joe Bates' *Art of the Atlantic Salmon Fly.*

As they stand, the instructions leave room for almost endless interpretation and unless some standard canon of fly-tying methods did exist in the fifteenth century, which is more than possible, anglers of the time would have been no more able to tie 'standardised' flies from the *Treatyse* than we can today. To add to the mystery, the most complete surviving manuscript copy of the *Treatyse*, dated about 1450, lacks the list of flies, as well as several other pages that appear in the printed version. This is the source of the speculation that the list of flies doesn't belong to the *Treatyse*, if such an accusation can seriously be made about a manuscript which seems to have been cobbled together from so many sources.

McDonald has described the patterns as launching the first period of classicism in fly tying in Britain, a point on which Skues, who had his own experience of the negative impact of classicism, agreed when he wrote, 'The famous twelve flies for trout and grayling are described as if they were the laws of the Medes and the Persians and altered not . . . '. And if the surviving literature of fly fishing is to be trusted, alter they did not. But is it likely that the literature describes every fly which was in use at the time? I think not.

As support, I call as my witness C. R. Pearce, who wrote a superb article on 'The Folk-tradition of Fly-tying' in *Trout and Salmon* (volume 16, No 185, Nov 1970, p 23-25; which was kindly copied to me by Kevin McKenna).

Pearce argues strongly that it is necessary to distinguish two kinds of tradition, both of which have contributed to the development of angling methods, namely the folk-tradition and the literary one. 'I doubt if anyone has bothered to separate them sufficiently.' He went on to say that the two traditions tended to separate and proceed in parallel instead of reinforcing each other, with the folk-tradition continually at risk of being 'swamped and extinguished', by the cultural might of the literary tradition. In essence, the creations of unknown local tyers, however effective or innovative they might be, stand little chance against mediocre patterns that are backed by the authority of the printed page.

I cannot agree more with Pearce, and my own view is that it is extraordinarily unlikely that English fishermen were so grateful for the *Treatyse* patterns that they accepted them without question for little short of two hundred years, but there is a distinct lack of any documentary evidence to the contrary. McDonald, for once, is wrong and I am convinced that anglers around the country continued to experiment with patterns that they had found best adapted to their local circumstances and which had been handed down by word of mouth; they just didn't write them down. So I don't think we should read too much into the *Treatyse* set, because it is likely that they are one of the first examples of Pearce's 'swamping of folk tradition' in action. Nonetheless, these dozen patterns are the earliest detailed tyings committed to paper and it is probably because they were so easily accessed that they had a long lifespan.

The 'Jury of Twelve', as the *Treatyse* flies have been described, was taken to heart by fishing writers and was recommended by Mascall[44] in 1590, and by Markham[45] in 1614. Izaac Walton himself faithfully reproduced the list, but he can be forgiven, because he was a bait fisherman at heart. But by the time Charles Cotton's chapters were added to the fifth edition of the *Complete Angler* in 1676 the twelve had had their day, most likely because an experienced fly fisher was writing. Richard Bowlker[46] relegated several to his list of flies that he didn't find useful, and it is probably a sign of the times that Thomas Best[47] discarded the entire series, leaving only the Dun Cut and that in his 'secondary' list of flies. After 1800, the twelve went into total eclipse and only two of the patterns survive, albeit in altered form, to the present day, the Stone Fly and the Wasp Fly. The fall from favour happened at an inconvenient time for us, half a century before the nineteenth century entomologist Alfred Ronalds might have explained what they were and so the origins of the patterns are surrounded by mystery.

The prominence of the *Treatyse* flies had encouraged a long roll-call of authors to amuse themselves speculating about which natural insects the patterns might have represented, a process which sometimes tells us more about the writer than it does about the flies. Despite the fact that he can't have had a clearer idea about what the flies looked like than we do, John Waller Hills was certain that he could identify all but one:

> . . . eleven can be identified. That is rather wonderful, but I believe it to be incontestable. The eleven are her first Dun Fly, which is a February Red, dressed with a partridge feather for wing and a brown body, as it is dressed today; her second Dun Fly, which is the Olive Dun; the Stone Fly; the Red Spinner, which is her fly made of roddyd (i.e. ruddy) wool; and her Yellow Fly, which is the Little Yellow May Dun. The Dun Cut of Dame Juliana is the Yellow Dun, the name having survived until the nineteenth century [in a footnote, Hills indicates that this is the Yellow Dun of Ronalds]. Then her Maure (mulberry coloured) Fly and Tandy Fly, with a body of tan coloured wool and wings of the lightest mallard, tied back to back, can be nothing but two dressings of the Mayfly in different states. The Wasp Fly, with a black body ribbed with yellow, speaks for itself. The Drake Fly, with its black body and dark mallard wing, is uncommonly like the modern dressing of the Alder. Lastly, the Shell Fly is the Shell Fly of Ronalds, with a dressing very similar, in spite of three and a half centuries. Thus it is possible to identify clearly eleven out of the twelve. The remaining fly is the Black Louper, appearing in May, which seems to have been a hackle fly, and corresponds to our Black Palmer or Coch-y-Bonddhu, but cannot be identified exactly.[48]

Hills' view was that the flies might have come from Shropshire or the Welsh borders, which is possible, but his identification was almost certainly biased by his devotion to the chalk streams and in my view it is questionable whether very many of the flies represented natural duns. Skues disagreed with Hills, as he might, and came up with a slightly different list, which leaves us with plenty of choice:

> I do not agree with Major Hills in all his identifications. For instance, I cannot identify No. 1 with either February Red or with the Partridge and Orange. In my opinion, it is the March Brown. No. 2 may be, as Major Hills says, the Blue or Olive Dun. No. 3, the Stonefly. No. 4, the Great Red Spinner, and No. 5, the Yellow May Fly or possibly Yellow May Dun, are recognisable enough. So is No. 6 as the Red Palmer.
>
> The Dun Cut I hold not to be the Yellow Dun but beyond question the fly which Mr. Halford persisted in calling the Welshman's Button, viz., the Sedge fly which appears in May and is known to science as Sericostoma personatum.
>
> No. 8, the Maure (or Mulberry Coloured) fly must be the Alder. No. 9, the Tandy fly, probably the Oak fly. No. 10, probably a Crane fly. No. 11, probably one of the green bellied Sedges and No. 12 I fail to identify.[49]

On the whole, I think Skues' list stands up to criticism better than Hills'. Even if he couldn't resist having a crack at his old adversary, Halford, Skues didn't miss very much and he made a remarkably perceptive observation: attempting to identify the patterns is all very well and good, but it does rather assume that they represent naturals which are found on English rivers. What if they don't?

Well? What if the patterns were imported from elsewhere?

Skues does have a point, and given our expanding knowledge of the development of fly fishing in medieval Europe, it remains a distinct possibility that the patterns weren't British at all, although there was more than enough time for fly fishing to have come to Britain and developed its own local and national characteristics. There is, however, one reason why Skues may be wrong, and that is the wool bodies of the *Treatyse* patterns. My personal opinion is that the use of wool is the most powerful argument for the flies having a British origin, quite simply because other European nations favoured silk bodies, almost to the exclusion of other materials. More than that is impossible to say, and until such time as a definitive source for the patterns, and some clue as to the conventions employed in tying them turns up, we might as well spit in the wind.

If the tying method assumed in the *Treatyse* eludes us, so to some extent do the correct shades the materials would have been dyed. The *Treatyse* gives detailed instructions on how horsehair should be dyed, but not the slightest hint about how the wool used to tie the flies should be treated. There was good reason for this, since the average fifteenth century fisherman wouldn't have needed to dye his own wool, given that almost every village of any size would have had its own resident dyer, who lived in a house near the river and happily polluted it with waste dye and worse. Because of the secrecy which surrounded what was a highly commercial process, we know relatively little of the detail of dyeing in ancient times. The mystery which enclosed the dyers' trade was enhanced by the plants they grew and the materials they needed. Some recipes whisper about the use of dead cats and even the most conservative dyer would have had a large barrel round the back of the house into which the men relieved themselves, rather than using the bushes. Most of the work would have been done out in the open in summer time, taking advantage of the good weather, for good reason, because depending on which way the wind was blowing, their homes must have smelt to high heaven.

All of this aside, the *Treatyse* flies were tied on home-made hooks and the author also gave advice on how to construct them. Then, the book being a no-nonsense manual, a description of how to whip a fly hook on to a line followed, outlining a technique which changed very little until the invention of the eyed hook and which appears to include a description of the whip finish:

> You must take fine red silk thread, and if it is for a large hook, then double it, but not twisted. And otherwise, for small hooks, let it be single. And with it, bind the line thick for a straw's breadth from the point where one end of your hook is to be placed. Then set your hook there, and wrap it with the same thread for two-thirds of the length that is to be wrapped. And when you come to the third part, then turn the end of your line back upon the wrapping, double, and wrap it thus for the third part. Then put your thread in at the hole[50] twice or thrice, and let it go each time round about the shank of your hook. Then wet the hole and pull it until it is tight. And see that your line always lies inside your hooks and not outside. Then cut off the line and thread as close as you can, without cutting the knot.[51]

Then - nothing. If we take the literature at face value, the combined efforts of British fly fishers was enough to make only one addition to the twelve flies in the next two hundred years, described here by John Lawson:

> The head is of black silk or haire, the wings of a feather of a mallart, teele, or pickled hen-wing. The body of Crewel[52] according to the moneth for colour, and run about with a black haire: all fastned at the taile, with the thread that fastned the hooke, you must fish in; or hard by the stream, and have a quick hand, and a ready eye, and a nimble rod, strike with him, or you lose him.[53]

Lawson's dressing is for a mayfly. Something about the picture accompanying the text suggests that the artist hadn't seen many artificials, but for what it is worth, it is the first illustration of a fly we have. Actually, I may be being a bit hard on the illustrator - though the execution is crude and it looks as if he has tried to draw a natural rather than an artificial, the picture has many points in common with the flies in the plate published in Sir John Hawkins' 1760 edition of *The Complete Angler*, a relatively thick body, a prominent head and widely split wings (see page 130).

Lawson's fly

In a subtle touch, Lawson advised that the colour of his pattern should be changed from dark white to yellow over the months:

> Your flie must counterfeit the May flie, which is bred of the cod-bait; and is called the water Flie: you must change his colour every moneth, beginning with a dark white, and so grow to a yellow, the forme cannot so well be put on a paper, as it may be taught by sight; yet it will be like this forme.

If the literature records every fly that was invented during this long period, this small detail brought a new level of sophistication to fly dressing, since it implied that the pattern was not static, and that the laws of the Medes and the Persians might be broken.

But perhaps we shouldn't read too much into this fly. I have already said that I suspect the literature only records a small fraction of the flies which were available to anglers prior to 1800 and we should be careful drawing too many conclusions from Lawson's notes. Quite why Lawson thought to mention this one fly and no other is a mystery, but it must have been important to him, since the scope of his notes is pretty concise. Though it is hardly credible that this was the only British fly to be invented in two centuries, it is the only pattern which has survived.

Other European Fishing Schools

It is traditional to present the *Treatyse of Fishing with an Angle* as the fount from which all subsequent fly fishing sprang, but as we know there were fly fishing traditions in other European regions, not least in Spain. Fernando Basurto's *Dialogue Between a Hunter and a Fisher* is the Spanish counterpart of *The Treatyse.*[54] Written in 1539, as Hernán Cortés, the fabled conqueror of Mexico sailed home - sadder and wiser, but very much richer – Basurto's work is remarkable because it is the first known work on fishing which relies upon the use of a dialogue, an extremely popular style of the time which would later be used in Samuel's *Arte of Angling* and most famously of all by Walton in *The Compleat Angler.*

Basurto's discussion takes place between a fishing commoner and his hunting patron, the subject being which of their sports should take precedence. The choice of the fisherman as commoner wasn't an accident, because one of the features of European culture of that age was that fishing had a lower status than other field sports, and while hunting and falconry were literally the pleasures of princes, fishing had much lower rank in the scheme of things. So Basurto's fisherman is daring in even speaking of fishing as a sport, let alone in the way he promoted it as the equal of hunting and, interestingly enough, this theme echoes the introduction to the *Treatyse of Fishing with an Angle.* Between the jigs and the reels, the text throws a little illumination on how the author fished: he had a rod with a wooden butt and a whalebone tip and he used silk-bodied flies. His fisherman recommended 'throwing down the stream and going up the stream with reasonable speed so that the feather goes along the top of the stream, for in such a manner the trout eat real flies and so we fool them with artificial ones.' The reader is told to capture naturals at the river, match them for colour and to use a representative artificial to catch his trout, a statement which echoes the theme of the Bodleian Library manuscript fragments and which points to a culture of matching the hatch which had either developed separately in many places, or had spread from a common source right across Europe by the sixteenth century.

In arguing for a common inheritance of all the European fly fishing traditions, there is no need to look any further than the similarities between the *Dialogue* and the *Treatyse*, but the flies they list are quite different. The one thing we do know about the *Treatyse* flies is that they were not palmered like Basurto's. The Spaniard's patterns were tied on spade-ended hooks, just like those recommended in the *Treatyse* but the materials used by the Spanish fishermen were silk (to wrap the bodies and again to rib them), the hackles of capons, ducks and an unidentified bird known as the 'bunal'. This use of silk to make bodies is typically Spanish and as I have already indicated, it is one of the key differences between British and flies originating elsewhere in Europe. Prior to 1900 the extensive use of dubbed animal fur or wool is almost exclusive to the bodies of the British patterns, with silk relegated to ribbing.

Fortunately for posterity, Basurto remembered to tell us how his flies were tied: the hackles were tied in at the butt with the tip facing forward, the first few wraps of the feather being taken over the butt toward the spade end of the hook, and finally the tip of the hackle was turned up and bound back in the finishing of the head. This is the first description anywhere in the literature of how to tie a fly which is good enough to follow today, and unlike any previous set of instructions, it includes precise instructions on where and how materials were to be applied to the hook.

We have to visit Switzerland for our next window into early fly fishing. In 1558, the Zurich physician and polymath Conrad Gesner published *Historia Animalium*, a profusely illustrated encyclopaedia of animal life.

Gesner was an interesting character. He came from very poor beginnings and was brought up by his great uncle, who combined his duties of canon of the church with a career as an amateur herbalist. With the support of his relative, Conrad studied Latin and Greek before he took up the study of medicine, qualifying in 1541, at about the time an obscure Polish astronomer called Copernicus was finishing *De revolutionibus orbium coelestium libri VI*; the work which stood Ptolemaic astronomy on its head and placed the sun at the centre of the solar system. Gesner's influence on the life sciences, though less seminal than that of Copernicus, was almost as pervasive.

Despite living in such auspicious times, Gesner doesn't seem to have had much luck as a doctor, and he managed to live in conditions of considerable financial hardship despite being made official town physician in 1554. Perhaps the reason was that he was more interested in his writing, and with good reason, because *Historia Animalium* was hugely influential and it guaranteed his immortality by becoming a standard work for many generations. The book was remarkable because it laid the foundation for standardisation of scientific terminology by listing the equivalent names of animals in a dozen languages. Gesner combined the classical and the medieval literature, adding his own observations and those of correspondents, and then organised the whole with extreme precision, including such facets as natural range, physical characteristics, habits, and use as food and medicine. By adding a large number of woodcuts he produced the first illustrated work covering the entire animal kingdom, the influence of which was to continue for two centuries through the numerous reprintings and translations. *De Piscium & Aquatilium Animantium Natura* – the fourth volume, is the one which interests us, because it contains a list of flies. There were patterns for grayling:

> Certain skilful fishers fabricate diverse kinds of worms and winged insects from the feathers of birds in various seasons of the year, and place such bait on the hook: for grayling indeed they make a kind of fly (in the month of April, I think) from partridge feathers, with a reddish head: body and wings white, from feathers (likewise) from the belly of a partridge.
>
> But in the month of May they represent the fly with a body partly of white and partly of black silk twined together in alternate layers, the head blue, the wings indeed from the back of the varied crow which our people name after the fog.
>
> Then in June they make up from feathers from the tail of the dark heron,[55] but the body green from feathers from the breast of the wild duck.
>
> But in July they shape a body from blue silk, a head from black silk, and they attach wings from feathers from the belly of the varied crow which our people name after the fog.
>
> In August they make the body from feathers of a crane's wings, (wings) from partridge feathers, [and the] head green.
>
> Finally in September they put together a body from blue silk, a head from red, and they assemble wings out of feathers from the back of the varied crow.

And for trout:

> ... (in the month of April, I think) you will fashion a fly in such a way that its body of silk be red, its head be green, with wings of red cock's [feathers] added.
>
> In the month of May, you will model the belly of the body from red silk and gold (gold threads), head black, but you add wings of red feathers of capons.
>
> In June, let the body be formed from silk blue and gold, let the head be yellow, but the wings from feathers under the wings of partridges.
>
> In July, you will fabricate a body from silk of green and gold, you will make a blue head, but wings from yellow feathers.
>
> In August, let the body be from the longer feathers of peacocks (prominently with the mirror or eye, as they say about the feathers of peacocks' tails) bound with a golden feather; head yellow, wings from the middle feathers between the wings of that wild cock which Germans name for the hazel.[56]
>
> In September, let the body be made from yellow and red silk, head dark, with wings from the back of the ptarmigan, which is called the white partridge.[57]

Gesner's writing is fascinating for more than this simple list of flies, though I can only wish he had written something about the way they were tied. First, he quotes as his authority 'a certain German manuscript on deceiving fish', yet another tantalising hint at a lost book (if all these vanished books were put end to end, they would cover a serious amount of shelf space). Second, he presents a completely new list of patterns only half a century after the *Treatyse*; flies which derive from a long central European tradition and which have absolutely nothing to do with the English list. All of this points to a considerable, and hitherto unsuspected diversity of patterns available to the medieval angler. And finally, although it is only an interesting footnote, he translated Ælian's *On the Nature of Animals* into Latin in 1556, a work which was the basis for every subsequent edition until 1858.

Reels, Lines and Rods in Medieval Times

Patient research in the latter half of the twentieth century has considerably advanced our knowledge of early flies and rods, but what about other fishing tackle? Hand-held spools have been used from time immemorial for the purpose of storing line, but curiously enough, despite the fact that it isn't an obvious invention, the history of the reel is almost as long as that of the rod. The reel was well known in the Middle East long before Europeans adopted it and the ancient Egyptians used primitive reels from about 2000 BC, but unfortunately, these reels were used for catching hippos, which, while it was one up on trimming for pike, isn't the sort of thing that gets one invited back on to a private beat nowadays.[58]

As usual, getting exact dates is tricky, so we can't be sure when the first reel was used. There are precious few clues in the literature and although it is possible that the ancient Chinese were using reels for fishing as early as AD 300 or 400, the references are pretty obscure. The Chinese certainly had the technology to invent the reel, given that they had invented the geared wheel by 200 BC, but very little is known about their early reel development.

Art is far more informative. A painting by Ma Yaun, dated circa 1195,[59] shows a man fishing from a boat, using a rod that seems to have a reel attached. The first indisputable illustration of a reel is a painting of a Chinese turtle fisherman who is clearly using a reel attached to a rod. The picture was executed in 1600,[60] which fits in very well with the first mentions of European reels, which begin to appear in the seventeenth century. However, we aren't on totally sure ground here, because a plate in the J. Paul Getty Museum has been discovered which seems to show a fishing reel attached to a rod; if the origin and date of the plate are correct, then we would have to move the first known use of the fishing reel in Europe back as far as the fourth or the fifth century AD.[61] Hopefully more evidence will emerge in the next few years.

Byzantine plate from the Getty Museum

Strange though it may seem, medieval fly fishermen didn't have much use for reels, even if they had heard about them. They found the combination of a long rod and a fixed line perfectly adequate for the majority of their fishing and the reel didn't come into common use for fly fishing until as late as the eighteenth century.

Lines

If reels are a bit of a mystery to us, we know much more about early fly lines. All the early European accounts talk of lines which are attached to the top of the rod - the first stage of fly line evolution. The *Treatyse of Fishing with an Angle* gives precise instructions on how such a line should be made: hair was taken from the tail of a white horse and then dyed, using, among other things, small ale, alum, vitriol, copperas, walnut leaves, tanner's ooze and soot. Tanner's ooze, by the way, is the liquid from a tanner's vats, which contains tanbark juices and God alone knows what else (keen as I am to try all of the early techniques, the idea of using tanner's ooze always stays my hand):

> First see that you have an instrument like this picture drawn hereafter. Then take your hair and cut off from the small end a large handful or more, for it is neither strong nor yet dependable. Then turn to the top of the tail, each in equal amount, and divide it into three strands. Then plait each part at the one end by itself, and at the other end plait all three together. And put this last end in the farther side of your instrument, the end that has but one cleft. And fix the other end tight with the wedge the width of four fingers from the end of your hair. Then twist each strand the same way and pull it hard; and fasten them in the three clefts equally tight. Then take out that other end and twist it sufficiently in whichever direction it is inclined. Then stretch it a little and plait it so it will not come undone. And that is good. And to know how to make your instrument, behold, here it is in a picture. And it is to be made of wood, except the bolt underneath, which must be of iron.[62]

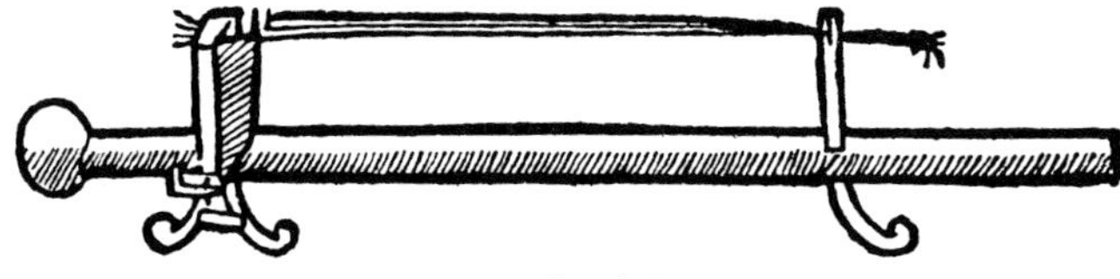

Line twister from the Treatyse

Have a good look at the woodcut, because the *Treatyse* line twister is a small masterpiece of design and it is considerably easier to make a horsehair line using it than it is to employ some of the devices which came on the market centuries later.

The fixed line was a significant constraint on tactics, but despite this, the field craft advice in the *Treatyse* differs little from modern books, and the angler was urged to stay out of the sight of the fish as far as possible and cautioned to avoid even his shadow falling on the water. When you bear in mind the length of rods and lines in use, a fisherman in the Middle Ages was unlikely ever to be much more than twelve yards away from his quarry; relatively close by modern standards. This proximity was a serious handicap and while we tend to think of early fly fishing as a clumsy affair, it can't have been, unless trout have got a great deal more wary in the last five hundred years; and yet, fifteenth century practitioners were highly skilled men and women, who caught good trout in numbers large enough to sustain the possibility of making a living out of professional fishing.

Where our forebears did differ greatly from us was in the type of fishing weather they looked forward to, a state of affairs forced upon them by the limitations of equipment they used. They hoped for enough wind not only to disturb the surface of the water but to hide their approach from the trout. This was a time when man was much more at the mercy of the seasons than he is now and an old Ayrshire minister summed it up when he prayed, 'Send us, O Lord, we beseech Thee, a fine wind: not a ratterin'-tatterin' wind, but a huddery-duddery, dryin' wind.' The cleric was thinking of the harvest, of course, but the fishermen in his congregation would have wanted exactly the same, and even when they did have the right strength of wind to fish, they still had to pray that it blew in the right direction, since the day when a fly line could be cast easily into the wind was centuries away. So the *Treatyse* and many other early fishing books devote an almost obsessional amount of space to the influence of the weather and season upon fishing, right down to relating baits and flies to months and seasons. Charles Cotton was no different, and the man whom many claim to be the father of our sport would rarely have felt the wind on his face as he fished a clear stream, fine and so far off.

Fishing Rods

The fishing rod is an ancient invention, though it may not be as ancient as fishing is itself, since hand lining seems to have preceded the rod by at least a thousand years. Once again, art comes to our rescue when writing will not. The first known angling scene comes from a tomb painting which dates to circa 2000 BC and shows a party of Egyptian fishermen at work. One of the group has a hand line and another a short rod.[63] This seems to be a bait fishing rod and we have to search harder to find a fly rod; although there are many references to fishing in ancient Greek, Assyrian, Roman and Jewish writings, the first mention of fly fishing with a rod was by Ælian.

Beni Hasan tomb painting

Judging from ancient murals, the Macedonian rod was the pattern for many centuries to come and it seems that many early fishing rods were multi-purpose weapons made from single pieces of wood or reed only a few feet long, though the first mention of a rod with joints was made by Martial in the first century AD and there is a reference to a longer jointed rod used by the Romans in the fourth century AD. However, despite the written and pictorial evidence, there is no logical reason why rods of ten or even eleven feet long were not used.

From Ælian's time until the *Treatyse*, there are few depictions of rods longer than six feet. The reason for this may be a purely practical consideration; rods are big 'long' unwieldy things and artists may have literally shrunk them to fit. In support of this theory, we can quote Homer's and Oppian's talk of long rods, although in Oppian's case at least, the rods in question were intended for sea fishing. Sadly, unless new material is discovered, our chances of discovering the truth are not so great. As it is, our small store of knowledge is pieced together from fragments and there are few enough to go on; for example, we know very little about early materials for rod making, although Pliny[64] mentions that the African arundo reed was much favoured. Other materials certainly were used, because Ælian also names the narthex and cornel wood. Narthex is very similar to ferula, a reed from which it would have been easy to make a light cane rod.

So once again, we have to wait until the *Treatyse* for a detailed account of a fly rod. At the time the book was published, Columbus had only recently discovered America, and Spain and Portugal were busy carving up the New World between them. Despite the fashion for voyage and invention, there were no tackle makers and imports of exotic woods hadn't really begun to make an impact, so anglers would have had to cast about near their homes to find the materials they needed. Every rod would have had to be home-made (or at least locally-made) and in keeping with the remainder of the book's philosophy, the author gave detailed instructions on rod making, right down to the correct time of year to cut the wood:

> And how you will make your rod skilfully, here I will teach you.
> You must cut, between Michaelmas and Candlemas, a fair staff,
> a fathom and a half long and as thick as your arm . . .[65]

Though making the rod strictly according to the instructions must have been quite a challenge, the materials were common to every English hedgerow. The author tells the reader to make the butt from hazel, willow or poplar and how to hollow it out so that it can be used to conceal the top, a design feature which was common to many fishing rods over the next four hundred years. The top was to be made of two sections; the lower of green hazel, and the upper of blackthorn, crabtree, medlar or juniper. The detail of the description may be open to question, but the basic design is not: a rod at least fourteen feet long, fishing a horsehair line that was fixed to the splice that joined the two sections of the rod top, and fed through a loop at the tip of the rod.

This wasn't a straightforward rod, and the *Treatyse* makes it clear that once the tops were stored in the hollow butt, 'you will have a rod so well disguised that you may walk with it and no one will guess that you are going fishing.' Now the element of concealment seems odd, but it is understandable when you realise that sport fishing was in its infancy. This was the day of the professional angler and only a fool would have been keen to advertise good water, an attitude which took a long while to change. Concealed rods still hadn't gone out of fashion three hundred and fifty years later – they had just become more sophisticated and were disguised as malacca walking canes.

The description of the *Treatyse* rod ends with the immortal words,

'And thus you will make yourself a rod so perfect and suitable that you can walk with it, and no one will know what you are going to do; and it will be light and full nimble to fish with.' And light and nimble it would have needed to be, because at the time the *Treatyse* was written, fences were a rarity and an angler with time on his hands could roam happily over millions of acres of heath and common, unrestrained by boundaries. It is very hard to imagine the English countryside as it was then; with strip farming blending into heath, animals free to wander on common land and wood pasture and little to stop the fisherman casting a fly wherever he pleased. Although there were enclosures in the fifteenth century, the fencing of land which so utterly changed the face of England did not start in earnest until the middle of the eighteenth century, so the author of the *Treatyse* can have had few concerns when he or she set forth, an inoffensive looking staff in hand and creel on back, in search of speckled trout.

The Seventeenth Century

CHAPTER TWO

The Seventeenth Century

THE DAWN of fly fishing as we know it occurred in the latter half of the seventeenth century. Quite suddenly, in the space of twenty years, a leash of books recorded a complete change in the face of the sport. Although it is tempting to assume that the authors concerned caused the change, it is more than likely that what they actually did was to record what had changed. Whatever the case, it is quite clear that fly fishing in the seventeenth century had moved on by leaps and bounds from the nursery years of the fifteenth.

Quite when the pace started to quicken is impossible to guess. Unfortunately, the years intervening between the writing of Basurto's *Dialogue Between a Hunter and a Fisher* in 1539 and the end of the first quarter of the seventeenth century are a blank. It seems quite odd that with all the excitement caused by the development of the printing press, no one thought to write anything about fly fishing for more than a century. But if they did, it has been lost and we should be grateful for the English angling writers of the seventeenth century, because they influenced the subsequent course of fishing more than any other writers have done before or since.

In many ways it was an odd time to set pen to paper, since England was still recovering from the bloody upheaval of years of civil war and there were plenty of other things to worry about besides fishing. It was a time of great change. At the beginning of the century, the population of England and Wales was about four million, nearly twice the total at the beginning of the previous century. The economy was still predominantly rural, with eighty-five per cent of people living in the country, but London started the century with quarter of a million souls and ended it housing nearly double that. The increase in population and the increasing needs of the towns put severe strains on the rural economy, which began the century in crisis, but as a result of enclosure and agricultural reform, produced sufficient surpluses to export grain by 1700. As usual, productivity was not bought without pain and the century was marked by revolts and starvation. To make matters worse, the vital cloth trade was in recession, partly as a result of the Thirty Years War, which engaged almost every major power in Europe, disrupting trade routes until hostilities finished in 1648; but the economy which England salvaged from this critical period was stronger as a result of a more diverse base.

At the beginning of the seventeenth century, Parliament was merely one of the king's councils, to be summoned only when the monarch needed to pass particularly contentious laws, or had to raise money at short notice. The day to day administration of government was carried out by the Privy Council, a completely unaccountable body which was hand-picked by the king. The arrangement seemed set in stone, but by the end of the century, most regal privilege had been swept away and England had its feet set firmly on the path to democracy. Like so much constitutional change, accident had more to do with it than purpose. From Charles' point of view, it all began innocently enough, with the 'Bishop's Wars'; a botched attempt to suppress a rebellion, which lost Northumberland to the Scots and forced the summoning of Parliament in 1640, after the King had succeeded in governing England for eleven years without it. It turned out to be the worst decision Charles ever made. The new Parliament was hell bent on a programme of reform and after the monarch failed to impeach five members of the Commons for treason in 1642, events spiralled out of his control, with the result that he had to leave London in a hurry. The country descended into civil war, which was only temporarily interrupted by Charles' arrest and execution in 1649.

Regicide did not endear the new regime to the other crowned heads of Europe and the Cromwellian era began with virtually every European nation's hand set against the government and English ships became legitimate targets for all and sundry on the high seas. Oliver Cromwell thrived on isolation and for a time he seemed unstoppable as he won wars against the Irish, Scots and the Dutch, but his military successes were not matched with the constitutional reform he expected. In 1653, unhappy with the way things were going, Cromwell marched on Westminster and dissolved Parliament; an action which led to the creation of the Protectorate, a governing regime which he held together by the force of his personality alone.

When Cromwell died in 1658 the country descended into chaos once more and it was with some relief that Parliament dissolved itself to make way for the restoration of the monarchy. Despite the settlement, feelings still ran dangerously high and political and military allegiances cast their shadow over even the most insignificant actions. From our point of view, the relationships between many writers of the period were poisoned by the fact that they had fought on opposite sides during the conflict; so while Walton could emerge from the shadows again, Franck had to sail into exile in America and Colonel Robert Venables faced the ruin of his career.

Of all the fishers who feature in this chapter, Venables had the most interesting life, and the rise and fall of his fortunes show just how much the pendulum could swing during those years. He was born in 1612 or 1613, to a landed family which had had its roots in Cheshire since the time of William the Conqueror. At the outbreak of the civil war he raised a company of infantry and declared for Parliament. Early on in the conflict, he was captured by the Royalists, but was released, fighting with some distinction in the remainder of the war and then in Ireland after that. Promoted to General, he was given command of an ill-conceived expedition to the West Indies where he presided over a disastrous and quarrelsome campaign, failing to take his main objective, Hispaniola. On Cromwell's orders, Venables was thrown in the Tower of London, where he spent several weeks cooling his heels before his release in 1655. He saw no further military service and we know little about his subsequent life, beyond what we can read in a series of increasingly sour letters inspired by his opposition to the marriage of one his daughters.

Even though one would assume that the tides of civil war would have swept the sands clean, the last half of the century was scarcely less troubled than the first, though for different reasons. The new schism was a religious one and mere rumour was enough to justify imprisoning Quakers and Protestants - for example John Bunyan had to compose his *Pilgrim's Progress* while he languished in jail. Catholics were no less discriminated against and there were plots against the king and rumours of renewed civil war. Matters came to a head after Charles II died in

1685, to be replaced by his brother James, a Catholic. The new monarch guaranteed the ascendancy of the Anglican church and suspended the penal laws against Catholics and Dissenters. Unable to come to terms with this, in 1688 a group of leading Protestants invited the Dutch William of Orange to come to England. The result was unexpected; although there was probably no intention to depose the King, James panicked, decamped with his family to France and William was crowned in his place. With French backing, James invaded Ireland in 1690, in a campaign that was initially successful but foundered with his defeat at the Battle of the Boyne.

Anglers in Dovedale

If reasons are to be found for the flowering of English fly fishing literature during the seventeenth century, they are intimately connected with the restoration of Charles II to the throne. Charles was the child of diplomatic intrigues, broken promises, unfulfilled hopes and exile, a combination which gave him a thick skin and an instinctive ability to compromise when the going got tough. His first act was to attempt to square every important political interest as part of his terms for resuming government, though he left it to Parliament to decide how to do it. A general pardon was to be issued, greater religious tolerance sought, and the security of private property guaranteed. It was a tall, and some feel cynical order, and though the reality fell somewhat short of Charles' grand aims, it gave new confidence to a weary nation which had weathered decades of uncertainty. One result was a flowering of literature: the novel, drama, biography, history, travel writing, and journalism all found their feet during this period - and so did our angling literature, which is particularly appropriate because Charles was a fisherman himself.

There must have been some secret alchemy hidden behind the curtain of this extraordinary period of English history, because at a time when the exhausted country was being ravaged by plague and by fire (events which some saw as divine intervention), three men wrote works which laid the foundation of the modern sport of fly fishing: Barker, Venables and above all, Cotton. The curious thing is that despite the international nature of fly fishing, all these writers were English and between them they established an English sporting tradition which completely dominated fly fishing literature until the late nineteenth century. The road they led their compatriots down was quite different from the path taken by the rest of the world and while it is clear that fly fishing for sport and the pot went on as it always had done in Spain, France, Italy, Middle Europe and Japan, the literature of sport fishing became an almost exclusively British preserve for the next two hundred years.

Rods

If I transported you back to the seventeenth century, the first thing that would strike you about the anglers you saw would be the extraordinary length of their trout rods. For all the changes in society during the hundred and fifty years which had elapsed since the publication of the *Treatyse*, fishing rods had altered remarkably little. The vast majority were still built to fish a float as well as a fly and, with few exceptions, dedicated fly rods did not exist.

If you had tagged on to an English landowner's party, he would have taken with him a rod which measured between fifteen and eighteen feet fully rigged, and as you rode out, he would no doubt have pointed out that a few even larger examples could be seen. The commoners and his farm workers would have been fishing with hazel sticks, more or less as they had always done. The thing that would have struck you particularly forcefully is that whatever type of rod was used, the line was almost always fixed to the tip, a choice which limited the area of water which could be covered and meant that to some extent rods had to be chosen according to the size of river to be fished.

Your host would have complained that getting hold of good rods was a problem. He could have pointed you to the premises of a few tackle dealers, but by and large they were confined to the cities and the majority of rods had to be home-made:

> . . . you need not be so exactly curious for your stocks as your tops, though I wish you to choose the neatest taper-grown you can for stocks, but let your tops be the most neat rush-grown shoots you can get, straight and smooth; and if for the ground rod near or full two yards long, the reason for that length shall be given presently; and if for the fly of what length you please, because you must either choose them to fit the stock or the stock to fit them in a most exact proportion; neither do they need to be so very much taper-grown as those for the ground; for if your rod be not most exactly proportionable, as well as slender, it will neither cast well, strike readily, or ply and bend equally, which will very much endanger your line.[1]

The detail about 'rush-grown' shoots is important, because it introduces a conundrum which was to exercise fly fishermen's ingenuity for another two hundred years. The top section of a fly rod has to be flexible enough to cast a fly, yet it also has to be strong enough to fight a fish and above all, it has to be light. Before the import of exotic woods began in earnest during the eighteenth century, fly fishermen got round the problem by cutting long, thin, whippy shoots from hedges to serve as tops and these were bound and left to dry in lofts until they were needed. Your host would have had a large stock, because tops like this snapped at the drop of a hat.

The pair of you would have had a long discussion about the appearance of rods, an important consideration in an era when every single one was custom-built and no two were alike. If the grip of an ordinary working rod wasn't left as a simple continuation of the butt section, it could be finished in a variety of ways: it might be made of cane; covered with thin leather or parchment; or painted after the fashion of the London makers at the time.

As for materials, he would have told you that hazel was the stuff for fly-fishermen, because it made for a long light rod that could easily be managed with one hand. But the expert that had made your companion's rod for him would have gone a stage further, and when you examined it, you would have seen that he had trimmed the last two feet of the top off and fitted a small shoot of blackthorn or crab tree on to it, the end of this shoot being cut off in turn and replaced with a small piece of tapered whalebone, a complicated construction, but one which made for a sensitive tip.

Whalebone found a new use in British rod building during the seventeenth century, and it became more or less a standard material for rod tips for the next two hundred years. Other countries had known the secret long before and the Spanish had been using whalebone for at least a hundred years by 1660, so it may well be that British rods had whalebone tips in the sixteenth century, but if so it can't be confirmed. The advantages of whalebone were that it was light, sensitive, elastic and very tough – unlike wooden tip sections, which had a tendency to smash easily if built too fine and which were stiff and unyielding if they were made thick enough to last. The disadvantage of whalebone was that it was relatively heavy, but its many other virtues ensured that it remained popular until the middle of the nineteenth century.

Your companion would have gone on at length about joints. Although there is some uncertainty about quite how these early rods were assembled, reading between the lines, it seems that both socket joints and splices were used. Cotton mentions Yorkshire rods made of six to twelve pieces which were 'tied together with fine thread below, and silk above,' which sounds like splicing to me, though the weapon he had in mind must have been a terror to assemble. Twelve sections sounds rather over the top to modern ears, but bear in mind that many rods were built for travelling and that transport was limited to horses or small ill-ventilated, badly-sprung carriages where a long, pointed package would have been about as welcome as a wasp, so fishermen were mindful to keep the overall length of broken rods as short as possible.

Socket joints were popular among anglers who needed to break down and assemble rods repeatedly, but the punitive weight joints imposed on a rod swung the scales heavily in favour of the splice, particularly for top sections, which were so thin that joints were impractical. On the whole, your friend would have been in favour of the splice for rods he used close to home, but if he had to travel, the socket was king.

One of the reasons we know so much about seventeenth century rods is that Venables does us the favour of giving an illustration of two in his frontispiece. Both have three sections and are built with socket joints, but the author doesn't give anything away about them in the text. The rod in front has three joints and is finished at the butt with a ball. The other rod is partially obscured by the first and though it has at least two joints, we can't see the base because it is overlaid by what appears to be a powder or bait horn (slight carelessness by the illustrator means that at first sight it appears that the rod has a butt almost like a modern shotgun.) Both the rods have the female joint on the lower, thicker section, standard practice in those days, as it was virtually impossible to form a joint the other way round without making the sections much too thick. Both the rods have rings tied to the tip of the top sections, the artist showing the lines tied to the rings, which may not have been correct, as loop to loop attachment of the line would have been easier. As far as we can tell, the pair were fairly typical good quality rods for the period.

Venables' frontispiece

Incidentally, though home made rods may sound crude, seventeenth century tackle had much care and attention lavished on it, since anglers couldn't exactly ring up a mail order house and order a replacement the way we can today and lifetime guarantees lay several centuries in the future. The trouble entailed in making a rod meant that even your landowner was unlikely to own more than one or two. Fortunately, rods did last pretty well if taken care of; as long as twenty years, if Walton is to be believed. It seems likely that some village carpenters ran a profitable side-line in rod building and although the majority of rods were made by amateurs, some were very practised and rods of the period could be quite sophisticated if it so took the builder's fancy. Chetham for example, mentions two different types of fly rod, a rod made of five or six pieces of hazel, whipped together and topped with six inches of whalebone; and a more sophisticated rod with a seven or eight foot deal butt (trimmed to shape by the local arrow-maker) with a six or seven foot hazel mid section, a two foot yew top, and a five or six inch whalebone tip.[2]

Lines

The fly line our landowner used would have been made of horsehair and it would have been quite familiar to fifteenth century eyes, if not to yours. Most fly lines were a few yards shorter than the length of the rod, and although lines approaching or exceeding the length of the rod did exist, they were reserved for downwind fishing on blustery days and would have been difficult to manage in still conditions. In practice, this meant that although lines varied from fifteen to thirty, or even thirty-five feet in length, fifteen to twenty feet was the norm. The lines were tapered so that it was possible to present a fly more delicately and this was done by increasing the number of hairs in each section of the line all the way from the tip to the butt, so that a typical example was built with a section made of two hairs nearest the hook, then three lengths of three hairs, followed by four lengths of four hairs and so on, until the line finished with up to forty hairs at the top. If the experience of modern fishermen who make horsehair lines is anything to go by, a practised hand could have made a line in a day.

One thing all early lines had in common, right across all of Europe, was that they were fixed to the top of the rod, and one of the big advances of the seventeenth century is the first use of the running line. All the accounts written prior to this date tell of lines tied or looped to the top of the rod, which was quite sufficient for catching most trout. But in 1651, Thomas Barker tells us that he was fishing with a running line, which is something quite new. Barker says that he fished for trout with a line that tapered to three or four hairs, but he boasted of using a line as light as one hair, saying, '. . . you may kill the greatest trout that swims, with sea-room.'[3] By the way, this quote, though inspiring, should be treated as the hyperbole it almost certainly was, because horsehair could be incredibly unpredictable stuff. The breaking strain of a single horse hair is under a pound, assuming that the hair is in good condition; if not it can snap like cotton.

Despite everything Barker said, the majority of his contemporaries used fixed lines for trout, for a very good reason. Braiding hadn't been thought of and their lines were made to the same recipe the *Treatyse* advised, knotted every couple of feet, and the knots caught on absolutely everything. If you think about the awful 'clunking' feeling a poorly-tied backing knot gives when it runs out through your rod rings and then multiply the sensation by a knot every two feet, you will get the general idea. Landing a big trout on a single hair attached to the end of a running line would have been a significant event, something that most anglers would have remembered for a long, long time; no matter how much sea room they had to play with.

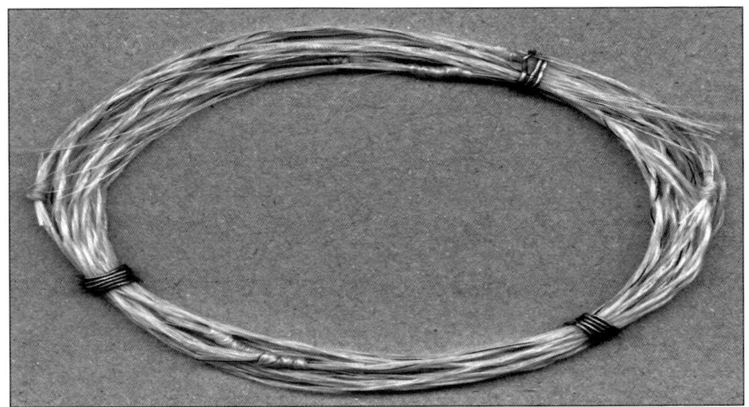

Horsehair line

Choosing horsehair and making lines from it was a great art and there was a simmering controversy over which type and colour was the best. There is a very good account of how to choose horsehair in the *Complete Angler*, which conveys very well how difficult it could be to find the right materials:

> And for making your Line, observe this rule, First, let your hair be clean washt 'ere you go about to twist it: and then chuse not only the clearest hair for it, but hairs that be of an equal bigness, for such do usually stretch all together, and break altogether, which hairs of an unequal bigness never do, but break singly, and so deceive the Angler that trusts to them.

> When you have twisted your links, lay them in water for a quarter of an hour, at least, and then twist them over again before you tie them into a Line: for those that do not so, shall usually find their Line to have a hair or two shrink, and be shorter than the rest at the first fishing with it, which is so much of the strength of the Line lost for want of first watering it, and then re-twisting it; and this is most visible in a seven-hair line, one of those which hath always a black hair in the middle.[4]

Once lines were made, many anglers dyed them; shades of green, brown, or yellow being the most popular. Very few authors ever agreed about the usefulness of different colours of horsehair and to make matters worse, there was considerable dispute about the sort of horse from which the hair should be taken. The consensus favoured stallions, for good reason, because mares' tails become soaked with urine and are liable to be rotten as a consequence. One nuance of selecting hair was that the best hair came from horses whose tails were combed reasonably frequently, as this lessened the chances of being let down by damaged hairs. Competition for good supplies must have been fierce, even in those days, when every man worthy of the description 'gentleman' would have kept at least one horse.

Given that it started in Walton's time, it is amusing to think that the argument over colour still continues, despite the fact that the materials have altered out of recognition in the intervening three hundred years. The only thing that has changed is that the advent of plasticised fly lines means that we have dozens of different colours to bicker over, instead of three.

Horsehair was so popular as to be universal in the seventeenth century, but as we have seen, it has its disadvantages, and even then there was a search for something better. A few fishermen had started using pure silk lines and other, more *recherché* materials:

> Further, I do not like the mixing of silk with hair, but if you please, you may, to make the line strong, make it all of silk, or thread, or hair, as strong as you please, and the lowest part of lute or viol strings, which I have proved to be very strong, but will quickly rot in water, you may however help that in having new and strong ones to change for those that decay; but as to hair, I like sorrel, white and grey best; sorrel in muddy and boggy rivers, and both the latter for clear waters.[5]

Musical instruments were stringed with catgut, so-called because it can be obtained from almost any animal except a cat. A few writers confuse catgut with the silkworm gut which became so popular in the nineteenth century, but catgut is a quite different material prepared from the dried and twisted intestines of the sheep, though horse and ass intestines are also used; the first references to it date back to the late sixteenth century. The name is a complete puzzle, as there is little evidence that catgut has ever been made from cat intestine. By the seventeenth century, catgut was freely available, and had all sorts of uses, ranging from driving bands for lathes, to clock belts. It was almost inevitable that fishermen would experiment with catgut sooner or later, but the material is too thick and stiff to present a really fine point and it has the terrible disadvantage of absorbing water like a sponge, with the result that it sinks. Despite these drawbacks, catgut seemed to have been relatively widely used for fishing lines, and Pepys makes a reference in his diary to a Mr Caesar, who fished with varnished catgut.

Early Hook Makers

Like the lines to which they were attached, early hooks were completely non-standard, with bends set entirely according to the fancy of the fisherman and their sizes were determined by the sort of needles which came to hand. But as books on fly fishing multiplied and the beginnings of a fly fishing industry appeared, so did the need for a scale that would allow authors to specify the size of their patterns. Establishing standards is never easy, but by the seventeenth century there was something of a defining force among tackle makers.

Kirby was the foremost hook maker for many years, trading from about 1650 until at least the 1770s in Harp Alley, Shoe Lane, London. When the elder Charles Kirby set up the business he was well aware of the poor quality of hooks of the day, which were often made for small profit margins and as a result tended to be extremely unreliable. Kirby hooks were of such good quality that the firm completely dominated the market in the late seventeenth and early eighteenth centuries, only losing its advantage when the crucible process for making steel became widely known. Kirby hooks were such a by-word for quality that it seems quite likely that Kirby used a hook scale to aid production, but if he did it is lost now.

Kirby's commanding position in the market didn't prevent other suppliers springing up and an international trade in hooks was well established by the early eighteenth century, with for example, the Shetland islanders importing their hooks from Bergen, and Kirby hooks being exported around the globe. By the middle of the eighteenth century, the Bergen hook industry employed no less than fifteen 'angle masters',who employed between them seven journeymen and sixteen apprentices. However, in general, quality control was very lax, and the manufacture of hooks was a hit and miss affair until the late eighteenth century, which explains the strong attachment that many writers had to particular suppliers like Kirby.

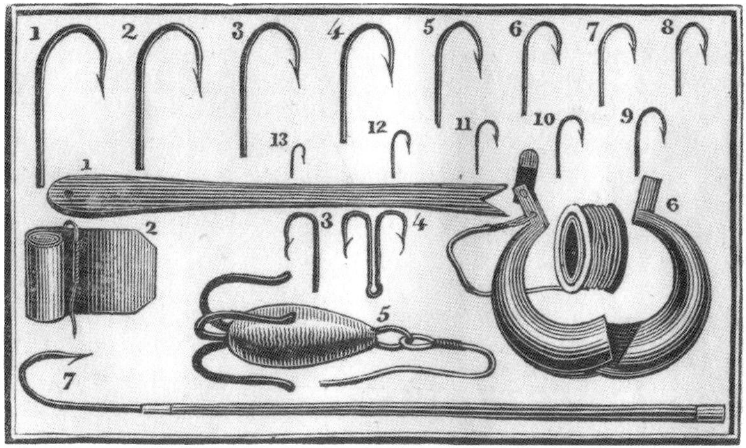

Kirby hooks

In fact, it was only after it was discovered how to convert iron into high quality steel on a large scale that fish hooks generally became strong enough to be reliable. Before this, all sorts of secret methods were used and Kirby's popularity was frequently put down to secret knowledge:

> It is reported that, the German Prince Rupert, well known for his experimental skill, in the reign of our Charles I, communicated to Charles Kirby a method of tempering hooks, which remained from that time a secret with Kirby's descendants, and even now the Kirby hooks are esteemed. Neither the London, the Birmingham, nor Dublin hooks are good, because they are manufactured to sell cheap.[6]

This is a good story if it is true – and it remains an intriguing possibility that the secret knowledge was an early version of the crucible process. Prince Rupert (1619-1682) was nephew to Charles I and the most talented Royalist commander of the English Civil War. After the end of the war, he was banished from England by Parliament, but continued to support Charles II, returning after the Restoration to become a privy councillor. He had a varied career, becoming the first governor of the Hudson's Bay Company in 1670 and Rupert is known to have had a penchant for carrying out scientific experiments. It would be possible to dismiss his association with Kirby as a contemporary urban myth if it wasn't for the fact that the Prince lived in Beech Lane, Barbican, at the time that Kirby had premises nearby in Golden Lane. It wouldn't have been that difficult for the two to meet, but at the same time it does seem rather unlikely that a hook maker, however prominent, got his know-how from a crown prince.

The steel for making hooks came from some odd sources in those days, and James Rennie in his landmark book *The Alphabet of Angling*, published in 1833, talks about the use of the nails from old horse shoes. These were converted to steel, presumably in a blast furnace, since charcoal was used:

> It is then formed into bars, or small rods, of a thickness varying according to the size of the hooks intended to be made. The bars for the fine hooks are a little flattened; those for the larger sorts are cut into lengths of from three to four inches, sufficient for two hooks, and are then in the form of a double-pointed spear. The artist requires a hammer, a knife, a pair of pincers, an iron semi-clamp, two files, one finer than the other, a wrest, a bender, long and short tongs, and an anvil. Let the rod be heated in a charcoal fire, when the barb or witter may be raised with the knife, taking care not to cut too deep. The point is then, after cooling, sharpened by filling it on a piece of hard wood, with a dent to receive the bar. The shank is next thinned, flattened, the upper part made square, and the whole worked off with the polishing file. Again, let it be put in the fire, and bent by a turn of the wrest round circular pincers. It is now cut from the bar, put into the fire a third time, and brought to a slight red-heat, and, taking it out suddenly, it is plunged into cold water. The temper is given by placing it on an iron heated in the same fire till it becomes bright blue, and while still hot it is surrounded with candle grease, which gives it a black colour.[7]

The next step forward came with the invention of the blast furnace, which as we saw in the last chapter seems to have appeared in Europe during the fifteenth century. By the middle of the sixteenth century, the demand for iron was so great and blast furnaces were so common that there was a scarcity of the type of wood needed for producing charcoal. The shortage became more and more pressing until the early eighteenth century, when it was discovered that coke could be used instead of charcoal. The use of iron only declined when it became possible to generate enough heat in commercial furnaces to produce steel during the mid-nineteenth century.

Fishing Techniques

As I discussed in the last chapter, the terms 'wet' and 'dry' are inappropriate terms as far as pre-nineteenth century fly fishing is concerned, as with few exceptions, the tackle and techniques in use kept flies on or very near the surface of the water, with patterns sinking a few inches at the most. This means that the greatest difference between you and our hypothetical landowner would have been the way the pair of you fished.

In the twenty-first century we take it for granted that we can keep our distance from the fish, which means that clear water holds few terrors for us. It was very different for the seventeenth century angler. Despite all the talk of fine and far off and the great skill that some anglers of Walton's day possessed, our idea of an idyllic chalk stream day would have sent them home in despair. They fished with much shorter lines than we are accustomed to, and they used a quite different technique, so getting close enough to fish to have a chance of catching them wasn't easy unless nature was prepared to lend a hand. The sort of conditions which seventeenth century anglers liked were rivers not quite cleared after rain, or windswept water under dark, scudding clouds. They had rods which cast long shadows and horsehair didn't fall that lightly, so caution and concealment were all. And when everything was against them, they hid behind bushes.

If the wind helped them by ruffling the surface and concealing them from the fish, it could also be a hindrance, because they couldn't cast into it as easily as we can. Our seventeenth century landlord would mostly have cast with the wind at his back and the sun before him, and like his ancestors, he would have fished downstream, or across and down, if he could. But he might, if he was an expert, have tried something quite new:

> And here I meet with two different opinions and practices, some will always cast their fly and bait up the water, so they say nothing occurs to the fish's sight but the line; others fish down the river, and so suppose (the rod and line being long) the quantity of water takes away, or at least lessens the fish's sight; but others affirm, that rod and line, and perhaps yourself are seen also.[8]

If you know anything about the history of fly fishing, you might be surprised to hear of casting up the water, because the honour for the first mention of upstream fishing in a book generally goes to William Stewart, a nineteenth century writer, simply because he championed it so vocally. But in fact Stewart was just formalising a tactic which had been known for centuries, though that isn't to say that it was widely practised.

Upstream fishing in the seventeenth century was known, but it wasn't easy; it was difficult to strike the fish, and the angler faced the tiring prospect of frequent casting with a long, heavy rod. All things considered, it was often too much effort, especially since the upstream man could cover far fewer fish in any given period of time. A typical day in a contrary wind would have involved several changes of direction, much cursing and a lot of cross-stream casts, as Cotton here recounts:

> In casting your line, do it always before you, and so that your flie must first fall upon the water, and as little of your line with it as is possible, though if the wind be stiff, you will then of necessity be compelled to drown a good part of your line to keep your flie in the water: and in casting your flie, you must aim at the further, or nearer Bank, as the wind serves your turn, which also will be with, and against you on the same side several times in an hour, as the River winds in its course, and you will be forc't to Angle up and down in turns accordingly; but are to endeavour, as much as you can, to have the wind ever more on your back.[9]

For some reason, none of the early writers ever described how they cast, so we have to skip forward two hundred years to get an insight into how it might have been done. A footnote in *The Book of the Axe*, of all places, describes what Cosmo III, the wonderfully-named Grand Duke of Tuscany, saw during a visit to England in 1669:

> . . . these [fishermen] keep it in continual motion, darting the line into the water like the lash of a whip, then, drawing it along a few paces, they throw it in afresh, repeating this operation till a fish is caught.[10]

Now compare Cosmo's memory with Venables' view of casting in *The Experienced Angler* (1662) that:

> You must keep your artificial fly in continual motion, though the day be dark, the water muddy, and the wind blow, or else the fish will discern and refuse it.

Both these accounts sound very similar to the method used by Fernando Basurto's sixteenth century Spanish fisherman, who threw 'down the stream and going up the stream with reasonable speed so that the feather goes along the top of the stream . . .' The knowledge that fish were most likely to take an artificial fly shortly after it landed must have had as much to do with this technique as the limitations of the gear they fished with, but the most interesting thing about all three authors is the way they refer to keeping the fly continually in motion. Quite clearly, drag didn't bother them as much as it does us and the long, drag-free upstream drifts that you and I are accustomed to making would have been quite foreign three centuries ago.

But the thing which would have impressed you most of all about your trip to Walton's era, is the important tactical advantage you lose when you fish with a fixed line. When we want to cast to a new fish which is slightly further away than our original target, we stay in the same position and work out a little more line. The only way they could lengthen line was to stop the rod in a lower position than before, but once the rod was horizontal and the line was fully extended, the only way to get nearer to the fish was to physically move towards it.

But it worked well enough, and one refinement that might give nymph fishermen pause to think is that some anglers fished dark stained lines, leaving the last few links in natural white horsehair, so that bites could be detected by the movement of the line alone.[11] They weren't daft.

The Complete Angler

And now fate took a hand in the development of fly fishing. By the time Izaac Filius Jervis Walton came to edit his last edition of *The Complete Angler*, it was obvious that he had a classic on his hands, and it was equally clear that he needed to expand the section he had written on fly fishing. In the fifth edition of the book, published in 1676, Walton included the work of Charles Cotton for the first time.

Walton is a key figure in the history of fishing, although his influence on fly fishing is limited. What of the man? For all Walton's fame, we know little of his early life, but he was apprenticed to a London iron-monger and soon bought a small shop of his own. In 1608 he was becoming prosperous and he was invited to become a member of the Ironmongers' Company. He published a number of biographies, in addition to *The Complete Angler*, and his writing gave him access to a wide circle of literary and society friends, including the vicar of

St Dunstan's Church, John Donne. The civil war was a trying time for Walton and he had to abandon London for Staffordshire, because he was a staunch Royalist and remained so despite Cromwell's victory. Despite this adverse turn of events, he seems to have been comfortably enough off, because he gave up his business after the war finished and devoted the rest of his life to literature, fishing, and his friends. The Restoration improved Walton's circumstances dramatically, as George Morley, the Bishop of Winchester, and a close personal friend, offered him accommodation in the bishop's palace, where Walton stayed for the remainder of his days.

Izaak Walton

Charles Cotton

At first sight, Walton and Cotton were an unlikely pair. There, on the one hand, we have Walton, a pillar of the church and community; and on the other Cotton, more than a little inclined to the high life and author of undeniably risqué poetry. Born in 1630, the brilliant and versatile Cotton was a teenager during the civil war and had a liberal education; becoming familiar with French and Italian, as well as the classics, and it is thought that he may have gone to Cambridge. He was a member of the rural gentry, an emerging class which comprised about five per cent of the rural population and which was expected to direct local government as well as to manage their estates in a paternal fashion. Cotton managed these two responsibilities with variable degrees of success after his father died in 1658 and he inherited the estates of Beresford and Bentley, on the Staffordshire and Derbyshire border. The Dove flowed nearby and it was there that Cotton naturally turned for his fishing. He became great friends with Walton and though the latter was old enough to be his father, their friendship became very close. The pair fished together many times and in 1674, Cotton built a substantial fishing hut on the banks of the Dove, perhaps in an attempt to tempt his elderly friend up more often.

The Fishing Hut

The hut was a substantial affair, distinguished by a carving on the stone above the door showing the entwined initials of the two men and the motto *piscatoribus sacrum*. By the time it was finished, Walton was very old, in his eighty-third year, and it isn't clear if he ever completely mastered fly fishing; so it is quite likely that his days on the Dove were spent gently dapping live mayfly. There is no record of what the pair talked about, though besides fishing, they had a love of literature in common and Cotton was a friend of Ben Johnson, Donne, Seldon and Sir Henry Wotton; connections which would have interested the older man greatly. Hopefully, whatever they discussed, it wasn't poetry, because here is an example of Cotton's finest verse:

If the all-ruling Power please
We live to see another May,
We'll recompense an age of these
Foul days in one fine fishing day:

We shall then have a day or two,
Perhaps a week, wherein to try,
What the best Master's hand can do
With the most deadly killing fly;

A day without too bright a beam,
A warm, but not a scorching sun,
A southern gale to curl the stream,
And (Master) half our work is done.

Then whilst behind some bush we wait
The scaly people to betray,
We'll prove it just with treacherous bait
To make the preying trout our prey;

This (my best Friend) at my poor home
Shall be our pastime and our theme,
But then should you not deign to come
You make all this a flatt'ring dream.

It probably isn't surprising that Cotton's poetry didn't make him rich and his spending always seemed to exceed his income, with the result that he was beset by financial difficulties in his later years. At the end, things got so bad that he had to sell Beresford Hall and he died six years later in 1687, of a 'fever', being buried with none of the fanfare that his revered friend received. If you want to find Cotton's grave, he is buried in St James' church, Piccadilly.

Cotton divided his sport into two disciplines: fishing with a natural fly, and fishing with an artificial fly. Dapping, a very old method of fishing with a live insect suspended below the rod tip, was a universal technique in the seventeenth century and I have always believed that it was the method which inspired early fishermen to tie the first artificial flies. Cotton suggested fishing with one of two natural flies, the green drake (mayfly) and the stonefly, and a line 'not much more than half the length' of the rod, but his heart wasn't in it and he disposed of the subject pretty quickly. Instead he made it quite clear that he was an artificial fly fisherman:

> The length of your line, to a Man that knows how to handle his Rod, and to cast it, is no manner of encumbrance, excepting in woody places, and in landing of a Fish, which every one that can afford to Angle for pleasure, has some body to do for him, and

> the length of the line is a mighty advantage to the fishing at distance; and to fish fine, and far off, is the first and principal Rule for Trout Angling.[12]

'Fine and far off' has become a cliché in the days of tapered plastic lines and 6X leaders, but it was far harder to achieve three hundred years ago. Despite Barker's earlier talk about using a single horsehair point, killing a fit wild trout with a leader built from even two strands of horsehair attached to a fixed line is no easy feat and it led to some interesting diversions from the 'true path' of fly fishing. One such was the highly effective and now illegal technique, of 'cross-lining'. This method got around the problem of concealing the line from the fish by suspending it clear of the water like a washing line, and it was first mentioned by Giles Jacob, who gave an excellent account:

> In Hampshire they have a method for trout-fishing, no where else practised, but the largeness of the rivers seem to make it necessary: their way of fishing there in the month of May, when the fly-fishing is at its fullest height, is thus; two persons, each being furnished with a long rod, go out together; when they come to the river they propose to fish, they separate one on one side of the water, and the other on the other side; then having a strong hair-line, in length twice the breadth of the river, one of the anglers is to fix one end of it to his rod, and by fixing a lead-plummet to the other end, throw it over to his companion, who likewise fastens that end to his rod, taking off the plummet; to this long line are fastened two short ones with hooks, the lines not exceeding two or three yards in length . . .[13]

Cross-lining techniques varied, but essentially two anglers held a line stretched across the river between poles which were between six and eight feet long. The line ran through a hole in the top of each pole and up to three droppers of up to six feet long dangled from it, a fly at the end of each. The pair walked slowly along the stream, taking care that only the flies touched the water and paying special attention to rising fish. Although many regarded it as little more than poaching, there is no doubt that it was an enjoyable and killing method, and huge bags could be made, so it took a long while to die out. No less a fisherman than the Reverend Durnford was still cross-lining on the Test in 1819 and so, I suspect, were many of his friends.

Flies

Silk is so crucial to fly fishing that we need to understand something about it. The Romans were the first to bring silk to England, but they could only get it by trading with the East, a difficult and dangerous process. Silk was big business, but from the European point of view its chief disadvantage was that for centuries it had to be imported over the many thousands of miles of the Silk Road. The reason it had to be imported was because the Chinese kept the production of silk a secret until the fifth century AD, when the peoples of the Eastern Roman territories found out how to make it. The spread of Islamic influence over the succeeding centuries allowed the techniques of sericulture to spread rapidly westwards, reaching Spain in the ninth century, Sicily by the twelfth century and Italy by the middle of the thirteenth century. Italy wasn't slow to capitalise on its commercial advantage and remained a leader in the silk trade for over a hundred years, adopting the Persian loom and even improving upon it by adapting it for water power.

British tyers tended to limit their use of silk to the thread they used, but that was not the case everywhere in Europe. Early Spanish fly fishing was at least as highly evolved as anything Britain could offer and was certainly evolved enough to have developed its own regional variations. The classic work of this period, known as the 'Astorga manuscript', is conventionally accepted to have been written by one Juan de Bergara in 1624, although there is evidence that at least two different authors were involved and like many works from this period, it may well represent the amalgamation of several earlier manuscripts. Bergara's patterns were intricate in the extreme and in many cases they are more complex than late nineteenth and even early twentieth century British patterns. But perhaps the most interesting thing about the Astorga flies is that they have nothing in common with other lists of the period. This shows better than any other example I can think of, the divergence between the different European traditions as they became increasingly sophisticated. There are good reasons why the early Spanish patterns are different: Leon, Bergara's homeland, is a place apart and even now the hackles Bergara used are difficult to get outside the area, an illustration of how quickly even the cottage industry which depended on fly fishing must have developed its own local traditions.

The Astorga patterns were probably quite densely tied, since some of them used up to five different hackles, and they would have been perfectly suited to the style of fishing recommended a hundred years previously by Basurto, although a note of caution should be sounded here, because Basurto was Aragonese and he may well have used quite different methods of tying and fishing from the Leonese anglers. I would like to be confident about what the flies looked like, but we are hamstrung by the fact that once again, we do not know exactly how they were tied. Although some of the patterns definitely use hackles wound near the spade end of the hook, the fact that later 'traditional' Spanish flies very often use a hackle fibre downwing makes me doubt that all of Bergara's patterns were tied with wound hackles as has often been assumed.

Now Juan de Bergara mentions that his manuscript, '. . . is an adaptation and carries weight from books written by anglers of vast experience,' a frustrating comment which is typical of early books on fishing in any language.[14] A detail of the patterns which makes me give credence to this claim is the way Bergara uses longitudinal strips of materials to form stripes along the body, a method which is also found on the *Treatyse* patterns and, curiously, in some of Venables' flies as well. This is such a strikingly unusual technique that it argues for some kind of common heritage to all the patterns, even though it was dying out in England at the very time Bergara was promoting it, but if there is a 'missing link' manuscript, it has never turned up. Apart from *Dialogue*, not a single earlier Spanish work has ever been found, although given that the Astorga Manuscript didn't come to light until 1935, there is a slim hope that other originals might be lurking in private libraries in Spain. Sadly, the original of Bergara's work is missing and it is presumed that it was lost with the major part of General Franco's library when his villa at Meiras in Galicia was burned.

The first good description an Englishman gave of how to tie a fly was written by Thomas Barker.[15] We know remarkably little about Barker, except that he came from Shrewsbury, knew Walton and was an expert fly tyer. All Barker's materials could easily have been found by a countryman: silk, wax, crewel, gold and silver thread, feathers from the mallard, cock or capon, peacock and plover, and fur from hogs, bears, cows, and bullocks; I presume that he also used wool. With the use of dubbed furs to make fly bodies, Barker marks another milestone in the British divergence from the tradition of other European nations; for the next two centuries, fur bodies would be a hallmark of English patterns.

This brings up another point of interest: as fly tying techniques modernised, so did the terms used to describe the methods. In the fifteenth century the phrase 'dubbing' a fly referred to the act of tying materials upon a hook, or to a hook which had a fly tied upon it (e.g. a dubbed fly). By the seventeenth century, 'dubbing' more often meant the process of twisting a material around silk thread, a basic technique which we still use today. While the method was almost certainly invented in Britain, because fly tyers elsewhere in Europe did not use it until much later, we don't know when it was discovered. There are certainly no mentions of the use of the technique prior to the seventeenth century.

Incidentally, authors prior to the twentieth century invariably used cobbler's wax to help dub their flies, which stained so heavily that all silks treated with it went a dark shade of brown, regardless of their original colour. This was such a problem that there were innumerable recipes for making 'soft' wax, which had the advantage of not discolouring the thread so much, but wax had to be used. There were two reasons for this: first, wax improved the grip of the fairly coarse threads then in use; second, stiff dubbing, like the pig's hair which was in common use, adhered better to waxed thread.

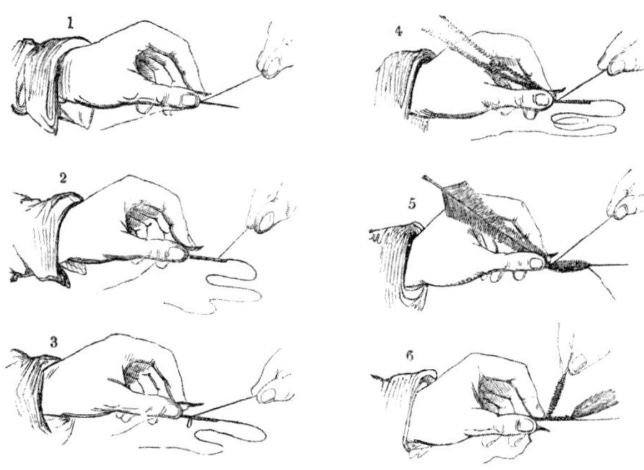

Tying a fly in the hand

The system of tying that Barker used was quite straightforward. First, the line was tied to the hook, then the wings were tied in at the head, points facing forward, followed by the hackle and body materials near the bend. The body was wound forwards, followed by the hackle. The hackle was tied off behind the wings, the wings parted with a needle and the silk was taken forwards between the winging material to keep them parted. The wings were then forced gently backwards and the silk whipped around the base to hold them there before the final tying-off. This is the classic reversed split wing technique and it results in a style of fly with an erect, slightly ragged-tipped wing and a relatively bulky thorax; quite different to the obsessively neat, backwards sloping paired quill wings found on what we regard as 'traditional' wets.

Barker divided artificials into two classes: 'palmers', which had a cock or capon's hackle wound in a helix down the entire length of the body, making for a bushy pattern; and streamlined 'flies', which were winged, without a hackle. These two classes of pattern dominate the British lists until the nineteenth century, when fashions changed, palmers fell from favour and the standard winged fly style changed to incorporate a few turns of hackle around the base of the wings. As a result, the contents of a seventeenth century British fisher's fly wallet would have been unfamiliar to our eyes, largely because of the presence of quantities of slim dubbed flies with no hackle and almost vertical wings; a type of pattern which has no counterpart today, except for Swisher and Richards' floating 'No-hackle duns', which are a modern re-use of a very old principle.

Wing styles

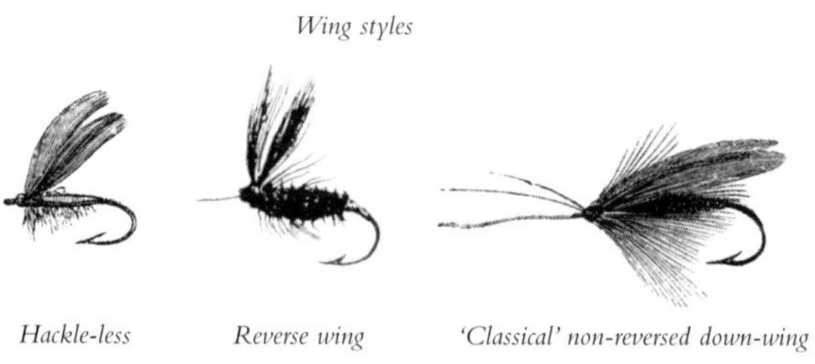

Hackle-less *Reverse wing* *'Classical' non-reversed down-wing*

Barker didn't list many patterns in his book for the simple reason that he expected people to make up their own. One explanation for why there weren't many lists of flies is that even in Walton's day, fishermen 'matched the hatch'; by spotting flies on the water and by occasional beatings of bank side vegetation to find out which flies were 'on'. If they took Barker's advice, the more obsessional kept three different shades of each type of pattern in their fly books - they even knew that they should wet the materials before tying with them to ensure that the colours were correct, a pearl of wisdom which seems to be lost on many modern fly tyers.

Of course, one way of finding out what the fish were eating was to catch one and open it up and the classic way of getting the first fish was to stick on a nondescript palmer and search the water with it. Despite the fact that modern authors are still spreading the word, autopsying trout is a very old habit; as far back as 1304 a Bolognese land owner was advising opening fish to find out what they had been eating, in a book on estate management written for Charles II of Naples. With such a long history behind it, by the seventeenth century, examining the stomach contents of trout seems to have been a fairly standard procedure:

> . . . note also, that both in this, and all other months of the year, when you do not certainly know what fly is taken, or cannot see any fish to rise, you are then to put on a small Hackle, if the water be clear, or a bigger, if something dark, until you have taken one; and then, thrusting your finger through his gills, to pull out his gorge, which being opened with your knife, you will then discover what fly is taken, and may fit yourself accordingly.[16]

However, despite all this match-the-hatch sophistication, the vast majority of early fishermen believed that flies arrived on the water because they fell there from above. Ludicrous though this seems now, it was probably an understandable mistake to make three hundred odd years ago. People thought differently in those days; do remember that this was an age when it was thought that ice was heavier than water and that the sun revolved around the earth. So next time you are out fishing, have a look at the river with seventeenth century eyes - the flies do seem to arrive as if by magic and why shouldn't they have fallen on to the surface rather than swimming up to it? Although Taverner had written an accurate description of nymphs in 1600, in his bewitchingly titled '*Certaine Experiments Concerning Fish and Fruite*', ignorance of the nymph was almost universal until about a hundred and fifty years ago, and it was this ignorance which, as will be made clear later, sent fly tyers down one of the longest blind alleys in history.[17]

To make matters worse, not only were Walton's contemporaries labouring under a sore misapprehension about the life cycle of the ephemeroptera, they also lacked a common language with which to discuss flies when they met. Being able to identify naturals precisely is something we take completely for granted and yet the development of a standard nomenclature for aquatic insects is one of the greatest triumphs among all the many developments which go together to make modern fly fishing as we know it. If I say to you, 'They were taking Iron Blue duns,' you know exactly which insect I am referring to. If I was being annoyingly pedantic, I could tell you that the fish were taking *Baetis niger* adults, but either way, you could still work out which fly pattern to use, and even if you were in Kuwait and had never seen an Iron Blue, you could still look it up in a book.

In the seventeenth century, no one had thought to give the smaller mayflies popular names, let alone classify them according to the binomial Linnaean system. I haven't made an exhaustive search of the literature, but I think that the first use of the name 'Iron Blue' is by George Scotcher, as late as 1809 or 1810, although the fly had existed all along. Cotton probably called the Iron Blue the 'Blue Dun' but I can't tell that for sure, and neither could a seventeenth century angler, because the fly didn't have an agreed name back then.

The absence of a precise nomenclature posed a constant challenge to early fly fishers and the dilemma wasn't completely settled until the nineteenth century. The naming systems which did exist were so localised that they were often completely useless outside the confines of a particular watershed, simply because the same insect was often known by different names depending on which part of the country it happened to hatch in. This lack of a universal classification system was an enormous handicap and it dogged anglers for another hundred and fifty years as Venables here intimates:

> But here I must premise, that it is much better to learn how to make a fly by sight, than by any paper direction that can possibly be expressed, in regard the terms of art do in most parts of England differ, and also several sorts of flies are called by different names; some call the fly bred of the water-cricket or creeper a may-fly, and some a stone-fly; some call the cadbait fly a May, and some call a short fly of a sad golden green colour, with short brown wings, a May-fly: and I see no reason but all flies bred in May, are properly enough called May-flies. Therefore except someone (that hath skill) would paint them, I can neither well give their names nor describe them, without too much trouble and prolixity; nor, as I alleaged, in regard of the variety of soils and rivers, describe the flies that are bred and frequent each: but the angler (as I before directed) having found the fly which fish at present affect, let him make one as like it as possibly he can, in colour, shape, proportion; and for his better imitation let him lay the natural fly before him.[18]

The predominance of 'hackles' and 'flies' in seventeenth century boxes didn't put the lid on innovation. This is the period in which we begin to see the use of 'horns' and tails on flies, and the stripping of one side of the hackle to encourage it to lie straight. A surprise or two is lying in wait: Venables' *Experienc'd Angler* features a frontispiece which includes an illustration of the first upside-down flies described anywhere. It isn't just a printer's mistake, because the text confirms it:

> ... if I turn the feathers round the hook, then I clip away those that are upon the back of the hook, that so (if it be possible) the point of the hook may be forced by the feathers (left on the inside of the hook) to swim upwards; and by this means I conceive the stream will carry your flies' wings in the posture of one flying ...[19]

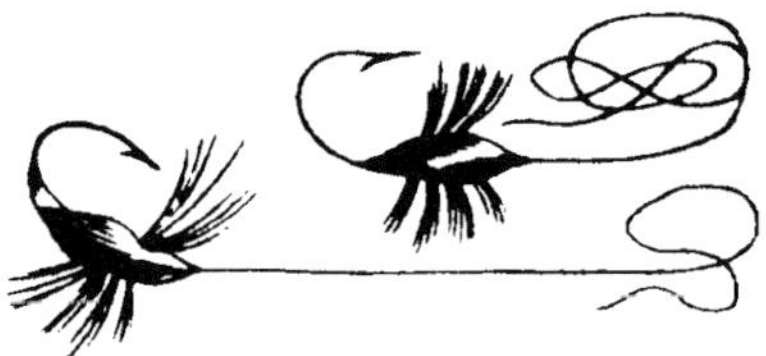

Detail from Venables' frontispiece showing flies

If an upside-down fly isn't enough, Venables had an even bigger surprise lurking in his fly book, a pattern which in my opinion transforms him from a capable angler to a great one. There is no reference to this secret weapon in the first edition of his book, but in the third he wrote the following:

> You may if you please place a small slender Lead upon the shank of your Hook, sink the Bait where the River is not violently swift, and draw the Cadbait over the Lead, you may make one the head of black silk, and the body of yellow wax; this you must be often raising from the bottom, and so let it sink again.[20]

There is no doubt that this is the first sinking fly, a lead-weighted caddis pupa. Venables had even worked out how to fish it, with the teasing sink and draw action that works so well for this type of fly. But the thing that makes his black-headed, yellow wax-bodied, sinking caddis so extraordinary is that it is absolutely unique. There wasn't another mention of anything remotely like it for almost three hundred years. This was a pattern which was designed to beat the limitations of horsehair and take the fly right down to the bottom, several feet deeper than his contemporaries' flies, to where the fish were; and it sets Venables in a class apart.

Regional Schools

Charles Cotton's patterns were an enormous influence on fishermen during the late seventeenth and eighteenth centuries, although there are clues in his writing that not all the flies he described were all his own inventions. He described sixty-five flies with original dressings, at one stroke exceeding the total accumulated in the English literature until then. His dressings show a new dimension of English fly tying, chiefly because they are so minutely detailed. He used a very wide range of materials when compared to other writers – various silks and wools, hen, coot, the tail of a black long-coated cur, marten's fur, hare's neck and scut,[21] hog's ear, white weasel tail, fox cub, rabbit, pigeon, squirrel, badger, peacock, bear, capon, heron, camlet,[22] mohair, tammy,[23] mallard, camel, sable, ostrich, greyhound, cow, cat, spaniel, black water-dog, and the hair of abortive calves. No dog was safe from Cotton; and they would have been pretty nervous in the company of most of the seventeenth and eighteenth century fly tyers. It is a sign of the sophistication of Cotton's patterns that he gave very specific instructions on how to obtain materials (e.g. black hair from a hog's ear, hair combed from the neck of a black greyhound, etc.), mixed materials to make dubbing and advised on the use of a needle to tease out dubbing and to show the underbody. Detail was Cotton's forte: he gave three different methods of dealing with a hackle.

Cotton was the first author to name his flies according to a classification which was to be used for another two centuries, although once again, it is extremely unlikely that he invented it. Under this system, artificials were classified as 'Browns', 'Duns', and 'Drakes', all of which could be classified as 'Hackles' and 'Flies', under the system we have already explored. This rough nomenclature would later be extended to include 'Spinners', although we have to wait until the mid-eighteenth century for that. There were various miscellaneous flies not accounted for in this rather loose arrangement, mainly terrestrials.

In the early days, no one attempted to set down any definitions for the classification, handicapped as they were by the rather hazy ideas of entomology prevalent at the time. The terms instead seem to have sprung from the convenience of common usage and the inevitable result was that there were serious inconsistencies between authors. In fact, it wasn't until much later that anyone made a serious attempt to set the principles of the thing down on paper, but by then it was long past its sell-by date and was already falling into disuse[24]. For what it is worth, 'Browns' were mostly members of the stone-fly family, 'Drakes' and

'Duns' were mayflies. The chief defect of this anglers' classification was the fact that in the end it found itself at odds with the scientific classification of natural flies and this, ultimately, was to prove its downfall.

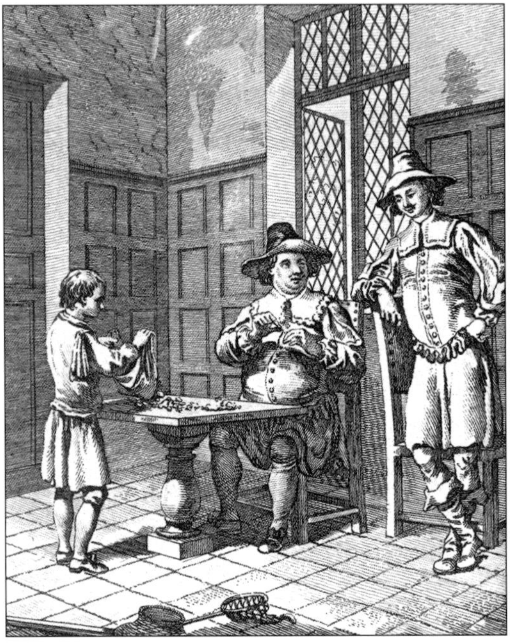

Tying a fly

Here is Cotton's method for tying a fly, a set of instructions which could have been used without alteration until the adoption of the vice. Incidentally, note his beer gut in the woodcut:

> In making a Flie then (which is not a Hackle or Palmer Flie for of those, and their several kinds we shall have occasion to speak every Month in the Year) you are first to hold the hook fast betwixt the fore finger and thumb of your left hand, with the back of the shank upwards, and the point towards your fingers ends; then take a strong small silk of the colour of the Flie you intend to make, wax it well with wax of the same colour too (to which end you are always (by the way) to have wax of all colours about you) and draw it betwixt your finger and thumb, to the head of the shank, and then whip it twice or thrice about the bare hook, which you must know, is done, both to prevent slipping, and also that the shank of the hook may not cut the

hairs of your Towght,[25] which sometimes it will otherwise do which being done, take your Line, and draw it likewise betwixt your finger and thumb, holding the Hook so fast, as to only suffer it to pass by, until you have the knot of your Towght almost to the middle of the shank of your hook, on the inside of it, then whip your silk twice or thrice about both hook and Line, as hard as the strength of the silk will permit, which being done, strip the feather for the wings proportionable to the bigness of your Flie, placing that side downwards, which grew uppermost before, upon the back of the hook, leaving so much only as to serve for the length of the wing of the point of the plume, lying revers't from the end of the shank upwards, then whip your silk twice, or thrice about the root end of the feather, hook, and towght, which being done, clip off the root end of the feather close by the arming, and then whip the silk fast and firm about the hook, and towght, untill you come to the bend of the hook: but not further (as you do at London; and so make a very unhandsom, and, in plain English, a very unnatural and shapeless Flie) which being done, cut away the end of your towght, and fasten it, and then take your dubbing which is to make the body of your Flie, as much as you think convenient; and holding it lightly, with your hook, betwixt the finger and thumb of your left hand, take your silk with the right, and twisting it betwixt the finger and thumb of that hand, the dubbing will spin itself about the silk, which when it has done, whip it about the arm'd hook backward, till you come to the setting on of the wings; and then take the feather for the wings, and divide it equally into two parts, and turn them back towards the bend of the Hook, the one on the one side, and the other on the other of the shank, holding them fast in that posture betwixt the fore finger and thumb of your left hand, which done, warp them so down as to stand, and slope towards the bend of the hook, and having warpt up to the end of the shank, hold the Flie fast betwixt the finger and thumb of your left hand, and then take the silk betwixt the finger, and thumb of your right hand, and, where the warping ends, pinch or nip it with your thumb nail against your finger, and strip away the remainder of your dubbing from the silk, and then, with the bare silk whip it once or twice about, make the wings stand in due order, fasten, and cut it off; after which with the point of a needle raise up the dubbing gently from the warp, twitch off the superfluous hairs of your dubbing, leave the wings of an equal length (your Flie will never otherwise swim true) and the work is done. And this way of making a Flie (which is certainly the best of all other) was taught to me by a Kinsman of mine, one Captain Henry Jackson, a near neighbour, an admirable Flie Angler; by many degrees the best Flie maker, that ever I yet met with.[26]

And there lies the first hint that the patterns which Cotton lists may not all have been his own inventions. He says that he was taught a particular way of tying a fly by his neighbour and relative, which confirms that there were methods of fly tying in common use which had not been described. This only stands to reason, given our knowledge of fly fishing elsewhere in Europe and as the next quote from Cotton shows, fly tying was established enough in England by the mid-seventeenth century that regional variation had already crept in:

> *Viator:* In earnest, admirably well, and it perfectly resembles a Flie; but we about London make the bodies of our Flies both much bigger and longer, so long even almost to the very beard of the Hook.
> *Piscator:* I know it very well, and I had one of those Flies given me by an honest Gentleman, who came with my Father Walton to give me a Visit, which (to tell you the truth) I hung in my parlour Window to laugh at.[27]

Walton provides independent confirmation of a diversity of patterns, with a quote in an introductory letter to the fifth edition of *The Complete Angler*, where he notes that, '. . . there are in Wales and other countries peculiar flies, particular to that place and country.'

As a final proof that Cotton drew his flies from a variety of sources, in his list of patterns, he describes one of his September flies as something '. . . for which we have no name, but is made of the black hair of a badger's skin, mixed with the yellow softest down of a sanded hog.' The sceptics might say that this is Cotton using the 'Royal we', but he doesn't give the word this usage elsewhere in the text and I am reasonably certain that here the word 'we' refers to fly tyers collectively, unless this is a reference to Robert Noble, from whose manuscript George Washington Bethune believed Cotton borrowed much of his material *(The American Flyfisher,* vol. 2, no. 1, page 14, Winter 1975).

Clearly, there had been considerable development during the years after the *Treatyse*; enough to allow large numbers of patterns and very different styles of tying to emerge. Such variation does not spring up overnight and so it is quite likely that many of Cotton's flies date back to the sixteenth century, though until now we have tended to think of them as belonging to his own era.

We are used to the idea of fly patterns being fixed, designed to be tied a particular way, because of pictures and detailed instructions we can easily find in books. Cotton's London fly shows that seventeenth century anglers were probably no different, and fly tying traditions were established. In addition, there seems to have been a very wide range of different flies available, and furthermore that each country and region could claim its own variants and unique artificials, so there is a persuasive argument for a substantial oral tradition of fly tying, otherwise they couldn't have reproduced the flies we see in the lists. This tradition was passed down from father to son and is almost entirely lost, except where we have been lucky and someone happened to set it down.

I believe that a large number of flies were passed down by word of mouth and that many of the patterns have been lost. It is simply not tenable that the *Treatyse* flies and Lawson's mayfly were the only flies available to English anglers until the seventeenth century and that Barker, Cotton and Venables invented an entire genre between the three of them; nor is it reasonable to suppose that the same goes for Basurto and Bergara in Spain. Which means that, assuming that the patterns that we know of were no more sophisticated than those which have been lost, by the 1670s there must have been hundreds, and possibly thousands of different flies across Europe. And if the flies were sophisticated, then so were the techniques that fly fishers used, but sadly we still haven't got enough pieces of our jigsaw of fly fishing history to discern the true picture with any real degree of certainty.

Reels

We know that the reel is an old invention, but the first mention of its use in Europe was made by Thomas Barker. In the 1651 edition of his book, he talks in passing about the use of the reel for pike fishing. Six years later, curiosity seems have overcome him and he must have tried the reel himself, because the text changes ever so slightly and the 'winder' is introduced with the words, 'I will now show you the way to take a salmon ...' Anyway, here is what Barker said:

> The first thing you must gain must be a rod of some ten foot in the stock, that will carry a top of six foot pretty stiffe and strong, the reason is, because there must be a little wire ring at the upper end of the top for the line to run through, that you may take up and loose your line at your pleasure; you must have your winder within two feet of the bottom to goe on your rod made in this manner, with a spring, that you may put it on as low as you please.[28]

The 'spring' was a spring clip fixed to a leather pad, which could be attached to the butt of any rod, and slid up and down until it was in the right position. This isn't much to go on, but it is quite likely that the spring clip was an early form of the clamp-foot that was to become so popular on reels in the eighteenth and early nineteenth centuries. An arrangement like this was essential, because rods of the period were made without any regard to whether a reel was to be used with them or not, and it was up to the angler to decide for himself how to fix his 'wheel' in place.

Barker's book includes the first printed European illustration of a fishing reel, which would be more helpful were it not the most maddening wood-cut ever to have been published.

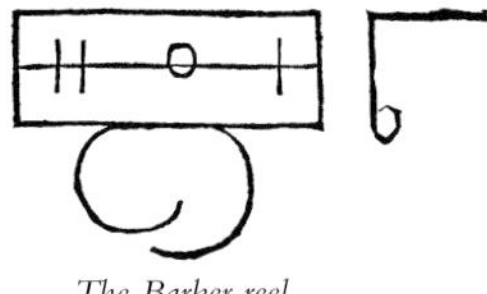

The Barker reel

If the illustration leaves you baffled, then you are in good company. I have never been able to decide what it is trying to depict and neither, as far as I know, has anyone else. The only reason that we know it shows a reel is because Barker says so. The cut has all the precision of something jotted down quickly on the back of a cigarette packet on a pub table and while it must have meant something to Barker, the secret hasn't travelled well down the years.

Now there is no mention of playing the fish off the reel, not because Barker left it out, but because no angler of the day would ever have dreamt of doing anything as daft as that. No, fish were played by hand and reels were used only for line storage. When a fish was hooked, the proper thing to do was to recover line as soon as the opportunity presented itself:

> You must be sure that you have your line of twenty-six yards of length, that you may have your convenient time to turn him, or else you are in danger to lose him: but if you turn him you are very likely to have the fish with small tackles: the danger is all in the running out both of Salmon and Trout, either on the right hand or the left hand, & wind up your line as you find occasion in the guiding of the fish to the shore, having a good large landing hook to take him up.[29]

And danger it would have been. Not only did twenty-six yards leave precious little room for error, but a fish that ran most of the line out would have left the angler at a serious mechanical disadvantage, chiefly because of the impossibly narrow spindles sported by early reels. The reel was a huge improvement on the alternatives, to be sure, but it brought with it a new set of problems. If a fish ran the angler down to his last few feet of line (backing lay a couple of centuries in the future), the fisherman was faced with an awful choice between winding like a madman, trying to recover line against a tiny winding diameter; or of hand-lining the slack in and trying to sort out the inevitable tangle later. Perhaps it isn't really so surprising that the majority dispensed with any of these new-fangled aids; they cost a fortune, there was little information about them and even Walton was none too clear about where one should go.

Fortunately, Venables, writing only a few years after Barker, saves the day. Without his book, we wouldn't have the faintest idea what seventeenth century reels looked like. *The Experienc'd Angler* thoughtfully includes an excellent illustration of a reel in the frontispiece.

Detail from Venables' frontispiece showing reel

Curiously, Venables only mentions the use of the reel in passing (and then only for trolling, which accords with Barker), which is rather odd, given the terrific piece of kit shown in the woodcut. The title was engraved by Vaughan, and it is possible that he may have known a thing or too about reels. Given that authors weren't often consulted about the woodcuts which illustrated their books, perhaps Venables' publisher, Richard Marriot, was responsible? Whatever the case may be, the reel in the frontis seems to be a class of clamp foot reel, with the wide drum and narrow spindle which characterises all early reels. Sadly, there isn't the slightest clue about what it was made from, other than the shape of handle and the clamp, which would have been difficult to make in anything other than metal, perhaps brass.

After Barker, apart from a few mentions by plagiarists, the reel might as well have vanished into thin air for a century, for all the attention it got. Why wasn't such a useful invention more uniformly adopted? Well, the key thing to take away from these early accounts is that the reel is only mentioned for trolling and for salmon fishing. This suggests that early trout fly fishers were happy to fish with the other two methods we know of: a fixed line; or with a short running one, which was passed through a loop at the tip of the rod. They were forced to resort to very different tactics to ours if a fish was caught. A large fit fish confronted the angler with four choices: to hang on until it played itself out; to run furiously up and down the bank in hot pursuit of his quarry; to throw the rod in the water hoping to retrieve it later; or to let the fish break him. Who says that fishing in Walton's time was dull?

It all seems totally irrational now, but there were plenty of good reasons why reels didn't catch on for trout fishing. First, and most important, trout were no bigger then than they are now and an eight-inch trout can be handled perfectly well on a fixed line if the rod is flexible enough. Second, knotted horsehair didn't run with quite the same facility that a modern plasticised double-taper will and allowing a fish to run was to risk a jam and a break. Third, the design of early reels was pretty awful; they weighed a ton and early brass alloys had a high zinc content and broke at the drop of a hat. The weight penalty and performance defects of early reels meant that they were reserved for situations where a long line had to be used, which boiled down to pike and salmon fishing. Even then, playing a salmon on a reel must have been a nerve-wracking experience and all things considered, it probably isn't too surprising that they weren't popular until the eighteenth century.

Anglers who did fish with winches had to be enthusiasts. As we know, early reels were basic affairs - they were single-action and lacked any form of drag or check - so fighting a fish off the reel was out of the question and hand-lining was the only way out for a seventeenth century angler who was lucky enough to find himself attached to a large and lively trout. To do anything else was to risk an over-run and a tangle. Lack of technological expertise meant that winch mechanisms were very plain and most were made out of brass; often to special order by local watch-makers, a practice which was, incidentally, still common in Ireland as recently as 1845.

The other puzzle the angler had to solve was how to fix the reel to the rod. Nowadays, reels have feet, but in Cotton's time brass collars that clamped around the butt were popular, and the alternative was a spike that went through a specially drilled hole. Fortunately, anglers didn't need to worry about changing reels too often, because one reel did for everything: fly-fishing, trolling, or bait-fishing, as the mood took its owner.

While the majority of early reels were made out of brass, some were carved or turned from wood. Early wooden reels varied from tiny thumb bobbins to enormous great things and once again, they served as line stores and not for the purpose of playing fish. A few survive – the majority of which are Scottish 'pirns', made of oak, mahogany, ash or walnut and intended for harling, rather than fly fishing.

One of the most interesting variations on the theme was the 'belly pirn', which was attached to a broad leather belt going around the angler's waist. Belly pirns were used with very long fly rods and while it seems crude, the arrangement had the undeniable advantage of letting the fisherman use his rod butt as a wading staff in heavy water. Yet another way of storing line, which was quite common in Scotland up to the beginning of the nineteenth century, was a short cross–piece nailed at right angles to the butt of the rod, on to which the line was wound in a figure of eight. Finally, there is an illustration in Fortin's *Les Ruses Innocentes* of a rather awkward contraption involving a line winder suspended just below the point at which the line was fixed to the rod tip, but this hardly counts as it couldn't have been used to lengthen or shorten line once a fish had been hooked.[30]

Early Salmon Flies

The origins of the salmon fly are almost totally obscure. I imagine that as long as fly fishermen have angled for trout, they must have caught the odd salmon by accident, and we do know that early fly fishermen saw the salmon as the ultimate quarry; though with fixed lines and home-made rods, their chances of hooking and landing one would have been pretty slim. Proof of this is easy enough to find, since the salmon was the first fish that the author of the *Treatyse of Fishing with an Angle* chose to deal with:

> Because the salmon is the most stately fish that any man can angle for in fresh water, therefore I intend to begin with him. The salmon is a noble fish, but he is cumbersome to catch. For generally he is only in deep places of great rivers, and for the most part he keeps to the middle of the water, so that a man cannot come at him. And he is in season from March until Michaelmas,[31] in which season you should angle for him with these baits, when you can get them. First, with an earthworm in the beginning and end of the season. And also with a grubworm that grows in a dunghill. And especially with an excellent bait that grows on a water-dock plant. And he does not bite at the bottom but at the float. Also you may catch him (but this is seldom seen) with an artificial fly at such times as he leaps, in like manner and way as you catch a trout or a grayling.[32]

The *Treatyse* doesn't give us the slightest hint about what salmon flies looked like, but it is clear that salmon were caught on flies five hundred years ago. They must have been challenging quarry, given that even a small grilse would make short work of a horsehair line fixed to the top of a fourteen foot rod and early salmon fishermen must have been reconciled to repeated smashes. We have to wait a hundred and fifty years before we can glean our first clue (from Barker) about how early salmon flies were tied:

> If you will angle for him with a flie (which he will rise at like a trout) the flie must be made of a large hook, which hook must carry six wings, or four at the least; there is judgement in making those flyes.[33]

I rather like that quote. It has a sort of wistful edge to it, as though the author had tried his hand at salmon flies and hadn't quite cracked it. Anyway, we're ahead, though not by much. Six wings must have made for a striking fly, but we lack the least indication of the sort of materials that might have been used to tie a pattern fit to take this king of fish. A quick peer into Barker's dubbing bag doesn't help us a lot; he used a pedestrian range of materials well suited to trout fishing, but offering little scope for complexity. On the other hand, his contemporary, Captain Richard Franck, had all sorts of mouth-wateringly exotic stuff tucked away:

> . . . silks of all sorts, threads, thrums,[34] moccado-ends,[35] and cruels of all sizes, and variety of colours; diversified and stained wool, with dogs and bears hair; beside twisted fine threads of gold and silver; with feathers from the capon, partridg, peacock, pheasant, mallard, smith, teal, snite, parrot, heronshaw, paraketta, bittern, hobby, phlimingo, or Indian-flush; but the mockaw, without exception, gives flames of life to the hackle.[36]

From the sound of it Franck was at least as skilled at catching salmon as Cotton was at catching trout. He was born in 1624 and educated in Cambridge, probably not at the University, although as Sir Walter Scott was later to point out, 'some degree of learning was necessary to have formed so very uncommon and pedantic a style.' As far as we know, Franck learnt to fish in the Cam and perfected his technique in the Trent, possibly while living in Nottingham, but he also seems to have caught salmon in the Thames. His creations were a world apart from the dull things some imagine the early salmon flies to have been.

Franck definitely was an authority, because he was one of the first authors who wrote from extensive personal experience of how to take a salmon with a fly. The trouble is that it is difficult to place him in the pantheon of salmon anglers. His book is about an expedition to Scotland which he began in 1656 or 1657 and it was no trivial exercise; in the seventeenth century, it took two and a half days to get from London to Birmingham, on apocalyptically bad tracks which barely deserved the honour of being called roads. Not many people made journeys of that length just to catch fish, but I suspect that Franck wasn't a typical fisherman.

Here I must admit that I have a sneaking regard for the boring old Parliamentarian. Scott is only one of many who have had a go at Franck because of his appalling style, but for all the leaden awfulness of his prose, his adventures show that he certainly could catch fish – not that it matters much, since he has been dead three hundred years now and can't object. Even the title of his book is a real treat:

Northern Memoirs
Calculated for the
Meridian of Scotland

Wherein most of the Cities, Citadels,
Sea-ports, Castles, Forts, Fortresses,
Rivers, and Rivulets,
are compendiously described

Together with choice Collections of various
Dis-coveries, Remarkable Observations, Theological
Notions, Political Axioms, National Intrigues,
Polemick Inferences, Contemplations,
Speculations, and several curious and industrious
Inspections, lineally drawn from Antiquaries,
and other noted and intelligible
Persons of Honour and Eminency

To which is added

The Contemplative and Practical Angler
By way of a diversion. With a Narrative of that dextrous
and mysterious Art experimented in England, and
perfected in more remote and solitary Parts of Scotland.
By way of Dialogue.

They certainly don't write them like that anymore. Now here is Franck's description of how to tie a salmon fly:

> For that end let me advise you, that the ground of your fly be for the most part obscure, of a gloomy, dark and dusky complexion; fashioned with tofts of bears-hair, blackish or brownish discolour'd wool, interwoven sometimes with peacock's feathers, at otherwhiles lap'd about with grey, red, yellow, green, or blewish silk, simple colours, or colours sometimes intermingled. For instance, black and yellow represent the wasp or hornet; and a promiscuous brown the flesh fly; and so the rest.
>
> And among the variety of your fly-adventurers, remember the hackle, or the fly-substitute, form'd without wings, and drest up with the feather of a capon, pheasant, partridg, moccaw, phlimingo, paraketa, or the like and the body differing nothing in shape from the fly, save only in ruffness and indigency of wings. Another necessary observation, is the wing of your fly, which ought to proceed from the teal, heron, malard, or faucon. The pinion and wing thereof ought to lie close, and so snug as to carry the point exactly downward.[37]

Franck agrees with Walton here; perhaps the only time they ever did. The Roundhead made much of an argument he had with Walton at Stafford on the rather unlikely fact related by the latter of pike being bred from pickerel weed, and he relates with barely concealed triumph that Walton fell back on quoting Gesner and then 'huffed away.' In fact, it seems unlikely that Walton had many opportunities to see fly fishing for salmon and he mentions a salmon fly only once, with a brief observation that it might be made with the 'red feathers of a Parakita, a strange outlandish bird; and he will rise at a fly not unlike a gnat or a small moth, or indeed at most flies that are not big.' To Franck, on the other hand, salmon flies were the bread and butter of his existence.

Flamingo, parakeet and macaw are pretty exotic materials for a seventeenth century angler to tote in his dubbing bag, but trade in feathers had been established as far back as the mid sixteenth century as a result of popular demand for ladies' hat making. Because of this, Franck would have been able to acquire exotic feathers without too much effort. He may have had access to even more unusual feathers, because he had travelled far abroad and the title pages of two of his books tell us that they were written in America. This probably accounts for the fact that although *Northern Memoirs* was written in 1658, it wasn't edited until 1685 and was only published in 1694.

We don't know exactly when Franck went to America. Cromwell died in 1658, and Franck would have been well advised to leave for America shortly afterwards. If this date is correct, the catalyst might have been the restoration of the monarchy in 1660, which would have been extremely bad news for anyone who had supported Parliament. On the other hand, there is evidence that Franck left for America as late as 1690, in which case, he would have returned at the latest by 1694, when we know he was living in London at the Barbican.[38] He was definitely in England in 1687, when his first book was published. This had the succinct title: *A Philosophical Treatise of the Original and Production of Things, Writ in America in a Time of Solitude*. Though this barely compares with the scope of the full title of *Northern Memoirs*, Franck rescued his form later with the snappily titled: *The Admirable and Indefatigable Adventures of Nine Pious Pilgrims, Devoted to Sion by the Cross of Christ; and Piloted by Evangelist to the New Jerusalem. Written in America, in a time of Solitude and Divine Contemplation; by a Zealous Lover of Truth, and a Faithful Admirer of the Sacred Mysteries and Historical Revelations, in the Old and New Testament, as the Holy Men of God were Heavenly inspir'd to Prophesie of the Divine and Holy Jesus.*

Sadly, neither Franck's first nor his last book make any mention of fishing at all, though it would be very odd if he hadn't fished in America. Strange as it is to think of it, the verbose old Roundhead may have been the first European to fly fish in the New World,[39] though it is likely that he was beaten to it by the Spanish, who are known to have encountered cut-throat trout in the Sangre de Cristo mountains of New Mexico during Francisco Vázquez de Coronado's exploration of the area in 1541.

The last of the early authors who has anything to tell us about salmon flies is Venables, and he left us yet another clue about early salmon flies:

> I shall only add, that the Salmon flies must be made with wings standing one behind the other, whether two or four; he also delights in the most gaudy and orient colours you can choose; the wings I mean chiefly, if not altogether, with long tails and wings.[40]

This is probably the same class of fly that Barker describes and it must have been a standard, because a hundred years later Brookes describes a pattern called the Horse-leech-fly which is uncannily similar to both Barker and Venables' idea of a salmon fly:

> . . . they are of various colours, have great Heads, large Bodies, very long Tails; and two, some have three, Pair of Wings, placed behind each other: Behind each Pair of Wings whip the body about with Gold or Silver Twist, or both, and do the same by the Head; with this Fly fish at Length, as for the Trout and Grayling: But if you dib, do it with two or three Butter-flies, of different Colours, or with some of the most glaring small Flies you can find.[41]

So despite an unpromising start, if we put all our knowledge together, we can picture a seventeenth century salmon fly: a dull body, made of bear's hair, perhaps wrapped in coloured silk, and hackled with cock, pheasant, partridge, or the gaudy feathers of macaw, flamingo or parakeet. The fly might have been left as a hackle, or it could have been dressed with one, two, or even three pairs of wings, taken from the teal, heron, mallard, falcon or peacock. Sizes would have ranged from that of a large trout fly upwards. Within this description there is scope for tying flies as dull as the old Tweed patterns, and as glorious as anything Traherne might have designed. Given the nature of the time it would have been surprising if some startling flies hadn't been tied; after all, these were the days of Shakespeare, Ben Johnson and of Milton. Momentous events must have moved the minds of the fishermen who wrote – Walton's lifetime alone saw the Gunpowder Plot, the Great Plague, The Fire of London and the English Civil War. But despite everything, the overwhelming impression we are left with is that there were very few people who knew anything at all about salmon fishing; hence the shortage of references and the frustratingly brief snippets of information on which we have had to rely so far. The salmon fly would have to wait another two hundred years before it reached its zenith.

The Eighteenth Century

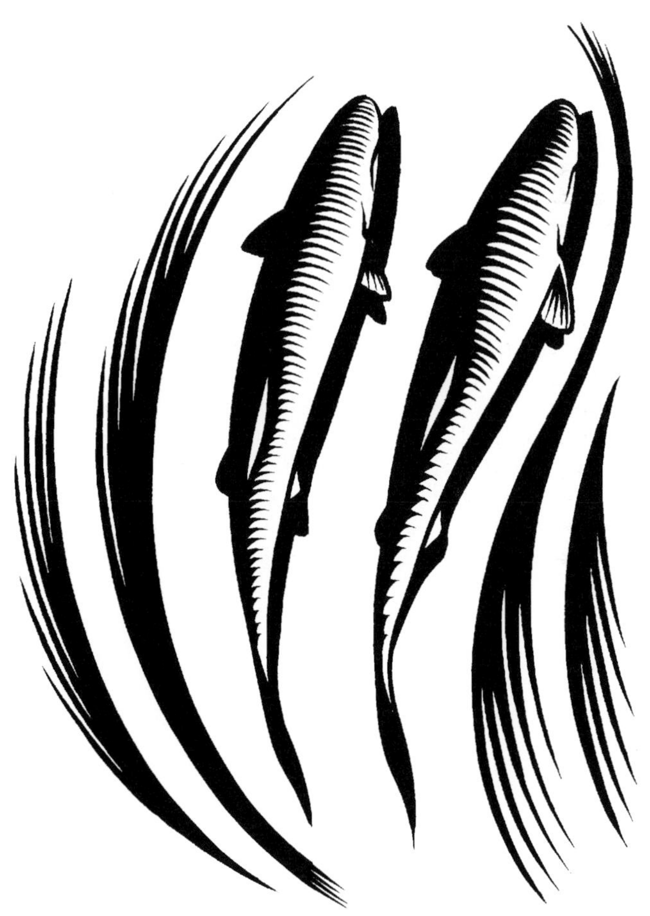

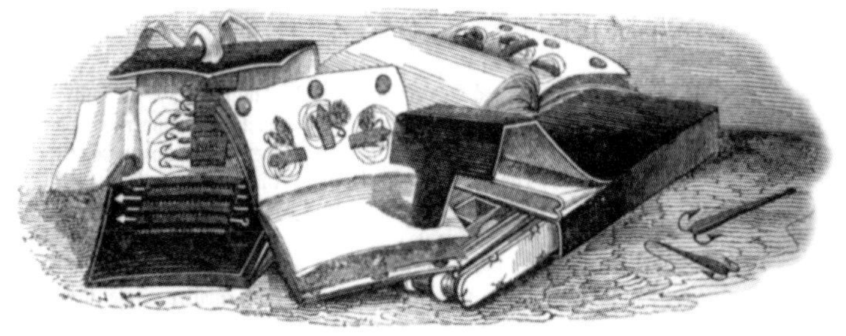

CHAPTER THREE

The Eighteenth Century

THE eighteenth century was a time of revolutions. Agricultural and industrial revolutions increased Britain's economic might several-fold and considerably improved the purchasing power of the common man. Abroad, there was an American rebellion, which lost Britain its most valuable colony; and a French revolution, which overthrew that country's monarchy and nearly pulled the British crown down in its wake.

When Queen Anne inherited the English throne in 1702, all of this lay in the future, but from a political viewpoint, she could hardly have chosen a worse time in which to reign. Political parties first appeared in 1679 and their teenage years were extremely trying for all concerned. It was Anne's misfortune that most of the worst aspects of party politics had been discovered by 1695, a situation which was aggravated by the fact that no fewer than nine general elections were held between then and the end of her reign. Part of the problem was that there was nothing like a universal franchise and despite all the political intrigue, England was hardly a democracy, given that only one in four of adult males were eligible to vote and the secret ballot was an unheard of refinement. On the other hand, thanks to Marlborough's brilliant campaigning and the capture of Gibraltar and Minorca, England was dominant on both land and the sea and a rather unexpected union with Scotland had also occurred. The authority brought by military success did much to counterbalance the weakness of political chaos.

By now Britain was increasingly a trading, rather than an agricultural nation and the population had reached seven million. On the whole, the people were more prosperous, though a third of the wealth was owned by the richest five per cent, many of whom were members of the great mercantile families which established themselves during this period. It was something of a boom time for the professions and also for store keepers, and though there were few shops in rural areas by the late seventeenth century, the numbers exploded during the eighteenth, prompting Napoleon's famous remark about a nation of shopkeepers. One consequence of this was a steady increase in traffic between town and country, although the roads were still very bad and even short journeys could be a sore trial if luck and the weather set their face against the traveller. To give some idea of the difference between then and now, it took at least a day to travel sixty miles to Cambridge from London, Edinburgh was a punishing ten day coach ride away and the remoter areas of Wales still relied on networks of Roman roads and ancient bridle ways, some of which were barely wider than sheep tracks and all of which were in an appalling state of repair.

There were some compensations, because communication was improving in other ways; London's first daily newspaper appeared in 1702 and by 1760 more than nine million newspapers were being sold in Britain every year. The effect of this communication revolution shouldn't be underestimated, because although papers cost the astonishing sum of three pence, each copy was read and re-read until it was worn out, some papers being shared by as many as two dozen people. It isn't surprising that advertising flourished in this environment and it wasn't long before angling products were being promoted through the press, freeing tackle makers from their previous dependence on reputation and yellowing adverts bound in the end-papers of books.

Anne's death triggered the Hanoverian succession and Britain entered a period of comparative stability under the guiding hand of Robert Walpole, who as Prime Minister took care to keep the nation out of war in Europe and also increased its prosperity. However, Walpole's star was in decline by 1739 and Britain was dragged into the War of Austrian Succession, which diverted many of her troops abroad and set the stage for the Jacobite Rebellion, in which the 'young pretender' Charles Edward Stuart made a grab for the English throne with French assistance. This revolt was put down with brutal efficiency by the Duke of Cumberland, who achieved a kind of immortality by crushing the Jacobite army at Culloden in 1746.

Colonies were conquered and lost in equal measure. By 1759, Britain was consolidating its grip on Canada and India and had seized Guadeloupe and several French trading posts on the west coast of Africa. Merchants looked forward to reaping the benefits, but the enormous national debt led Parliament to levy extra duties on the colonies, resulting in the American War of Independence, which broke out in 1775. The new war nearly ruined Britain, given that it cost more than £200 million and lost it untold natural reserves, but the economy bounced back astonishingly quickly and the country was happily at war with revolutionary France by 1793.

Historians give us many reasons why a British revolution didn't occur, the major one being increased prosperity, which improved the lot of the working man significantly. Part of this increase in wealth was linked to industrialisation and although by 1800 the industrial sector was still small compared to the agricultural one, Britain had become the most industrialised nation in the world. Plentiful raw materials and a well-developed infrastructure were part of this, the best example being the thousand miles of canal which had been dug in Britain by 1760, and the colonies acted not only as sources of cheap imports, but also as a captive market for exports.

The full impact of higher standards of living which industrialisation brought in its wake wasn't felt until the nineteenth century, but as the opportunities for leisure began to grow, so did fishing with a fly become more and more popular. It was particularly unfortunate that this growth in the number of anglers happened to coincide with the peak of the enclosure movement, in which land was fenced off, closing many traditional rights of way and limiting anglers' access to water. This is a very important point, because in many ways enclosure is the foundation of the current system of riparian ownership in the UK, and it played a very large part in the social shaping of British angling after 1700.

Prior to enclosure, there was very little distinction between farmland and heath or common and by and large, fishermen were free to roam and to fish wherever they pleased. The reason for this is that prior to 1700, in a system which was common throughout Europe, farmland was only under the control of an individual from seeding until harvest; the remainder of the time the land was open for grazing by livestock belonging to the community, with the result that fishermen were pretty much free to come and go as they pleased. However, by the mid-nineteenth century, six million acres of English fields had been fenced in and were no longer accessible to the general public, a concept which still survives, backed up by the law of trespass. With the fencing of newly private land there came a new idea: the enforcement of riparian rights, and this had a major impact on the availability of fishing. While some owners were happy to let commoners fish from their land, many were not and fishermen began to find access to good water more and more difficult, as more and more fields were fenced off. As you can imagine, enclosure was deeply unpopular, because it stood a whole way of life on its head. For the first time, local people found that they could not fish local water, and it isn't surprising that poaching became common as frustrated anglers began to take the law into their own hands.

Although the enclosure of land was happening throughout Europe, it was in Britain more than anywhere else that a peculiar interaction of culture and literature resulted in fishing becoming a popular sport. With public access becoming more and more limited, fisheries began to acquire value and status, because plenty of anglers were prepared to pay for access to productive water that had previously been freely available. Rising rents were bad news for the common man, whose purse would not stretch to paying for good fishing, and who increasingly found himself barred from the best waters by restrictive laws such as the Waltham Black Act of 1722. One of the best examples of economics coming into play in fishing that I can think of is the effects of the sharp rise in popularity of salmon fishing at the beginning of the nineteenth century. This is dealt with at length elsewhere in this book, but in essence, once landlords discovered how much competition there was for good salmon water, they simply raised the rents as much as the market would stand, effectively shutting out the local fishermen who could not afford to compete with wealthy visitors.

Ultimately, all this enclosure of land proved socially divisive to fishing in Britain, with waters becoming divided into those which contained game fish; and those which did not, which were less valuable and therefore more accessible to the common man. From this dichotomy came the division of British fishing into 'game' and 'coarse', a split which continues to mystify our European neighbours, although an exactly similar split can be seen in America. Though the schism occurred in the nineteenth century, its foundations were laid in the eighteenth and while the working man was never totally denied access to fly fishing, it is worth bearing in mind that he would have found it more and more difficult to get access to good water as fences sprang up in inconvenient places throughout the century.

Materials for Fly Tying

In some ways enclosure was the least of all the challenges which the fly fisher faced in the eighteenth century. We know that they tied a wide range of flies, but given that tackle dealers were thin on the ground, where did the early tyers get the wide range of materials they used? If we stick our noses in one of their dubbing bags, the contents indicate that no farmyard animal was safe, and the fly tyer who didn't shoot would have done well to be on good terms with the nearest gamekeeper. Fortunately, that sort of thing was easily done in the eighteenth and nineteenth centuries, when the country was in the grip of great estates with their obsessive sporting interests; but there was another, slightly more exotic source of hackles - cock fighting.

The origin of cock fighting is uncertain, but all our present strains of domestic fowl are agreed to have been descended from wild jungle fowl found in India and we know that man has kept birds for eggs and meat for upwards of five thousand years. The historical record shows that almost every civilisation which has kept fowl has attempted to selectively breed them for its own purposes and the Romans alone were known to have established half a dozen breeds. Given the pugnacious characteristics of jungle and domestic cocks, it was inevitable that some of the breeding effort was diverted into producing birds that would fight. The result was that cock fighting had a very long history by 1700 and though the first mention of it as a sport in England was made in the twelfth century, we know from archaeological digs that fighting cocks were common long before that.[1]

Cock fighting

Cock fighting was at the height of its popularity in the eighteenth century, so much so that it was becoming a concern to a government worried that it was nurturing a nation of gamblers. The sport transcended class boundaries and commoners were as likely to rear birds as nobles. To begin with, it wasn't even considered to be an unsuitable occupation for a churchman, and from the perspective of our own times of concern for animal welfare it is difficult to convey just what a grip the sport had on the popular imagination.

Fly tyers took hackles from any suitable bird, but the reason why fighting cocks were of such peculiar interest was that they were closely feathered with long, shiny, stiff hackles, often of strikingly beautiful colours. Each variation of plumage had its own name and it isn't surprising that some of these have come down to us over the ages, including 'Blue Dun', for example. Other varieties, including Black-breasted Red, Polecat, Ginger-Red, Birchen-Grey, Silver Duckwing and the bewitching Treacle-Breasted Marigold Duckwing have faded into obscurity, but we know of at least sixty different strains of fighting cock and thirty approved crosses.

Good hackles were just as highly prized then as they are now, and in the absence of our modern tradition of 'genetic' hackle farms, the only way to get them would have been to pluck them from individual birds. Fly fishers and feather dealers would have haunted farms and cock pits and it is easy to imagine the tough deals which must have been struck in dimly-lit ale houses over particularly choice hackles.

Hackles

I say tough, because fishermen had very specific requirements of hackle, even two hundred years ago. Their level of sophistication was greater than has generally been supposed and fly tyers had already begun to differentiate between the properties of different types of hackles as early as the fifteenth century, a trend which is particularly apparent if one examines Spanish lists of flies. The *Treatyse*, for example, recommends the use of capon hackles over hen. Bantam hackles were also used when they were available.

The grandfather of all discourses on hackle is found in Chetham's book:

> Hackles (which are Feathers about a Cock or Capons Neck, and such as hanging down each side, next a Cock or Capons Tail) of all colours, as the Red Dun, Yellowish, White, Orange coloured, and perfect Black, these are of especial use to make the Palmer-fly, or Insect called by some Wool-beds.[2]

Now, the strict definition of a hackle is: 'A long shining feather or series of feathers on the neck or saddle of a domestic cock, peacock, pigeon etc., which is erected in anger,'[3] but being practical people, fly fishermen respect no linguistic boundaries and the word has been bandied about no end. These days, the term hackle has come to mean just about any feather, as it has done for many years. For example, in 1766, Brookes wrote:

> . . . the best are the Lapwing-topping, the Feathers of a Hen's Neck, (from which you will get the greatest variety), and not much used, though they are the very finest Hackle but the Lapwing's top, the same Feathers of a Cock, the long Feathers of a Swallows tail, the Crown of a Peacock, a Wren's Tail, a Pheasant's Neck, a black Cock's ditto.[4]

While there aren't any mentions in British texts of the 'complex' hackles that came into favour later (furnace, cuckoo, grizzly and so on), eighteenth century fly fishers' first choice came from a cock's neck - the area we describe as the cape - and from near the tail. They aimed to use stiff, well-coloured hackles which had a fibre length of less than half an inch and the greatest prize was to find a dead cock with strong brown red hackles, a treasure trove which would last the finder many years.[5] Tyers valued a rather different type of hackle to the long parallel-sided 'genetic' hackles we love so much today, and there was a brisk market in spade shaped hackles which were wound in by the tip to produce a complex layered effect which was still valued even in

Halford's day. Within a hundred years, fly fishing would become so popular and good quality hackles so scarce that it was possible for a major importing industry to be founded upon the demands of fly tyers alone. From then until the late twentieth century, the supply of good quality cock hackles would be barely adequate to keep pace with demand.

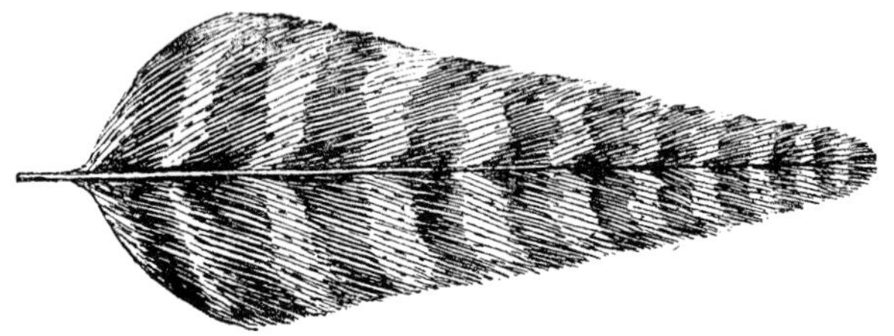

Spade-shaped hackle

Two developments had a profound influence on the availability of hackles. First, cock fighting was made illegal in America in 1836 and England in 1849, an absolute disaster for fly fishermen, since it dried up a major source of supply at a stroke; and second, the ever increasing popularity of fly fishing meant that by the 1870s many types of ordinary cock hackle were becoming extremely scarce, as Ogden complained when he lamented the rarity of good furnace hackles:

> When I was a lad I could find this bird at any barn door; but now you may travel a hundred miles and not see one the right colour, which I think must be owing to the decrease in the breeding of game fowls.[6]

There was one source of line-bred cock hackles which did remain available and still does to this day, though it is localised to one region of Spain; the birds which are known in the English-speaking world as 'Coq de Leon' and which were first mentioned in the Astorga manuscript of 1624. The supply of these roosters has never been plentiful and they almost died out in the 1960s, but since then they have recovered strongly and are a living example of how birds have been bred by amateurs for the purpose of producing hackles since time immemorial. The management of this Spanish breed couldn't be more different from that of the factory bred 'genetic hackle' we favour today, but the result is unique hackles of the most extraordinary shades, none of which are exactly cheap and many of which are highly prized. As far as I know, the Leonese cockerels are the longest surviving line of birds bred for fly tying and they are a superb illustration of the way in which amateurs must have bred birds for feather quality since the jungle fowl was first domesticated.

The Astorga manuscript lists a fascinating series of flies, many of which are tied with Coq de Leon hackles. The centre of breeding of these birds then, as now, lay in a tiny area comprising a few towns in the north of the province of Leon, cradled in the valley of the river Curueño, a couple of hundred miles north-west of Madrid.

In complete contrast to modern western farming methods, which sacrifice the bird to produce a cape, the roosters of Leon live the privileged existence of old-time cocks, only having to put up with the indignity of the occasional bout of selective hackle harvesting. Most of the birds learn to put up with this outrage with an air of haughty resignation, since hackles are plucked every ten to twelve weeks from the moment they reach the age of six or perhaps eight months to the day they die. The Leonese roosters give us one of our only insights into the way hackles may have been harvested in the English countryside; a single plucking may produce more than a hundred saddle hackles and up to a hundred and twenty spade hackles.

Current estimates put the total number of birds involved at around five thousand; a far cry from their mid-century trough when it is thought that fewer than three hundred existed and the line was in danger of extinction. The hackles have a wonderful terminology all of their own, but there are two different main types: *colgadera*, which are long soft spade hackles; and *riñonada* which are shorter, more rigid saddle hackles. Then the trouble begins. All Coq de Leon are divided into *indios* and *pardos*. Indios are plain brown or dun hackles which are subdivided into: *acerado* (steely); *plateado* (silvery); *palometa* (almost white); *negrisco* (black); *rubión* (a rich chestnut); *sarnoso* (a dirty grey – literally 'mangy'); and *avellanado* (a sort of mousy medium dun). *Pardos* have a black central list and they are usually shot through with the most incredibly seductive black speckles, making them, in my view at least, the most attractive hackles available anywhere at any price. *Pardos* may be *flor de escoba* (golden – literally 'broom flower'), the most brilliant of which are known very aptly as *pardo encendido* (burning brown); *corzuno* (very dark grey, almost black); *sarrioso* (silvery gold); *crudo* (almost transparent – literally 'cream'), some of which lack any speckles and are known as *palometra de pardo*; *rubión* (a rich teak); *aconchado* (a startling grizzled whitish silver); and *langareto*, an almost mythical feather the colour of which is understandably rather hard to define. We would call it grizzled, but the word does it no justice. This is an ancient terminology and it challenges the English naming system for gamecocks in its subtlety and inventiveness.[7]

Trout Flies

After the publication of the *Treatyse of Fishing with an Angle* in 1496, every century has produced a standard work. The most influential work of the eighteenth century was Richard Bowlker's ever so slightly dull and plodding *The Art of Angling*, a fishing manual which made few improvements on the advice given to fishermen in the previous century, but which nonetheless ran to at least twelve editions, which is a good measure of the popularity of its subject. Like most books of the period, *The Art of Angling* was small enough to fit in a pocket, so the fishermen could stuff it in a jacket and whip it out at times of crisis. Many copies of this and other similar works were lost, or damaged beyond repair, when their owners went one step too far and took a header into the deeps. The well-thumbed pages of my copy testify to ownership by at least one under-confident angler and the ancient water-stains that crinkle the pages to another, over-confident one.

The patterns in *The Art of Angling* were organised into two short lists, which though they were nothing new, remained popular standards for another fifty years:[8]

The Red Fly	*The Large Black Ant*
The Orl Fly	*Black Caterpillar Fly*
Blue-dun Fly	*Welshman's Button*
Sky-colour'd Blue Fly	*Iron Blue Fly*
Brown Fly	*Little Red Ant*
Cadis Fly	*Sally Fly*
Cow-Dung Fly	*Little Black Ant*
Fern Fly	*Canon, or Down-Hill Fly*
Stone Fly	*Little Whirling Blue*
Red Spinner	*Shorn Fly*
Granam Fly	*Little Pale Blue*
Blue Gnat	*May Fly*
Spider Fly	*The Willow Fly*
The Large Red Ant	*Grey Drake*
Black Gnat	

Bowlker's flies. In particular see how the use of the 'reverse wing' method makes the wings stand very upright. These were flies for fishing on or very near the surface. This is a nineteenth century illustration.

Two things make this rather conventional list interesting: one being that for the first time we have a clear idea about what the flies looked like. Prior to the eighteenth century, there are very few illustrations of artificials and those we do have are so lacking in detail or execution as to be almost useless. But by good fortune, Sir John Hawkins chose to illustrate his 1760 edition of *The Complete Angler* with a group of plates over which are scattered half a dozen flies and although these are by no means the first etchings to show flies, they are certainly the first good illustrations of early patterns.[9]

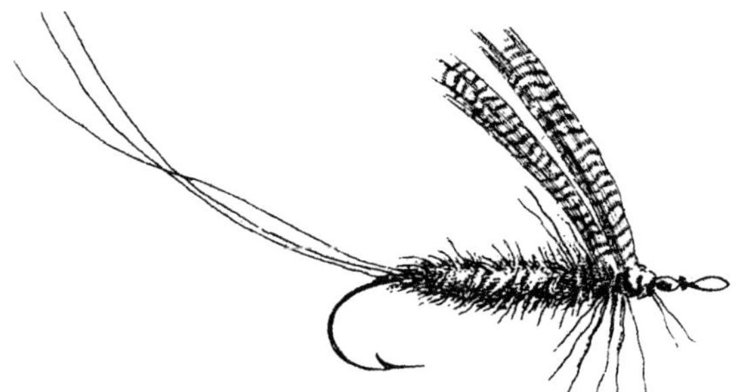

Detail of fly tied on eyed hook from Hawkins' Complete Angler

Hawkins' plates must have caught everyone's eye, because the pictures had a very long career and appear in several other books. The frontispiece of Thomas Best's book shows an idyllic fishing scene of small interest other than six surprisingly familiar flies huddled at the bottom; these are Hawkins' patterns, now collected into a cosy group.[10] The flies shown are: an Ant Fly, the Dun Cut, a Palmer, the Great Dun, the Hawthorn fly and the Green Drake. The selection, while probably random, is quite fortuitous, because several of the flies are listed by Cotton and at least one, the Dun Cut, can trace its parentage right back to the *Treatyse*.

I cannot work out what made them so attractive, but elements of the Hawkins plate had a much longer life than the publisher intended, because besides Best's work, they also turn up in Duhamel du Monceau's *Traite General des Pesches*, published in 1769, *The Sportsman's Dictionary* (1792), Osbaldiston's *The British Sportsman* (1792), Daniel's *Rural Sports* (1807), *British Field Sports*, by Scott (1818), Rennie's *Alphabet of Angling* (1833) and last, but by no means least, Blaine's *Rural Sports* (1840), though by then the woodcut was getting a trifle long in the tooth and Blaine did at least have the grace to modernise the images slightly. Nowadays lawyers would have waxed fat on the litigation that followed, but copyright was a relatively new idea in the late eighteenth century and was limited to a mere twenty-eight years by the Statute of Anne, which was passed in 1710. All publishers were frontiersmen then and if nothing else, it all goes to show that you can't keep a good woodcut down.

Best frontispiece

Plagiarism aside, at long last Hawkins' much copied plates give us a good idea of how early flies were tied, albeit as interpreted by eighteenth century tyers, but at least the artist who first drew the flies was much nearer to the origin of the patterns than we are. There is a surprise: the fly which Best identifies as the Great Dun appears to be tied on an eyed hook, which is very odd, since although they had been discovered in antiquity, eyed hooks didn't become popular in Britain for another hundred years. It is possible that this fly is actually tied with a very early form of loop eye, because there is a note by Hawkins elsewhere in the text that the angler should be provided with 'hog's bristles for loops to your flies.'[11]

The other thing worthy of note about Bowlker's list is that six of the flies are tied with hackle wrapped only at the base of the wings. This is a new method and other lists published in this period show the same thing; the shy entrance of a half-way house between the hackleless reversed winged flies of the seventeenth century and the nineteenth century ideal of a sloping wing tied facing backwards and wrapped with a few turns of hackle at the base. It isn't quite clear which method Bowlker used to tie his wings, but looking at the available woodcuts, I suspect it was the reversed wing, which accounts for why the wings of the patterns we see stand so tall. But the method of winging is a mere sideshow compared to the entrance of this new method of tying in the hackle and it immediately raises a question: what was the thinking behind it? Was the new 'wing base' hackle supposed to represent the legs of the insect, as it was subsequently rationalised, or did some deeper philosophy lie behind it? Sadly, the literature gives us no clues about the theoretical motivation behind this particular style of tying, which is a pity, because it is one of the key techniques in fly dressing and without it whole classes of artificial, such as dry flies and many nymphs, could not be tied. Within the space of a century or so, the 'wing base' hackle would prove so successful that the palmer style of tying would completely fall from favour and the style remains a cornerstone of modern fly tying techniques. But we have no idea why it was invented.

The changes in British patterns were mirrored by those in Spain and it seems likely that it was during the eighteenth century that the 'classical' Spanish tying methods began to be consolidated. The finest examples of Spanish patterns of this period come from a manuscript written in 1825 by Luis Peña, first published by Carrère in the middle of the last century.[12] In what must have been a memorable encounter, Carrère came by the manuscript almost by accident, when he met with one Fr Felipe Sanchez in Madrid. The old priest came from a small village called Boñar in the heart of Leon and the manuscript he brought with him contained a list of very old patterns, some of which are contemporary with Bergara's flies and some of which are more modern, probably dating to the eighteenth century. Peña lists forty-one detailed wet patterns, the majority of which have silk bodies and down wings which combine mixtures of different colours of Leonese cock hackle fibres in a variety of beautiful and subtle ways. These flies represent the Leonese school at its absolute peak and they show a mastery of the fly tyer's art that probably remains unchallenged. Here are examples of a few of the dressings:

> PARDO CRUDO - needs one feather from a Boñar riverside rooster, with nearly black spots over a black and blue background, the spots must be small and show well on the fibre of the feather. The hook must be thin and small. The body is made of raw hemp like the last.
>
> NEGRISCO – this mosquito is tied with the feather of a smoky negrisco rooster, but very translucent, such that, when the feather is held to the light, it has a colour like polished steel. The body is formed from black linen. The rib should be one thread of white silk. The hook, fine and small.
>
> MARTINETES - are tied with a smoky negrisco, another blue kingfisher feather; another of glowing brown which is closely spotted. From all the feathers we take enough beard to make the mosquito, in equal parts mixed, except the kingfisher ones, and twelve fibres are enough. The body, of white silk with a pack-saddle at the back of dark silver silk. The rib, of silk the colour of smoked pine.[13]

A down-wing version of a fly tied in the 'classical' Spanish style

On the face of it, the few books published in the eighteenth century suggest that little had changed in the English-speaking fly tying world, but drawing together all the evidence, it appears that tyers were using a much wider range of materials than ever before. If a seventeenth century tyer could pack all his dubbing in one bag, by the eighteenth much more space was needed. Tackle dealers must have rubbed their hands in glee when they read this sort of thing (by Best):

> Before I proceed to give the angler a list of the articles he is to provide, let me advise him to have a small cabinet made to keep them in, with sixteen drawers in it, and a few pigeon holes, and on each drawer, let there be a written label intimating the contents of it, which he will find to be much better than putting them indiscriminately into a dubbing bag; because when he wants to use them he can go to each separate article without any trouble.[14]

The sixteen drawers were to hold the following materials: hog's down; camel's hair; badger's hair; bear's hair; spaniel's hair; sheep's wool; seal's fur; mohair; cow's hair; colt's or calves' hair; camlets; furs from squirrel, fox, fox-cub, otter and otter-cub, fulimart (polecat), mole, black cat tail, house mouse, water rat, and marten; cock hackles (red, dun, yellowish, white, orange and black); feathers (mallard, partridge, cock pheasant, starling, jay, land-rail, blackbird, thrush, fieldfare, coot, hen, plover, peacock and ostrich); material tweaked from carpets and blankets; silk wrapped on little reels; flaw silk; gold and silver thread; flattened wire (known as twist); various colours of wax; needles; a sharp pen-knife; and a small pair of scissors. This is quite a list and although some of the materials are no longer in common use, it could still be used by a modern fly tyer.

Hidden in there is an important new development; seal fur, which went on from this small beginning to be the most popular dubbing material for another two hundred years. Seal fur may well have earned its place because it could be got quite easily from trunk makers, who were churning through vast amounts of seal skins at the time. This new material could be dubbed with comparative ease and dyed any colour under the sun, which soon made it very popular. Calf and cow hair, which seal fur replaced, were useful materials, but they were rather tricky to dub and after a long period of decline, they fell into disuse during the early nineteenth century. Despite its new-found popularity, seal's fur didn't completely take over and some of the old materials persisted for quite a while. For another few decades, while the bodies of small flies were tied with seal's fur, the bodies of larger flies called for bear's fur, and materials like squirrel and fox were still being used in some patterns in the mid-nineteenth century.

Palmer Flies

The contents of fly boxes were still very different to anything we are used to seeing. A large portion of every eighteenth century fly box was reserved for 'hackles' or palmer flies, which had been part of the very bedrock of fly fishing for at least two centuries. Palmers are still in use nowadays, often fished on the top dropper to attract fish to the surface, but I doubt that many readers are aware that they trace their lineage from flies tied to represent furry caterpillars. Caterpillars were extremely popular live baits in Walton's time, a fact which is confirmed by Chetham and others, who list many hackles, and also by Franck in *Northern Memoirs*:

> So that if at any time the fly fails of success, as frequently it has happened to myself and others, let the angler then have recourse to the ash-tree-grub, the palmer-worm, caterpillar, green or grey drak, the depinged grasshopper, or that truculent insect, the green munket of the owlder-tree.[15]

But where did the term 'palmer' come from? There is a clue in the very word itself: crusaders and pilgrims returning from the Holy Land were referred to as palmers because of their habit of bringing back palms with them on their return. The same word was used to describe itinerant monks who travelled under a vow of poverty. By association, the term was applied to many-legged insects such as woodlice and caterpillars because of their wandering habit. The caterpillars in particular were rumoured to travel great distances and so they were called palmer-worms.

For at least a century, the palmer was a dominant style. Artificial caterpillars had a lot going for them compared to their live brethren - durability, longevity and very little tendency to escape. The patterns were easy to tie and so effective that the incontrovertible fact that trout rarely come across woolly caterpillars on the water was held of little account. Then, in the late eighteenth century, fashions changed for some reason, and caterpillar live baits began to fall out of favour. By the second half of the nineteenth century, although palmered dressings were still very popular, their origins had become obscure. Here is Michael Theakston, writing in 1862, barely a hundred years after Best:

> It is the general impression that they represent, or are derived from, hairy worms, or those caterpillars that are hairy, to which they bear a kindred and very striking resemblance; but the angler never uses the hairy worms as baits, and they are never seen upon the water; if they were, the hackles (for excellence of imitation) when immersed in the water would take the lead of all artificials. The appearance of the hairy worms may be natural to the fish – like the maggot, clapbait, and other larvae – although the fish never see them. Close as the hackles imitate the hairy worm, they seem to be or have grown into ingenious theories more than original imitations. Their attractions as baits has adapted their brilliant materials into many fanciful varieties – without foundation and probably no semblance to anything on the water – which, in the absence of originals, cannot be other than casual or trial baits, which at best are but a precarious dependence.[16]

The decline in the use of palmered patterns during the nineteenth century reflects the increasing emphasis on imitative patterns tied to represent emphemeroptera during that period. As the number of winged patterns in fly boxes grew, so palmers were diluted out and many patterns fell by the wayside. Today, though we still fish a few palmers, the link with woolly caterpillars has long been forgotten. It is a sobering thought that the influence of early fly fishers can still be seen in our fly boxes – though time, as Theakston charitably pointed out, has hallowed the palmer fly and its descendants still continue to catch fish today. The Soldier Palmer is still extremely popular, even with cutting edge lake fishers, as are classics like the Zulu, the Bumbles and the Woolly Bugger. The rise and fall of this type of fly makes a fascinating cameo of fly fishing history and shows to perfection how difficult it is to keep a good pattern down – even after the original rationale for using it has long since been discredited.

The other type of fly which dominated early fly boxes was imitations of items used as live bait. There is no doubt in my mind that many early trout artificials were tied in an attempt to liberate anglers from the tiresome problem of finding reliable supplies of fresh insects. There is some objective support for this theory because patterns derived from insects which were fished as live bait form a high proportion of early lists of flies. The reason for this is obvious: by and large, winged insects have a short shelf-life and they die at the drop of a hat. As a result, fishermen who wanted to dap with live mayfly or stonefly had to collect their bait on the morning of their expedition, keeping their prizes in specially designed boxes. All in all it was a difficult task which must have been

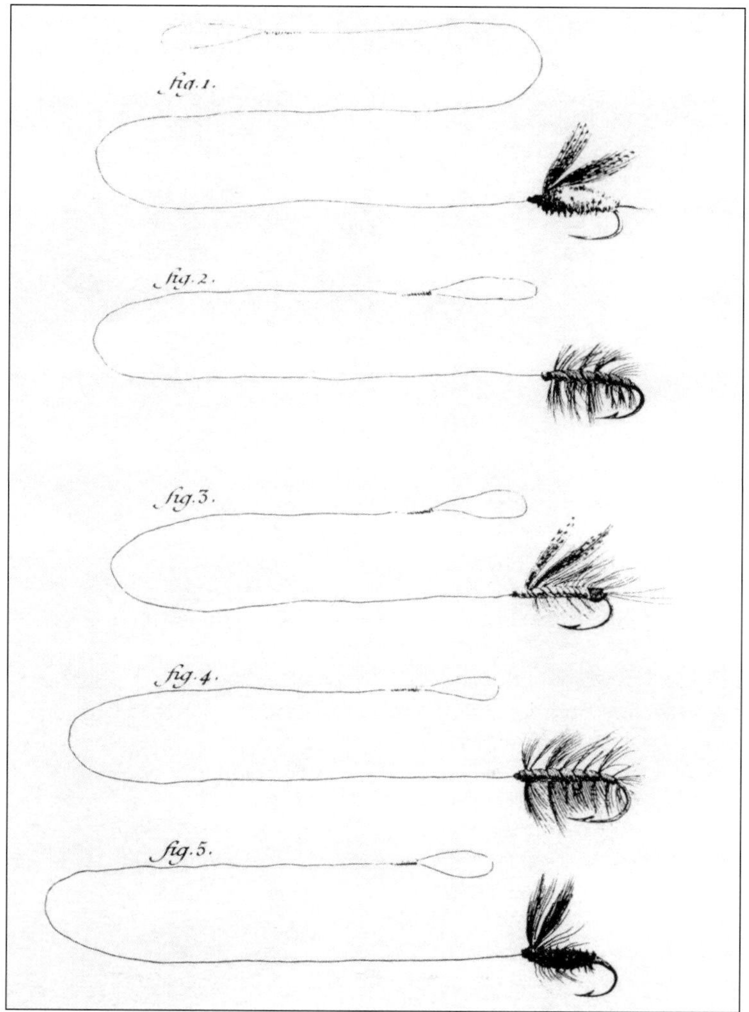

A mix of palmer patterns and flies

hard on the soul with the water lying so invitingly by. Collecting a good supply of naturals would have been time-consuming on a good day, but it would have been a sore trial on a bad day, when there were few to be found and the understandable response would have been to substitute imitations when the going got tough.

Few insects large and hardy enough to impale on a hook escaped the attention of early fly fishermen and the breadth of imitations in the lists reflects this. Absolutely nothing seemed to escape the ambition of our forefathers, whose taste in terrestrials was refreshingly catholic. They imitated anything that flew, crawled or wiggled, and stonefly, oak fly, mayfly, cow dung fly, housefly, bluebottle, wasp, caddis and other imitations abound. Although they were very effective, they, like the palmers, fell into eclipse in the nineteenth century in the face of the fashionable *ephemeroptera* patterns. By the twentieth century, flies tied to imitate live baited insects had largely disappeared, which is one of the reasons why old lists of patterns look so odd to us. Terrestrials have deservedly made a comeback in recent years, and while I haven't yet read a modern magazine article which suggests imitating a dung fly, given the rate at which new, improved killer patterns are being published, it is probably only a matter of time.

Until now, all I have been able to talk about have been European flies, but things were set to change. The first settlers in America had been careful to bring hooks and flies from the Old World, although they didn't take many rods, because they knew raw materials were abundant in their adopted home. It was only a matter of time before they began to tie their own flies, but to begin with they used copies of patterns which had worked well in the Old World.

Edward Pole was probably the first American trader to advertise flies, amongst a comprehensive range of other fishing tackle, in advertisements placed in Dunlap's *Pennsylvania Packet*.[17] Despite the geographical isolation in which the new colonists found themselves, old habits died hard and it wasn't until the late nineteenth century that a distinctive American style began to emerge, but nevertheless, the first steps towards fly tying independence were taken two hundred years ago.

Rods

One area where eighteenth century anglers did push the frontiers forward was in the way they began to draw a distinction between fly and bait rods. With the exception of Chetham, the majority of seventeenth century authors used one rod for everything, be it float fishing for perch or fly fishing for salmon. But by the latter half of the eighteenth century, increasing specialisation of rods was evident and there was much greater choice of materials for the sections. A typical all-purpose rod from the early or middle eighteenth century would have been between fourteen and seventeen feet long, with an ash butt, seven foot long; a hazel mid-section, seven foot long; and a top made of two foot of yew, with a six inch whalebone tip; not that different from its seventeenth century predecessor. Ash, which is straight-grained, strong, springy and relatively light, remained a standard for rod butts until at least the middle of the nineteenth century.

Compared to their grandfathers, eighteenth century men could be incredibly sophisticated in their choice of rods. The 'modern' fishermen used a selection: a twelve footer for fishing with two or more hairs; a nine foot rod for fishing single hairs 'for the small fly'; and a strapping seventeen footer for salmon, the latter using a 'wheel'. This was an important development, because it was the beginning of increasing specialisation of rods and the separation of salmon and trout fishing into different disciplines. Differentiation of rods brought a wide range of new materials into use; deal, ash or willow were favoured for the butts, and hickory or hazel for tops, with the standard whalebone extension. Hickory, a new material, came from any one of about eighteen different trees that comprise the genus *Carya* of the walnut family, commonly found in the North American deciduous forests. A few traditionalists still used juniper, bay tree and elder for butts; and yew, crab apple and blackthorn were used for tops, but these native woods were becoming distinctly old fashioned as they were displaced by imports. The adventurous salmon fisherman could even try some new-fangled Indian stuff called 'Bambou cane' for the construction of his tops.

One of the most useful discoveries made during the eighteenth century was the invention of the intermediate rod ring. Rings didn't spring from the ether, fully formed: their ancestor was a loop tied to the tip of the rod, through which a running line was slipped and a few early rods were built with tip rings. Running rings can instead be seen as a natural development of this loop and they began to appear on salmon rods at the beginning of the eighteenth century.[18] The method of attachment was brutally simple; loops of iron wire were bent round a former, leaving a spike which was hammered into the wood of the butt sections. Middle and top rings were constructed from loops which were lashed on flat, before being bent out at right angles to the rod. Together with the differentiation of different types of rod, the intermediate ring had a profound influence on the subsequent course of fishing, if only because it made it so much easier to fish with a running line and also because it improved the mechanical advantage of the rod when a fish had been caught. We are used to handling the line as it comes out from the bottom ring, just above the rod hand, which allows us to control the tension on the line very precisely, either by feeding line or by moving our hands further apart. Without any intermediate rings, the line bowstrings from the line hand to the rod tip and introduces instability into the arrangement.

The development of the ring gave anglers much more control over the line while a fish was being played, but the nature of the knotted horsehair in use made the invention much less useful than it might have been. Horsehair hung up on rings at every opportunity and it wasn't possible to 'shoot' much line during casting, a drawback which would eventually sound the death knell of this type of line. Perhaps because of this, the ring didn't seize the imagination of the fly fishing world overnight and early salmon and pike rods were far more likely to have rings fitted than trout rods. Quite apart from the problems with horsehair, the other drawback of this less than universally acclaimed invention was that early rings were incredibly unreliable and if one failed, the domino effect meant that the rest were likely to pull out in sympathy, whereupon they ran down the line like curtain rings, leaving the hapless angler playing the fish directly off the reel.

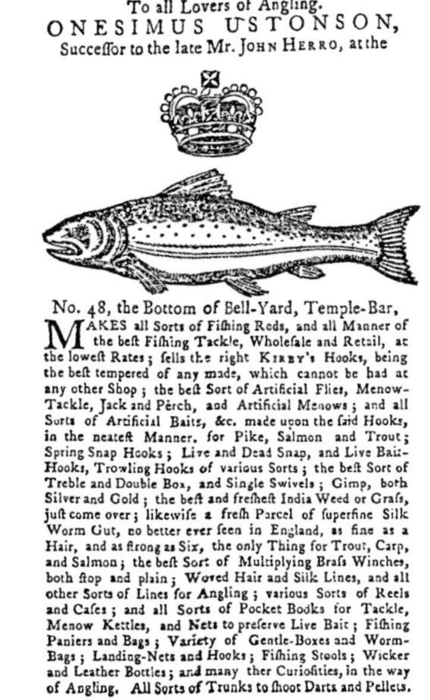

Advertisement for Onesimus Ustonson, tackle maker.

It will come as a relief to DIY-haters that it was hardly necessary to build your own rod any more. Traders are known to have been in business as early as 1600 and Gervase Markham suggested to his readers that they should buy their rods in haberdashers' stores, where he said there was a 'great choice', but retailers didn't become common for at least another hundred years. By the eighteenth century, the tackle trade was well established and shops sold every conceivable article that a fisherman might need, as well as numerous items which he didn't, a tradition which they have selflessly carried on until today.

Mentions of pioneers in the trade aren't too hard to find: John Hobbs, who traded from 1650 until at least 1676, is described in Barker's *Delight* as 'the man for you if you would have a rod to beare and fit neatly' and Walton mentions two tackle dealers in the *Compleat Angler*: 'I will go with you either Mr Margrave, who dwells among the book-sellers in St Paul's churchyard, or to Mr John Stubbs, near to the Swan in Golding lane; they be both honest men, and will fit an angler with what tackling he lacks.' John Margrave traded from circa 1650 to 1676 at The Three Trouts, St Paul's churchyard, but we know next to nothing about Stubbs. A multitude of dealers sprang up during and after Walton's time, including the great firm Ustonson, which began trading in the 1760s and which was to supply tackle to King George IV.

Reels

In this heady commercial atmosphere it wasn't long before the economic possibilities of reels were recognised. Kirby was advertising 'the best sort of Winches' in local papers by 1726, and he wasn't alone. Graham Turner's valuable study of a collection of trade cards held at the Guildhall, the GLC Records Office and the British Museum, has revealed that brass winches of various designs were being advertised for sale by many dealers throughout the eighteenth century.[19] Much of the expansion of the tackle trade during this period was driven by the popularity of fishing with the emerging middle class of merchants and shop keepers so derided by Napoleon.

But it wasn't all plain sailing. In the last half of the century, there came an interesting development – the multiplying reel. The multiplier was exactly the sort of gizmo which appeals to people with money to burn and leisure to repent, so reels of this type sold like hot cakes. In 1770, Onesimus Ustonson advertised that he was selling 'the best sort of multiplying brass winches, both stop and plain'.[20] At the time it must have been a fairly recent invention, as the first mention of the multiplying reel in the literature was made barely twenty years later:

> Your fly line should be about thirty yards long, and wound on a small brass multiplying winch which is to be placed on the butt of your rod; then you must run the line through the rings before mentioned, and you may always command any length without the trouble of changing the line, and shorten it when you come to places encumbered with wood.[21]

In many respects, the multiplier was an unfortunate development chiefly because most of them were so unreliable; a case of an idea made metal before its time. There were some good products, but the trouble was that reels were made of brass, and the small brass gears of many multipliers were too soft to stand the strain of winding in under the pressure of a large fit fish, even if the fisherman remained level-headed enough to take care. But, for the moment, the multiplier was in its honeymoon period.

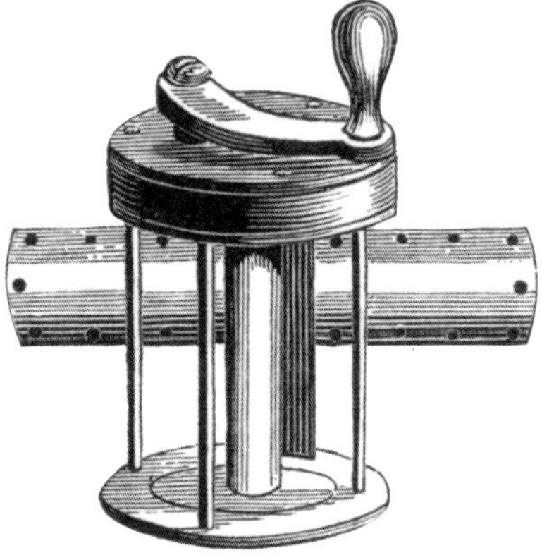

An early multiplier from Salter's Guide

The appearance of the multiplier was paralleled by developments in fly lines and towards the turn of the century several other important advances were made. By the last quarter of the century, fishermen were using thirty yard lines for trout, and much longer ones for salmon. They were also able to make use of a 'newly invented engine' for twisting horse hair which is first mentioned by Brookes in 1766 – since this author doesn't talk about it as if it is anything new, the invention may well have dated back to the early years of the eighteenth century. But the twisting engine was almost superfluous, because thanks to the development of machines used in the textile industry, a variety of manufactured tapered knotless lines had come on the market and these must have transformed the average fly fisher's existence. No longer did anglers have to beg, steal or borrow horse hair; no longer did they have to spend endless evenings preparing and knotting their own tapered lines, they could just go out and buy them in a shop.[22] The snag was that the lines on offer weren't cheap and neither were they totally reliable, but for those who could afford them they were understandably popular.

Few woven horsehair lines seem to have survived, but the Flyfishers' Club in London has an excellent example, which was donated by Professor J. W. McNee – it is a slim tapered trout line, about twenty yards long and remarkably well preserved despite its great age. It may even be one of the very earliest tapered woven horsehair lines made, because according to the Professor's note, written in March 1949:

> . . . it is certainly well over one hundred years old. My father was born in 1852 and when still a boy this line was passed on to him after considerable use by his father. It was handed to me about fifty years ago and I used it as my first line. It had to be soaked in water before use which made it straight and reasonably heavy.[23]

Getting rid of the knots must have made a considerable difference to the utility of pure horsehair lines and it goes some way to explaining why they stayed popular as long as they did. The Flyfishers' line still seems to be in fishable condition, which is what my limited experience of horsehair lines has taught me to expect: the plaited ones handle very well and if they are cared for properly they last almost forever.

Hooks

By the late eighteenth century, hook making in Europe had become a sophisticated manufacturing process, helped to a very great extent by Benjamin Huntsman's 1740 discovery of how to make high quality steel on a small scale using the crucible process. Huntsman used his method to manufacture watch and clock springs and it was so successful that it spread to every area of steel manufacture and all best-grade steel was subsequently made by the crucible process until the electric furnace replaced it in the twentieth century. It is probably no coincidence that around this time authors began to give hook sizes for some of their patterns and we get our first clue as to the size of early flies. Though hooks had been commercially available since before Walton's day and the famous firm of Charles Kirby had made its name by selling quality hooks from at least 1655, Thomas Best was one of the first authors to give sizes. Unfortunately Best didn't think to tell us which scale he used, though in all probability it was the early Redditch, but he was one of the last to leave his readership in the dark; from 1800 onwards, authors began to give hook sizes for patterns, a sign of growing standardisation.

A measure of how sophisticated hook making had become in the eighteenth century can be gathered from a trip to the Patents Office.

In 1789, patent No. 1719 was granted to Mr John Andrews, who lived in Tardebigge, a village a few miles from Redditch.[24] The invention was described as 'Making and completing fish-hooks of superior strength and polish to any other fish hooks.' While the technique appears to be derived from the method used at the time for polishing needles, the fascinating thing about this early patent is that it describes a method of mass producing steel hooks which wasn't so far removed from the techniques in use two hundred years later:

> The fish hooks are first formed of steel wire, as in common cases, and completed by the following process, namely: they are first, being cold, spread upon thin cap paper and covered with thick yeast of barm to prevent the fire penetrating too quickly into the steel and injuring the beard and fine point of the hook, and they are then put into a smooth iron plate five inches wide, seven inches long, and one eighth part of an inch thick, which is then put into an iron case open at each end, six inches wide, three inches deep and ten inches long, and then put into a slow clear fire made in a brick stove, seventeen inches long, twelve inches wide and twelve inches deep, and there remain until the fish-hooks are heated of a warm red; they are then taken from thence in the iron case by a pair of tongs, and emptied out of the case into a small tub of water milk warm, and there remain for the space of one minute and then taken from thence and put into fine emory or drift sand, heated in an iron pan two inches deep and nine inches diameter, over a brick stove or tunnel over a slow coal fire, and they are kept till perfectly dry, and then put into a fine sieve to separate the hooks from the sand or emory; from thence they are emptied upon brown paper, and put loose into a barrel or barrels, there being three, which are fastened together with screws, head to head, without any communication with each other; the middle barrel being capable of containing four gallons, the two outside barrels five gallons each, all which said barrels run upon two iron spindles fixed in a wood frame, one at each end of the two outside barrels, and turned with a windlass by one man. In each of the two largest barrels there are put two gallons of water, a quarter of a pint of castile soap, and three pounds of white emory pounded small, and in the small barrel one gallon and a half of water, three ounces of castile soap, and two pounds and a half of white emory pounded small.
>
> There are then ten thousand of the fish-hooks put into each barrel, and secured therein by a round cork fixed in a bunghole made in each barrel, four inches in diameter, and the barrels are then turned with the windlass and kept in continual motion for twenty hours, by which time they will be sufficiently bright

> for polishing, and by which mode there may be scoured twelve sizes of hooks at one time by equally dividing them, namely: number 1 to 8 inclusive in the two largest barrels, and number 9 to 12 inclusive in the small barrel.
>
> The hooks are then taken out of the barrels and dried by putting them in a tub that is capable of containing six gallons, and therein mixed up with one gallon of dry ash sawdust, and there remain for the space of five minutes, and from thence they are put in a machine called a tray, and fanned until the sawdust is separated from the hooks, and the hooks are then spread upon a table and picked from the emory by hand and put into leather bags (made of sheep skin, yellow dressed) fourteen inches long and five inches wide, and shook by hand for two hours, and then picked, each size separate.
>
> And in order to temper them, six pounds of fine sand, called hour glass sand, made hot in the same iron pan as before mentioned, must be kept stirring till it is of proper heat to temper, which will generally be in eight minutes, but will be accurately known by putting a waste hook or piece of wire of the size of the hooks that are to be tempered into the sand, and then the fish hooks are put loose into the sand, and kept constantly turning and moving; and of those hooks which are size 1, 2, 3, and 4, the temper will come in five minutes; and of those which are in size 9, 10, 11, and 12, in three minutes; by which means the fish hooks will become of a beautiful dark blue colour, which is the proper temper, and as soon as that appears they must be immediately put out of the iron pan into the wire sieve to separate them from the sand, and when so separated they must be put into a leather bag, as before mentioned, and shaken by hand for five minutes. When that is done they are put into yellow paper, and are then complete, and are of superior strength, colour and polish to any other fish hooks, and will keep any length of time without the common application of oil.

The last sentence highlights an important point: early hooks made of untreated metal rusted at the drop of a hat and fishermen had to go to great lengths to ensure that flies were dried out after use if they didn't want to lose them. The patent is interesting, not least because it is so discursive, which must have marked it out in the days when patents were typically only a few lines long, and it may well indicate the importance that Andrews knew attached to the patent. The fact that a supplier could contemplate making thirty thousand hooks in twenty-four hours gives some idea of the size of the potential market, a far cry from the small scale home production of the late fifteenth century.

The shape of hooks was changing, as well as the quality of the metal from which they were made. In the eighteenth century, anglers began to question the design of the blind or spade-ended hooks which had been standard for so long. Had they but known it, the answer was staring them in the face, as the eyed hook had had a long pedigree even then, but for some reason its day did not come for another hundred years. The first illustration of an eyed hook I know of was printed in France in 1660[25], while the first English illustration appeared in 1760.[26] However, the metal eye has a much longer history than is often thought. Fred Buller has some bronze second century AD eyed hooks which were made in Palestine, the smallest of which is about a number ten; interestingly enough, they were found with a collection of hook making tools. These are not the only ancient eyed hooks, because the British Museum has a number of bronze hooks in the William Hamilton collection and several of these have an eye formed by bending the shank back upon itself. Hamilton was the ambassador to the Kingdom of Naples at the end of the eighteenth century and although the hooks he collected have never been dated, they were already old when Hamilton acquired them and it is thought that they are probably Roman. The fascinating thing about this particular collection is that it contains an eyed quadruple hook.

A rather exotic collection of barbless hooks, some of which were eyed, was recovered in 1925 during mining operations in the bed of the Saija river in Colombia, some of which were as small as three-eighths of an inch in length and all of which were made from gold or gold/copper alloy. These hooks were judged to have been forged before the Aztec and Inca civilisations were founded, fixing their probable origin to around 500 BC,[27] but even this set may be relative newcomers in the history of the eyed hook, because the Museo Civico di Archeologia Ligure, in Pegli, Italy, boasts a Neolithic bone hook which has two holes bored through the shank, one of which can hardly have been anything except an eye.

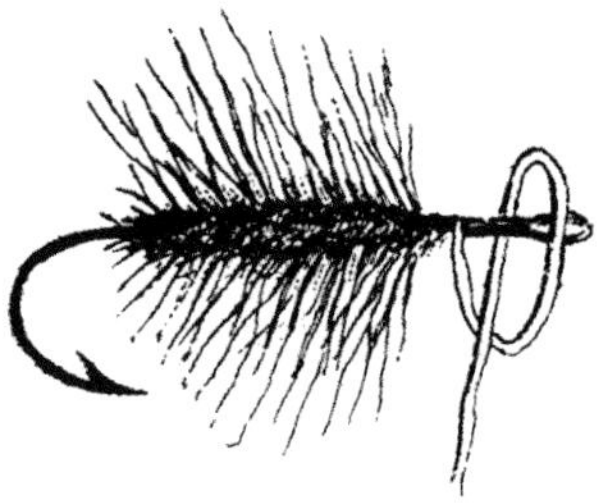

Detail of an eyed hook from Hawkin's Complete Angler

The only reason I can think of to explain why eyed hooks did not come into common use much earlier than they did is that they aren't that easy to make. Bending fine metal in a small circle isn't easy to do if you are using poor quality steel and lack assistance from machines, and technical problems may well have held the eyed hook back. The saga is probably the best example I know of why it is dangerous to assume that just because a thing had been invented, it would be widely used. In fact, it wasn't until H. S. Hall began his work on improved hooks for dry fly fishing that the virtues of the eyed hook were taken for granted. But for that, we will have to wait another hundred years.

Casting

Perhaps because of the availability of tapered lines, we begin to see the first decent descriptions of how to cast in the eighteenth century, for example in Bowlker:

> The Art of managing your Rod and throwing your Fly is no more to be learned by rules than that of making it; only I would advise the young sportsman never to encumber himself with too much line, not longer at most than the breadth of the River he Fishes in. In raising your Line, observe to wave your Rod a little round your Head, rather than bring it directly backwards; and take care not to make a return of your Line 'till it is gone to its full length behind you, otherwise you will be very apt to whip off your Fly. The greatest skill is to make your Line fall as light as possible on the water, especially in smooth gliding Streams, for if it falls heavy so as to dash the Water, you will be sure to affright and not catch the Fish. When you see a Fish rise at the natural Fly, the best way is to throw a Yard above him, rather than directly over his Head, and let your Fly move gently towards him, by which means you will shew it to him more naturally, and he will be the more tempted to take it; but nothing but your own practice and experience can make you a Master of the Art, so as to throw exactly behind Trees and Bushes into holes and curls of the Water where the best Fish commonly lie. [28]

Printed descriptions like this meant that at last a beginner didn't have to rely on his friends to teach him everything and the era of the modern fishing manual wasn't too far off. But although the advice above sounds reasonably up to date, it is only necessary to read a few of these accounts to realise how different fishing styles were in those far off days. For example, where presentation was concerned, the good fisherman laid great emphasis on avoiding anything but the fly and the cast falling on the water. Some unusual techniques evolved to achieve this, a common trick being to stop the forward stroke of the cast with the rod tip much higher than we would, and rely on the 'back spring' of the rod to throw the reel line up and clear of the water. Pulling off this kind of manoeuvre is only necessary, or possible, if an excessively soft fly rod is used and it makes casting awkward. Stiff rods weren't universal until split cane appeared in the late nineteenth century and because of this the casting action used by many eighteenth century anglers would have looked very strange to our eyes.

In spite of this, improvements in rods and lines meant that anglers could cast significantly further than they could in the previous century. A good fisherman could throw twelve yards of line with one hand, and seventeen with both. It is a moot point whether anyone would actually have wanted to cast single-handed all day with a sixteen foot rod, but do note that casting distances had roughly doubled from the time when fixed horsehair lines were in use, and that they were beginning to approximate to the distances the average present day angler can achieve.

This extra distance meant that the fisherman could relax a little, because he was that bit further away from the fish. The impact that the routine use of reels, tapered running lines and intermediate rings had on fly fishing field craft is a subject on which one seldom finds any references, but it was profound. All that was needed now was for materials and manufacturing methods to improve and anglers would be fishing with recognisably modern equipment.

Salmon Flies

There is a frustrating gap of very nearly a century between Barker's and Venables' accounts of the salmon fly and the next time we hear of it again. In that time, if we take the literature at face value, very little had changed, because both Fairfax and Brookes describe exactly the same fly, with minor variations:

> But for a greater salmon, if your fly be artificial, make it very large, with six wings, one behind another, that by that and the different colours, he may suppose it, as indeed it will appear in the water, a cluster of flies.[29]

This is the Horseleech fly, which was probably at the last gasp of its popularity by then. It would be rather surprising if the pattern was actually intended to imitate a horseleech, *Hæmopsis sanguisorba*, which differs from the common leech only by virtue of its larger size, and in the detail of the formation of its jaws. There used to be all sorts of fables about horseleeches and it was commonly believed that the bites of half a dozen were enough to kill a horse stone dead. Quite apart from this interesting, though useless fact, the reason why anglers might have wanted to imitate horseleeches was because (in one of those extraordinary errors of inference which make reading old books on fishing such fun) they were thought to hatch from dragon fly eggs – and dragon flies were held to be very significant prey for the king of fish.

In a sense it is quite extraordinary that this one, rather impractical-sounding fly should be the only pattern which was so faithfully transcribed by all these authors. If there were other flies in popular use, you would have thought that at least one of the four authors mentioned above would have described them – but they don't, although they give hints that salmon would take flies intended for trout. The key here is in the word 'popular', because fly fishing meant fishing for trout, chub and dace until the late eighteenth century, which isn't to say that no one fished for salmon with the fly; it is just that it wasn't very common.

Fishing for salmon was a risky undertaking, with broken tackle the penalty for the slightest mistake and as a result it wasn't a popular sport. Quite apart from the fact that salmon were difficult to catch, they simply weren't fashionable as a sport fish. Until the end of the eighteenth century, the vast majority of salmon were taken in nets, traps, or by spearing on the spawning beds. Perhaps as a consequence, prior to the nineteenth century, detailed salmon fly patterns are excessively rare, but the wind of change must have begun to blow in the middle of the eighteenth century, because Richard Bowlker hints at a couple of patterns, which are described here in detail by his son Charles.

> DRAGON FLY
>
> The wings are made of a reddish brown feather from the wing of a cock turkey, the body of auburn-coloured mohair warped with yellow silk, and a ginger cock's hackle wrapped under the wings; the hook No. 2 or 3. Or it may be varied thus; the wings of a rich brown feather from a heron's wing; the body drab, or olive-coloured mohair, a bittern's hackle under the wings, and a forked tail. This fly is about two inches in length.
>
> KINGS' FISHER, OR PEACOCK FLY
>
> This is also a salmon fly, and is seen at the same time as the Dragon Fly. The wings are made of a feather from the neck or tail of a peacock; the body of deep green mohair, warped with

> light green silk; and a jay's feather striped blue and white, wrapped under the wings; the hook No. 2 or 3. It may be thus varied; the wings of a dark shining green feather from a drake's wing; the body of green mohair warped with chocolate silk; and a bittern's hackle under the wings.[30]

The Dragon fly makes a nice bridge between the Horseleech fly and modern flies and these two patterns are very important, because they are quite different from anything that preceded them. For a start, they have many of the characteristics of nineteenth century salmon flies, with complex designs and wings which vault over hackled bodies. The King's Fisher in particular is a striking fly, with the electric blue of the jay contrasting sharply against the deep greens and chocolate of the remainder of the fly, and it would have stood out in any fly book.

The Bowlker patterns definitely marked the start of something, because within a relatively short space of time, more salmon fly patterns appeared in print, in a book written by a man called Samuel Taylor. Taylor is largely forgotten now, overshadowed by Bainbridge and Blacker (whose books were distinguished by colour plates, hence their popularity) but his contribution shouldn't be underestimated. He was one of the first to deal with the increasingly popular sport of salmon fishing at length. Taylor gave us three detailed salmon fly patterns, the first good description of how to tie a salmon fly and our first reference to the vice, which is quite enough for one author. His description of how to tie a salmon fly not only includes a description of the mixed wing which became such a feature of nineteenth century flies, but it is also a vast improvement on Franck's:

> It must be observed, that the salmon hooks for summer fishing should be about No. 3, and strong made; and if the shanks are too long, there must be some taken off, according to the length and size of the fly you intend to make; and that your feathers must be intermixed with different gaudy shades, such as golden and other pheasant's, parrot's, peacock's, and in short, of all other birds that are fit for the purpose, either foreign or domestic; and others dyed, including hackles of various colours, as well as your mohair and other fluff for the body; but to render these flies more light in clear water, let the body be made quite thin, of silk of a suitable colour (for it must always be suited to the fly you make); a bit of gaudy feather at the tail, with narrow gold or silver plating according as it matches, instead of twist; and the hackle for legs, the blue spotted feather from a jay's wing (the other part of it being stripped away) worked up, only from about half way below the wings, but pretty thick under them.

> I have here mentioned this hackle in particular, because it is very excellent; but your hackles must always be suited to the shades of your other materials. Further observe, that before you begin to make the head of the fly, you should take two gaudy strips of feather, and lay one on each side of the shoulders, to stand something longer than the other feathers, and whip them there, and finish the head; and the fly, when thus placed in proper order, will appear very beautiful. For the better convenience of making these large flies, you should be provided with a very small vice, for the purpose of holding the hook, that you may have both hands at liberty to put in your materials, which will enable you to dress the flies more neatly as well as more perfectly.[31]

Taylor didn't say any more about the vice, leaving just that one frustrating fragment; the first reference anywhere in the literature; but in making use of the tool, he set himself one hundred years ahead of his time.

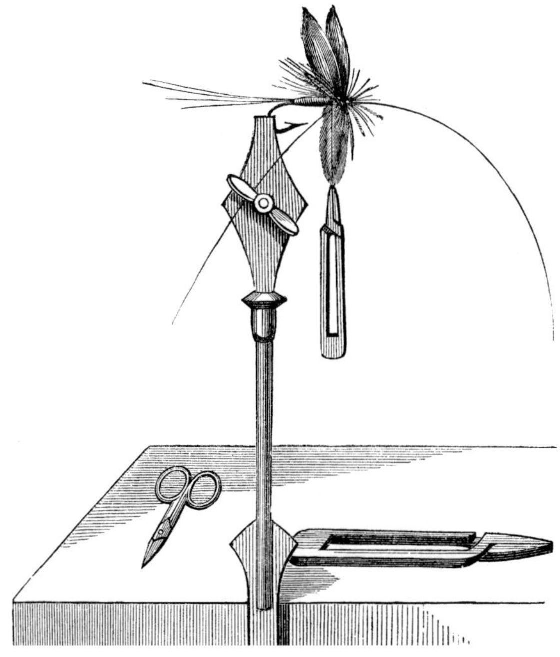

An early vice

Why then, if the tool was available, didn't other fly tyers take up the use of the vice earlier than they did? It has been suggested that early models were non-specialist vices made with soft cast-iron jaws, which were too soft to grip a hook properly, but the evidence for this is equivocal. More likely the same kind of conservatism which discriminated against the eyed hook came into play here. People were used to the idea of tying flies in the hand, using a skill which was passed down from one angler to another and there was nothing to be found in books about tying with a vice. On top of this, adapting hand-tying methods for use on a hook held in a vice is remarkably difficult, particularly if you lack modern instruments like bobbin holders and hackle pliers. Hand tyers were used to letting the end of the silk dangle free, catching it and other materials under their fingers to maintain tension, but if you try this method with a vice, the tool gets in the way. Adopting the vice meant learning an entirely different way of tying flies, and while patterns were relatively simple, there wasn't much reason to go to all the trouble of learning new tricks. Besides, a hand tyer could sit down and make flies anywhere, provided there was a patch of sun and a glass of beer to hand, while the vice shackled him to the bench. The ability to tie a new pattern by the waterside is one of the great advantages that we have sacrificed to progress.

Origins of the 'Gaudy' Salmon Fly

One of the interesting things about Taylor is the way he used materials like parrot and golden pheasant, advising that as the season progressed, flies should be made steadily more gaudy, until they were to be adorned with 'the most glittering plumage' at the height of summer. At a stroke, he raised the stakes in the level of detail with which salmon flies were tied, by introducing such subtleties as horns, although he doesn't mention these by name.[32] This raises a question about the origins of the 'fully-dressed' salmon fly; which seized the imagination of nineteenth century fly tyers, leading to an explosion of complex and colourful patterns tied with increasingly exotic materials. It is commonly held that Ireland is where this type of fly found its origins, but the trouble is that if early native Irish fly tyers wrote at all, they wrote in their native tongue, printing being controlled at the time by royal licence. While it is possible that early Irish manuscripts still exist, at present all we can say is that we know very little of writing about Irish flies before 1800. Recently, a cache of early Irish material has been found in the archives of the American Museum of Fly Fishing and it will be interesting to see what this holds.

The earliest authenticated Irish flies date to about 1797[33] and even then, these are trout flies. In his seminal book on Irish flies, Ted Malone[34] conjectures that fly fishing was brought to Ireland by English officers manning the garrisons, which is very likely right, but if this is correct, they would have brought English flies with them and despite a few gaudy English originals, the vast majority of eighteenth and early nineteenth century Scottish salmon flies were dull in the extreme. It seems unlikely that early Irish flies were any different. As witness, I would point to the selection that Frederic Tolfrey fished in Canada in 1816; a very early list of Irish patterns. When Tolfrey tried to establish the origin of the patterns, many years later, he asked no less an authority than William Blacker, who confirmed that he had fished the same flies on the Bann. Here are three of the flies:

> No.1. Body, yellow tag, next to purple, cinnamon-brown mohair, or pigs-down at the shoulder, reddish-brown hackle for legs; wing, hen pheasant's tail, two strips of Mallard wing, for tail; either ribbed or not with gold or silver twist. Hook 8 or 9, Limerick.
>
> No. 2. Body, brown pig's hair full slightly ribbed with gold twist. Wing, from the wing of a hen pheasant. Tail two strips of mallard wing. B.B.
>
> No. 3. Body, tipped with yellow, then dark blue pig's down up to the head; black hackle wound from the tail up, and silver twist. Wing, teal-feather. Hook 8 or 9.

I hope that you will agree with me that these are not gaudy flies. They lack macaw horns, are bereft of jungle cock, haven't the merest hint of cock of the rock and can't boast a sprig of gallina between them. So when were the flies designed? The latest date the patterns could have been created was 1816, when Tolfrey fished them. Since it is unlikely that they managed to cross the Atlantic in the year that they were invented, my own opinion is that these are very early nineteenth and possibly even late eighteenth century Irish patterns. This puts them firmly among the earliest known Irish salmon flies and while they lack the solemnity of Scottish patterns tied during the same period, neither are they exactly showy.

The other problem we face when we try to make a judgement on this subject is that there is a complete dearth of salmon fly patterns of any description before 1800 and very few before 1825. The logical explanation for the lack of flies is that there were relatively few salmon fishers to invent them,yet there is old Franck's dubbing bag, stuffed to bursting with macaw, flamingo and parakeet. One possibility is that the expansion of salmon fishing led to the creation of numbers of unrecorded patterns in the late eighteenth century and these flies were the inspiration for the revolution that followed, rather than the ones we see in the books. If these early pioneers were anything like Franck, they might have found that salmon had a penchant for brightly coloured flies and have indulged it without ever writing the patterns down, yet left a legacy of their experiments in the imaginations of the Irish tyers. If I were to advance any evidence for this hypothesis at all, I would quote this passage:

> The greater part of our English anglers make a great fuss about the proper flies for salmon; whereas the Scotch anglers, who are very skilful, and possess many admirable qualifications for the sport, content themselves with either a heron's or a bittern's hockle, or the red feather from the wing of a turkey-cock, which answer for the wings; while a little fine wool, of a sulphur yellow (sometimes rather deeper), makes the body of such a fly as the salmon seem to relish greatly. The Scotch anglers all busk their own flies, for so they call the art of manufacturing them.

By inference, Williamson, writing in 1808, would seem to indicate that by the early days of the nineteenth century, English anglers were fishing noticeably brighter flies than the Scots, and this may have provided the basis for an accelerating trend as the years wore on.

Whatever the truth is, we do know that the first signs of that revolution were found in Ireland. In 1830 Belton wrote:

> The Limerick flies are almost always very gaudy and have silk bodies; whereas those tied in Dublin are usually of mohair or fur, and much more sober in their colours, although infinitely more showy than Scotch salmon flies.
>
> The fly I found the most successful here, as almost every where else that I have tried it, was one of O'Shaughnessy's, a deep orange, silk body, with broad gold tinsel, rich mixed wings, and macaw horns.[35]

Later he gives another pattern, tied small and fished in pairs on single gut: 'orange to violet bodies, mixed wings, with either grouse, or jay, or Gallina hackle, whipped under them; the latter either plain, or stained yellow.' This isn't to say that every Irish fly was bright, and there were marked regional variations, so that on Lough Screeb, the locals favoured 'very sober colours, such as olive mohair, or a mixture of brown, yellow and purple; with a dark mallard, or grouse, or turkey wing.'

On the scanty evidence we have, it seems likely that it was the Limerick and perhaps the Erne patterns which crossed the Irish sea and had such a profound effect on English and Scottish fly fishing. This process was catalysed by improvements in travel and tackle which meant that salmon fishing suddenly became immensely popular. The demand for different flies exploded, no doubt egged on by local tackle dealers who had much to gain from parting the new breed of travelling salmon fisherman from their money.

We don't know for sure who kicked the new fad off, but O'Shaughnessy, perhaps the most famous Irish fly tyer of all time, is a possibility. O'Shaughnessy established his business in Limerick in 1795 and his name is mentioned too often in conjunction with early gaudy flies for it to be a coincidence, given that his hooks were so prized that fishermen travelled from far away to obtain supplies of them. O'Shaughnessy would have been well placed to start the new trend. The Limerick tradition catered for the Shannon and its surrounding fisheries and at the time, Limerick was a large seaport, into which exotic materials, including feathers would have been imported every week. Although they seem to have had an entirely separate tradition, the Erne tyers were equally likely to have been involved in setting the new trend, and certainly Ballyshannon had an active export business in eels and salt fish during the eighteenth century. Even allowing for the fact that the sandbar in the estuary meant that larger ships had to anchor and unload some way out, the success of the more northerly port would have brought traders from far afield, as the Irish historian Kevin McKenna wrote to me recently. Among the Erne tyers, James Rogan and Pat McKay certainly made their names tying gaudy flies, and who knows what sort of creations their predecessors tied?

Whatever the origins of the gaudy fly may have been, within a very few years, the dull traditional salmon fly was swept away in a flood of brilliant new creations. The fact that these flies were completely unnecessary didn't have the slightest impact on the near hysteria with which salmon fishers adopted them. With few exceptions, the sombre traditional patterns, which had done such faithful service, were swept aside by bright new substitutes. It took the gaudy fly another hundred years to reach its zenith and we will catch up with it later on.

Fishing Techniques

There is very little written about how eighteenth century anglers fished, but we can make an educated guess, thanks to David Webster's delightfully eccentric book, *The Angler and the Loop Rod.* This strange publication first saw the light of day in 1885, and was most likely authored by a Dr Livingstone, but does describe how to fish with tackle an eighteenth century angler would have recognised.

On reflection, perhaps eccentric isn't quite the right adjective to describe Webster. If we take him at face value, he regarded a day's fishing as a dismal failure were he to kill 'less than from ten to fifteen pounds of trout between ten in the morning and four in the afternoon.' This wasn't a vain boast, because when the book was written, the Scotsman had been a professional fisherman for forty years, and he lived on the proceeds of selling his catch.

Webster's tackle? His favourite trout rod was thirteen and a half feet long, with an ash butt, hickory mid section and lancewood top; truly a late eighteenth century weapon if I ever heard of one. His hand-held line ran through a loop at the top of the rod, a setup which would have been totally familiar to Barker and one which dates the origin of Webster's technique to the seventeenth century. The line itself was braided from horsehair, tapering from forty-five hairs at the loop down to five or six at the point, where he tied a long gut cast. The total length of the line was about thirty-seven feet including the gut.

The Scotsman cast with extreme delicacy using this arrangement, aiming to keep his flies afloat, or at the very least, close to the surface. He grasped the rod in both hands, the left near the butt and the right eight or nine inches higher up. His upper arms were kept close to his body, so that only the wrists and forearms were brought into play. Once he had made a cast so that the line began to fish down below him, he began gradually to raise his rod towards the perpendicular, bringing the tip around in what he described as a 'horse-shoe shaped curve' (which sounds a bit like a switch cast to me) until he flicked it backwards and switched the cast forward again. His aim was to ensure that the first part of the line to touch the water was the middle point of the horsehair, the gut carrying the droppers parachuting in gently so that all nine flies landed almost at once. Nine flies! I have enough trouble with three! The flies didn't spend much time on the water, because Webster only allowed them to fish down a few yards before casting again, a technique which Charles Cotton would have felt quite at home with. The use of droppers on a fly cast is by and large a nineteenth century invention, but with the gut cast substituted by a horsehair point and a dramatic reduction in the number of flies he used, the Scotsman's method would have been recognised by any eighteenth century angler.

It is only the fact that Webster's book was published in Halford's era that makes his method seem obsolete, as if a passing time machine had accidentally deposited him in the wrong century. While his contemporary laboured long hours to develop his dry fly patterns, the Scotsman was cleaning up with tackle that the chalk stream men would have dismissed as antiquated. Amazingly enough, a very few old men were still to be seen on the Clyde in the late 1950s fishing with long double-handed hollow-butted rods and horsehair lines. Their bibles were Edmonds and Lee's *Brook and River Trouting* – and *The Angler and the Loop Rod*. Old habits do indeed die hard, especially when they work.

Fishing for 'Coarse' Fish

Having digressed once, I might as well digress twice, and discuss fly fishing for chub, roach, dace and pike. Nowadays most fly fishermen regard dace with extreme irritation, and I confess that I once totally lost it and threw rocks at a small shoal to which I had cast for at least an hour, having laboured under the mistaken impression that they were grayling. I suspect that coarse fish have been pursued with a fly for as long as any of the salmonids, but it has never been terribly popular and fishermen have been surprisingly coy about writing on the subject.

Early writings about coarse fishing with a fly are particularly scarce. The *Treatyse of Fishing with an Angle* mentions fly fishing for dace; the Tegernsee manuscript talks of fly fishing for carp, pike, catfish and burbot; and there is a passing reference to fly fishing for dace in *The Arte of Angling*, published in 1577. Apart from these, the general lack of references is rather odd, since there is no particular reason to fish for trout with a fly in preference to any of the other fish mentioned. However, by the seventeenth century, when the literature on fishing started to take off, there was reasonably general agreement about which fish would take a fly well. In 1662, Venables commented that:

> . . . for such fish as will rise at the fly, viz. Salmon, Trout, Umber, Grayling, Bleak, Chevin, Roach, Dace, &c. Though some of these fish do love some flies better than other, except the fish named, I know not any sort or kind that will ordinarily and freely rise at the fly, though I know some who angle for Bream and Pike with artificial flies, but I judge the labour lost, and the knowledge a needless curiosity; those fish being taken much easier, especially the Pike, by other ways. [36]

I tend to agree with him about bream. Incidentally, Venables, no purist, suggested that fly fishing for chub, roach or dace could be improved immeasurably by putting a caddis on the point of the hook - that's the sort of tip you never seem to see in *Trout & Salmon*, or *Fly Fisherman*. It is a shame that Venables held such a low opinion of fly fishing for pike, but it seems to have been a commonly held prejudice and few other seventeenth century writers have anything else to add on the subject. Mind you, this was the time when the smart set thought there was no better sport than to tie a baited hook to the foot of a pinioned goose and settle down to watch the fun when a pike struck. Fishing with small wet flies didn't stand much chance against that class of entertainment.

Chetham, who angled for just about anything that swam, seems to have been an enthusiastic coarse fly fisherman. From the way he wrote, it is clear that 'dibbing' with a natural fly was a popular method, with artificial flies as an alternative and while he didn't give any patterns, we can guess which ones he might have favoured, because the natural he suggests for chub is the fern fly, with caddis, palmer worms, caterpillars, grasshoppers, oak worm and hawthorn worm as alternatives. This list would go a long way towards explaining the tradition, adhered to even in our century, of fishing palmered flies for chub. Incidentally, by the beginning of the nineteenth century, dibbing artificial flies for chub was so popular that artificial moths, bees, butterflies, cockchafers, and grasshoppers tied specifically for the purpose could be bought quite easily in the shops.

Brookes makes reference to a 'Caterpillar fly' used for dace in 1766, which might be Bowlker's Black Caterpillar Fly (also known as the Black Palmer) but otherwise the earliest specialist fly for coarse fish is Best's Humble Bee, which was concocted to seduce the wily chub. This fly, dating back to the last quarter of the eighteenth century, was tied on a number two hook. The body was best black spaniel's fur, with a black cock's hackle over it (presumably palmered), the tag deep orange, and the ensemble was winged with crow wing feather. It was by no means the last word on chub flies and by the middle of the nineteenth century they had reached a stage of daring sophistication. Hofland suggested a red hackled palmer ribbed with gold, a black hackled palmer ribbed with silver, the Marlow Buzz, and a fly with a peacock's herl body and a mallard wing as essentials in the chub fisherman's fly box. By this time one can begin to see a growing formalism in choice of chub flies and twenty years after Hofland, Francis Francis still recommended large rough red or black palmers, although he added an imitation bumble bee, alder fly, and the Cinnamon fly to the list. Chub flies don't seem to have advanced much further since then and neither do the tastes of their quarry, because the last one I caught fell for a Soldier Palmer.

Chub flies from the Journal of A. J. Lane 1843

By the end of the nineteenth century, fly fishing for coarse fish had a well established place, although changes in fashion meant that it was doomed to become something of a minority sport. Nonetheless Bickerdyke[37] was spoiled for choice for chub patterns:

> As to the fly, I hardly know what to recommend, there are so many good ones. The favourite of Mr. W. Senior ("Red Spinner"), is dressed on a Snecky Limerick grilse hook. The body is of chenille tinsel, with a tail $^{1}/_{8}$ inch long, of white kid.

> Close to the head is wound a long coch-y-bondu hackle. For dark days this fly should, I think, be dressed with a dark shade of tinsel and the coch-y-bondu hackle, but for bright days with a brighter body and ordinary red hackle. The favourite chub-fly of the late Mr. Francis Francis was of grilse size; body, silver tinsel, a furnace hackle (dark red with black centre) wrapped round it, a few turns of black heron over that at the shoulder, an under-wing of a few sprigs of emerald peacock harl, and an over-wing of dark turkey; and for a tail, a tag of white kid glove or wash leather. Another favourite of his had a yellow crewel body, with red hackle and a dun turkey wing.

Choosy things, the chevin. By the 1920s there was general agreement that they liked a large fly, Sheringham going as far as to suggest that flies up to an inch long guaranteed success. Bickerdyke's chub selection included a fly dressed with a palmered badger hackle, a large Coachman, leaded to sink if necessary, a beetle imitation, sundry artificial bees, wasps, cockchafers and the long-fabled Alexandra. He wasn't averse to fishing a dry fly for chub, or dace, for that matter and neither was he above fly fishing for rudd (he gives a couple of half-hearted recommendations of patterns, before remarking that rudd aren't particularly fussy about their flies, a fact which I can confirm, having encountered unbelievably ravenous shoals on at least one occasion.) Sheringham suggested a dry Wickham or a wet kid-tailed Alder as the right stuff for rudd, adding that he found roach took dry flies almost as well as chub in shallow water, rising much the way that dace will.

Fly fishing for pike is an old pastime which has come back into favour recently. Pike certainly seem to have been a popular quarry in central Europe during the late Middle Ages, but for some obscure reason many early British writers laboured under the impression that they could not be caught on a fly. This view came under attack once salmon fishing became fashionable in the early nineteenth century, probably because salmon fishers inadvertently took pike quite frequently and found out what a sporting quarry they made. Pike flies were certainly available for sale at the end of the eighteenth century from tackle dealers like Ustonson and Chevalier, because Mackintosh tells us so. He even gives a pattern:

> The fly must be larger than even those used for salmon; it must be made on a double hook, formed of one piece of wire fastened to a good link of gimp; it must be composed of very gaudy materials, such as the feathers of the gold and common pheasant, peacock, mallard, &c. with the brown and softest part

> of bear's fur, a little dark and reddish mohair, with yellow and green mohair for the body, and four or five turns of gold twist slanting round the body; the head must be formed of a little dark brown mohair, some gold twist, and two small black beads for the eyes; the body about three inches long, and made rough, full, and round; the wings not parted, but to stand upright on the back, and some smaller feathers continued thence all down the back to the end of the tail, so that where you finish they may be left a little longer than the hook, and the whole to be about the thickness of a tom-tit, and near three inches long.[38]

Quite apart from being an overdressed horror that must have been exciting to cast on period fishing tackle, Mackintosh's pike fly is notable because it makes the first use of bead eyes that I am aware of – these are usually thought of as a modern invention.

Another early pike fly is pictured by A.J. Lane, in a manuscript which is thought to have been written in 1843. Once again, the fly is a fearsome thing that would have posed more danger to the angler than the fish. With a completely straight face, Lane tells us that one of the best flies was an imitation of the sand martin and he added that pike:

> …rise tolerably freely to flys dressed very largely & of gaudy peacock feathers, sho'd be made up on large double, or even sets of hooks. They are commonly fished for in this manner on the Irish lakes with a boat and four or five rods with flys on different lengths of line and then rowed very gently over the lake.[39]

Pike fly from the Journal of A. J. Lane 1843

This was the beginning of a tradition in truly frightful pike flies, because only twenty years later, no less a fisherman than Francis Francis gave a very detailed description of a nightmare fly specially designed to take pike:

> Pike are also taken in some waters with an artificial fly, and it is not a very uncommon thing for the angler to hook one on his salmon fly, nor to lose fly and all in consequence. The kind of fly most commonly employed is one of large size, with a pair of big, out-spreading hooks, the body composed of divers coloured pig's wool, blue, yellow, and green, as thick as a man's little finger, with a large heron's or other hackle for legs; and for the wings two eyes from a peacock's tail, with a few showy hackles, wide gold or silver foil; and a tail of various coloured hackles; at the head two glass beads are strung on to represent eyes. This which is more like a good sized hummingbird than anything else, is cast and worked like fly, and when pike are inclined to take it, it is the most sportıng and agreeable way of fishing for them in shallow pools, where there is very little water above the weeds, it will be found the most serviceable. There are many such places which are full of jack, and which it would be found very difficult perhaps to fish in any other way.[40]

The trend has, of course, been towards even more specialised, if less impressive, pike patterns in recent years, but the sport is growing so fast that it is difficult to sort the wood from the trees and I am going to have to leave it to some later author to have the final word.

The Early Nineteenth Century

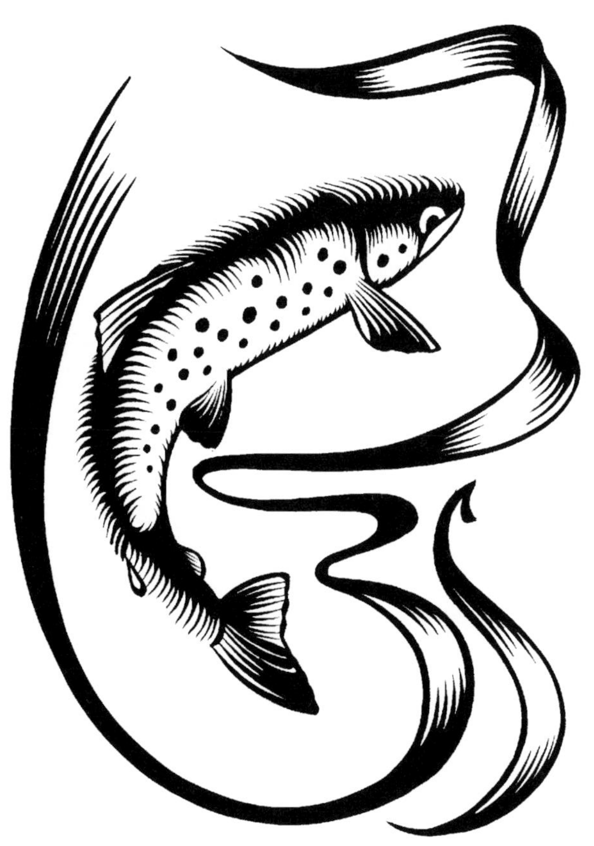

Chapter Four

The Early Nineteenth Century

When the new century dawned, England was at war with its old adversary France again, a conflict which dragged on until the defeat of Napoleon in 1815. The hostilities were fabulously expensive, a measure of which is that by the time they had finished as many as a quarter of British men had worn military uniform. Things did not improve after Waterloo, because the post war economy was weak and a cycle of boom and bust followed. Despite the passing of the 'Corn Laws' – legislation intended to maintain grain prices – poor harvests and unemployment caused by industrial recession troubled the country. It did not help that the industrial revolution was in full swing and that the movement away from uncertain employment on the land to jobs in new steam powered factories was causing the break up of traditional village communities in favour of unplanned urban sprawl. The result was that although the economy grew strongly, by the 1830s social unrest was a real danger. The Corn Laws, poor laws and game laws came under attack and Earl Grey's government responded by passing reform bills which modified the poor laws, abolished slavery and extended the franchise (although admittedly with the cynically narrow aim of giving the emerging middle class an opportunity to back the Whigs.)

In 1837, Queen Victoria came to the throne and the early years of her long reign saw the popular repeal of the Corn Laws under Peel and the establishment of a modern national banking and credit system. This was presented as a move to bring increased financial stability, but the truth was that the repeal of the Corn Laws was partly a response to the appalling famine which had struck Ireland after the disastrous failure of the potato crop in 1845-6. While the government wrung its hands in committee, at least half a million Irish men and women died and a further million emigrated.

Despite mainland Britain's apparent indifference to the sufferings of the Irish, much progress was made with social improvement with the appointment of school inspectors; the passage of the first national Public Health Act; and various Factory Acts which improved the lives of workers, not least the many children who were often employed in abysmal conditions. These Acts were highly necessary, as there was a lot of labour to exploit: by 1851 the combined population of England, Wales and Scotland stood at 21 million.

The middle years of the century were very eventful and 1848 stands out as the year of Europe-wide revolution, which miraculously left the United Kingdom untouched. In February the Parisians took to the streets against the government and within a short space of time similar uprisings occurred in Vienna, Milan, Venice and Prague. The uniting theme behind all these revolutions was discontent with government policies which had failed to deal with the far-reaching effects of industrial revolution, a restricted franchise and the powerlessness of the working man to influence his lot.

Britain's escape from revolution is all the more remarkable because of the extent to which its economy changed during the nineteenth century. By the middle of the century, agriculture accounted for less than a quarter of the gross national product and textiles were the flagship of a financial system which depended on international trade for its lifeblood. Products were carried overland by rail and overseas by steamship, using coal hewn from the great mines in the north of England and the demand for iron was so buoyant that by 1850 Britain was producing half the world's total output.

After that came the boom years. From 1850 to 1870 wages and profits rose so strongly that the economy was barely dented by the Crimean war. It was an era of scientific renaissance, with businessmen debating key discoveries like Darwin's theory of evolution in open challenge to the teachings of the Church, while on the other hand they financed missionaries to scour the globe in search of converts. There were many more converts to make, because this was the era of empire and while Gladstone struggled with the 'Irish question' at home, he quietly consolidated the sphere of British influence in Africa. The empire wasn't won without a struggle and conflicts necessitated the use of British troops in India in 1857 and South Africa in 1899. In spite of its territorial expansion, by the last quarter of the century, Britain was in eclipse as an industrial power, paying the penalty for having invested too soon by finding itself lumbered with outdated industrial plant. The ageing British foundries produced less steel than either Germany or the United States and to make matters worse, textile exports were falling. The boom was over and from now on Britain's share of the world economy would decline slowly.

America also had its share of troubles. In 1861 civil war broke out after many years of disputes between the northern and southern states. The catalyst was the disparate economies and socio-political structures of the more industrialised northern states and the predominantly agricultural, slaving southern states. The North, with its greater manufacturing capacity, better transportation and larger population, won an historic victory and while slavery was abolished, the Union was preserved. America was set firmly on the path towards becoming a superpower and before long opportunity and prosperity meant that it would overtake its mother country as the pace-setter where fly fishing was concerned.

Fishing

Against such a background it is probably inevitable that the nineteenth century was a period of unparalleled progress in fly fishing, the pace of development in some ways exceeding that of our own time. The period was dominated by advances in entomology, tackle design, the shift to upstream fishing and the adoption of the dry fly. In McDonald's words, a fisherman born in 1800 stood at the brink of 'the greatest revolution in fly-fishing history since the sport has been known'.

The change started quietly. Nowhere was this more apparent than in the enforcement of riparian rights. In some respects, the early and middle years of the century can be seen as a transitional period between the *laissez faire* era of the seventeenth and eighteenth centuries and the tight control of angling rights which characterises modern Britain. But when it happened, change was rapid and quite profound; Scotland makes a good example. The vast majority of Scottish salmon were netted until comparatively late in the century and as a consequence fly fishing wasn't a significant source of income until the 1840s at the earliest. It is a sad fact that on many rivers the nets were so efficient that only grilse reached the upper streams and in consequence it was common for the water above the nets to be let out to 'tacksmen' at quite low rents. To give an example, in the 1830s the entire Makerstoun beat on the Tweed was let for only £20 per annum to a man called Rob Kerss, a tenth of the price similar water would fetch only fifty years later. The tacksmen depended on the fish for their living and their methods were brutally efficient. Like his fellows, Rob would wait until a spate had brought large numbers of salmon through the nets, and then he would be out with his boat, spearing fish for all he was worth. The slow run off that was characteristic of Scottish rivers in pre-drainage days meant that an alert tacksman could have days of good killing when the fish were concentrated in the pools and a single man could kill hundreds of salmon at a time.

As more and more fishermen appeared on the banks, it didn't take long for the tacksmen to discover that they could augment their income by guiding and to begin with their charges were modest. In 1839 a day's fishing, including an oarsman and boat, could be had for five shillings.[1] This was tradition in the making: although wealthy anglers had paid assistants to net fish for them since at least Cotton's day, the profession of ghillie has its roots in the tacksmen's practice of assisting fishermen. Incidentally, the word 'gillie' is far older and relates to a derogatory lowland Scots term, *gillecasfliuch* - literally 'gillie-wet-foot' - for the servant who carried a highland chief across a stream in order to keep his feet dry.[2] No one seems to know why it came to be applied to fishing guides, who, if my experience is anything to go by, find it riotously funny if their client falls in.

This comfortable state of affairs was not to last. As net catches fell and the number of salmon fishermen increased, landlords turned their eyes to the bottom line and the tacksmen found themselves squeezed out by rising rents, after the middle of the century. But in the early years of the century, salmon fishers were still few and far between. As Francis Francis pointed out, in the 1840s, a fisherman who had fished salmon was looked upon as a tremendous creature. It was, as he said, 'something like killing a gorilla, was this killing of a salmon with a fishing rod.'[3] Yet salmon fishing for sport would ultimately become a bigger industry than netting, and the symptoms of this can be detected very early in the nineteenth century. Where once the angler had been free to roam, he now found himself hemmed in by rights and regulations, and ghillies had little option but to become employees of the lairds. It was a trend which accelerated until, by the end of the century, there was very little water left in Britain which wasn't firmly controlled either by landlords or clubs.

Rods

A British fisherman at the time of the Napoleonic wars would have found little difference between much modern equipment and that left to him by his great grandfather. In particular, the materials used for rod making had changed but little:

> The best rods are made from ash, hickory and lancewood; ash for the bottom piece, hickory for the middle, and lancewood for the top joints: real bamboo is preferable to lancewood, if it can be procured of good quality, which is extremely difficult: logwood is sometimes used for the tops, and answers extremely well for Salmon or trolling rods; but this wood is not frequently to be met of straight grain in pieces of sufficient length for rods; but if it should be it is not equal in elasticity to well seasoned lancewood.[4]

Apart from the addition of lancewood and perhaps bamboo, the materials listed had been the mainstay of rod building for two centuries, and they would remain so for another thirty years. Hazel had faded away; it had been a favourite material of the earliest anglers and of amateur rod builders, but the increase in professional rod making meant that it wasn't much used after the late eighteenth century. Lancewood, which replaced it, is a straight-grained wood obtained from a number of different species of the enticingly-named custard-tree family (*Annonaceae*). True lancewood (*Oxandra lanceolata*) comes from the West Indies and the Guianas and from a rod-maker's point of view it has the virtue of being stronger and lighter than any of the native alternatives.

As it happens, lancewood was particularly easy to get in Britain after Napoleon's defeat, because a combination of military adventurism and diplomacy had expanded the colonies of Demerara, Berbice, and Essequibo to form British Guiana. Lancewood has the merit of being tough yet extremely elastic and though it was too heavy to be much use for building butts, it was valuable for making small joints, was ideal as a tip material and had the additional merit of looking highly attractive when polished.

Other woods in use at the time included rosewood and 'partridge' wood, which were both imported from Brazil, as well as yew and briar. To begin with, the emphasis was still very much on home-grown woods, but it wasn't very long before it became impossible for rod builders to ignore the virtues of the imported materials that were flooding into Britain and they began to abandon the less adaptable native materials.

The new materials were very different to the tried and tested woods that they replaced and tackle dealers took a while to get used to making rods from them. George Bainbridge's comment that the quality of bamboo was unreliable tells us why 'exotic' woods were not taken up faster – importers hadn't worked out how to choose the best bits and quality was notoriously uncertain. For example, the bamboo Bainbridge knew was 'Calcutta' bamboo (*Bambusa arundinacea*), a thin-walled, fine-grained material with leaf nodes about ten or fifteen inches apart, which was in common use in the early nineteenth century, though it was a pale shadow of the much stiffer Chinese bamboos that were discovered several decades later. According to William Mitchell, all Calcutta bamboo was burned with a red-hot elliptical iron before export, with the result that about a fifth of the tough outside 'enamel' fibres on the rod were destroyed.[5] Though it is only an interesting footnote, bamboo may have been in use for fishing rods long before the nineteenth century. Venables makes a passing reference to preferring 'the cane or reed before all other' for rods, although he could have been referring to sugar-cane, rattan or one of the many other canes found in the West Indies.

The rod ring, which had given eighteenth century fishers such a hard time, was perfected in the nineteenth century, but it wasn't until the end of the century that anglers could absolutely take it for granted. By now the majority of rods were fully ringed and there was plenty of scope for things to go wrong. O'Gorman left us with a hilarious description of a bad ring day:

> I have seen an entire set of loops torn down to the wheel by a large salmon of the Shannon, greatly to the surprise of the gentleman who was playing him, and who beheld his rod pointing straight to the sky, and the line level with his hands.[6]

Unreliable rings were not the only problem with which anglers had to contend. There were joints to worry about as well and, if anglers are to be believed, even in the early nineteenth century there wasn't such a thing as a good one. By then, the joint had a long history, going back to at least the *Treatyse*, even if technical problems prevented their confident use for about another hundred years. Wooden joints were thoroughly unsatisfactory, since they could only be formed if the female section of the rod was made unduly thick, and even then, they had an alarming propensity to swell and jam if they got wet. And if wooden joints were unreliable, metal joints were a complete nightmare.

It wasn't that the idea of making joints out of metal was a bad one per se; it was just that the metallurgy of the age wasn't up to it. Finely made joints were too weak, while joints which were strong enough to do the job were too heavy. Needless to say, much ingenuity was applied to finding a solution to this troublesome impasse, and it shows in the enormous variety of joints which were in use by the nineteenth century. We find female brass sockets taking a wooden male end, brass female sockets accepting brass-coated male ends, and screw joints, to name but three. It took a long while for rod makers to hit on a design for the ideal joint and our forebears had no option but to grin and bear it as they worked loose or seized up tight. Worse still, early jointed rods had an irritating tendency to snap off in the socket or just below the joint, usually at the most inconvenient moment possible.

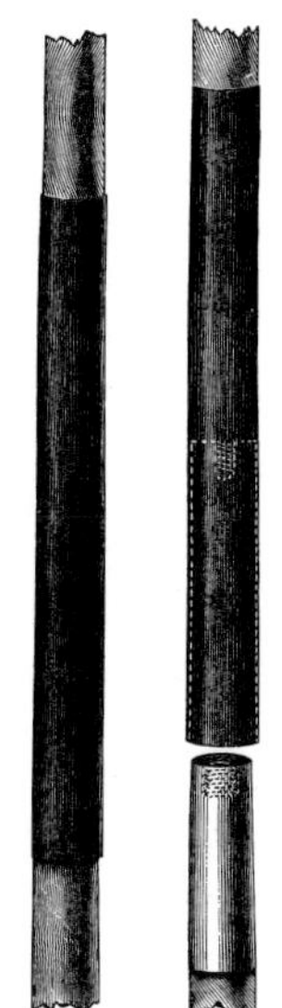

Irish joint - from Fishing, Salmon and Trout, *Badminton Library, 1885*

The limitations of the materials in use meant that joints were constructed quite differently to the way they are today and while we are accustomed to finding female joints on the upper section of a carbon fibre rod, in the days of wooden rods it was normal for the female socket to be on the lower section of the rod, a design which was technically easier to make, given the greater thickness of the lower section. This arrangement wasn't universally the case and Stoddart indicates that the Irish very sensibly put the female socket on the upper section, in order to keep the rain out.[7] One way around the problem was to avoid joints completely and to splice the sections of the rod together, another was to reduce the number of joints down to the minimum necessary, but the penalty of the latter type of design was that the angler had to put up with overly long rod sections which in turn, were awkward to transport. Rods with sections no longer than two and a half or three feet long were quite common and for reasons which escape me, many anglers actually preferred to fish with them.[8] But while more spacious transport meant that the length of sections did gradually

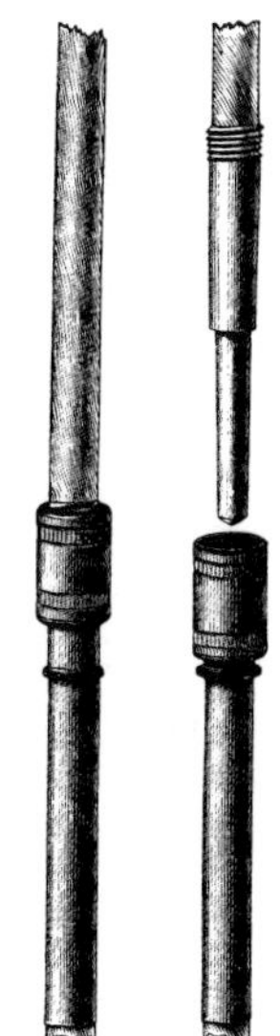

Farlow joint

lengthen towards the 1850s, the quest for the ideal joint remained a consuming interest of tackle makers and the search didn't finally end until it became possible to manufacture strong, thin-walled suction joints late in the nineteenth century.

Professionally built tackle was still very dear. For example, Bainbridge had some of his rods made by Henry Swann, of Langholm, North Britain. Swann's rod came in five pieces, with screw joints at each ferrule. A rod of this description, with two tops, cost him eighteen shillings in 1807; a considerable sum of money at the time, but then Bainbridge, disparagingly referred to by his neighbour, Sir Walter Scott, as a 'dog of a banker', could presumably afford to pay for quality. In his retiring way, Scott went on further to say that if he had still had a 'certain Highland piper' in his service, he would have had Bainbridge 'dirked to a certainty . . . as it is I must think of some means of poisoning his hot rolls and butter, or setting his house on fire . . .' but he seems to have got over it, as Bainbridge died of natural causes . . . as far as we know. The less well heeled had to content themselves with locally built rods costing between ten and eleven shillings fully finished, and brass jointed fly rods which retailed for up to sixteen shillings. The working man had to make do with the best his village joiner could come up with.

The early nineteenth century was the last refuge of the amateur rod maker, and the vast majority of rods were shop bought by the 1860s. This shift to manufactured rods is important because it coincided with yet another leap in casting distances, and also because it was part of the road to the six-strip split-cane rod, a development which couldn't have happened without a strong manufacturing base.

It seems quite odd, in view of all the other advances that had been made, but it was quite normal for rods to have a whalebone tip of up to four or five inches long, a legacy of rod construction which had its roots at least two hundred years before. Rods were still quite long overall and the length of a salmon rod was virtually unchanged from Walton's day, at seventeen or eighteen feet. However, this was not to last. The impact of the industrial revolution meant that by the middle of the nineteenth century, attitudes had changed a great deal and rods were shortening towards the modern ideal. At the beginning of the period, the length of trout rods hovered between twelve and fourteen feet, although some experts[9] were sure that a double-handed trout rod shouldn't be less than sixteen feet long! Albeit in somewhat shorter lengths, the double-handed trout rod remained popular with more conservative fishermen until the last two decades of the nineteenth century, although single-handed rods became steadily more common throughout the period.

Lightness was not necessarily viewed as a particular virtue, and they must have had bigger biceps in those days, if what Theophilus South wrote is to be believed:

> I have fished from five in the morning to nine o'clock in the evening, the greater part of the day against a strong wind, with my single handed trout-rod, – measuring fourteen feet, three inches, and a half, and weighing one pound two ounces, and generally throwing from twenty to thirty yards of line, and never experienced any trouble from its weight, or the exertion required for its free use.[10]

This triumph of compact early nineteenth century design would have been at the upper end of the weight range and a lighter rod mentioned by 'Arundo', built of pine and logwood and twelve foot long overall, weighed a more reasonable eight and a half ounces. Notwithstanding such a heroic defence, the long trout rod was in terminal decline and it would be phased out over the last half of the century. Again, this is an important step, because it led the way not only towards rods which appear to be modern to our eyes, but towards rods which could be fished with modern techniques.

Irish Rods

In Ireland, where everything has always been different, different design considerations applied:

> They are much more elastic than the English rods, and consequently throw a long line better. The perfection of a salmon rod (for it matters little where or how a single-handed rod for whipping out minnows be made) in my poor judgment, is a twenty foot rod, made in four pieces, by Kelly, or Murray, with a top joint manufactured by Ustonson, or Chevalier. But, wherever it be bought, let the angler remember that the but must be solid, and the top spliced. No two-handed rod, in fact, ever ought to have a hollow but, or its top joint fixed with a brass ferrule.[11]

The major objection to hollow butts and ferruled tops was that they broke, and salmon anglers must have heard the sickening crunch of splintering wood with monotonous regularity. This was a problem that wasn't solved until split cane became widely available and it probably accounts for the persistence of spliced rods. An enormous variety of solutions were tried, and older jointed rods frequently have a spliced top to avoid creating a potential weak spot. The one piece of amateur rod-making know-how that was vital for any early nineteenth century angler, whether he bought his rods or not, was how make his own tops. Tips broke so often that it was essential to carry a supply of spares, and going on a fishing trip abroad would have been inviting disaster if the wherewithal to make or procure new tops wasn't available.

The zenith of Irish salmon rod design was the Shannon rod, popularly known as the 'Castleconnel' rod, a basic design which seems to have been used for many years by amateur makers on the Shannon before the rods started being made commercially at Castleconnel. Typically, these beasts were between sixteen to eighteen feet long, though a really unrestrained example might run to twenty-five or twenty-six feet. Nowadays, the Shannon is only a shadow of its former self, running tamely in man-made channels, but it is likely that the great width of the river in those days influenced rod makers to produce the huge weapons they did, even though much of the fishing was done from boats known as 'cots'. These Shannon rods were made entirely of greenheart and although they were light and flexible in the butt, they were top-heavy, with the result that they would not cast well against the wind unless in the hands of an expert.

The defining feature of a Castleconnel rod was the reverse taper in the butt, which gave the rod its characteristic action; a good specimen actually flexed between the fisherman's hands. The rods were almost universally spliced and made in two pieces, ten and a half feet in the butt, and nine, or nine and a half in the top. Despite this, the enormous length of the sections wasn't a problem in Ireland since the railways were all broad gauge in those days and the rods would easily fit across a compartment. There were other reasons why Castleconnel kit was quite distinctive, because a heavy reel was thought necessary to 'balance' the rod, and to hold the large amount of line needed to play the large Shannon fish. Incidentally, if you are ever lucky enough to pick up one of these early Irish reels, you will find it appears to be made with a left hand wind, because the fashion was to place the reel on the rod so that the handle was on the right when the rings were upward, as convention had it that fish were played with the reel above the rod.

Shorter Shannon-style rods were also made for grilse and trout fishing in toothpick-like lengths from eleven to thirteen and a half feet. In the 1880s, suppliers of these outstanding pieces of kit included Enright of Castleconnel, Kelly and Flint of Dublin, Haynes of Cork, Hilliard of Templemore and Nestor of Limerick.[12] Amazing though it is to relate, the Castleconnel rods were themselves dwarfed by rods in use on the

Blackwater in the 1840s, which were sometimes as long as twenty-seven or twenty-eight feet! It seems that these amazing beasts were used to literally dangle the fly over the head of the salmon, and it is universally agreed that their casting abilities were pretty limited.

Mass Production of Hooks

By 1800, although metallurgy hadn't advanced enough to solve the problem of the joint, is was good enough to allow hook manufacture to become a routine affair. Once high quality steel could be made reliably, needle and hook making became a much easier and a large industry sprang up in the British Isles, with rival centres in Kendal, Redditch and Limerick. Variety being the spice of life and the source of profit, hook-makers experimented with an enormous variety of bends: Needle point, Round bend, Sproat,[13] Kendal, Limerick (of which there were at least three varieties: Dublin, Pennell and Crystal), Sneck, O'Shaughnessy, Aberdeen, Kinsey and the Kirby were the most popular, but there were literally hundreds of variations, each with its own devoted band of admirers, and many an argument must have been fought out over amateur stress diagrams sketched out on scrap paper.

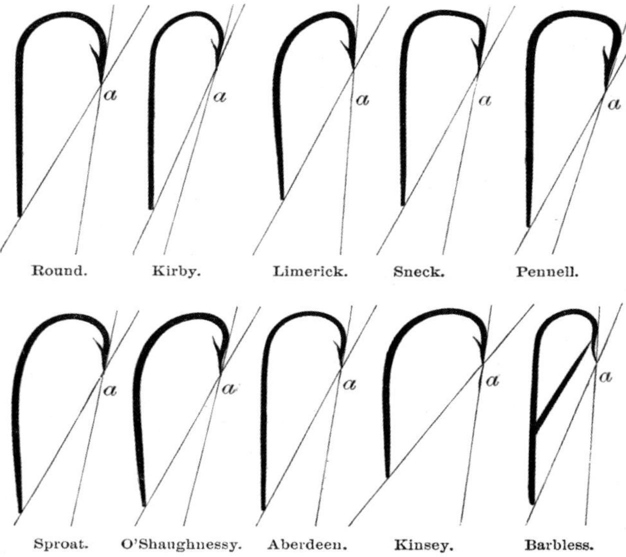

Different hook bends

The industry boomed and by 1823, when Redditch alone could boast seventeen firms of hook makers, the Limerick hook industry had been in existence for nearly thirty years. It is said that Redditch owes its history as a needle making centre to the monks of Bordesley Abbey, who were evicted during the Reformation and taught the local people their skills, which they had learned as a result of links with Toledo in Spain. The Redditch firms of 1823 included Allcock, Bartleet, Boulton, Clarke, Cook, Cooper, Harrison, Hemming, Holyhoake, James Jos., James R., Milward, Mills, Prescot, Reading, Smallwood and Tandy. Other hook makers established in the same period included Beard, Davies, Gould, Hall, Moore, Rimmer, Sealy, and Woodfields.

Hutchinson, a needle maker, started making hooks in Kendal as early as 1745, being joined by Adlington during the mid-nineteenth century. It was not very many years later that the great European names became established, for example Mustad, which was founded in 1876, although it wasn't always a fishing company and it made nails and axe heads to start with. The Mustad story is told very well in Hans Jørgen Hurum's Book, *A History of the Fish Hook.*

Hook making was soon refined into a routine production process. Mustad stole a march on the market by employing hook making machines, but hand-made hooks were still the rule, made by a process which was used without much alteration for many decades:

> First, then, the wire is struck off in given lengths, in accordance with the size of hook required; next, the point is formed and the shank reduced by a few strokes of the file; and next, the barb is cut by means of a large knife. All is now ready for bending, which is one of the most particular items in the construction, as the operation decides the shape, and, consequently, the particular species of hook to be produced. This is quickly done by means of a small steel block around which the wire is bent, the shape of the block varying according to the particular bend required. Now comes the final operation, viz., that of tempering. This is done in a large pan over a slow furnace. Millions of hooks are frequently tempered in one operation . . .[14]

Mass production it might have been, but the quality of hooks still remained very variable. Most hook-making businesses relied on a considerable amount of subcontracting, which was part of the problem. The process of putting bends in the needles was often delegated to local families as piece-work, while sharpening and polishing was carried out in nearby mills. The Redditch hook makers, for example, did their polishing at the water mill at Temple Mills, on the Lead Mill river, which is a branch of the Lea. Even then, the mill had a long history, because it had been built by the Knights Templar.

One major source of complaint was the deep cut which many hook makers used to turn up a barb. The word 'barb' is derived from the French '*barba*' or beard, and the exaggerated barb of some types of Limerick bend, as well as Sneck and Kendal bent hooks, led to anglers becoming resigned to hooks breaking off at this place.

Batch tempering was a particularly unreliable part of the process and fishermen became proficient at recognising soft hooks by colour alone; the low carbon content meant they were light-blue instead of purple-blue. Japanned hooks were a different matter, and the standard way of detecting a faulty one was to stick the point in a cork and put strain on the shank, a test which stresses the bend so severely that many perfectly good hooks fail it. In the late seventeenth and early eighteenth century it was not uncommon for entire batches of hooks to be sold with inadequate tempering and it was a careless angler who did not test his hook thoroughly before tying a fly on it.

Irish Hook Makers

No history of the hook would be complete without mention of the Irish. Irish hook makers enjoyed an international market, and the use of their products was *de rigeur* among expert salmon fishermen in the late eighteenth and early nineteenth centuries. 'Limerick' hooks were said to be the best, and there were three sources of them: Phillips of Dublin; Blacker's favourite; Sell, of Quay Lane, Limerick; and O'Shaughnessy.

Limerick and O'Shaugnessy hooks

Most writers of the day favoured the Sell and O'Shaughnessy hooks because they were less prone to failure, but if a choice had to be made between the two, the O'Shaughnessy product was very definitely the Rolls Royce of hooks. The family seem to have established their business in 1795 and they were soon very well known to the fishing fraternity, being able to count James O'Gorman among their friends. No less a person than Sir Humphrey Davy, the greatest chemist of his day, author of *Salmonia*, and former president of the Royal Society, wrote a testimonial to the quality of their hooks in 1828. With this kind of backing, the family developed a formidable reputation for quality and their products soon reached the unfeasibly high price of sixpence a dozen, as a result of being recommended almost as a matter of course by nineteenth century authors. Much of the reason for their well deserved fame is that the original O'Shaughnessy hooks were hammered out and forged, with the barbs filed out from the metal, rather than being cut out and bent up as was the case with the majority of their rivals. The design of the O'Shaughnessy hook was so widely admired that it became universally known as the 'Limerick' bend, a style which can still be seen on hooks today. Inevitably, the firm's good fortune was not to last; the founder died in about 1820 and by 1834 the business had been taken over by a watchmaker, who carried on the tackle making business, continuing to turn out Limerick hooks after the original pattern. But the magic had gone.

O'Shaughnessy's son was also a hook maker and set up a separate business, but he did not do as well as his father had and he ended up as an employee of a man called Glover, perhaps because of his tragic fondness for hard liquor. Sadly, the early Irish hook makers had very few opportunities to gain an education and because of this either they wrote very little, or they were illiterate. The result is that we would know virtually nothing about Irish hooks had not writers commented on them in passing; and we owe a great debt of gratitude to 'Theophilus South', who upon a quixotic whim that I simply do not understand, did us the favour of measuring the major supplier's offerings. His careful measurements, given in the table below, were taken 'from the shank end to the extremity of the bend'.[15] Had he not done so, we would know very little indeed about the dimensions of the hooks.

Sell's				*O'Shaughnessy's*				*Phillips'*			
Salmon				Salmon				Salmon			
No		in.	16ths	No		in.	16ths	No		in.	16ths
1	measures	2	12	1	measures	2	4				
2	....	2	10	2	....	1	15	4†			
3	....	2	5	3	....	1	13	5†			
4	....	2	3	4	....	1	8	6	....	2	4
5	....	1	15	5	....	1	7	7	....	1	14
6	....	1	14	6	....	1	5	8	....	1	12
7	....	1	10					9	....	1	7

Sell's No	in.	16ths	*O'Shaughnessy's* No	in.	16ths	*Phillips'* No	in.	16ths
Grilse			Grilse			Grilse		
1	1	7	1	1	3	BB	1	2
2	1	5	2	1	0	B	1	0
3	1	4	3	0	15	CC	0	14
4	0	15	4	0	14	C	0	12
Trout			Trout			Trout		
1	0	12	1	0	10	fff	0	10
2	0		2	0		ff	0	8
3	0		3	0		f	0	7
4	0	6	4	0		fe	0	6
5	0		5	0	6	midge	0	5½
6	0		6	0				
7	0		7	0				
8 midge	0	5	8	0				
			9 midge	0	5			

† *Added from* The Book of the Salmon, *Ephemera, 1850. Nb. that Fitzgibbon describes the Phillips' 'C' hook as 'CC (small)' and renumbers the hooks for the convenience of his own readers.*

When Belton visited the two shops in 1834 he was able to see hooks being made according to a process which had altered little since the publication of the *Treatyse*:

> . . . I was shown the hooks in all their several stages of manufacture. They are at first small straight bars of the very best iron, and of the requisite length, with a kind of rude head at one end. They are first barbed, sharpened and rounded by the file, then bent with circular pincers to the proper degree of curvature: next they are steeled by the application of fire and charcoal, and then, after a little final polishing, are placed on a smoothing iron, heated to 580 degrees of Fahrenheit, which gives them the blue colour and temper; and are, lastly, immersed in grease, to prevent them from rust. In point of quality, I think there is little difference between them, and Kelly's of Dublin: but, in consequence of their forming a somewhat larger curve, and projecting more than his, they are more certain to strike the fish; while, for the same reason, they do not admit of equally neat tying. They are all of them, however, incomparably superior to the best London hooks, and are the only ones to be depended upon for large fish; but they are dear.[16]

They certainly were dear: by 1845 a dozen cost between one and four shillings.[17] But for his money the angler got a fantastically strong hook filed from best German steel, rather than the softer and less reliable wire hooks which were the rule from Dublin and London firms. By comparison, Sell's hooks only fetched between nine pence and three shillings a dozen.

Several decades later, Peard gave a description of what was probably a very old Robert O'Shaughnessy at work at 18, George Street, Limerick:

> We climbed the rickety and dirty stairs, and in an upper room found the old artiste hard at work.
>
> On a table before him lay several fine triangular files, a few pairs of pliers, a piece of boxwood, and a tray divided into several compartments, combining small bars of Swedish iron,[18] of sizes suitable for hooks of every number. Now he takes one of the bars and cuts out the barb; then turning the iron in his hand, shapes the back. Again he turns the half-finished hook, and carefully completes the barb, giving it a spherical point as fine as a darning needle. Lastly, he puts on his glasses, and carefully examines what has been done, adds a few finishing touches, and with the pliers gives the exact shape according to pattern, remarking, with a severe glance at the luckless inventor, "Some gentlemen are a little self-willed, and like to spoil a good thing by their improvements." Nothing now remains to be done but the tempering. I have used these hooks for many years, and have killed salmon with every size, the two largest and smallest excepted; as one fracture only occurred, I feel bound to bear testimony to their excellence. The price is high, but when it is remembered they can be used season after season, in a series of new flies, they are cheap at the money.[19]

The price certainly was high, but not so high that Peard didn't think it worth his while going well out of his way to obtain a supply of the genuine article. Faulty hooks were one of the many irritations anglers had to cope with, and poor tempering of commercial hooks was so common that O'Gorman, a man sorely tried by unreliable equipment, thought it necessary to give detailed instructions on how to re-temper hooks in an emergency. As a result, the individually made O'Shaughnessy hooks were so highly prized that it was common practice to strip the fly from a hook after it had been mauled by fish: not only did the hooks last for ever, they were simply too valuable to throw away.

Lines

By the early nineteenth century, fishermen were beginning to take much more of an interest in rod action as the combination of better rod design coupled with increasing use of mixed silk and horse-hair lines allowed them to cast further. By now, lines were of good enough quality that the average fisherman could not only aerialise more line, but he could also shoot it to a limited extent, a development which had a significant effect on fishing, because it meant that flies were being fished further away and had more time to sink. At the beginning of the nineteenth century, a decent caster could:

> . . . throw with a sixteen feet rod, from eighteen yards to two or three and twenty neatly; and also will be enabled to throw ten or twelve yards in the wind's eye to the opposite bank . . .[20]

Twenty-three yards was five or six yards further than the average cast even fifty years previously, which shows just how much things had changed. Mass production had had a profound impact.

By the turn of the century, the price of manufactured lines was falling and there was an extensive choice of different types and tapers available:

> The lines for reels are to be purchased of every length from fifteen to one hundred and twenty yards, or even longer,[21] at the tackle shops throughout the kingdom, and at a much cheaper rate than a private individual can manufacture them, if his time and trouble are considered to be of any value.
>
> Single handed rod fishers prefer their reel lines to taper to a point, so that they may, by merely fixing their foot length of gut to the line, wind it up close to hand; and where the stream is narrow and bushes frequent, this is certainly a good plan. But for bold streams, the line should be of equal thickness throughout, and not too fine, in order that a taper hair line of ten yards in length may be attached thereto.[22]

In 1854, Pulman quotes prices as: silk and hair woven, two pence a yard; silk and hair spun, one and a half pence a yard; horse hair one pence a yard, which would have been well within the reach of anglers of moderate means. But the tackle makers were still feeling their way, and their experimentation meant that there were some real abortions on the market. Some lines tapered too sharply, others were too thick, and the cheapest lines rotted almost the instant they were wetted.

The mixed silk and hair line, mentioned above, was an unhappy compromise, because the two materials had quite different properties, but nonetheless this mixture was reasonably popular. Why it should have been is a mystery, though price may have entered into it, since the lines combined all the worst faults of horsehair and silk: they were relatively expensive, wore out quickly, lacked strength, kinked at the drop of a hat, and owing to the protrusion of countless points of the horsehair, ran very badly through the rod rings. But they were part of a long tradition and some fishermen loved them.

Plaited silk lines first appeared during this period, and they were an important development, because they represented the first step on the way to manufacturing techniques which would produce the waterproof, rot-resistant fly lines which paved the way for the dry-fly men. O'Gorman first mentioned an eight-plait silk line as a recent invention in 1845, which provides a convenient date to anchor them by.[23] The best lines were plaited from Indian or Persian silk, and these were thinner and stronger than their twisted counterparts. More important still, they were available in lengths of eighty or even a hundred yards, although the typical fisherman still used lines which were rather shorter than those we would fish with nowadays: twenty yards for trout in rivers, forty to fifty yards for lake trout, and eighty or a hundred yards for salmon. Eight-plait silk rapidly took over from horsehair and silk/horsehair mixes, because once it had been well dressed it ran through the rings more smoothly, was less liable to kink or catch, did not hold so much water and was easier to cast against the wind.[24]

These longer plaited lines are further evidence of the way fishing was beginning to benefit from the industrial revolution. From time immemorial, wool had been turned into threads by hand spinning, a process in which single fibres of wool were twisted together from a mass twisted around a stick known as a distaff. This technique was superseded in the Middle Ages, by the spinning wheel, which probably came from India and spread to Europe via the Middle East. The wheel made it possible to form yarn of a more even thickness and this machine in turn was modernised in the sixteenth century by the introduction of the Saxony wheel, a device which made it possible to spin coarse cotton and wool yarn much more efficiently and was undoubtedly used to manage silk thread as well. The advent of the Saxony wheel meant that up to five spinning wheels could supply a loom, but it wasn't until the late 1770s that a series of breakthroughs made it possible to spin very large amounts of very fine yarn and it was this development that ultimately made it possible to make long plaited silk fly lines. The critical machine was probably Samuel Crompton's 'Mule' which enabled a single operator to control more than a thousand spindles simultaneously.

Silkworm Gut

There was another development that had a profound impact on fly fishing during the early nineteenth century: the discovery of silkworm gut. The adoption of gut changed the path of fly fishing as much as the discovery of nylon would, a hundred years later.

So what was this material that revolutionised the face of fly fishing? According to William Radcliffe, the Chinese discovered gut, and they were fishing with it as early as the fourth century BC:

> By making a line of cocoon silk, a hook of a sharp needle, a rod of a branch or bramble or dwarf bamboo, and using a grain of cooked rice as bait, one can catch a whole cartload of fish.[25]

Legend has it that the Chinese have cultivated silk since before 3000 BC, when the emperor Fo Xi taught his people how to raise silkworms on mulberry trees. By 1000 BC the Chinese were exporting some silk, and Europeans were familiar with it as a material, although the process was kept highly secret, and no one but the Chinese knew how silk was made, or even what it was. It was such an important material to Western civilisation that speculation, as one might imagine, was rife, and crack-pot theories as to its origin abounded. Pliny, like many of the ancients, assured his audience that silk grew on trees, 'The Seres [Chinese] are famous for the wool of their forests,' he wrote. 'They remove the down from the leaves with the help of water.' If he had but known it, the old savant wasn't too far from the truth, but other popular theories were way off beam, and one held that silk was a vegetable, perhaps a member of the cabbage family. Exports to the West started in earnest in about 200 BC, with the opening of the 'Silk Road', a caravan route that linked the great civilisations of Rome and China. Although the emphasis was on trade, with wool, gold and silver going east, while silk came west, the route was used for the export and import of everything from inventions to armies. A branch of this old route chances to pass through Macedonia, where Ælian heard of that first fly being fished, two millennia ago. Today, if Macedonian shepherds lift their heads, they can see the stark condensation trails painted by air liners unwittingly following the same route.

Four thousand miles long, the Silk Road began in Sian, in Northern China, swung north-west to hug the Great Wall, split into two around the desert of Takla Makan, then climbed into the Pamir mountains, crossed Afghanistan, before finishing in the Levant, from where goods were shipped across the Mediterranean Sea. Because of the route's length, few people travelled it in its entirety, and goods were passed in relays from one caravan to another. The decline of Rome and the rise of Arabian power made the road increasingly unsafe and it fell into disuse for thousands of years before being revived in the thirteenth century by the Mongols. It is still possible to travel part of the road today using a highway connecting Pakistan with the Sinkiang Uighur region of China.

Silk was so useful and so expensive that it was inevitable that Western civilisations made determined attempts to steal the Chinese' secrets, and it wasn't long before they were successful. No one knows exactly how sericulture reached Europe, although there are numerous legends to fill the gap. You can take your pick, but my favourite tale tells of two priests who smuggled silkworms out of China in hollow bamboo walking sticks, after they had been sent to China by the emperor Justinian in an attempt to find out how silk was made. They are said to have brought their precious find back to Anatolia in the fifth century AD. There is some logic to the story, because it is set exactly at the time when brigandage on the Silk Road began to make it difficult for the West to obtain supplies easily, but the obvious problem with it is that given monkish walking speeds, they would have brought back some very old worms with them, unless of course, they exported ova.

However it first came to Europe, silkworm gut was first mentioned in England in an advert placed by Kirby in 1722, the text stating that it was 'newly come over.' Word of this new material spread quickly in local publications, because by1724 James Saunders, was writing of the Swiss and Milanese:

> These, they tell us, make a fine and exceedingly strong hair or line, resembling a single hair, which is drawn from the bowels of the silkworm, the glutinous substance of which is such, that like the cat's gut which makes the strings for the viol or violin, of an unaccountable strength, for this silkworm gut will be so strong, that nothing of so small a size will equal it in nature; for it is rather smaller than a single horsehair ordinarily used in fishing, so that with their lines, they secure the strongest fish in the rivers, where they have some trouts very large. I have seen mention of these worm-gut lines in England, and indifferent strong too, but not like that I have mentioned in Italy. Yet they will hold a good fish too, if she is not too violent and does not too nimbly harness herself among weeds and roots of trees.[26]

Despite the lack of any serious competition, the uptake of gut was relatively slow to begin with, though by the middle of the nineteenth century it was in reasonably common use. There were good reasons why anglers were so cautious about the new material. For a start, early natural gut was quite thick and thinner gut remained expensive and difficult to get until good quality drawn gut became widely available in the late nineteenth century. Availability aside, part of the reason why anglers failed to adopt the new material more quickly was that gut behaved quite differently to the horsehair casts to which they were used. Gut needed soaking before it was elastic enough to be used, a minor inconvenience perhaps, but one to which many anglers found it difficult to adjust. So gut didn't find many takers in the eighteenth century, but on the other hand, once it did gain a place in angler's hearts, it knew no rivals until the 1930s when nylon was invented.

Gut wasn't a perfect material and it had many drawbacks; some of which I have already mentioned, but it also had a tendency to rot, and its lack of longitudinal stiffness meant that a gut dropper was much more likely to spin around the cast than its horsehair counterpart. Neither did gut fall as lightly as horsehair, and it lacked as much 'stretch', which meant that it was more likely to break on the strike. On the other hand, gut did allow the presentation of the fly on a nearly transparent point, was resistant to damage, and didn't share the tendency of horsehair casts to 'pink' – that is to spring slack loops of hair out of the side of a twisted cast. In the end, the greatest selling point of the new material was that with time it became far easier to get good quality gut than it was to get good quality horsehair.

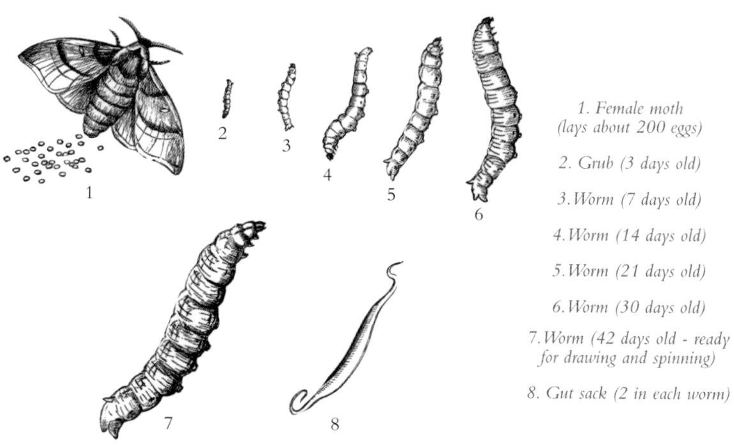

Illustration of the life stages of a silkworm from Kelson's The Salmon Fly

With the adoption of gut, fishermen had a first class opportunity to indulge in a completely new argument, and they drew up their battle lines with great enthusiasm. There was much debate about whether thick, round gut was better than flat or thin gut - and gut did vary:

> If fresh, transparent and flawless, of course it is the best; but I have seen flat gut and thin gut stronger than thicker or rounder links. I prefer quality to rotundity or stoutness – tackle of fine and compact material, to that which is massive and porous. I have had slender grilse-lines with which I should not fear to lead the "wickedest" salmon within reach of the gaff or landing-net. Gut that has been long exposed in shop windows should never be purchased, and links that have light rusty-coloured spots on them should be rejected.[27]

Gut did catch on in the end and by the mid-nineteenth century, it was big business, with imports to Britain coming from far afield. Spain, Portugal, Italy and Sicily all had their own industries, and gut could even be had from Syria if you knew where to find it. Roundness, thinness and transparency were regarded as the hallmark of good gut, but authors complained that the combination was less often found than one would wish. Spanish gut was generally agreed to be the best, but Syrian gut was longer, sometimes as much as twice the length of its European counterpart, which measured between ten and twenty inches (usually fourteen or fifteen inches) long.

Gut had a wonderful nomenclature all of its own. The thickest gut was called 'Hebra', the second thickest 'Imperial', and there followed 'Marana 1st', 'Marana 2nd', 'Padron 1st', 'Padron 2nd', 'Regular', 'Fina', 'Refina' and 'Refinucha' – the thinnest and most expensive. The nuances of the system didn't end there. Within each thickness of gut, there were three different qualities, the best being 'Selecto', the second best 'Superior' and the worst, 'Estriada'.

Estriada is a most descriptive word: in Spanish it means fluted, or grooved, and it describes the appearance of inferior quality gut very well indeed, but then gut was very variable stuff. The existence of the classification didn't guarantee quality, and fishermen were well advised to check their gut carefully before parting with hard cash. There was quite considerable variation in the thickness of different pieces of gut and a thin piece of Royal Hebra could easily be classified as Imperial. The more unscrupulous dealers were naturally inclined to be optimistic about the class of gut they were selling, and they were helped by the fact that even a piece of 'Selecto' was inclined to vary a little in thickness along its length, so the classification was at best a general guide for lower quality hanks.

The preparation of gut was a painstaking process, which meant that it wasn't easily adapted for mass production. In particular, the time and concentration of the solution the worms were exposed to determined the fineness of the strand of gut which could be produced, and the whole process was notoriously temperature dependent:

> Take the largest and best [silk] worms you can procure, just when they begin to spin. This may be known by their refusing to feed, and by having a fine silk thread hanging from their mouths. The worms must be kept in strong vinegar, and covered close for twelve hours, if the weather is warm; if not, two or three hours longer will be necessary. When taken out, they must be pulled asunder, and you will see two transparent guts of a yellowish green colour, as thick as a straw, bent double, the rest of the inside resembling boiled spinage; you can make no mistake. If you find the guts soft, or break upon stretching them, you must let the worms lie longer in the vinegar; when fit to draw off, you must dip one in the vinegar, and stretch it gently with both hands to the proper length. The gut thus drawn out, must be stretched out on a thin piece of board, by putting each end in a slit therein, and placed in the sun to dry. This is the real gut, and the mode of dressing is the cause of the ends being cramped.[28]

Gut was the basis of an important peasant industry in some areas, with Murcia alone producing nearly a hundred million pieces a year, but this rather sanitised account doesn't quite do the process justice. The business of breaking the vinegar-soaked worms open, extracting the glands and stretching them to their full extent before hanging them out to dry was diabolically messy, and houses where it was done must have stunk to high heaven in mid-summer. The next stage was quite disgusting, with the female members of the family drawing the gut through their teeth and spitting the residue on to the floor. After that the glutinous skin which covered the gut was removed by boiling it in soap and water and finally the gut was bleached, hand polished and sorted. It was highly seasonal labour. In Spain, production of gut was compressed into the period between June and August, the Italian crop reaching fruition about a month later. Despite the high price of the end product, the peasant labourers made relatively little, the proceeds instead enriching the inevitable series of middle men.

The popularity of fly fishing meant that supplies of gut were always ill-matched to demand, and there was fierce competition within the tackle trade to secure supplies and to buy the best hanks. Needless to say, the very thick gut used for salmon fishing and fine long Refina used for trout fishing were in the shortest supply. Inevitably, market forces led to the development of methods of making gut thinner, a process known as 'drawing'. This was a tricky job, and the craftsmen and women who performed it were paid skilled rates of pay for drawing natural gut through jewelled plates. Drawn gut was inclined to be rougher in texture and rather less transparent than natural gut, but it was also more expensive, costing from ten to sixteen shillings for a hank containing about a hundred threads. With demand always exceeding supply, there was plenty of room for dealers to exploit the public and many hanks were slyly packed with inferior threads.

Drawn gut diameters

Gut line diameters	*Inches*
1/4 drawn	0.12
Strong 1/2 drawn	0.11
1/2 drawn	0.108

Gut Loops

Gut had other uses besides the making of casts. The classical method of attaching a fly to gut was, of course, to whip the fly on to horsehair or gut, but both materials were prone to fray just in front of the end of the hook, rendering what might well have been an expensive fly completely useless. Much ingenuity was devoted to solving this particularly frustrating problem, including the ingenious suggestion of turning up the end of the shank to keep it clear of the snell,[29] and at some time in the first quarter of the nineteenth century an alternative solution was found. Salmon flies began to be tied with a gut-loop formed at the head of the hook, to which the leader could be attached.

Loop attachment of flies reduced the difficulties fishermen faced at a stroke: it made the carrying of flies much easier, it eliminated the problem of patterns snapping off their own gut, and it made changing flies much easier. Naturally, it was seen as a great threat to world order and some fishermen fought a rearguard action against such a perversion of nature's laws for almost another thirty years. Despite this, the gut loop became standard on salmon flies by the end of the third quarter of the century. Gut eyed salmon flies persisted long after it became the rule to tie trout flies on eyed hooks, and they only started to become difficult to find in the 1920s.

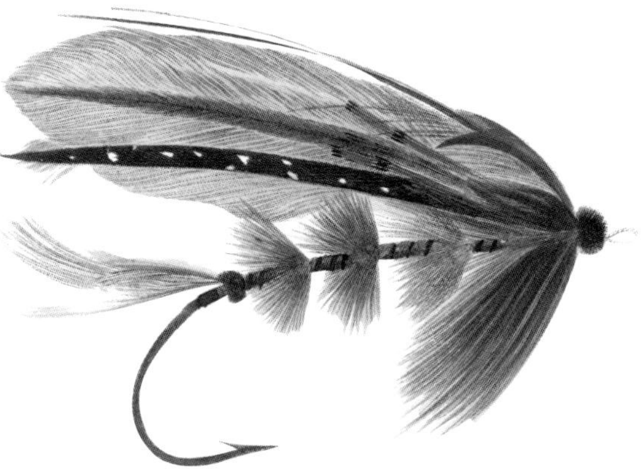

Salmon fly with a gut loop

> As regards the salmon-fly, one great improvement, of recent date, consists in the substitution, as a mode of attaching it to the line, of a small loop or eye-hole of gut at the head or the shank-end of the hook, instead of a full length of the same material. This loop, as in the case of the length in question, may be formed either of triple or of single gut, according to the size of the wire. It is of advantage in at least two respects: first, its adoption renders an assortment of salmon-flies capable of being carried without crushing or disarraying their plumage; and again, while hooks tied on the length or strand are apt to become chafed or weakened at the neck, or to crack off altogether, the substitution of a loop prevents this evil – for, should the strand it was originally fitted to appear worn or damaged, one only has to remove it and attach a new one in its stead. The loop in question ought, on every occasion, to be made as small as possible, just sufficient to allow the passing and repassing of a triple or single gut length through the eyehole.[30]

The question most people ask about gut loops is why they were so seldom seen on trout flies and the answer is that it was impractical to construct them on anything except the largest sizes of hook; but John Betts has raised the even more interesting question of why loops were always tied with the broad axis of the loop lying horizontal. I have to say that I have never been able to come up with a good reason why this should be so, apart from the dictates of fashion. If any reader has a good answer, both John and I would be only too glad to hear it.

Indian Weed

To begin with, gut had a rival, called 'Indian Weed'. Various adverts offered Weed for sale, the earliest appearing in 1689,[31] and it was recommended by Howlett[32] in 1706, who called it 'China or Indian-Grass'. The last reference I can find is by Bainbridge, who mentioned weed in 1816.[33]

Advertiſement.

AT the Sign of the *Fiſh* in *Black Horſe Alley*, near *Fleet-Bridge*, liveth *Will. Brown*, who Maketh all Sorts of *Fiſhing-Rods*, and Selleth all manner of *Fiſhing Tackle*; alſo *Charles Kirby's* Hooks, with Worms, Gentles, and Flies; and alſo the *Eaſt-Indian* Weed.

Indian Weed advert from Chetham

Weed had the advantage of being strong and fine and so it was harder to see under water than either horsehair or silk, but it was extremely brittle, and needed even more soaking than gut did to make it supple. Indian Weed was made from jute, but otherwise we know very little about it. The most complete reference is in Brookes:

> INDIAN, or SEA-GRASS, makes excellent Hook-links; and though some object to it, as being apt to grow brittle, and to kink in using, with proper Management it is the best Material for the Purpose yet known, for large Fish, especially if ordered in the following Manner:
>
> Take as many of the finest you can get, as you please, put them into any Vessel, and pour therein the scummed Fat of a Pot wherein fresh, but by no means Salt Meat has been boiled; when they have lain three or four Hours, take them out one by one, and stripping the Grease off with your Finger and Thumb, but do not wipe them, stretch each Grass as long as it will yield, coil them up in Rings and lay them by, and you will find them become near as small, full as round, and much stronger than the best single Hairs you can get. To preserve them moist, keep them in a Piece of Bladder well oiled, and, before you use them, let them soak about Half an Hour in Water; or, in your walk to the River-side, put a length of it into your Mouth.

> If the Grass is coarse, it will fall heavily on the water, and scare away the Fish; on which account Gut has the advantage. But, after all, if your Grass be fine and round, it is the best thing you can use.[34]

Reels

The multiplying reel, which had been developed in the eighteenth century, was in common use by the early nineteenth. Tackle dealers still hadn't got them right and multipliers were very unreliable, but nothing seemed to deter the gadget freaks. But by now, many of the experts had decided against them:

Early multiplying reel

> Although the multiplying reel is now in general use, the advantages which are set forth in its favour are more than counterbalanced by the frequent disappointments which the Angler is liable to from its imperfections. The fact is that the power of the wheels, as now arranged, is inadequate to move a small weight at a trifling distance. To be convinced of the truth of this observation, it is simply necessary to fasten a piece of wood of a couple of pounds weight to the end of a reel line and throw it into the water, letting the line run out to a distance of twenty yards down a stream. On winding up the line, the person who tries the experiment will be annoyed by the frequent stopping or catching of the wheels, as if the cogs were choked up; and it will not be without considerable difficulty that he succeeds in accomplishing his object. With respect to greater weights, when supported by animated resistance, it will be found almost impossible to succeed; and should a Salmon of tolerable size be hooked, and the line attached to a multiplying reel, it will require the utmost skill and attention of the Angler, by occasionally drawing up line with his left hand, and then winding it, to secure the fish; and this is the only remedy he has, for should he rely on his reel, and persist in forcing the wheels round, the main pillar or support of the engine will certainly break, and leave him to ruminate upon his rashness.[35]

James O'Gorman held absolutely nothing back and wrote: 'I must say that I totally detest, abhor, and repudiate all click wheels, lock wheels, and multiplying wheels.'[36] But despite his imprecations, multipliers remained incredibly popular, for the simple reason that the need for reels which could retrieve line quickly was as great then as it is now. The problem anglers faced was that single action reels of the time were based on a completely defective understanding of mechanics, and if a large fish ran out a lot of line, the fisherman was left dementedly trying to wind it back in on to a spindle with a tiny diameter. By contrast, although they shared a similar design, multipliers could take up line at speed. The problem was that multipliers couldn't stand a lot of winding against a weight; quite simply, the metallurgy wasn't up to the job. Time and time again one reads of unfortunate anglers grinding the expensive brass gears of their reels flat while they tried to wind in a lively fish.

Despite a great deal of experiment, British tackle dealers didn't ever seem to get multipliers right, but they doggedly kept on making them all the same, and this almost wilful inability to develop better technology seems to have been a serious fault of the tackle trade of the day. British reels of this period that survive are often badly made and it is easy to see why so many people disliked them.

An advert in the 1846 Farlow's catalogue shows the sort of reels that were available at the time. Note the very small diameters - not a single reel over three and a half inches and there are no less than five with diameters under two inches:

Plain		*Multiplying*	
1¼"	1/6d	1½"	4/6d
1½"	2/6d	1¾"	5/6d
1¾"	3/6d	2"	7/-
2"	4/-	2¼"	10/-
2¾"	5/-	2¾"	11/6d
3"	7/6d	3"	13/6d
3¼"	9/-	3¼"	16/-
3½"	10/-	3½"	20/-

To make matters worse, poor distribution networks meant that it was particularly difficult for countrymen to get quality single action reels. It was around this time that writers began to press the case for what became known as the 'contracted drum' reel; a design which did allow quick retrieval of line. In 1836, Alfred Ronalds suggested that a reel with a diameter of three and a quarter inches and a width of one and a quarter inches would be a great advance. In 1841, George Pulman went a stage further, suggesting that the distance between the plates should be as little as half an inch, remarkably modern proportions for a reel,[37] but though they were uncommon, well designed reels could now be had, if only you knew where to look:

> A great improvement has of recent years taken place in the form and construction of the reel, or winch. By reducing the length of the barrel and pillars, and enlarging the diameter of the brass plates between which they are confined, the line can be wound up with much greater speed and regularity than when the plates used were narrow, and the distance betwixt them considerable. The catch, also, or rack, is generally abolished, although some anglers naturally enough retain a prejudice on its behalf. This appendage, however, and all machinery intended to assist the winding up, can be beneficially dispensed with. The simpler, in fact, in these respects, the reel is, the better; it not only lets off the line more readily, but is less liable to become deranged in its action.
>
> Among other improvements recently made upon the reel or winch, are those which relate to the handle. This is now constructed so as to fold over or be readily detached, according to the pleasure of the angler, and thus facilitate the carrying or packing up of the machine. Checks, also, have of late years been introduced, and the mode of affixing the reel to the rod altered and improved. A still more recent improvement consists in the substitution of a thick hollow barrel for the slender one commonly in use. The advantage of this contrivance is twofold. First, the air confined in the hollow tube or barrel assists to dry the line and to preserve it free from rot. Again, should a large active fish threaten to exhaust the contents of the reel, the improved barrel will give off freely to the end, and recover with the desirable speed and regularity; whereas, in the case of the winch ordinarily in use, the extreme end of the line, at such a crisis, is generally at fault in its movements, yielding, if at all, with constraint and hesitation, and occasioning, on its being wound up again, considerable delay, at the moment, too, when expedition is most required.[38]

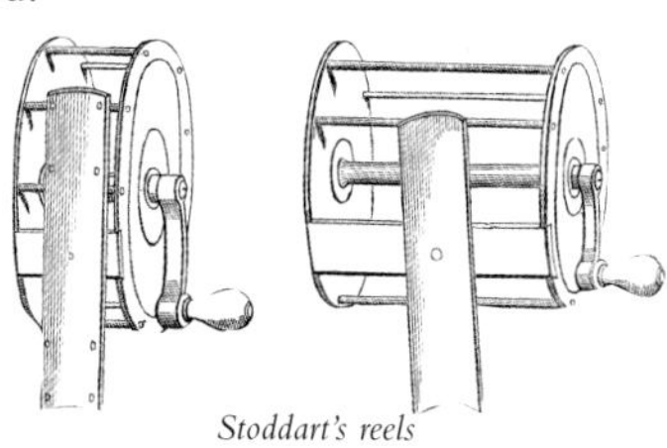

Stoddart's reels

Neither was it a good time for a fisherman who needed to swap a reel quickly from one rod to another. Spike and clamp foot reels were the rule, as they had been the century before, but spike reels could only be moved from rod to rod with difficulty, because butts had to be specially drilled to take them; and clamp reels had an annoying habit of working loose at exactly the wrong moment.

None of this was helped by the sad fact that although the reel had been in use for almost two hundred years, there was still a spirited dispute about where it should go on the butt. Many fished with the reel on top of the rod, with the handle to the right. As late as 1885 Bromley-Davenport was playing fish with a single-action reel on top of the rod, but by then he was bucking the trend. Others favoured an under-slung reel fixed low on the butt, while yet a third school favoured a position higher on the handle. It must have seemed that it would never be sorted out, but by the 1830s a new light had dawned and the plate foot reel emerged. The plate foot solved so many problems that it replaced the spike almost overnight, and spike reels became curiosities within a short space of time. Just to be contrary, the clamp remained a firm favourite for much longer than you would think, and firms like Pfleuger were still marketing clamp-foot reels in the final years of the nineteenth century.

Clamp foot reel

To begin with, rods had to be individually modified to take the modern plate foot, but the new design had so many advantages that it wasn't long before there was demand for a universal reel seat. In the end, the rod suppliers gave in, but it wasn't until the last quarter of the century that anglers could be sure that a new rod would have a standard reel seat.

Reels in America

In America, a separate line of reel design was beginning to emerge and from small beginnings it built itself into the industry which dominates fly fishing today.[39] The earliest known American reel was found on a beach in 1918. This reel had the date 1753 cut into one side, and appears to have been hand made, which is typical of the majority of early American reels, which were mostly home-made affairs built with crude wooden spools attached to iron seats, although it is true that there was a significant trade in imported products. In the early nineteenth century, old timers often fished with discarded wool spools, bound into frames by the local tinsmith, maintaining a noble tradition of making-do that many of them had brought to America when they emigrated. But the native industry was gearing up, and single-action brass or German silver[40] reels with curved handles soon became common.

In such a vacuum, it wasn't long before entrepreneurs saw the possibilities. George Snyder, a watchmaker and silversmith from Paris, Kentucky, is believed to have made the first quality reels in the United States sometime between 1805 and 1810. Snyder was born in the 1780s and died in 1841 in his sixtieth year. Described by his friends as a 'good practical angler', Snyder realised that there was a great need for a reliable multiplying reel designed for fishing the live minnow to black bass. With typical perseverance, he set out to invent one. His first reel was built for his own use, but it was so well made that it attracted a lot of notice and it wasn't long before he was making reels for other members of his club and even clients from farther afield. Some of Snyder's reels were extremely sophisticated, and Henshall comments that he once owned a Snyder reel which ran on garnet jewelled shaft bearings.[41] Within a few years, other firms had set up and were exploiting the market, including Meek, Hardman and Milam, and these firms were between them responsible for the further perfection of the design of the American multiplying reel. One thing which differentiated these 'Kentucky reels' from British multipliers was the fact that they actually worked, and it wasn't long before designs emerged that were capable of casting a line directly from the spool; a trick that you didn't try with a British reel unless you were patient with tangles.

It isn't clear why the American reel designers succeeded where their British counterparts so signally failed, but it may be that the fighting characteristics of the Black Bass in the Kentucky River had much to do with it, not to mention other hard-fighting fish like Stripers. Perhaps

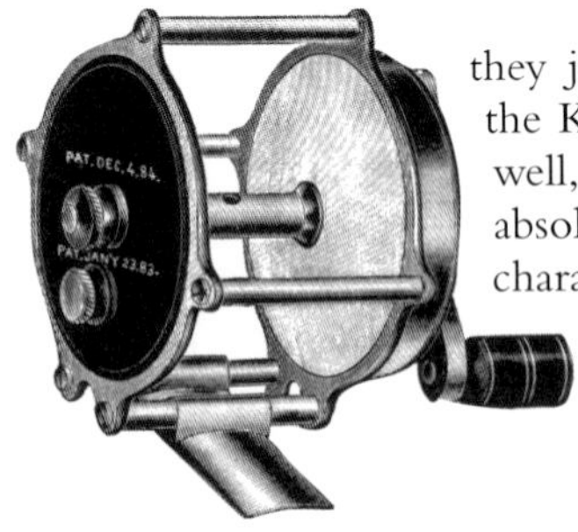

The New Gem.

they just listened to their customers more, but the Kentucky reel makers chose their materials well, and the best of their products were absolutely bomb-proof. Kentucky design was characterised by innovation, and several innovations were first seen on American reels, among them the balanced crank handle and the first free-spool mechanism.[42]

The Crossroads

Startling progress was also being made in other fields, and by 1800, fly design was perched at an important crossroads. George Bainbridge's *Fly-fisher's Guide* is a good example of how much fly tying had advanced: it gives a list of materials running to four pages, far beyond early tyers' wildest dreams. It was no coincidence that the publication of the *Guide* coincided with an obsession with trout and salmon fly tying that launched thousands of new patterns, and some of the author's ideas seem radical even now. He introduced the idea of winging flies with exotic materials such as horn shavings, apple core and thistle down, although he did his readers the favour of conceding that the latter material wasn't terrifically durable. As for fly-tying instruction, well, he left his predecessors flat-footed, and colour plates showed tying materials, life-size fly patterns, and the natural insects which they represented, an approach which is still followed today. Although Bainbridge tied without a vice and many of his patterns use a rolled split wing, his method was an advance on anything used before, and he mentions hackle pliers for the first time - before that the only tool tyers used was a pair of scissors.

Bainbridge does highlight a radical change in the way trout flies were being tied: he published the first colour plate which showed wings being made from paired quill slips and tied on with the tips facing backwards (towards the bend of the hook). Prior to 1800, wings on British trout flies were usually formed from a single rolled segment of quill fibres tied on with the points facing forwards (away from the bend of the hook), following which the bunch was then folded back and over-wrapped at the base to keep it secure – the reversed wing style. This resulted in a relatively upright wing, which sat at an angle greater than forty-five degrees to the hook shank and it is shown very well in early woodcuts.

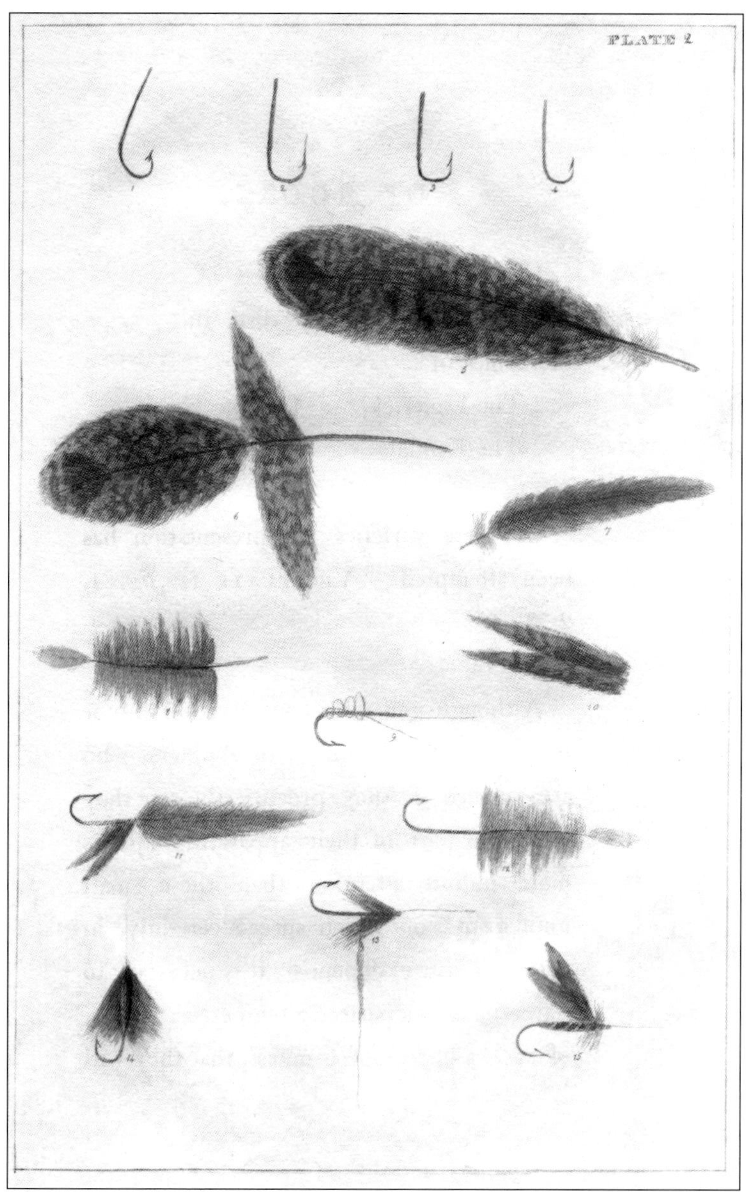

Early nineteenth century Bainbridge plate showing paired slip method

After Bainbridge, flies were increasingly tied with a down-wing that was set on with the tips facing backwards and the whole of which lay at an angle of around forty-five degrees to the shank – the classic down-wing tie which we are familiar with today. One of the main advantages of this method is that it produces patterns with far neater entries than their reversed-wing ancestors and the down-wing also makes them swim better underwater. John Betts, the well known American historian, has recently put forward the view that the change in style was inspired by the opportunity to design flies that sank better, an opportunity afforded by changes in tackle. Before 1800, the majority of anglers used a relatively short horsehair line which held the fly suspended on the surface and few flies would ever have fished more than a few inches down.[43] After 1800, longer casts coupled with the use of tapered silk lines made it possible to fish flies very much deeper.

Although it didn't occur overnight, this change in depth is important, because it marks the beginning of the new era of specialised sunk or 'wet' fly fishing. We take it so much for granted that the wet-fly technique has always been around that this is a startling concept, but I agree with John Betts that the wet-fly fishing school we know had to evolve just like dry-fly fishing, and that the technique found its roots in the middle years of the nineteenth century.

One of the great themes of this book is that in the beginning flies were fished floating or awash and that the deeply fished wet fly and the dry fly came much later. Remember that the way early anglers fished, using frequent casts and the short line method, meant that their flies did not have much opportunity to go down very far. The deepest that anglers like Barker and Cotton fished a fly under normal circumstances was a matter of only a few inches and the short lines they used meant that they had to go to some trouble to get flies to sink any deeper. Wind was a particular problem with horsehair and anglers actually had to drown their lines on stormy days to keep them in the water. It was only when silk lines and gut casts came along – a combination which not only sinks much like a modern intermediate once its components are waterlogged, but can be shot, allowing much longer casts to be made – that the deeply fished wet-fly method we know and love became possible.

Quite simply, silk and gut forced anglers to begin to reconsider their tactics, because they could fish further away and their flies could be allowed to sink to a depth at which takes could not be easily seen. John Betts' view is that the classic down-wing tie is a symptom of that change, and while further research is needed to confirm this, it is fortunate for us that the down wing appeared when it did, because a side-effect of the redesign is that it allows us to spot the impending separation of the wet-fly and the floating-fly schools simply by studying the patterns they tied. By the middle of the nineteenth century, most wet flies were being tied with classical down wings, and when the upright wing appeared again, it would be on dry flies.

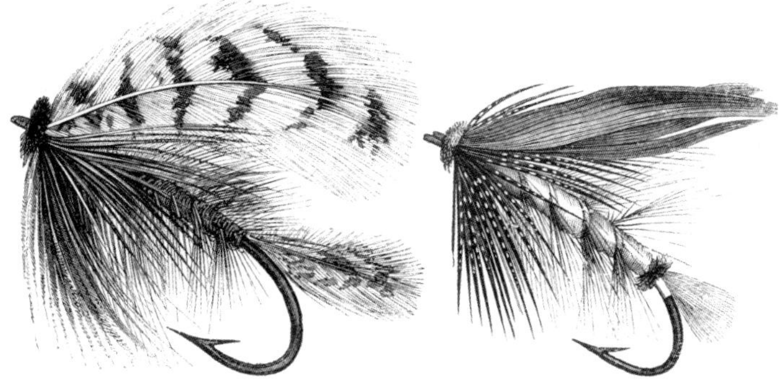

Early nineteenth century flies showing different wing types

In 1836, a book appeared which really did change the contents of fly boxes forever; a work which became so popular that it was still a standard a century later, and which marks the appearance of fly patterns which look relatively modern to our eyes. On the face of it, it is a bit surprising that fly fishing waited until the early nineteenth century to make the leap that Alfred Ronalds' book represents; after all, the premise of *The Flyfisher's Entomology* is so simple it is odd that no one had thought of it before. What Ronalds did was precisely to identify the insect that each fly represented and then illustrate it together with a dressing.

Earlier authors, from Barker to Bainbridge, had tied flies to imitate naturals, but with a very few exceptions, they left the angler no idea which natural each fly was intended to represent and there was little science behind their observations. It was the linkage of flies to a structured classification of naturals that made Ronalds' work such a ground-breaker and the measure of his success is that the book ran to twelve editions. The *Entomology* sold by the shelf-load because it solved the problem which had baffled fly tyers for centuries: the lack of a standard fisherman's nomenclature for waterside insects, a deficiency which meant that anglers from widely separated waters faced an impossible communication problem, as it was more than likely that they called the same insects by completely different names.

The lack of a key linking pre-nineteenth century flies to naturals is a problem we face even today and it is the biggest obstacle that any student of early patterns has to overcome. Frequently, it simply isn't clear which natural fly a particular antique fly pattern is supposed to represent and the conventions adopted in fly tying make it very hard to guess. Ronalds saved the day by making the link between natural and imitation explicit and his book was justifiably popular for this reason alone. However, there was much more to it than that, because in each case, his fly-tying instructions were keyed to an illustration, an innovation which was taken up by many of his successors. His system makes such good sense that very few authors fail to use it today. And as if this new method of presentation wasn't enough, Ronalds linked his patterns to a credible entomological classification of the naturals, rather than using vulgar terms such as 'cow lady' and 'whirling dun', which were not necessarily guaranteed to describe the same insect in Dovedale as they did on Tweedside.

This bald summary disguises the extraordinary efforts that Ronalds went to in order to confirm his theories – he built an octagonal observation chamber hung from a bridge above his beat on the river Blythe in Staffordshire and spent much time sweatily closeted within its claustrophobic confines. The chamber hung only a few feet above the water and it was carefully designed so that the occupant could observe trout in the river below without disturbing their activities. We all owe him a debt of gratitude for the cramped limbs and aching joints he must have suffered during the long hours in that stuffy chamber, scribbling notes that constitute one of the first systematic surveys of trout behaviour ever made by a fisherman.

Perhaps it is because of his detailed observations that Ronald's flies represent a considerable step forward, an improvement even on Bainbridge. They are recognisably 'modern' and the palmers are reduced to a few token entries – fallen from the dominant position that they had built up during the eighteenth century. The caterpillar fraternity must have breathed a sigh of relief.

This is a convenient point to put the spotlight on nineteenth century trout fly philosophy. Many of the ideas which we take for granted were already in place, and just about every fly fisherman from Venables onwards favoured imitative patterns. But even in the middle of the nineteenth century, the majority of anglers still laboured under the peculiar misconception that the flies they saw on the surface of the

Early nineteenth century Ronald's flies

water had fallen there from above. For centuries, this hadn't mattered, because anglers had ensured that flies fished on or near the surface, where they behaved like the duns they were supposed to imitate. But the gradual adoption of silk and gut slowly began to turn everything on its head, because the angler who used such modern tackle could cast further and could present flies that sank more quickly, dragged down by the line during much longer drifts, so that they fished much deeper than their inventors had ever intended. This raised a knotty philosophical problem, because with a few exceptions, such as the dun of the Dusty Yellowstreak, the nymph of which undergoes eclosion under water, and *Baetis* spinners, the duns of the upwinged flies are never seen deep beneath the surface. You would think that the powerful minds which turned their attention to fly fishing during this period would have solved the problem, but the universal response of fishermen was to ignore this incongruity. After all, it worked.

Extraordinary though it may seem and despite the fact that they were increasingly fished in what we now know as the wet style, late nineteenth century classical down-wing wet flies weren't tied to represent nymphs; instead they followed a tying tradition which had its roots in antiquity. It is a peculiar fact that although Ronalds knew all about the life-cycle of the ephemeroptera and even goes so far as to mention nymphs by name, all his patterns were tied to represent duns. I don't think this was a problem for Ronalds, because critical analysis of his book implies that he fished his patterns as floating flies and must have intended others to do so, but the reality was that as the nineteenth century wore on, Ronalds' patterns found themselves being fished more and more as wet flies and by the time the tenth edition of *The Flyfisher's Entomology* was published, the change was complete.

For all Ronalds' careful observation, hung in his tiny observation room, he missed a golden opportunity and unintentionally lead fly fishermen into a dead end; because if his down-wing wet patterns weren't intended to represent nymphs, they didn't imitate duns very well, either. I'm probably being a bit hard on him, because much as the word 'imitation' might have been bandied about, fishermen were in the iron grip of the tying conventions they used. But Alfred Ronalds was the one person who was in a position to see what everyone before him had missed, because he had spent so much time observing the habits of trout, and all the creatures they fed upon. Yet despite all his laborious observations, this great man missed his chance. Ronalds had seen enough to be able make an inspired leap and discover nymph fishing, but he did not.

The natural conservatism of fly fishermen meant that a new orthodoxy emerged after Ronalds, with the 'imitative' winged classical fly ascendant, and the artificials which didn't fit into it slowly fading away. The decades that followed were characterised by a sea change in the contents of fly boxes as the palmers were diluted out by winged patterns. There was also a degree of rationalisation and so we find Walbran of Mickley, the great fly fisher of the Ure, abandoning his palmers, simply because they didn't imitate specific naturals. We shouldn't be too tough on Walbran, because his mistake was the same one made by many others, including Halford and Gordon, who rejected good flies purely because they didn't fit into whatever theory prevailed at the time. It can hardly have been Ronalds' intention, but his following was so strong that the publication of his book marked the beginning of the end of the *laissez faire* imitative school founded by Cotton, which tolerated impressionist flies, and the start of a new era of formulaic fly tying which was only ended many decades later by Skues.

It is interesting to think that the arguments which raged over almost every aspect of fly design later in the nineteenth century studiously avoided the inescapable fact that winged duns are not to be found several inches under the surface, breasting the current. To be fair, the emergence of the modern wet-fly style was insidious and the changeover doesn't seem to have been completed until perhaps the 1880s, just in time for Halford to begin to question it. But however slow the pace of change was, it doesn't alter the fact that all the effort which was put into exact imitation was, where the wet fly was concerned, by and large, a complete and utter waste of time until after Skues, and so a serious question does arise as to why so few patterns were designed prior to 1850 which represented a sub-aqueous creature. In effect, the whole elaborately-constructed thesis of wet-fly fishing rested on quicksand. But no matter, fish were being caught, because trout have to take what they are given.

Flawed though it may have been, Ronalds' approach to fly tying brought new subtleties with it. His careful match of silk and dubbing, often coupled with instructions that the silk should show through the dubbing, is a good example. The only earlier authors to show such an interest in this kind of detail were Scotcher, Juan de Bergara and Luis Peña, none of whom were in a position to exert as much influence as Ronalds. This presented tyers with a problem, because in the early nineteenth century, specialised fly-tying silk didn't exist. Fishermen had to find their own, and it was almost impossible to come across fine enough thread, which made tying small patterns much more challenging than it is now. Quite a variety of silks were necessary, a typical list of colours including: straw; brimstone; fawn; light and dark Easterhazy; light and dark orange; light and dark purple; dark puce; black; different shades of yellow; crimson; red; and brown:

> The strongest in proportion to its substance, the finest and best silk for fly-dressing, is to be procured at Worcester, and you must ask for that sort which is used by glovers in stitching ladies' finest kid gloves. The silk of this sort, which is composed of two twists, will be found the most useful for general purposes.[44]

Although Ronalds missed the opportunity his observations gave him to radically redesign the fly, he did bring a scientific spirit to fly fishing, which may well have been a reflection of the spirit of the age. It was during this period that Dalton drew up the first table of atomic weights, Stephenson built the first locomotive, the electric motor was invented and a man called Charles Babbage had a visionary idea of a calculating machine, which inspired the development of the computer in the late twentieth century. Against this background it was probably inevitable that the general spirit of scientific enquiry would affect fishing, and angling advances would increasingly rely on observation from now on.

As an example of this, tirelessly inventive as he was, Ronalds was among the first to draw fishermen's attention to the problems posed by the refraction of light as it passes through the water's surface. Nowadays we expect fishing manuals to have an irritating chapter on the physics of light to divert us from the good stuff; but in Ronalds' day, refraction wasn't much taken account of, and it wasn't until the early twentieth century that it became an accepted part of fly fishing tactics. Alfred Ronalds and James Rennie (who wrote a few years before him) were the pioneers who took fly fishing into the age of science. In doing this, the pair laid the foundation for modern fly-fishing field craft.

Origins of Saltwater Fly Fishing

Although most people believe that saltwater fly fishing is the invention of our own era, it has as long a pedigree as any other branch of the sport and flies have undoubtedly been cast in the sea for thousands of years. The only reason why saltwater fishing seems such a newcomer is because we keep losing our place with it, chiefly because so little has ever been written about the subject. The unsettling thing is that it doesn't take a great deal of research to discover that saltwater fly fishing has gone through so many renaissances that one might assume every generation has set out with the perverse intention of reinventing it.

Paradoxically, there isn't much dispute about who dipped the first fly in the salt, because there it is in Ælian, paraphrased here by Radcliffe, in *Fishing From the Earliest Times*:

> . . . one of the crew sitting at the stern lets down on either side of the ship lines with hooks. On each hook he ties a bait (perhaps not a bait in our modern technical sense, but rather a lure) wrapped in wool of Laconian red, and to each hook attaches the feather of a seamew.[45]

Does a hook with two feathers lashed to it constitute a fly? And I admit there is no mention of a rod, but I think the important thing is that the principle of fly fishing in the sea was established millennia ago. I doubt that it was lost as an art during the Middle Ages, but the trail goes cold for a long time afterwards, which is one reason why saltwater fly fishing is seen as a comparatively recent invention.

After Ælian the earliest reference I can find to saltwater fly fishing was by Brookes in 1766, in his *Dictionary of Angling*.[46] The doctor makes a very brief reference to fly fishing for mullet, stating that they 'are to be caught with most flies that allure the trout.' Otherwise, the first detailed reference to the subject was made in 1840 - at least a century before it is conventionally assumed that the sport found its origins. This is in the form of an otherwise unremarkable entry on the subject in Blaine's *Encyclopaedia of Rural Sports*, which blandly advises fishing when the tide is flowing, at which time:

> . . . excellent sport is often gained with almost any moderate sized fly; but in this respect they are capricious, and a variety of flies should be carried, both as to size and to colour. We have known them one day take nothing but a palmer, and a second the smallest winged flies. A pair of wings on a hook No. 5., with its barb covered by a bright gentle, will often prove killing.[47]

Perhaps the most startling thing about Blaine's entry is that he insists that fly fishing for mullet was practised 'along the whole lengths of the Sussex, Hampshire and Devonshire coasts,' which suggests that it must have been a popular form of entertainment.

There is evidence that saltwater fishing was practised elsewhere in Europe and there are illustrations of flies in Sañez Reguart's *Diccionario Historico de las Artes de Pesca Nacionales* published in 1795, which leave little doubt about how far advanced sea fishing in Spain was, since the plates show a jig and a streamer.

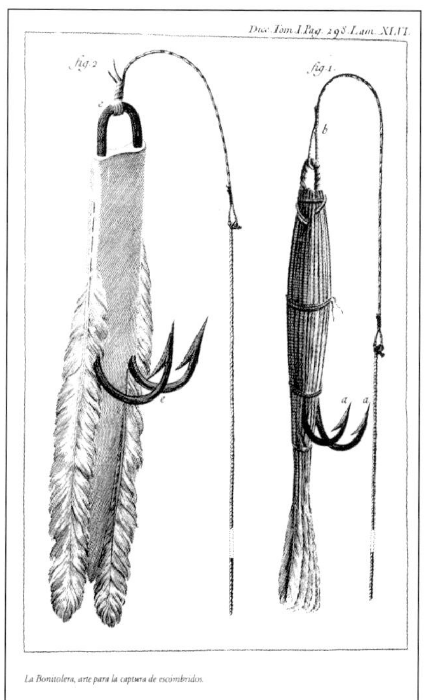

Plates from Reguart's Diccionario Historico de las Artes de Pesca Nacionales

A decade after Blaine wrote, we are treated to an even more detailed description of British fly fishing.[48] It has been suggested, though never confirmed, that the author of the piece in question was a Mrs Hutchinson, which would add another twist to the story, if the sex and name of the writer are ever established for sure. The patterns described in the book are unique and highly evolved; one of them is an upside-down fly, and all of them are incredibly gaudy, marking the beginning of a trend for saltwater flies. The author describes fly fishing for pollack, bass, and grey mullet, using up to seven flies at once, with this advice:

> Your snoods or casting lines for fly fishing for pollack must be either twisted gut stained grey, or twisted wire covered with paint of a leaden colour, that will stand the salt water. The casting-line should have two swivels; and when there is a good breeze, sufficient to enable you to use your largest flies, the swivel nearest your wheel-line should be a very large one. You should always be prepared with your strongest as well as your finest tackle, that you may be properly appointed, whatever the weather may be.
>
> Your rod for this fishing should not be more than three yards and a half long, with a strong stiff top, and very large rings; and the rod should consist of two pieces only, spliced, as the sea-water would soon destroy a rod with ferrules. Your lines should be of hemp, some of them very stout, for rough weather, and finer ones for calm weather. The manner of using your rod when under an easy breeze is this; - you dip about half a yard of the top of the rod in the water, holding the rod perpendicularly, and when you feel a fish strike, you immediately reverse your rod and play your fish as on any other occasion.
>
> No. 1. This was a favourite fly with plenty of wind. Tail: about half an inch of gold twist around the shank of the hook, then red feather of cock-of-the-rock. Body: lower part red worsted, upper part blue worsted or shag, gold twist, orange hackle lower part, bright dark crimson hackle upper part. Wings: under wings cock-of-the-rock's red feather, tipped with white, upper wings two white feathers from under the wing of wild fowl stained yellow. Head: large blue jay's hackle.
>
> No. 2. Tail: gold twist, then some strips of swan or white turkey mixed, stained red, orange, blue or green. Body: same as No. 1. Wings: under wings mixed colours of swan or turkey stained, upper wings brown turkey tipped with white.
>
> No. 3. Tail: gold twist round shank of hook, then mixed, small scarlet hackle, small blue ditto, silver-pheasant black and white

feather, ditto stained orange. Body: same as No. 1. Shoulders: blue jay. Wings: lower wings stained, mixed, scarlet, blue, orange, upper wings mottled feather of peacock's wing, light buff with black bars.

No. 4. Hook reversed. Body: same as No. 1. Tail: mixed. Wings: two white feathers from under wing of wild fowl, stained green. Head: Blue-stained hackle twisted round.

No. 5. Used when the weather is bright and not much wind, and made on large trout hooks, two link twisted gut. Tail: two turns of gold twist, then a small cock's hackle stained blue for tail. Body: rich red worsted, gold twist, rich bright red hackle. Wings: mixed; stained mallard, red, yellow, green. Head: guinea-fowl hackle twisted round.

In the light of Blaine's comments, Mrs Hutchinson can't have been quite the pioneer of sea fishing with a fly that some have suggested, but her choice of patterns does give an idea of what may have lain in the fly wallets of British sea fishermen.

Salmon were also taken in the salt in the early nineteenth century and there is an extended discussion of this in Chitty's *Illustrated Fly-Fisher's Textbook*, which covers salmon and mullet fishing with a fly, not only in the brackish waters of estuaries, but in the sea itself. There is a terrific description of a Highlander standing on the rocks 'hitting them off in fine style,' which just makes you want to go to Loch Swin and try it all over again.[49]

Salmon Fishing

We've seen that salmon fishing started to become popular in the early years of the nineteenth century. The patterns that began to be tied during this period were the dawn of an explosion of creativity which produced a galaxy of exquisitely detailed flies, drove several birds near to extinction, and launched a fashion for salmon fishing which ultimately made it the most expensive of all the branches of the sport. But all of that lay in the future. The sudden increase in the popularity of salmon fishing in the early 1800s is difficult to understand until one realises that the great achievement of the new century was the establishment of the coaching system.

By 1810, it was possible to travel the entire country on roads which were vastly better than the rutted tracks of a century before, though few anglers would have been adventurous enough to travel very widely.

The downside of a long journey was the iniquitous system of rapacious toll houses, and highwaymen were considered an occupational hazard, but at least it was possible to think of travelling longer distances. Riparian owners were quick to notice the change, and as more and more fishermen descended on their doorsteps, the old tradition of freely granted access to the 'right sort of person' began to be replaced with a formal system of letting.

Prismatic Rarities

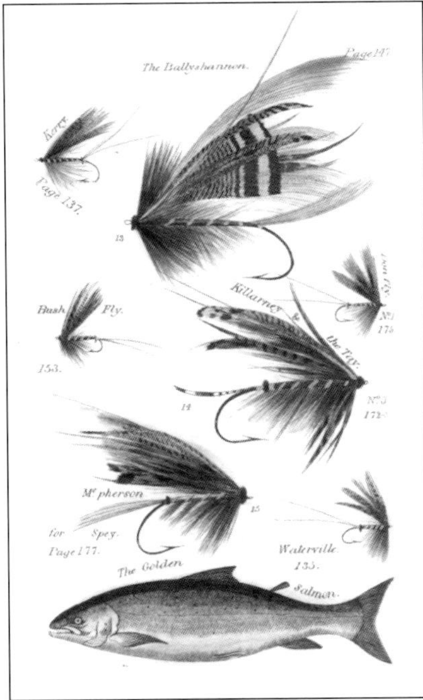

Blacker flies

Into this great melting-pot came a man of great talent, William Blacker. Blacker was born in Cronebane near the village of Redcross in County Wicklow, but later emigrated to England and he published his *Art of Angling, and Complete System of Fly-making and Dyeing of Colours* in 1842, extending it to issue what was in effect a second edition in 1855. The book was a tour-de-force, featuring coloured plates and specimen trout flies, tied by Blacker himself, and it is believed that an edition containing salmon flies was presented to the Palace. Blacker, a tackle dealer, didn't just sell the book, he sold flies and materials, reels, rods, gut and just about every other thing the fly-tyer might need, capitalising on the brisk rise in popularity of salmon fishing which started in the 1840s.

Blacker's advice on fly tying was a radical departure from his predecessors. For a start, he gave totally different methods for tying trout and salmon flies, and much of his writing was taken up by a manual devoted to the details of how to dress individual flies. Like Ronalds, the tying was illustrated at several different stages, but Blacker differed from the authors preceding him because he was a professional fly tyer. There were many professional tyers working at the time, but few of them could write and even fewer could think of charging a guinea a fly, as the dextrous Irishman did whenever fortune gave him the chance.

Where the salmon fly is concerned, Blacker was the torch that illuminated the night and the patterns he created suddenly lifted the sights of many of his contemporaries. His fame spread so far and wide that it wasn't long before he could afford to charge three pounds for a month's tuition of four hours each day at trout and salmon fly tying. His trout flies were very traditional, but few anglers had seen anything like his salmon flies.

Blacker's instructions are very complex and not at all easy to follow. Even really good fly tyers find them trying, and this has led to a simmering controversy. Years later, Francis Francis complained that:

> The flies sold by Blacker were so beautifully tied, and his reputation as a tyer stood so high, that one has a right to expect first-rate directions from such a master; but I confess I am disappointed in them, and that many of them appear to me not only puzzling but almost impracticable.[50]

Interestingly, Francis' derogatory comment referred to the only fly which Blacker gave instructions to tie 'in reverse', that is, starting with the wing. In fact, Blacker was following a convention first discussed by Taylor. Shipley tied his flies the same way, and it may have been in an attempt to keep the body of the fly as thin as possible. There is a deal of logic behind this approach, because a right handed tyer who doesn't use a vice would find it the most natural way of tying a fly, as long as the wing is kept out of the way.

Various explanations have been put forward to explain the difficulty of following Blacker's instructions, including the intriguing possibility that Blacker intentionally made them confusing in order to preserve his sales. One reason why they may look odd to modern eyes is that Blacker's instructions only make sense if flies are tied in the hand and it seems hardly likely that someone who went to such trouble to illustrate his book actually intended to conceal how his flies were tied. Whatever the explanation, Blacker deployed a range of materials that would have stopped earlier tyers in their tracks. Take his No. 2 salmon fly:

> The wings are composed of golden pheasant tail feather, mixed with the following: strips of bustard, scarlet macaw, wood duck, mallard, yellow macaw body feather, silver pheasant, and a topping

> over all, extending a little longer than the other feathers; blue and yellow macaw feelers. The wing, as above, should be laid out on a piece of paper, ready to tie on after the body and legs are formed, the jay rolled over the head in this fly, and the head tied on last, of black ostrich. The tail is a topping, mixed with a strip of wood-duck feather, tipped with silver twist, a tag of gold-colour floss, and black ostrich; the body puce floss to the centre, and the remainder orange pig hair or mohair, ribbed with broad silver tinsel, and a guinea-hen rump feather rolled over the orange beneath the jay hackle. The hook No. 6 or 9, Limerick.[51]

Sadly, Blacker died of tuberculosis in 1856, depriving fly fishing of a genius at the height of his creativity - he was only forty-two years old. Fitzgibbon was present at the bedside and with his death only a year later, two of the salmon fishing greats were dead. Who knows how many wonderful flies we were denied?

Blacker is strongly associated with the rise in popularity of the class of salmon flies which matured into the 'classical' fully dressed flies which find themselves framed on so many walls today, but the trend had started before he was born, with the import of so-called 'Irish' flies into Scotland. The patterns which we now regard as 'traditional' or 'fully-dressed' salmon flies are quite distinct from flies of previous centuries and they are distinguished by the complexity of their design and a concentration on minutiae which sets them apart from anything seen before or since; for example the jointed bodies and built wing which become so *de rigeur* during the late nineteenth century. Classical flies were the result of a completely new approach to tying which utilised a far greater range of exotic materials in each pattern than had previously been the norm, coupled with absolutely specific fly recipes which brook no alteration; it is these features, rather than their gaudiness, which sets classical salmon flies apart.

The 'Irish' flies stood out among their contemporaries because they arrived at a time when the popular Scottish flies were particularly sombre, as a look through the contemporary Scottish experts, Younger or Stoddart's, lists will confirm. The flood of complex and colourful new patterns displaced the old favourites, guaranteeing them a frosty reception from the many experts who quite rightly could see no logic to them. Nevertheless, the majority of anglers loved them to death and the market was so insatiable that it wasn't long before there was a startling variety of patterns on offer.

We can date the arrival of the new breed of salmon fly in Scotland quite precisely. According to Younger, the first contingent of 'Irish' flies were seen on the Tweed around 1810,[52] and the colourful interlopers were so successful that they swept the indigenous competition away within a few years. The traditionalists were not amused by the eclipse of their favourites, and even Thomas Tod Stoddart, a man who was fated to be the bane of the establishment's life, was provoked into a shrill fit of apoplexy. To be fair, Stoddart understood all too well what the Tweed stood to lose; while the local flies may not have knocked anyone's eye out, they had a subtle grace that was the product of many generations of development. The same fate befell the beautiful long hackled flies that Spey anglers favoured. In the process Stoddart did us the great favour of naming the advance guard of the revolution:

> Answer me - Where in thy day was the Doctor? where the Parson? where the Butcher? where the Childers? - where, in short, all those prismatic rarities that stock so amply the tin and vellum of a modern salmon-fisher? You possessed them not. It was neither your wish nor your interest to employ them.[53]

We might add the Dundas Fly and the General to the shortlist of miscreants, but Stoddart's despised list of prismatic rarities formed the foundation for an explosion of creativity which would only be stopped by a world war. 'Auld Tom' Stoddart might not have approved of the trend, but from that moment onward, salmon flies could never again be accused of being nondescript.

The Late Nineteenth Century

The Hardy Perfect

CHAPTER FIVE

The Late Nineteenth Century

THE MIDDLE of the nineteenth century marked a watershed in fly fishing technology and techniques. Before 1850 anglers like Cotton and Venables would have been comfortable with the tackle in everyday use and they wouldn't have had to adapt very much, but in the last half of the century, they would have been lost; everything had changed and fishing was beginning to 'modernise' quite rapidly.

In Britain, the middle of the century coincided with the beginning of the split in the ranks of fishermen which placed the followers of each branch of the sport firmly on either side of a social divide. Salmon and trout ('game') fishers became the sporting elite; a marked contrast to previous centuries when the vast majority of salmon were trapped, netted, or speared. The rest angled for non-salmonids, which became collectively known as 'coarse' fish.

To a large extent the schism mirrored the rigid social divides of English society at the time. Salmon fishing was becoming the sport of the middle and upper classes and competition for the best water soon drove prices beyond the means of the working man unless he was lucky to live in the right place. This increase in the popularity of salmon fishing happened quite quickly in the middle two decades of the century [1] and those who did live by salmon rivers increasingly found themselves denied the right to fish water which flowed past their back doors; a rising tide of resentment was the result. The best trout fishing suffered a similar fate, as riparian owners realised the value of their properties as sporting assets and started charging for access. Salmon rents increased by a factor of ten between the 1830s and the 1870s and out of sheer self defence, the less well-off banded together to form fishing clubs, renting, leasing, or on occasion buying fishing in order to preserve it. Within a few decades virtually all the water in the British Isles had been spoken for, in almost exactly the same way that the land had been enclosed. If nothing else, it was a reflection of the increasing popularity of angling among those who could afford it.

Salmon Rods

After centuries of slow change, during which salmon rods had barely changed, other than sprouting intermediate rings, progress was made by leaps and bounds after 1850. In Britain, this was fuelled by cheap materials sourced from the Empire, but other Western nations saw similar increases in their economic power, particularly the US. Living standards rose strongly in the two countries and leisure time was on the increase - at least among the moneyed classes.

Rods built at the beginning of this period were quite long by our standards, many of them being over sixteen feet. With a rod like this, twenty-five yards would have been a good cast by an amateur, while an expert might have managed thirty or even thirty-five yards with a deal of effort. Part of the reason why casting distances hadn't improved more was that tackle was still very traditional and rods were heavy and comparatively soft-actioned. Most butts were still built of well-seasoned ash, which had the advantage of being as tough as old nails, even if it was rather on the heavy side. In those days there was an abundance of good, if slightly romantic sources of ash, such as the shafts of old gigs, and even the handles of surplus boarding pikes. Norway deal[2] was an alternative, while hickory was widely used on smaller rods. The middle section of 1850s rods was usually made of hickory or lancewood, and the top of whole bamboo cane, or cane and lancewood spliced together.

To give an idea of what rods were like, Francis Francis mentioned an eighteen foot three inch hickory rod made by Bowness and Chevalier, which must have been a real pig, given its weight of three pounds, but although this might seem very heavy to us, it wasn't out of line for a rod of its day. A best-quality salmon rod came with three tops, and in an important development, rent and glued cane top sections started to appear on the very highest quality examples, marking the beginning of a long period of experimentation which would ultimately end in the perfection of the six-strip split-cane rod.

Exotic materials were flooding into Britain from the newly established Empire, and one of those was a wood called Greenheart. Greenheart belongs to the laurel family and is found in the rainforests of the Guianas, on the north-central coast of South America. Greenheart is densely grained, moisture resistant, and very elastic, but it is also incredibly hard and it blunts tools very quickly. To begin with it was mainly used for rod tips, rather than complete rods. Later, when tastes changed, it ousted hickory and lancewood and was used for rod butts and middle sections as well. After that, progress was rapid; greenheart had pretty much captured the hearts of British fishermen by the 1870s and after that it was used to make the majority of salmon rods and many trout rods.

Greenheart's popularity is hard to understand now, because even compared to cane, its action is rather deliberate, but it was perfect for salmon rods, and nowadays older fishermen, long since converted to carbon fibre, say that there was nothing quite like it for Spey casting. But it was a blind alley that stopped tackle makers looking at other materials; in the end, this love affair with greenheart would cost Britain its lead in the development of fishing rods.

Prices for good salmon rods at this time varied from three to five guineas, and some idea of what they weighed can be gathered from the following:[3]

Late nineteenth century rod

18 feet, greenheart, ferruled, weight 2 pounds 10 ozs.

19 foot, hickory butt, and the rest greenheart, ferruled, weight 2 pounds 9 ozs.

19 foot, all greenheart, ferruled rod, weight 3 pounds.

20 foot, all greenheart, and spliced rod weight two pounds 13 ozs.

This was the last gasp of 'traditional' rod design, and rods often had features which would have raised eyebrows only a few decades later. In the middle of the nineteenth century, it was still quite common for butts (particularly of Scottish rods) to be hollowed out to take two or three spare tips, a feature which had it roots as far back as the fifteenth century – indeed the rod described in the *Treatyse of Fishing with an Angle* was made this way. It was a wise precaution given the regularity with which tips built from native woods were smashed. Boring out a butt was a tedious process, and was accomplished using a machine known by the unlikely, but rather menacing name of phipple bitt (the cognoscenti may care to know that they were called 'schulops' in Scotland). The method of boring out butts seems to be a lost technology nowadays, despite having been such a popular technique and I have failed to find a single modern reference to how it was done. The whole thing is a mystery and it would be interesting to know if the phipple bitt or something like it has survived in some corner of the world, because it is key to making accurate reproductions of period rods.

The biggest problem with hollow butts was that they required that the lower section of the rod be made overly thick and hence rather stiff. Neither was the hollow butt the perfect solution for protecting top sections, because despite every care being taken, tips were often damaged as they rattled around inside. Because of this, many English anglers took to storing their tip sections in the hollow handle of a landing net, or gaff, and some even carried tips strapped to a piece of board, but nonetheless hollow butts were relatively common on rods right into the 1870s. General frustration led to some interesting variations on the theme, not least a rod sold by the American firm Conroy in the 1840s, which had a butt made out of cast iron, painted to look like wood. Somehow I can't imagine it had a very pleasing action.

Trout Rods and the Upstream School

Where trout rods were concerned, great changes were in the wind. To gain a sense of perspective, it is worthwhile stopping for a second and remembering that in 1850, multipurpose rods were still very common, the more sophisticated ones having interchangeable butt sections so that they could be used for fly and bait fishing, and the whalebone tip, which had endured from the seventeenth century, was still to be seen. The first stirrings of change were seen at the beginning of the nineteenth century, when rods began to shrink, but the trend was given a powerful boost by a young Scot.

When William C. Stewart wrote *The Practical Angler* in 1857, one of the most influential books ever published on fly fishing, he was only twenty-four years old. Practical was a good description of Stewart's angling and when a ghillie was reminded of Stewart's boast that any good angler ought to net at least twelve pounds of trout in a day, the old man studied his feet and remarked sourly, "Aye, ane one o' Stewarts' days – twenty-foor hoors o' creepin' an' crawlin."

Stewart seldom lost an opportunity to put his views forward, managing to put a lot of backs up in the process. It wasn't only his youth that irritated his critics, it was the fact that he was quite insistent that the majority of them were using completely the wrong method:

> The great error of fly-fishing as usually practised, and as recommended to be practised by books, is that the angler fishes down stream, whereas he should fish up.
>
> We believe that we are not beyond the mark in stating that ninety-nine anglers out of a hundred fish down with the artificial fly; they never think of fishing in any other way, and never dream of attributing their want of success to it.[4]

Stewart listed four advantages of fishing upstream: the angler is unseen by the trout; fish are hooked more easily; the water isn't disturbed (hooked fish can be played down stream towards the angler); and the presentation of the fly looks more natural to the fish. This was a radical viewpoint, and it flew directly in the face of fly fishing orthodoxy, not that Stewart probably cared very much. He expounded a philosophy which may look quite sensible now, but then it was a dangerous heresy aimed at the very heart of the fly fishing establishment.

In the 1850s, the majority of trout fishermen used long rods with soft actions. They fished much as their ancestors had done for centuries: starting at the head of the pool, they cast across and down, raising the rod tip as the flies were swept round down stream, then took a step or two down and recast. Everyone took good care to wet as little of the line as possible in order to ensure that the fly stayed in the upper layer of the water, and some worked the fly into the bargain, a combination of tactics which is ideally suited to long rods, and which combined to ensure that the venerable rod design they favoured had no need to change. So the young Scot's wisdom was not universally well received; here was Stewart telling them to turn around and to fish shorter, stiffer rods and the man only just out of short breeks!

A combination of outright opposition and natural conservatism meant that although the argument about upstream fishing was three centuries old, Stewart's ideas took many years to take a firm hold. Stewart must have taken some comfort in his own lifetime, because his book became a classic, was reprinted many times and served as a textbook well into the twentieth century. However, fishermen love the comfort of clinging to old saws, even if they are plainly wrong, and despite all of Stewart's evangelism, the establishment stood united against him. In one of the most sustained attacks Stewart ever suffered, he was attacked in print by Cholmondeley-Pennell, who took considerable licence in order to promote his own views:

> In spite of Mr. Stewart's able advocacy, most anglers have now arrived at the conclusion that fly-fishing up stream, always, or even generally, is a mistake in practice. In my general observations on fly-fishing I have pointed out one or two of the reasons which have led me to consider it so in theory also. With a strong wind up stream it is sometimes a necessity, though, even then, I cannot but think an unfortunate one.[5]

To give an idea of the gulf separating the two men, Cholmondeley-Pennell did much of his trout fishing with a double-handed trout rod which measured no less than fifteen feet one and a half inches from butt to tip.[6] The fact that Pennell, a sensible all-rounder, could get away with writing such utter tosh confirms how ingrained the old ways were; many years later Arthur Ransome summed up the futility of the situation, when he wrote in *Rod and Line* '. . . they have both been long dead and, I suppose, fish the Styx, one fishing up and one fishing down and pass each other without speaking.'

One of Stewart's bugbears was the excessive pliability of trout rods of the period, which was a major limit on the distance the average angler could cast. The majority of rods were built with an unbelievably soft action, a state of affairs which was encouraged by some experts who thought it was a good thing if a rod could be bent until the tip touched the butt. If Scottish rods were excessively pliant, English and Irish rods were even worse, but the tackle makers doggedly stood their ground. It took a long while for Stewart's views to be accepted and even then it was upstream dry-fly fishing which caused the final defection to the stiff single-handed rod that we now take so much for granted. Public taste is a fickle beast.

Stewart's ambitions didn't end with the conversion of fishermen to upstream fishing and single handed rods; he was convinced that rods were far too long. He foreshadowed Ogden's thinking on short rods and line speed and discussed rods as short as six feet, although it is doubtful if many like this were built in his own time. A trickle of single-handed rods did start to become available and their introduction forced a rethink of rod design. By the 1860s the whalebone tip was well on the way to being displaced by greenheart and cane, and the battle between the single and double-handed trout schools had been well and truly joined. It was a conflict which divided the establishment and it filled the pages of angling periodicals.

From a modern perspective it is difficult to imagine why long rods should have lasted as long as they did, but double-handers did have advantages such as greater power; easier playing of fish; the ability to lift a trout over weeds; and a higher back-cast, which must have saved many fishermen from embarrassing encounters with hedges. The majority stuck to what they knew and the double-handed trout rod was still in widespread use in the 1880s, even on the chalk streams. It is easy to understand why. If you have to cast repeatedly for hours on end, as in the traditional downstream wet-fly style, it is much easier to bear the weight of a heavy double-handed rod than a heavy single-handed one. To Francis Francis, the ultimate arbiter was weight, '. . . to fish a whole day with a single-handed rod is very tiring to the fore arm, and more particularly to the grip of the right hand.' In his own terms he was quite right, because the majority of single-handed rods of the day, at twelve feet, were far too long and heavy to fish comfortably for any length of time. Stewart was interested in shorter, lighter, single-handed rods for precisely this reason, but by and large the manufacturers couldn't deliver light single-handed rods until six-strip split cane was perfected.

It wasn't that light rods couldn't be found, but they certainly weren't common. Henry Wade, the redoubtable one-armed secretary of the Wear Valley Angling Association, fished for trout with a 'three-pieced splice-rod, only eleven feet in length, its weight being eight ounces' in 1861.[7] His finest fly rod was a four piece, eleven foot four inch weapon which weighed a mere five and a half ounces. Contrary to what one might expect, this rod was very traditional, with an ash butt, hickory middle joint, and lancewood top. The maker might have been catering for Wade's disability, but it shows just what could be achieved by a talented builder working with the old materials.

Unfortunately, the majority of rods were anything but light. Below is a selection of Francis' double-handed trout rods from the period, fairly standard rods all:

> *Gould* - A hollow cane rod, with ash butt, twelve feet eight inches long; weight, thirteen ounces twelve drams.

Cheek - A common hickory rod, of the usual make, rather stout in the butt, but very handy and well balanced, eleven feet seven inches long; weight, fourteen ounces six drams.
Bowness - Ordinary hickory rod, rather light and whippy, eleven feet eight inches long; weight, thirteen ounces four drams.
Aldred - This is one of the glued-up triangular-spliced rods, that is, the joints consist of three long pieces of bamboo cane, carefully fitted, glued-up, and tied every inch and a half. This rod, though a beautiful specimen of workmanship, is rather tiring on the arm, being a little top-heavy, and lacking the free spring of the last two, though it has great power of resistance with a heavy fish. Length, twelve feet four and a half inches; weight, thirteen ounces eight drams.[8]

Note that without exception the weights of Francis' rods were more than twice that of Wade's rod, even allowing for length. Yet Francis thought the Bowness was 'rather light and whippy.' It just goes to show what you can get used to, if you try hard enough.

It seems quite extraordinary now, but the dry fly was quite commonly fished on a double-handed rod in the early years, a fact which Halford remarked upon as late as 1889. No wonder it was regarded as a difficult art. Striking a small trout rising to a mayfly imitation attached to a rod that resembled a young telegraph pole must have required a nicety of judgement. Needless to say, Halford was firmly on the side of the single-handed rod, though he took a good deal of flak for it, at one time finding himself in the opposite camps to Francis Francis. Anyway, Halford won the day, not least because he reckoned to cast up to thirty yards with an eleven foot rod, and 'into the teeth of anything short of a positive hurricane' with a nine foot six inch rod. No one with a long rod could have made such a boast, or at least not in the restricted spaces available on some of the chalk streams.

As if the dispute over the length of rods wasn't enough, by now fishermen were obsessed with 'balance,' which turns out to be another blind alley in rod development. A single-handed rod was expected to balance if it was lightly held about a foot above the handle, and a two-hander about two feet above the handle. Convention dictated that if a rod didn't balance like this with the reel attached, lead was added until it did, regardless of the effect on the overall weight of the rod. This must have been one of the most senseless fads ever to afflict fly fishermen - not only was there absolutely no advantage to be gained from it, but some delightful rods must have been completely ruined this way. It is yet another good example of how fashionable ideas can blind us to common sense.

Split Cane

American tackle still owed a great deal to its British counterparts, but by 1850 demand for imported tackle was falling in the US as the home market geared up. In 1845, John J. Brown was able to talk of imported hazel and hickory rods as 'little adapted to our modes of fishing' and fallen into disuse. His preference was for native ash, bamboo, Calcutta reed, or lancewood rods, which the country's dealers had by then brought to perfection. By and large, American fly rods were still spliced and made of lancewood, bamboo and whalebone, just like their British counterparts, but suppliers experimented with a vast list of materials including: ash, hickory, maple, basswood, ironwood, service-berry, hornbeam, cedar, barberry, memel, washaba, mahoe, greenheart, bethabara, noib, lemonwood, snakewood and dagama. Prices for complete rods ranged from five to fifty dollars.[9]

And then something quite extraordinary happened, a development which catapulted rod design on to an altogether higher plane. Rods began to be built entirely out of a single material - bamboo. Bamboos are incredibly diverse and more than a thousand species have been proposed over the years, though botanists disagree about exactly how many of them are unique. With such a wide variety it is difficult even for an expert to differentiate two species, let alone a dealer, and the latter usually lump many species together, because in practice it is almost impossible to tell the prepared culms apart.

The real advance here was the discovery of a new way of preparing bamboo. Here I am going to have to apologise to American readers; every British book of the period refers to the result as 'split cane' and I shan't depart from tradition. The term is derived from the way that bamboo culms were split with a sharp knife before the sections were straightened and planed. In the beginning it was thought that rods built from sections which had been split along the grain were stronger than sawn sections, but there were other reasons for using a knife. One consideration was that the very hard steel alloys we know today had not yet been discovered and bamboo was so tough that it blunted saws quite quickly; another was the loss of valuable bamboo caused by the width of the saw blade itself. In the fullness of time, manufacturing economics and improvements in machine tooling meant that the splitting was abandoned by the majority of manufacturers. This process was more or less complete after the First World War, by which time almost all culms were machine cut without any noticeable loss of strength, but the name still remains.

Splitting bamboo might have been a radical way of building rods, but it was an old idea, even in the 1850s. The Chinese knew how to eliminate the hollow centre of bamboo by splitting and gluing it as long ago as 950 BC,[10] and the technique has been used for making furniture in India since the second century AD. It is possible that the use of cane in rod making has a longer history than most people think; and John James Hardy believed that Indian Army officers might have brought back bamboo for rod-making as early as 1700.[11]

Early whole cane rods were built with Indian bamboo and weren't very sophisticated. Lack of experience with the material meant that rods built from it were heavy and very stiff, which goes a long way to explain their lack of success. On the other hand, the virtues of thin bamboo sections didn't escape the suppliers and whole bamboo became popular for rod tip sections, the only problem being the rarity of long sections of Calcutta cane without leaf nodes. The process of splitting and mitring sections of material together had already been pioneered with hardwoods, and although rods built this way were never very successful, the technique transferred to bamboo extremely well.

The first reference to the use of split cane for any part of a rod is generally taken to have been made in 1801.[12] This is based on J.W. Hills' reading of the paragraph written by Snart; but a more critical analysis would suggest that the latter was actually referring to end-to-end splicing of bamboo after the nodes had been cut out, and to the quartering of thick bamboo so that the individual sections could then be rounded. Snart refers to four-section split-cane tip sections made from planed and glued bamboo and wrapped with silk. There was a good deal of experimentation after that and rods with split-cane tops and even middle sections were being built by Mr Little (rod-maker to Prince Albert) as early as 1847.[13] Some manufacturers were even more adventurous:

> In my opinion, rods made entirely of lancewood are the worst; and those made entirely of rent and glued jungle cane are the best. They must be most carefully fashioned, and no maker can turn them out without charging a high price. I am also of the opinion that they will last longer than any other sort of rod, and are far less liable to warping. I have a high opinion of their elasticity, and Mr. Bowness, fishing-tackle maker, of 12 Bellyard, Temple Bar, showed me once a fly rod, made in this, my favourite way, that had been for many years in use and was still as straight as a wand. I never saw a better single-handed rod.[14]

But although rods made entirely of split cane were being produced in Britain by 1847, they weren't common, and the use of split cane was largely confined to the manufacture of rod tops for another twenty years.

For anyone who has difficulty understanding why split-cane rods didn't catch on overnight, there were good reasons why anyone would have been cautious about buying one, not least because a cane rod usually cost several times as much as its greenheart counterpart. Then again, early split-cane rods were much heavier than they might have been and to cap it all, they lacked much of a reputation. Greenheart, on the other hand, was a superb material for rod-building and much easier to join; allowing the production of cheaper, lighter rods with a far better action than three- or four-strip split cane of the period. The other problem with split cane is working with it: John Betts told me once that when he was working for Orvis, filing the flats on a cane rod would completely remove the teeth from a milling machinist's file in about thirty minutes. This must have been a serious deterrent to experimenting with the new material.

It isn't easy to decide who built the first rod entirely from split cane. Clearly, the Bowness rod mentioned above wasn't new in 1847 and it is possible that Ustonson was building split-cane rods as early as 1830, because Courtney Williams refers to the Earl of Craven having a twenty year old Ustonson cane rod repaired in 1851.[15] On the other hand, this particular rod could have been a 'solid' Calcutta bamboo rod, because these were widely available at the time. William Mitchell wrote that the first split-cane rod he ever saw was in 1852, and that it had originally been made to order by Blacker for a well-known angler called James Stevens, the implication being that the rod was no longer new at the time Mitchell saw it.[16] Yet another candidate, Mr J. D. Dougall, of Glasgow, had three-strip split-cane rods on display at the Manchester Free Trade Bazaar in 1845, and maintained that he first produced a split-cane rod between 1838 and 1840, but there is also good evidence that Aldred built the first rods of this type.[17] John Waller Hills, showing a typically patriotic bias, awards the accolade for the first British rod made completely from split cane to Higginbotham, a tackle maker at 91 Strand, London, but this is on the slim evidence of a reference in Wright's *Fishes and Fishing*, published in 1858:

> At my request he introduced me to an old Welshman, named David Williams, whom Mr H. had drilled into making rods according to his plan; this Williams was acquainted with Clark, the unrivalled maker of glued-up bamboo fly rods: the most excellent of all rods.[18]

The evidence for this last claim is pretty dubious, since it is impossible to know whether the rods were made entirely from split cane, or whether they were partially made of cane, like Little's rods. Part of the confusion lies in the fact that there was no shortage of partial cane rod builders; by the time of the Great Exhibition in 1851, not only Aldred and Bernard, but Farlow had three-strip rods for sale.

I tend to believe Mitchell's opinion that the Aldred rods were the first three-strip cane rods ever built, given that he was a rod maker himself and had made a comprehensive study of the subject in the 1880s. Incidentally, the Aldred three-strips suffered from some serious faults which illustrate to perfection the difficulties builders had with early split cane. The tips were made from many small sections of male Calcutta cane sawn from between the nodes, with the sections spliced together to form continuous lengths. Although it seems almost unbelievable now, for some extraordinary reason Aldred, like others of the period, elected to put the hard enamel surface of the cane on the inside; and the rods were all extremely heavy as a result.

Other suppliers, including Blacker, were quick to market three-strip rods, but all of them were technically wanting and they didn't sell. By now the British angler favoured greenheart so completely that the initiative moved to America, and the British did not convert wholesale to cane until the twentieth century.

Samuel Phillippe

Historians generally follow the line that the inventor of the split cane fly rod was Samuel Phillippe, a gunmaker in Easton, Pennsylvania, though the memories of the men who wrote on the subject were uncertain, even a few decades after the event.[19] A portrait of Phillippe shows an elderly man with magnificent mutton-chop whiskers, a long face and steel framed spectacles balanced high on his balding crown. Phillippe was an angler of some note who fished with Thaddeus Norris from time to time and it is significant that unlike many of his rivals, he was motivated by the idea of making a rod that was lighter than anything else available. In this he certainly succeeded, because an eleven foot four inch rod of Phillippe's, made in three sections, weighed only eight ounces. Compare this with later English rods, which weighed about an ounce a foot.

Phillippe started by making tips and the second joints of rods out of two and then three sections of split cane, and he finished them with solid ash butts. The three-strip rods wouldn't cast true, so he experimented with four strips, which he thought were an improvement. The first four-strip rods weren't 'pure' cane, because Phillippe used white ash for the butts, but a year later he eliminated the ash and built one entirely from split cane. The early rods weren't intended for sale and he didn't put the design on the market until 1848. Quadrate rods built to his specification were shown at the Great Exhibition at the same time as some of the first British three-strip rods, which shows how much Phillippe was well ahead of his time; by comparison Farlow's didn't advertise their first four-strip rods until some twenty-four years later.[20]

Samuel Phillippe

Four-strip cane rods are still being built by specialist suppliers, but it takes a talented angler to cast well with them and this must have become apparent to Phillippe fairly early on, because he dropped the design. We don't know if he built any five-strip rods, but given that it took the talented R.W. Crompton fifty years to discover how to make five-strip tapers work properly, we can assume that Phillippe didn't stay with them for long. The first six-strip split-cane rods were built by Phillippe in either 1848, or 1849. He did this very quietly, without any fanfare, and sold them to Andrew Clerk & Co., in New York. Clerk was Phillippe's source of bamboo, so it was natural for the pair to do business, but I wonder if Clerk had any idea what he was taking on when Phillippe delivered his first six-strip rods. Whether or not he had any inkling of his brush with immortality, the business arrangement did Clerk a great deal of good, because the firm subsequently became the patrons of the rod makers Leonard, Green, and Murphy. Of the three, Leonard was the one who would build the best rods and the greatest reputation. Ebenezer Green built split-cane rods in small numbers from 1860 onwards and Charles Murphy made them in quantity after 1863. Murphy was a superb craftsman and he was an early influence on Leonard, but his cantankerous nature mitigated against his success. Even his friends said that he would rather quarrel than eat, and it is characteristic of the man that he muddied the waters of split-cane history with a steadfast claim that he had invented split-cane construction, despite all the evidence to the contrary.

Hiram L. Leonard

Like Phillippe, Hiram L. Leonard set out to start up a gunsmiths, but he found demand so low that he turned instead to making fishing rods. It turned out to be an inspired choice, for he could make rods like no one else before and possibly since. Leonard was born in Maine in 1833, but he grew up in Pennsylvania, where he worked for a time minding the machinery at a coal mining company before he returned to his home state. These were hard times and in addition to gunsmithing, Leonard tried his hand successively at taxidermy, hunting and fur trading, before he hit on the idea of making fishing rods. Hiram was a striking individual and when Thoreau met him in 1857, he described him as a tall, handsome man, faultlessly groomed and of 'gentlemanly address'.[21] Leonard was also an accomplished musician, played the flute and the bass viol, and was possessed of the peculiar belief that no man could make a good fishing rod unless he could play at least one instrument. Maybe he was right, because few other rod makers ever approached him for quality.

It was Leonard who took Phillippe's invention and perfected and popularised hexagonal rods in America early in the 1870s. Leonard's break came in 1871, when Bradford & Anthony, a Boston sporting shop, saw a rod Leonard had made for his own use and commissioned him to build split-bamboo rods for them. At the time, Leonard was forty years old, and it wasn't long before had more work than he could handle. The names of the men he hired to help out in those early years became the roll-call of the great American rod makers: Fred Thomas, Thomas Chubb, Ed Payne, Billy Edwards, and Hiram and Loman Hawes. All of them subsequently went their separate ways, but not before they learned some special magic from the master.[22]

Quite how Leonard's men learned the magic is a good question, because Hiram kept his cards quite obsessively close to his chest. His greatest secret was a bevelling machine of his own design, which first went into use in 1876 or 1877. The beveller cut the six strips needed for each rod with incredible precision and unerring accuracy; and there wasn't another manufacturer who had anything like it. Well aware of the consequences for his business if the secret ever leaked out, Leonard kept the machine in a locked room and only he and his nephew Rube Leonard ever used it. Fred Thomas must somehow have gotten a look at it, because if he hadn't one of the secrets of building split cane rods would have died with his mentor.

But there was more to Leonard than a fancy machine: he was the first rod maker to build rods with compound tapers which were calculated mathematically, and it seems that he discovered Chinese 'Tonkin' cane long before anyone else guessed how much better it was than the Calcutta cane in such universal favour at the time. The story goes that in 1877 Loman Hawes bought an umbrella with struts of such high quality that they couldn't possibly have been Indian cane. It didn't take Leonard and Hawes long to trace the supplier, and the discovery of the material gave Leonard's products an edge which they didn't lose for thirty years.

It wasn't all plain sailing. Leonard ran into financial trouble in 1878 and had to sell a controlling interest in his business to the Mills family. Mills moved the factory south from Bangor, Maine to a spot in Central Valley, only fifty miles from Manhattan, in 1881. In retrospect, this relocation was the catalyst that spawned the American split-cane industry, which began when Thomas Chubb decided against going to New York and set up instead at Post Mills in Vermont. By the time Leonard died in 1907 at the age of seventy-six, Thomas, Payne, Edwards and the Hawes brothers had all set up businesses of their own, which preserved the tradition of the master's way of rod making, but Leonard went to his grave with the secret of how he calculated his rod tapers, and it was several decades before the rest of the industry worked out how to make a good rod great.

Whatever the truth of it, by the mid-1870s, six-strip split-cane manufacture was in common use for quality rod building in the United States. Britain had to wait rather longer and the first hexagonal rods were marketed by Allcocks as late as 1879. The 1881 Allcocks catalogue lists 'Hexagonal Built or Split Cane Rods' made in England in lengths from 10 1/2 to 18 feet. These rods had two tops and cost from £4 17s. 6d., for the trout rods, to a dizzy £12 for a salmon rod. This sort of pricing explains why cane wasn't terrifically popular to begin with, since by comparison, an eleven foot 'best quality' greenheart trout rod cost only 23s., while a twenty foot hickory salmon fly rod retailed for a paltry £5 5s. The reason for the high pricing was that split-cane rods were complex things to build compared to their wooden cousins, as the following quote shows:

> In making a rod, some ten or twelve feet of the butt of the cane is sawed off and split into thin pieces or strands. These pieces are then bevelled on each side, so that when fitted together they form a solid rod of about half the diameter or less of the original

> hollow cane. This bevelling is done with a saw, or a plane if preferred, but more expeditiously by having two rotary saws or cutters set at an angle of 60° to each other, in case the rod is to be of six strands. The strip is fed to the cutters by means of a pattern which, as the small end of the strip approaches, raises it into the angle formed by the cutters. This preserves a uniform bevel, and still narrows each strand toward its tip end so as to produce the regular decrease in size of the rod as it approaches its extreme end. These strips can, if desired, be filed to a bevel by placing them in triangular grooves of varying depths in a block of lignum-vitæ. The pieces are then filed down to the level of the block, which is held in a vise during the operation. The six or twelve strips as required, being worked out, and each part carefully tested throughout its entire length by a gauge, are ready for gluing together, a process requiring great care and skill. The parts should be so selected and joined so that the knots of the cane "break joints." The parts being tied together in position at two or three points, the ends are opened out and hot glue well rubbed in among the pieces for a short distance with a stiff brush. A stout cord is then wound around the strands from the end glued towards the other portions, which are opened and glued in turn, say eight or ten inches at a time. A short length only is glued at one time so that slight crooks in the pieces can be straightened and this is done by bending the rod and sliding the pieces past each other. During the gluing all inequalities and want of symmetry must be corrected or not at all, and so the callipers are constantly applied to every side at short intervals, and any excess of thickness corrected by pressing the parts together in a vise. Figure 1 shows a section of a length of bamboo cane from which the strips indicated by spaces marked off are to be sawed. Figure 2 is an end view of the six strands properly bevelled and glued together. This length or joint of the rod is made up of six sectors of a circle whose diameter is greater than that of the rod, and hence it is necessarily what in common parlance might be called six-cornered . . .
>
> The ferrules are water-tight and expose no wood in either the socket or the tenon part. Bamboo is so filled with capillary tubes that water would be carried through the length and unglue them, if it could once reach the ends where the joints of the rod are coupled together; hence the necessity of careful protection at this place. The entire rod when finished is covered with the best copal coach varnish. By taking care to renew the varnish from time to time, no water need ever get to the seams.[23]

Six-strip split cane didn't cross the Atlantic without a deal of subterfuge. According to James Leighton Hardy, employees of Hardy

Brothers actually took a kettle to an American rod, probably an early Leonard, in the late 1870s and patiently steamed the product apart in order to discover how it was made.[24] Flushed with the success of their espionage, Hardy Brothers exhibited six-strip split-cane rods at the International Fisheries Exhibition in 1883, as did Farlow, but they had trouble selling them. Quite apart from the premium price tag that split-cane rods carried, discrimination against split cane may have been the result of bad experiences anglers had had of poor quality American imported rods, which were quite common at the time. It wasn't until the 1890s that split cane began to make much headway against greenheart in Britain.

After 1890, the advance of cane for the building of trout rods was rapid. By 1900, competition for supplies of bamboo was fierce and the sources of the best material were jealously guarded. By then it was universally acknowledged that six-strip rods comfortably outclassed the opposition, and after the turn of the century, it was unusual for cane rods with fewer sides to see the light of day, although good modern four and five sided rods do cast extremely well.

The discovery of six-strip split cane did not prevent a certain amount of 'design overshoot' from occurring. Initially, it was quite common for six-strip rods to be planed to a round section, a fashion which was abandoned when it was found that it weakened the rod, and there was also a brief vogue for reinforcing blanks with various materials. This was quite understandable, given that early fish and animal glues weren't totally trustworthy and multiple intermediate wraps were a vital insurance policy against delamination. Linen over-wraps were tried, as were wire spirals on the outside of the rod, and two rather under-confident American companies made rods which were closely wound with silk from butt to tip. Six sections weren't enough for some; and a few eight, nine or even twelve section rods were made, but they suffered from excessive dampening, besides being terrifically expensive to manufacture, and since there was no real merit in them they never caught on.

Rods were becoming much more reliable as a result of advances made in several different areas, for example the practice of staggering the bamboo nodes so that they did not line up around the rod sections in order to eliminate weak points. At the end of the century, not only were ferruled joints the rule on better quality rods, but several different types of ferrule were competing for supremacy, including Hardys' spiral lock-fast joint, the older socket joint and Mr R.A. Anderson's 'patent capped ferrule'. Even in this area, English rod design was beginning to lag behind the better American designs, which used the metal suction joint, perfected by Orvis of Manchester, Vermont, an invention so good that it hasn't been improved upon since. Although there were still many improvements to be made to the joint, notably the use of lighter alloys and carbon fibre, from this period on we hear very little about unreliable joints from anglers and all the major problems had been solved. At this point it should have been possible to say that another great angling controversy had finally been put to bed - except that a rearguard action was being fought for the splice, of which we shall hear more later.

Although we are in sight of modern design at this stage, rod handles looked quite different to the highly shaped cork rings that we are used to today; hardwood handles were very common, and higher quality rods were often clad in pigskin, or fine sheets of cork glued to the butt section, turned on a lathe, and sand-papered smooth. Another difference was that from the mid 1800s onwards, it was quite common for rods to have a detachable 'spear' stored with the point hidden in the butt cap, which could be taken out, reversed and screwed back in so that the rod could be stuck upright in the ground, in order to avoid it being trodden on and smashed.

In the end it was the popularity of dry-fly fishing which brought split cane into favour in England, but British salmon fishermen favoured greenheart right to the end of the century:

> Beautiful pieces of handiwork are the split cane rods which have come into favour in late years, and admirably they do their work in casting a fly and playing a fish; but it is doubtful if they possess enough advantage over good greenheart to balance their far greater costliness. In trout fishing, especially with dry fly, split cane is without doubt the very best material that can be used; but in the larger sizes of salmon rod, it is not very easy to discern any superiority that split cane possesses over greenheart, except perhaps in appearance, and the cost is at least three times as great. Nor indeed is there any particular merit in split cane for smaller rods of 15 feet in length, such as may be used for grilse or sea-trout, or in boat fishing for salmon. The most that can be claimed for them justly is that a good split cane rod is quite as serviceable and trustworthy as a good greenheart. Let every man please himself in the matter; if he chooses to give ten or twelve guineas for a split cane salmon rod, instead of three or three and a half for a greenheart, nobody but his wife has any right to complain.[25]

But the attitudes which had seemed so fixed slowly changed, and despite intense competition from greenheart, the merits of bamboo weighed heavily in its favour. In the end, as prices began to fall a little, even the most conservative British fishermen found bamboo rods hard to resist. The manufacturers responded quickly and for example, by the early 1880s Hardys offered a huge range including single-built, double-built and steel-centred cane rods. Their single-built rods were made from six sections of cane; double-built had an inner core of six sections of cane around which an outer six sections were glued. Similar rods were offered sooner or later by other suppliers. The attraction of 'double-building' was that it made stiffer rods possible by eliminating the pithy section of the bamboo which is normally concentrated at the centre of a single-built blank, substituting instead another layer of the hard outer bamboo 'power fibres' at the heart of the rod. Rods with 'hardened spring steel centres' were proudly listed and claimed to be virtually indestructible – but despite special treatment, the centres oxidised gently away in time, leaving the owner with a hollow-centred double-built rod filled with expensive rust.

In spite of its disadvantages, steel had an awful fascination for rod-makers, and not only did they use it to reinforce rods; they experimented with collapsible hollow-steel rods. In one design, the line was threaded into the tube from the reel, via an aperture a few inches above the reel seat, emerging from the top of the rod. This arrangement had many problems; the line was tricky to thread, particularly if the interior of the rod had rusted to any degree, and neither did the line feed easily when it was wet, a problem which must have driven anglers to distraction when they were trying to change lines in a hurry.[26] On the other hand, steel rods had their attractions, since they didn't break or warp under pressure. While steel ceased to be used for anything except the cheapest rods, the idea of threading the line up the centre of the rod refused to die, and rods with a hollow centres still appear now and again. However, steel could not compete with cane, and it vanished from the quality rod makers' catalogues very quickly.

Hooks

Although eyed hooks had been known for centuries, for a long time they weren't at all easy to make in quantity, with the result that it isn't until 1845 that we begin to hear serious talk of them and even then it wasn't always favourable. O'Gorman, for example, denounced them as 'another Scotch invention', which was pretty mild language for him, and God alone knows what curses he would have resorted to had he known the eye was a Neolithic Ligurian invention.

From time to time, various authors and dealers tried to push the idea of eyed hooks, but with very little success. Hewett Wheatly marketed a series in 1849, but couldn't sell them. Warners and Son patented an eyed hook in 1866, but there was little interest and the venture fell by the wayside; and Allcocks of Redditch manufactured eyed hooks for J. S. Holroyd (a tackle dealer in London) in 1867, but again, there was no demand and the idea dropped.

It wasn't until H. S. Hall's eyed trout hook came on the market in 1879 that blind hooks faced a serious challenge. Hall was a friend not only of Halford, but also of Marryat and the success of his hooks was only partially due to good timing, because he also went to extraordinary trouble to promote them. The design of the new hook was actually a joint effort between Hall, who lived in Clifton, Bristol, and a Captain George Bankart of Leicester; a venture which ended in a sad, interminable and acrimonious exchange in the columns of the *Fishing Gazette*.[27]

Hall and Bankart were inspired by the eyed hooks which appeared in Aldam's *Quaint Treatise on 'Flees and the Art a' artyficiall flee making'*, which was published in 1876. The *Quaint Treatise* was an odd little book, bound into which are twenty-five actual flies, two of which are mayflies tied on japanned straight-eyed hooks with Limerick bends. Not realising that the hooks had been specially made for Aldam by W. Bartleet and Sons of Redditch, Hall and Bankart corresponded with the author and obtained a supply of eyed hooks from him in 1878.

Interestingly enough, the mayfly patterns were tied by James Ogden or his daughter Mary, which is significant, because Ogden claimed to be one of the first anglers to fish a dry fly and the patterns deserve a second look if only for that. Anyway, Hall and Bankart conducted experiments with Ogden's hooks, but weren't at all satisfied with the design, which they found to be too heavy in the wire. It was an intensive process and the two hundred and forty letters sent to Bankart by Hall during this period are an indication of the incredible lengths to which they were prepared to go in order to find a working design. The pair ended up having some hooks made to their own specification by Hutchinsons, which were delivered in 1879.[28] Their final model had a Limerick shape with a skewed point, an upturned eye and bronzed finish; and it was the ancestor of all the up-eyed dry-fly hooks in use today.

Although no less an angler than R. B. Marston, the editor of the *Fishing Gazette*, cast doubt on the venture, the public had other ideas and the new hooks sold like hot cakes. Uncharacteristically, Marston had missed a trick: the reason tht Hall and Bankart's hooks succeeded where similar designs had failed before was the increasing popularity of dry-fly fishing. Repeated false casting tried gut beyond its limits, and the new hooks appeared just at the right moment for the dry-fly men. Furthermore, anglers could not help but know about this new product, because Hall was an assiduous publicist. In particular, he pointed out that the benefits of eyed hooks were that they:

1. Were almost impossible to whip off
2. Could be tested before a fly was tied
3. Could be re-tied if the gut leader wore
4. Could be switched between point and dropper
5. Could be tied on varying thicknesses of gut

Hall mischievously added that on the whole, eyed hooks were more economical, particularly given that the gut was frequently spoiled by fish which tried to escape by plunging into weeds. After initial scepticism by the angling public, it didn't take long for eyed hooks to become popular, particularly after Turle developed a knot suitable for attaching them to gut, and the enthusiastic approval of angling heavyweights like Francis Francis and Frederic Halford sealed the future of the new hooks.

The value of the eyed hook had been established and only a few years later, Cholmondeley-Pennell introduced a down-eyed model. By the end of the century, partly as a result of interest generated by Hall's articles in *The Field* and the *Fishing Gazette*, up and down-eyed hooks were freely available in both salmon and trout sizes and the use of the vice for tying became increasingly *de rigeur*. A third variety of hook, sometimes called 'needle-eyed' was also available, with 'a hole drilled perpendicularly through the end of the hook shank like the eye of a needle',[29] but this was fiddly to use and failed to attract much of a following.

As usual, the old designs enjoyed a long sunset. Blind hooks were still being manufactured in the 1930s:

> There is still a school of anglers who prefer their salmon-flies dressed on gut-loops, because they maintain there is less strain on the cast through having an elastic joint between metal and single gut. I think this is distinctly the better argument in support of the gut-loop, but I do not recommend it in preference to the well-designed metal eye, except for large flies (3/0 upwards) and for fishing in a strong and gusty wind.[30]

The trout men converted to the new hooks with enthusiasm, but the tradition of tying salmon flies on blind hooks with gut loops persisted until the beginning of the First World War. After that it began to die out: by 1920 tackle suppliers offered eyed hooks by default and flies tied with gut loops as an option; by 1930 flies tied to gut were difficult to find.[31]

In the transitional period, some peculiar experiments were carried out. For a time in the 1930s an odd practice of whipping metal eyes to a class of long shanked hook known as 'Long Dees', was followed. Very little has been written about the subject, but it seems that the reason was that Long Dees were markedly hog-backed and it has been conjectured that it was necessary to whip an eye on in order to improve the line of pull, but fortunately both the habit and the hooks died out, so I shall say no more of them except that I would very much like to see one.

Finishing Methods

Early hooks rusted at the drop of a hat and much ingenuity went into preventing it happening. If hooks were finished at all, they were blued, but all that did was to slow the rusting process down. There was a short vogue for silver and even gold-plating hooks, but the expense and the flashiness of the finished products was enough to ensure that they didn't catch on. The practice began to die out in the last quarter of the nineteenth century, at which time some hooks were being finished with an enamel coating (usually black, but red, green, blue and yellow were available from Allcock & Co. of Redditch in the 1880s); by lacquering, tinning; or in a few cases, like H. S. Hall's post-1885 hooks, using the modern technique of bronzing.

Our present-day hook making processes owe much to earlier methods. Modern hooks are made from wire, usually with a high carbon content steel, but occasionally from alloys. The wire is cut to the length required and then pointed, either by grinding, or by cutting on the diagonal. After this, the barb is formed by cutting into wire. Next, the hook is bent around a former, the shape of which determines both the bend of the hook and the offset of the point. Following this, the hook is sometimes 'forged' in a press which flattens the wire slightly, starting at a point just behind the barb and continuing a little way up the shank. Forging increases the strength of the hook and is a critical part of the manufacturing process. Finally, the eye is made by bending the wire around another former and turning it up or down as required. Hooks may be treated by a further process known as 'chemical sharpening' where acid is used to remove any minute snicks, burrs and defects that the other processes have left. The basic shape of the hook is now finished, but the untreated metal is far too soft to use, so it must be 'tempered'. The hooks are placed in an oven, brought up to an even heat, and then cooled rapidly in liquid nitrogen which reduces scale. The tempered hooks are cleaned by tumbling them in an abrasive, checked for quality and finally 'bronzed' by coating them with lacquer and baking them in another oven. Almost any colour can be achieved using pigmented lacquer, and some hooks are electroplated gold or silver, although fortunately this is not common.

Hook Scales

With the exception of the scale which I presume Kirby used, and the woodcut of hooks in the *Treatyse*, the earliest reference to a hook scale that I know of was made by Bowlker in 1746,[32] who mentioned numbered hook sizes just once in connection with a fly dressing, unfortunately without leaving us the slightest idea which scale he meant. The lack of any earlier references thus dates the first known hook scale to some time in the middle of the eighteenth century. The first scale of which we have clear illustrations is the 'old' Redditch scale which went from a small number 13 to a large number 1.

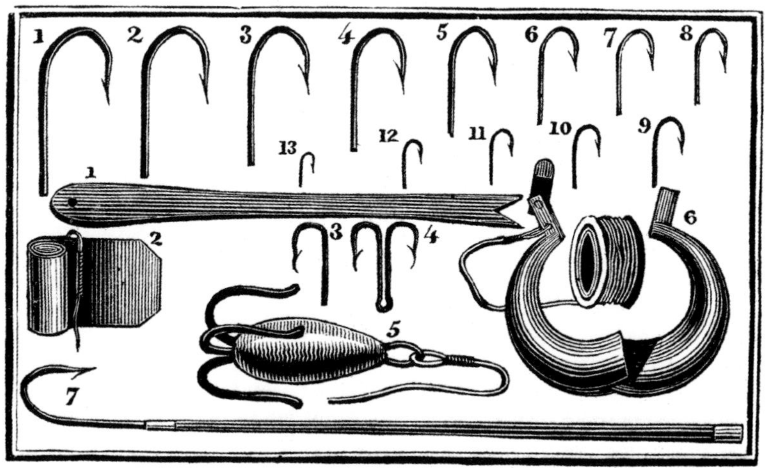

Robert Salter, old Redditch scale

This scale seems to have been used from the eighteenth century until at least 1867 when it was reprinted in an edition of *The Complete Angler.*[33] After that, things rapidly became confused as several competing scales emerged. The 'modern' or enlarged Redditch scale came into use at some time during the middle of the nineteenth century with the first reference I can find to it being by Stewart in 1857. Yet a third scale, originating in Kendal, was popularised by Adlington, gaining its first mention in 1836[34] and first being illustrated in 1842.[35] All three systems were used in parallel.

Early nineteenth century hooks were made of finer wire than is commonly supposed and were smaller than any scale numbers given would suggest. Illustrations of early hooks are given by Brookes,[36] Bainbridge,[37] Williamson,[38] and in various plates in Daniel's *Rural Sports.*[39] Almost every one of these authors depicted the old Redditch scale, but for reasons best known to themselves, they seldom showed the entire series.

The logic behind some of the scales is baffling, and the late Jack Heddon speculated that many suppliers relied on measuring hooks by the width of their gape rather than shank length.[40] On first sight this seems a pretty odd idea, but there is a degree of logic behind it because blind hooks were often trimmed to length by the tyer, so the length of the shank of a finished fly could vary; some manufacturers use the same system today. By comparison, the old No. 13 was about 1/16" gape, the No. 11 was about 1/8" and the No. 9 was 3/16", corresponding to Nos. 17, 15 and 12 of the modern Redditch scale.

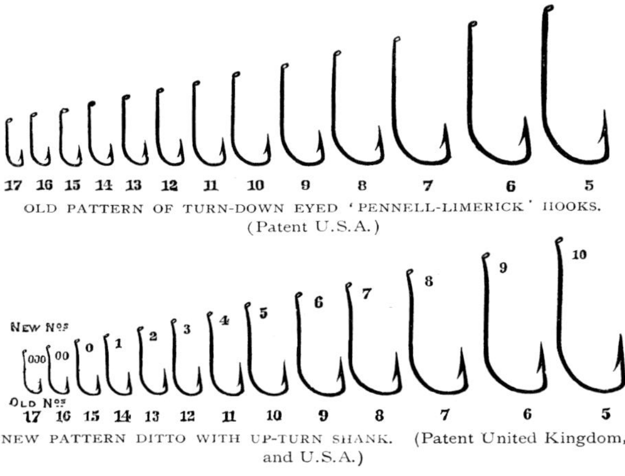

Hook scale

While hook manufacturing remained a cottage industry, confusion between scales wasn't too much of a problem and this may be why early authors shied away from mentioning them at all, but the perfection of manufacturing techniques in the early nineteenth century made it possible for hooks to be made in large numbers and distributed very widely. This brought a new problem; by the late nineteenth century there were at least five different hook scale systems in common use: Carlisle, Kendal, O'Shaughnessy Limerick, Dublin (or Phillips) Limerick, and Sell of Dublin. A growing market in conversion tables was the result and although eyed hooks fixed the shank length at long last, things hadn't improved very much by the 1930s:

> Hooks are still sold without any attention being paid to a standard of length; the No. 1 hook, for example, of one manufacturer is equal to the No. 0 or No. 2 of others. Limericks are always a size larger than their corresponding number in other makes. And in spite of many attempts outside the trade and one or two inside it there remains to this day a hopeless confusion of numbering, because there is no unit of length to which size has a definite relation.[41]

Sea Fishing

Although very little was published on the subject in book form in the late nineteenth century, a great deal of interest in saltwater fly fishing was being shown in the pages of the *Fishing Gazette*. Numerous articles were published in early *Gazettes*, including this one by 'Old Sportsman':

> As to salt-water flies, the one I consider superior to any is made with the pure white hair of a goat's beard, a portion of which is selected of a size and length to resemble a sprat or a sand eel, and tied on just as the wings of a salmon fly are, but to let the tying extend at least half an inch along the hook; a little red or yellow or light blue mohair is wound along the hook in the manner of the salmon fly and ribbed with broad gold or silver tinsel.[42]

Incidentally, the same author mentions in passing that mullet and bass, 'will not take the bait or fly... but they may be easily shot, and are frequently when they run about in the shallow water along the mud at the flood tide...' which shows, if nothing else, that early saltwater fishers had open minds on what made for good sport. If the range of killing methods was a catholic one, the range of quarry species was incredibly wide and columnists discuss trolling flies from a boat for pollack, lythe, mackerel, codling, mullet and sea trout, but without going into much detail about the patterns they used, suggesting that they weren't thought to be terribly important. So Dr Brunton, for example, mentions using 'a large dark brown salmon fly', a fly made from a white feather with a scarlet body and sundry yellow and dark grey flies, a casual approach which contrasts particularly sharply with the attention to detail which was being vested in trout flies at the time.[43] The general impression is hardly one of sophistication, although a lot of fish were being caught.

Things had not moved on very much by the end of the century and while British fishermen continued to fish flies in the salt, they did little to develop the sport and the subsequent history in the UK was one of decline. This is probably a reflection of the sad fact that few British fish have the power to compare with North American species like striped bass or bonefish. Given the type of tackle in use at the time, it would have been hard to work up much enthusiasm for a day's lythe-bashing, especially when fresh-water salmon were available as an alternative. The state of development of sea fishing everywhere was generally poor and no one seems to have made any attempt at a systematic study of the subject, with the result that by 1895, the author of *Sea Fishing* (part of the Badminton Library) was driven to remark that 'Fly fishing in the sea is a lottery.' He observed that the flies he fished imitated 'some marine insect or small fish', but it is clear that much less thought had gone into the patterns he quoted than was the case for fresh water flies of the time. His favourite was the 'whitebait' fly, which was an imitation of a small herring.

> The overwing is a strip of white feather from a swan's quill, the underwing being some strands of peacock harl. The hackle is of the same material, and the body, which is well padded, is covered with broad, flat, real silver tinsel. A few strands of harl form the tail.

The gear British anglers used at the time wasn't the sort of thing that was likely to attract bright young anglers to sea fishing. *Sea Fishing*, advocates backbreaking old Victorian tackle: a fifteen or sixteen foot two-handed greenheart rod, or an eleven foot six single-handed rod, fitted with either hardened German silver or phosphor bronze snake rings. Tackle of that sort of description seems laughable now, even in the era of ten to fourteen weight nine-foot saltwater rods, and we can only admire the men and women who were prepared to cast with it.

Interestingly, the same author wrote about catching salmon in saltwater, and cited a case where Sir John H. Morris caught five salmon on the fly in Loch Roag, Isle of Lewis in 1888, picking up on a practice first highlighted by Chitty earlier in the century. The text makes it clear that sea trout were caught in salt water in the late nineteenth century, and it seems to have been fairly common practice in the Scottish islands, with a few flies being developed specially for the purpose. One Orkney sea-trout fly of the period was dressed with a palmered fiery-brown cock hackle, and was intended to represent a sand hopper; another, rather more dubious in its claim to being a fly, was assembled by mounting a mouse tail on a hook. Rubber tube sand eel patterns were also used.

Sea Fishing is well worth reading, not only because the advice it gives is extremely sensible, but also because a couple of recent books published in Europe haven't done very much to advance upon it. In common with so many aspects of the sport, sea fly fishing lost its creative momentum in Europe at the turn of the century and from now on, the salt would belong to the Americans.

Casting

Authors writing before the nineteenth century show a curious reluctance to describe how to cast a line. One reason is that they lacked any established terminology with which to discuss it; a deficiency which must have made it a terrifying prospect for any writer. The other explanation is that there wasn't much reason to describe how to cast in much detail, since anyone who had sat behind a coachman could work out the basic principles for himself. But by 1850, 'whipping', the simple pick-up-and-lay-down cast which had been standard practice for so many centuries, had given way to a sophisticated range of specialised casts. This is a very good example of how outwardly simple changes in tackle can lead to radical developments in technique. The catalyst in this instance was the adoption of long, tapered silk lines which couldn't be fully extended with a single cast. These lines forced fishermen to explore new types of cast, in particular styles which allowed the shooting of a small amount of line, and methods which controlled how far the fly went behind the angler on the back cast. For almost the first time, fishermen found themselves in possession of lines too long to be cast by the average angler, yet were long enough to tangle with a distant tree on the back cast and the result was the invention of the majority of the casting styles we know today.

Anyway, one of the first really good descriptions of the mechanics of the overhead cast was made by Williamson in 1808, and as he might well have done, he remarked that it was odd that no one else had done so previously.[44] Williamson seemed to open the floodgates and after him we are spoilt for choice, but Fitzgibbon's account of casts, written nearly forty years later, is the most complete set of early descriptions.[45] Here we find overhead casting off the right and left shoulders, the switch cast, the 'Welsh throw', a brief description of the Spey cast, and the side cast. This is a wider range of casts than many anglers are capable of today, and since Fitzgibbon gave no hint that any of the methods he described were unusual, we can presume that they were all fairly well established at that date.

Working out exactly when these casts were invented is difficult. Switch casting and Spey casting require a relatively long line; at a guess these methods must date back no earlier than the eighteenth century, and the invention of the twisting engine. Side casting is a different matter, since it can't be done easily with a double-handed rod, and I suspect it didn't become a standard method until shorter single-handed rods became popular. Nevertheless, all the descriptions Fitzgibbon gave were good enough to follow, with the exception of the Spey cast. I'll leave you to make up your own mind about his explanation about that one:

> There is an under-handed throw much in use on the Spey, which prevents the line from circling behind. Of course this is a great advantage among trees or other obstacles. It is generally practised upstream, and the line with its 'swish' upon the water, goes over all the fish before they see the fly, which appears to me to be a great objection. These Spey fishers can throw this under-handed cast as far as an expert hand in the ordinary way. A peculiar rod is necessary, which must be very stiff. Indeed, a common salmon rod would be apt to break in the hands of these fishers. The cast is easily learned, but must be seen to be thoroughly understood.[46]

If Fitzgibbon had witnessed Spey casting, he can't have devoted much time to studying it, because although Spey rods of the day did have an odd-looking curved top, they certainly weren't stiff and in general they were as loose as an old whore's stays. Spey casting was a well-kept secret, and it seems that very few people outside Scotland actually knew how to do it before the 1890s, by which time very few of the casting styles which we rely on today remained to be discovered.

Casting methods may have been in a different league to the previous century, but they hadn't completely cracked it in 1850 and despite the many advances in technique that had taken place, casting into the wind was still fraught with difficulty:

> We recommend the beginner never to endeavour to cast a line against the wind. It is an extremely difficult and dangerous operation, and can only be performed by an old practitioner, and even by him, not satisfactorily unless he use a stiff rod and a hair reel-line.[47]

Salmon fishing methods were very different in those early days of mass addiction to the sport and some of the methods in use would have looked very strange to us. 'Working' the fly was so popular that it was almost universal, chiefly because it was thought important that the wing of a salmon fly should 'open and close', so many anglers enthusiastically jiggled their rod tips up and down to give the lure a lively action, a technique which was still being advocated by Joe Brooks as late as 1972. When a big fish was caught the angler 'butted' it, by pointing the rod far back over his shoulder, and literally showing the butt to the fish. Butting was widely held to put great pressure on the fish, although a moment's thought about the laws of physics should have knocked that one on the head. Butting did on the other hand, make for distractingly beautiful etchings and in any event, logic didn't carry any more weight among anglers then than it does now. In a way, the use of butting was understandable, given the soft rods which were in general use during the middle years of the century, and the classic picture in any book of the period is of an heroic angler with his rod thrown back over his shoulder, the tip bent in an impossible curve, a great swirl in the water, and a villainous-looking ghillie lurking nearby, ready to reach out and snag the prize with a vicious gaff.

Butting a fish

Silk Lines

In the 1860s and 1870s, thirty yards 'from the reel to the fly' would have been a very good cast for a salmon angler. The longest cast that Francis Francis ever witnessed was thirty-eight and a half yards from fly to reel, which was achieved using a twenty foot salmon rod, and the longest cast he ever made personally was thirty-four and a half yards, a distance which few anglers could achieve today. Cast your eye back to the distances fishermen could achieve in the 1850s, and you can see what an improvement had occurred. Part of this increase in distance could be put down to greenheart, but as much of it was due to developments in fly lines. The new-found ease with which tapered lines could be manufactured was a milestone in fly fishing, but it took quite a while for the new lines to establish themselves, which was partly because the vast majority of them were made entirely from silk. Tapered fly lines had been around for at least a hundred years, but low quality meant that they weren't popular until late in the nineteenth century.

Good horsehair became increasingly difficult to obtain after 1860 and very few quality horsehair lines were made after that date, although it is still possible to buy them if you know where to look.[48] The result was that the use of horsehair lines began to die out after the 1870s, although the material still had vocal adherents many decades later. The fact that anyone was prepared to defend a superannuated material like horsehair may seem perverse, but good braided horsehair lines lasted decades if cared for properly; whereas early silk lines were very prone to rot. Nevertheless, by the third quarter of the nineteenth century horsehair's day was done. It didn't happen a moment too soon, because at long last fishermen could buy large diameter single-action reels. Braided lines of a hundred yards or more were needed to fill them, and this was beyond the limit of anything that could be achieved with horsehair.

By the mid-1880s, a great revolution of thought had occurred and a forty yard fly line and one hundred to one hundred and twenty yards of 'thin back line' were reasonably standard issue for the 'modern' salmon angler. Before the late nineteenth century, the majority of anglers saw no distinction between the fly line and the backing, which were one and the same. Thinner backing meant that more line could be wound on the reel and a fish could be allowed to run much further without the risk of a break caused by the drag of a thick drowned line.

Horsehair was not the only victim of industrialisation. With the price of labour beginning to rise, the dominance of hand-made materials could not last forever. By the late 1850s, the majority of fly lines were machine made, and eight-plait silk lines were in common use, usually combined with a tapered gut 'cast' or 'collar' between the fly and the fly line. The 1890s saw the early enamelled silk lines, which kinked horribly and sometimes cut rod rings, begin to be replaced by technically superior oil dressed silk, with the dry-fly men taking the lead. There was a substantial trailing edge to this succession and enamelled lines were still available in the 1930s and 40s.

Oil dressed silk lines were wonderfully supple and a joy to cast and although they became the bench mark for fly lines between 1890 and 1960, it can't be said that they were perfect. The great advantage of oiled silk was that it made for a thin, dense line, which could be cast with great ease, but the finish was soft and wore away with the result that lines had to be dressed almost every day if there was to be any hope of them floating well. The finish had a strong tendency to oxidise and soon became tacky, which ruined its casting properties, and the only cure was to wash the line in an alkaline solution and then go through an incredibly tedious routine of refinishing the line with repeated coats of linseed oil. If lines were carelessly stored, they rotted and grew eye-catching multi-coloured fungi. To add insult to injury, many of the new silk dressed lines were hollow, and these had a horrible tendency to rot secretly from the inside out, sometimes within days of their first use. Perhaps the best lines of the day were made by Eaton and Deller, who had the distinction of manufacturing the first braided silk fly lines with an oil dressing.

Many anglers ended up buying two lines, winding one of them on to the drier each night so that it would be ready the following day. Obsessional line care might have been a necessity, but silk offered so many advantages over the competition that fishermen were prepared to go to enormous trouble. A typical treatment involved boiling raw linseed oil and copal varnish until the mixture singed a feather, cooling it and then soaking the line in it for a week or more. On a fine day the line was stretched out between two posts and all the superfluous dressing removed with a cloth. A week of good weather was needed for the line to dry thoroughly and if it was rained on in the early stages the dressing was likely to wash off, which must have been a bit of a trial for anyone living anywhere in the British Isles. After another fortnight, the line had to be re-dipped in the solution, stretched and re-wiped, and allowed to dry again. And at the completion of all this patient preparation, conventional wisdom said that the line shouldn't be used for six months, but was instead to be hung up indoors and put out in the open air whenever the weather was favourable. It truly was a time for patience.

The reason why people were prepared to go to so much trouble to care for silk lines was that tapered silk gave a huge advantage over level horsehair. Once anyone had ever fished with silk they were reluctant to go back to the traditional materials; silk could be cast further, mended, and generally controlled so completely that it altered the face of fly fishing. Silk lines were a revolutionary invention, and only the development of floating PVC lines would have more impact on casting distances and angling techniques.

Silk was not the only game in town. In the search for the ideal fly line, all sorts of ideas were tried, which lead inventors up some entertaining, but otherwise completely blind alleys. By the 1880s, it was possible to buy fly lines made from an extraordinarily wide range of materials. This experimentation was driven by the cost of state of the art braided silk lines, which were very expensive, fetching between ten and fifteen shillings (for the benefit of American readers, there were twenty shillings to the pound). Mixed silk and horsehair lines were still available, and although they were no better than they had been a hundred years previously, they were popular because they were cheap, fetching between about four and eleven shillings each. Astonishingly, lines made of human hair were available for a brief period, but they failed to do well since they cost twice as much as a line made of any other material, absorbed a great deal of water, and stretched particularly badly.[49] Twisted or plaited hemp lines enjoyed a brief period of use, if not popularity; although they had the advantage of being very cheap indeed, they were thick, required special preparation and rotted quickly. The copper wire-centred silk line was another short lived innovation, made available in the early 1880s by Foster Bros. of Ashbourne, Derbyshire. Doubtless there were other, even more improbable solutions, but fortunately all record of them has disappeared.

For the first time, the distances that experts could achieve began to vastly exceed those of amateurs, and during this period casting competitions enjoyed a period of tremendous popularity. Forty-three yards was a typical winning tournament cast between 1880 and 1936 (by 1915, the salmon fly overhead cast record stood at fifty-four yards, with the Spey cast at little over forty-one yards.) In 1896, Mr Grant of Inverness, a man well known for his 'Vibration' series of greenheart rods, cast fifty-six yards using one of his twenty foot rods, though for various reasons this wasn't classified as a record. Grant later achieved the astonishing distance of seventy-four yards with a switch cast, but this was accomplished on grass.[50] The 'Vibration' rods were made by planing down the wood until the rod gave the correct note when struck with a tuning fork, a process which Grant publicised in the pages of *Land and Water* magazine during 1893. A variety of suppliers made Vibrations, at least some of whom are said to have sourced their timber from peculiar places such as the water-soaked timbers of the redundant Tay bridge and the pilings of the old docks at Aberdeen.

These records show how far equipment had developed from the days when the angler was entirely at the mercy of the wind direction, and they were a huge improvement on the distances achieved even twenty years earlier. By 1900, everyday casting distances had approximated to those achieved today, and Hardy was able to talk of twenty to thirty yards as an 'easy' cast with a salmon rod, a distance which would have challenged Fitzgibbon only half a century previously. Trout casting techniques had reached a level of considerable maturity by the time the First World War broke out, a measure of this being the forty-four yard world record cast established in San Francisco in 1902.

Mrs and Major Grant

Salmon Fishing

By the last quarter of the nineteenth century, salmon fishing had come of age. It was no longer a great adventure, as it had been in Scrope's day; it had rapidly accumulated a burden of tradition and convention, and there was much less sense of an exciting venture into the unknown. Salmon fishers still cast down and across, as they had since the discovery that salmon would take a fly, but the sport was well enough understood that angling manuals dealt with it as a matter of course, and books begin to be littered with the sort of diagrams that virtually promised a hooked fish if the angler could only cast to point A and fish patiently around to point B. This isn't to say that there wasn't anything left to discover, far from it. One of the advances made during this period was the introduction of mending, a technique which was probably discovered in the 1840s or 1850s.

Major John Traherne was one of the first to advocate the mend in order to avoid the line bellying and pulling the fly head-first downstream. It was a novel concept at the time. The majority of salmon fishermen seldom worried about what the fly was doing once it had sunk out of sight, unless they concentrated on 'working' it. Traherne seems to have been ahead of his time and it seems that the widespread adoption of mending can be dated to the 1870s, although a few individuals had practised it for very much longer. Once the mend was widely adopted, salmon fishermen became more concerned about the path the fly took under water, the size of fly, and the dressing, until it became a subject of obsessive interest. A symptom of this is the alteration in the way casts were made between 1850 and 1900. In the middle decades of the century, tapered gut casts were the norm, built from seven or eight lengths of the longest threads of triple gut twisted together using machines which could be found in any fishing tackle shop. After twisting, the lengths were joined, building in a taper as the line was constructed. Single slip knots were used, 'lapping the ends over' with waxed silk thread which was varnished at the finish. After the triple gut line came four or five lengths of hand-picked gut, tapered in thickness to the end where the fly was to be attached. The fly gut was normally attached with a loop, but some writers suggested a 'common knot' as it disturbed the water less.

All this knotting and whipping was fiercely complicated, and the last years of the century brought a move away from the use of treble-twisted or plaited gut. Instead, fishermen resorted to a couple of untwisted strands of round gut, whipped together and looped on to the fly line, or they relied on single gut. A properly soaked, well prepared cast made this way was expected to have a breaking strain of twenty pounds, compared to a knotted cast that might snap at seven and a half pounds. But in spite of every precaution, gut was so temperamental that casts had to be checked several times a day for defective links, and it was wise to discard a cast entirely after three or four months use. Thank God for nylon.

During this period, really good fly fishing equipment became available for the first time, and anglers were freed at last from the constant worry of tackle failure. Firms like Hardy, Farlow and Orvis supplied equipment that had attained a measure of perfection, and from now on rods, reels and lines would be regarded merely as the method of delivering the fly to the fish. This allowed minds to concentrate on the 'hows' and 'whys' of salmon fishing in a way that had never happened before.

Reels

Despite the many voices calling for a fundamental redesign, narrow diameter spindles remained a common feature on reels until at least the 1890s. There were some exceptions, of course, and it wasn't long before Eaton were producing a five inch diameter narrow reel with a spindle an inch in diameter, but many anglers had to resort to winding pack thread around narrow spindles in order to increase their working diameter.

Manufacturers did retool in the end and the development of the reel was financed by the enormous increase in the popularity of salmon fishing, an effect which was felt in all areas of the tackle trade. Well-heeled salmon fishers travelled widely, and the money they spent led to an explosion of ingenuity. Some beautiful products were produced, so much so that this period can be regarded as the apogee of brass winch design. The pick of the bunch were the 'return handle' reels (whose handles could be unscrewed and reversed to lock the reel and avoid damage during transport.) The ultimate design of the era was perhaps the Jones' folding handle reel, which did away with the need to unscrew the handle for travelling thanks to a clever locking joint. However, these leading-edge products were pricey and they were far beyond the pocket of the majority of fishermen.

Developments in Britain were mirrored in America, where by 1845, indigenous reels had almost completely replaced imported products. By the mid-nineteenth century, the American fisherman was dependent on Europe for little more than gut. American reel design equalled, and in some respects surpassed, its British counterpart during this period. The outstanding reel of the era was known simply as the 'Orvis Reel'. In 1856 a young man had established a tackle business in Manchester, Vermont, that would ultimately become one of the icons of fly fishing. Charles F. Orvis chose his location well, because by the mid 1800s the Green Mountains had attracted a vacation trade among affluent young Americans who came to take their ease in a town which boasted the most beautiful main street in North America. Within twenty years, the shop where he had once served over the counter became too busy for him to manage alone and he had to hire his daughter Mary to run the fly tying trade, but somewhere along the line he found time to sit down and design one of the first recognisably modern reels.[51] Available in a trout model for $2.50 and a bass model for $3.00, the Orvis reel was deep and narrow between the plates, a combination of features which allowed a very fast retrieve. It first appeared in 1874, and was modified

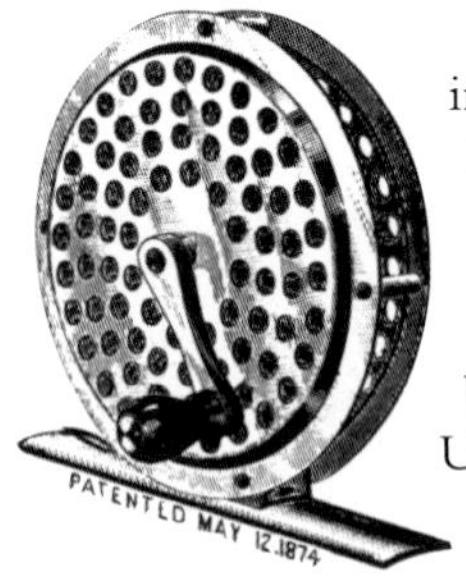

The Orvis reel

in 1875 to build in a check. The plates were ventilated, and apart from its lack of an interchangeable spool and crank arm, the Orvis product was a thoroughly modern design. From now on, there would be an increasing trend for fly reel development to be dominated by American machine technology. US firms like Chubb, Leonard, Orvis, Pflueger, Meisselbach and Vom Hofe catered for every pocket and their designs gave the American market a momentum that it never lost.

By now, in Britain at least, multipliers were becoming curiosities, but despite the consolidation of the market, some oddities were still being produced. Typical of the kind of experimentation going on at the time were Holmes' rods, which had the winch fitted into the butt. Bizarre though this invention seems now (or so it did when I began this book; Sage have just rediscovered the idea), it sold well enough that the design continued to be available in various guises for many years. Foster of Ashbourne's 'Skeleton centre winch', is another good example of an 'advance' which didn't quite take the market by storm. Another invention which didn't catch on was the side-mount reel, which put the reel foot on the side of the reel frame, rather than the top, with the result that the reel sat horizontally on the butt of the rod. A design of this sort was patented by Billinghurst of Rochester, New York. It was modified and refined so much by many other tackle makers that it became quite popular for a short period, though quite why escapes me.

Reels were getting lighter, as a result of the use of new metals, particularly aluminium. This spelt the death knell for brass, which had been the mainstay of reel manufacture for several centuries, because it was so easy to work with and attractive to boot. Aluminium had been around for a while; it was discovered as early as 1709, but it was very hard to extract, and its properties weren't appreciated for another two hundred years. The first experimental casting began in 1855, but at that time the metal cost more than gold to refine, so it was hardly popular. It wasn't until the early 1880s that production of aluminium became possible at commercially viable prices, when it was discovered that it could be smelted using electrical power.

Tackle makers were quick to realise the advantages of the new material, but the early alloys were brittle, and at first aluminium made little ground. Instead, there was a brief vogue for all sorts of exotic materials. Gun-metal was popular for a while, but since it was almost as heavy as the brass it replaced, it didn't last long. Curious though it may seem, rubber was a mainstay of fly reel construction between 1851 (when Goodyear put in his first patent for rubber processing) and about 1925. The hard rubber which was used to make reels isn't necessarily easy to recognise and it went under various brand names like Ebonite, Xylonite, and Vulcanite.

Ebonite, a material formed from rubber with a twenty to thirty per cent sulphur content, was extremely popular, chiefly because it was hard enough to take a polish, so well that in some cases the result looked almost like a metal. Ebonite reels were very common from the 1870s onward, but the material faded back into obscurity after the end of the First World War, although it continued to be used for reel handles for a little while after that. Ebonite was light, which is why it was so popular, but it was also fragile. It was replaced to a certain extent by Bakelite, a phenolic plastic, which was used in cheaper reels from 1909 until 1950 or so. But rubber was a diversion: from 1914 onwards, the vast majority of quality reels were made from aluminium alloy.

Vom Hofe Hard Rubber Reel

Another advance made during this time was the elimination of the crank handle. Cranks were common on reels and they were the bane of fishermen's lives, because the line was inclined to tangle around the lever at awkward moments. Fixing the handle to the side-plate was a major contribution not only towards reel design but to anglers' sanity. A few suppliers went one stage further and eliminated the handle as well. Ronalds mentioned an automatic reel which used a spiral spring to wind up the line; it is possible that this was the Chesterman self-winding reel that Shipley wrote about in 1838.[52] In 1880, Yawman & Erbe, of Rochester, New York, advertised an automatic reel, an invention that would become immensely popular in its land of origin. Shakespeare also produced an automatic fly reel which was very successful.

The 1880s were the golden age of fly reels, and many of the most collectible reels were designed or manufactured during this period. There is no shortage of examples. Vom Hofe, a German immigrant to America, marketed a range of reels including the imposingly-named Celebrated Trout and Bass Fly Reel, which had an on/off, non-adjustable drag in addition to a sliding check, an unheard of degree of sophistication. The Vom Hofe reels of the 1880s were made of high quality steel, featured hand-cut countersunk screws, phosphor-bronze springs and axle, and boasted a commitment to quality which has rarely been matched since.

The Adjustable Drag

We don't know who invented the first adjustable reel drag, though Pulman recommended an early version in 1851, but one of the best examples was designed by George Kelson and marketed by Farlow and Co. Ltd. of 191 The Strand. After a shaky start, Farlow boasted an excellent track record of development of reels, having paid particular attention to them since the 1860s.

Kelson's reel was sold as the 'Patent Lever Winch'. This product was a small masterpiece of design, with the handle fitted in a counter-sunk bearing, screwed (rather than bolted) fittings and, of course, an adjustable drag. The 'handle' side of the reel was constructed of three discs, the middle disc fixed as part of the reel frame, the outer and inner revolving together. Although it was initially made from brass, later versions of the reel were built of aluminium. The Patent Lever embodied all the features of a modern reel, save for an exposed rim and wide spindle, but the one feature which made it stand out was the brutal efficiency of its drag mechanism. Fully tightened, the Patent Lever could stop a runaway brewer's dray, and the smoothness and power of the drag compares very well with disk drag reels designed and built a century later. Prices for this small marvel of Victorian ingenuity ranged from 42s. 6d. for a three and a half inch reel, to 70s. for a five inch one. If you wanted yours built in aluminium alloy it was available at a twenty-five per cent premium. The biggest model, large enough to carry a hundred and twenty yards of plaited silk line, was almost as light as a feather at a mere fourteen and a half ounces.

The Patent Lever Winch from The Salmon Fly *by Kelson*

Kelson's reel was very successful; Farlow marketed it into the 1920s, but it was eclipsed by a design from an upstart rival:

> Messrs. Hardy, of Alnwick, have designed a reel of which I can only speak from hearsay, but those who have used it declare that the title it bears – the 'Perfect' – involves no exaggeration. It runs on ball bearings, and is made of alumin, an alloy of aluminium, weighing very slightly more than the pure metal, and far stronger. The reverse plate is perforated, whereby damp is allowed to evaporate from the line, and above the handle is a screw to regulate the pressure of the check. These reels are produced at a wonderfully low price; one with a diameter of $3^1/_2$ inches, weighing $12^1/_2$ oz., costs 35s.; with a diameter of 5 inches, weighing 27 oz., costs 60s.[53]

The Perfect was a milestone. As James Leighton Hardy recently pointed out, Hardys did not make their own reels prior to the Perfect, preferring to re-badge Peter Malloch's products instead. The Perfect was their first home grown product and it catapulted the young company from the status of bit player into the major league. Within a very few years it became the standard by which all other reels were judged.

Forster Hardy's design was introduced in 1891 and included most of the improvements that fishermen had been requesting for fifty years: it was narrow between the plates, deep in the drum and had an adjustable check. It had a plate foot mounting, a patent 'revolving ring line guard' and it ran smoothly on ball-bearings. Best of all, it could be taken apart for cleaning. This ease of disassembly was part of the key to the Perfect's success. Until the Hardy design appeared, the side plates of reels were held together with screwed intermediate bars, and a reel with grit inside it was a nightmare to clean. The only thing the Perfect lacked was an exposed rim - though it could have had one. William Senior, angling editor of *The Field*, wrote about this very improvement in correspondence with Hardys, but for some reason his suggestion was never taken up.

The Hardy Perfect

The Perfect marked a decisive break from the old-fashioned narrow spindle, wide barrel reel, and it was the forerunner of a modern generation of well-designed, adjustable drag, single-action devices. Hardys can rightly claim that the Perfect is the most successful reel ever made, and it has remained in production for the best part of a century, during which time many dozens of variations and improvements to the original design have been made.

From now on, reel manufacturers were able to concentrate increasingly on detail and there were few major design changes. There were still a few tricks left to learn. Hardys scored another first with their release of the 'Halford' improved St George reel, which had finger-operated catch for releasing the spool; a modification of which is used on the majority of modern reels. Yet another innovation was produced by the Perth firm P. D. Malloch. Their 'Sun and Planet' reel was named after the gearing arrangement within the casing. The handle was attached to a small cog, so arranged that when a fish took line, the side plate of the reel didn't revolve – the handle simply span on its own axis until the angler gripped it. The gear design was brilliant; solving several problems at a stroke, but otherwise the reel was no match for its rivals and the Sun and Planet never achieved much by way of sales. But it wasn't forgotten, because the design inspired the 'anti-reverse' fly reels which began to appear after the Second World War, and which are currently so popular for saltwater fly fishing.

Trout Fishing: the Wet-Fly Schools

Ronalds had more or less fixed the southern English tradition of winged wet-fly fishing in the 1830s, but the regional schools retained their strength and the Scots were foremost among the dissenters:

> What, I naturally ask, are the notions of such anglers with respect to the tastes, or, it may be, the optics of the trout? Do they suppose this fish, in regard to its surface food, so singularly capricious as to refuse all others but the insect of the day, so whimsical as even to resist the claims of hunger itself, unless wrought on by the appearance of some peculiarly streaked water-fly? Do they fancy it discriminative of every shade or hue in the wing, body and feelers of its prey? – keenly sensible of the smallest deviation in colour, more so than of a defect in shape, from the natural insect? If such their conclusions, I cannot help affirming that they give credit to the fish in question for possessing a power of discrimination, not less than a degree of daintiness, altogether extraordinary.[54]

It was a fair question. Thomas Tom Stoddart, who posed it, fished with a very small variety of flies, limiting himself to a red or brown hackle, with or without wings; a black hackle, with or without wings; and a winged hare's lug. This dependence on only a few patterns characterises the Scottish school and although it is often assumed that it worked because of a lack of education or the gullibility of native trout, nothing could be further from the truth. Proof of this is that the flies were used by a large number of professional fishermen in Scotland, including David Webster, who was introduced in a previous chapter; Stoddart was effectively one of them and he had learned his craft the hard way. Some measure of his character can be gained from his famous reply to an innocent query by his friend, Sheriff Glassford Bell. When the latter asked what he did, Stoddart was so taken aback that he was momentarily lost for words, "Doing?" he exclaimed. "Man, I'm an angler!"

At the age of twenty-three, Stoddart abandoned the law for a lifetime devoted to fishing and poetry, settling, in rather uncertain financial circumstances, on the banks of his beloved Tweed. His best known book on fishing was published when he was thirty-seven and quickly became a classic. Stoddart's opinion was echoed by Stewart, who had equally little time for the conviction that it was necessary to closely match the hatch, and invariably fished a lightly-dressed palmer or 'spider'. Stewart certainly caught his share of fish, and in true Scottish style, he had awards to prove it. On the other hand, some of his theories had a slightly crackpot air:

> The artificial flies in common use may be divided into two classes. There is first the winged fly, which alone, properly speaking, merits the appellation; and there is the palmer hackle or spider, by the last name we mean to call it, believing that if it resembles anything in the insect tribe, it is a spider. As a means of capturing trout, we rank them higher than the winged imitations.[55]

Stewart's spiders are interesting, because he used them with his upstream short-casting technique in a very similar way to the method used by anglers in the north of England, who used an unrelated set of spider patterns. This parallel development of similar flies for different reasons is fascinating, but it is also important because it marks the beginning of a glacially slow collective realisation that the traditional winged fly didn't represent the last word in the evolution of the wet fly. Although this change in attitude didn't bear fruit for nearly a century, it paved the way for modern patterns.

The 'North Country' school was a strong one, and to a large extent, it still exists, with traditional patterns still available from many local tackle dealers. The beginnings of the school and its distinctive patterns can be found in a manuscript written by John Swarbrick, who farmed near Ilkley in Yorkshire at the beginning of the nineteenth century.[56] Swarbrick's selection of flies was modified and refined by later generations of northern anglers including Pritt, Jackson, Theakston and Edmonds and Lee.

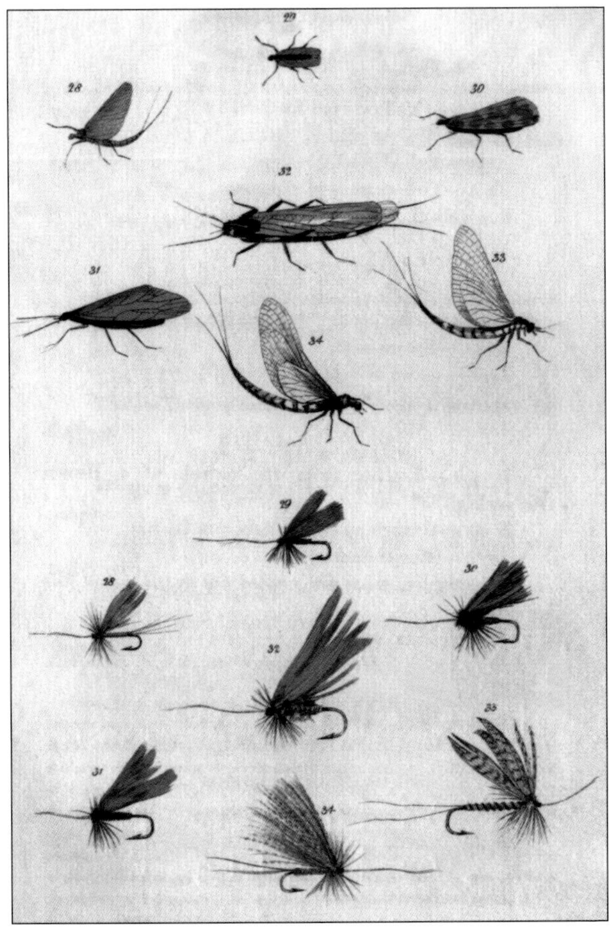

North country flies from Jackson's Practical Fly Fishing

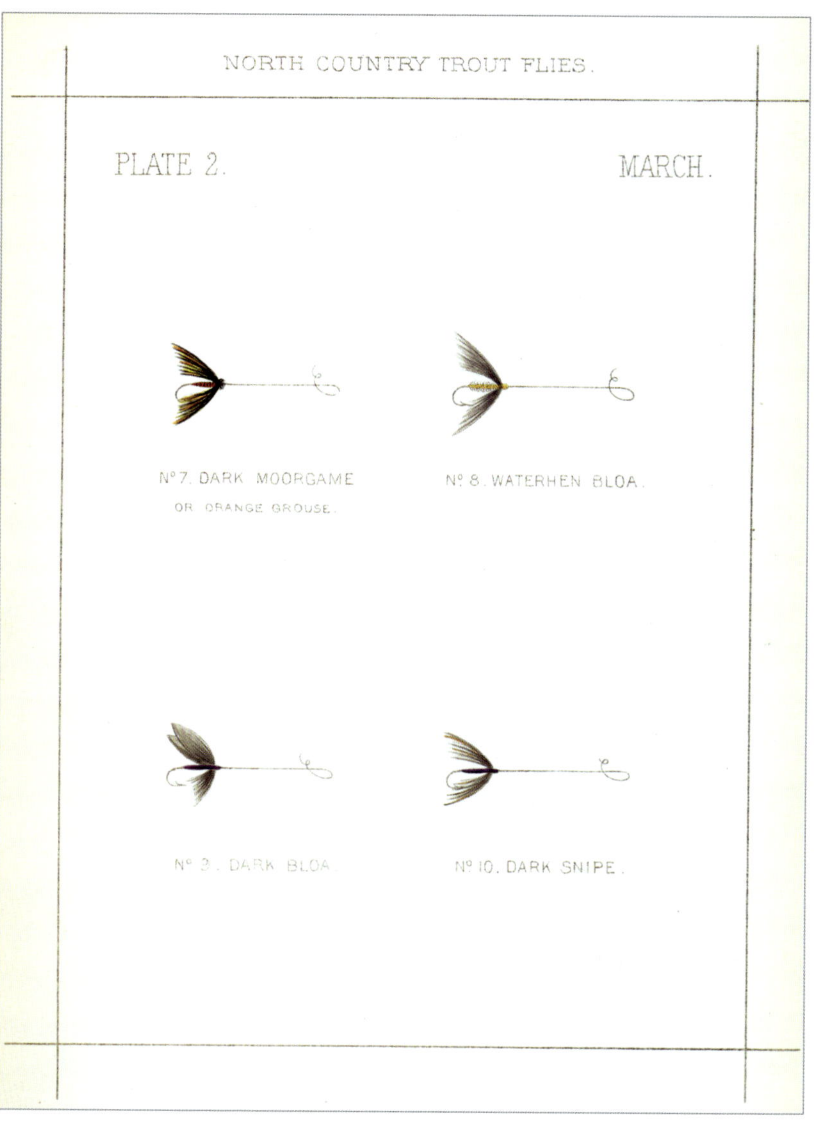

Pritt. A selection of English north-country flies of the late nineteenth century.

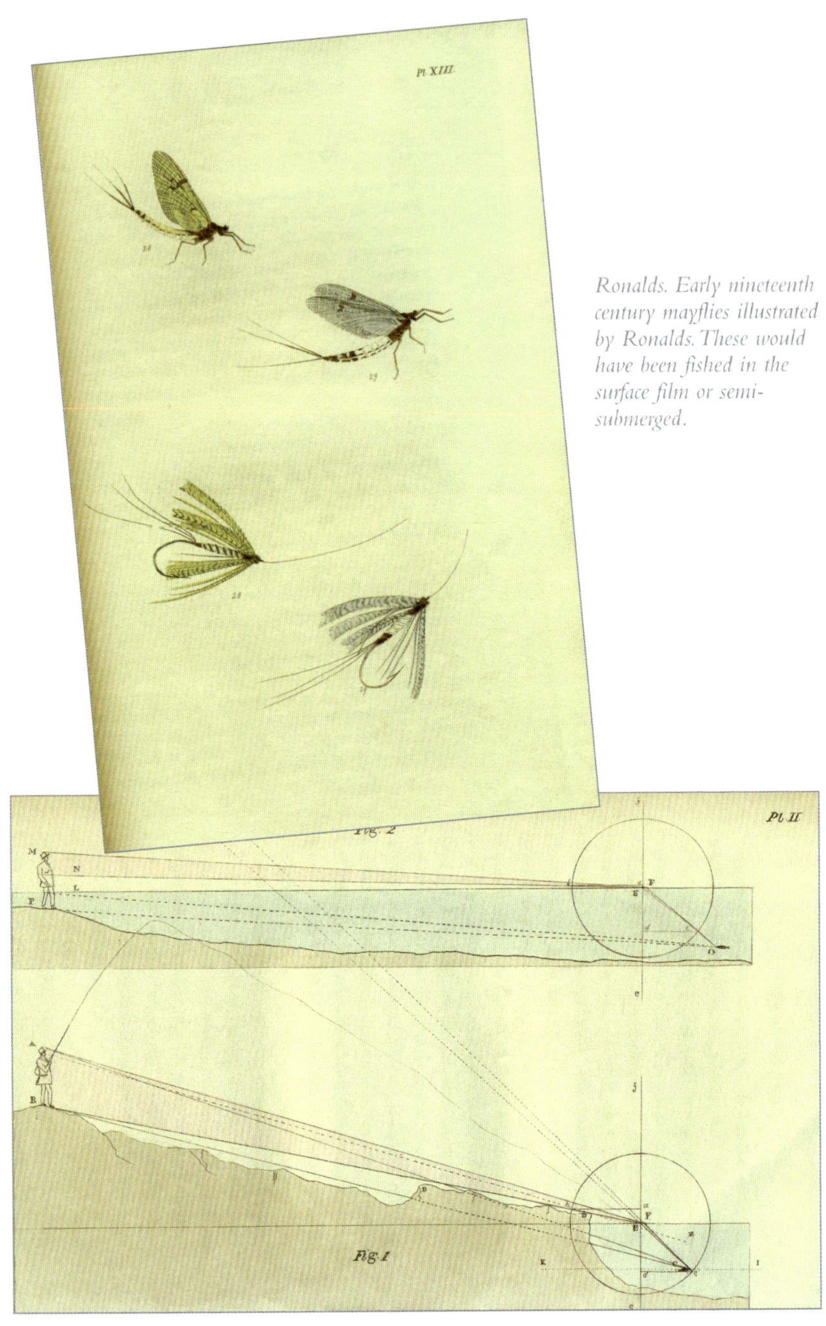

Ronalds. Early nineteenth century mayflies illustrated by Ronalds. These would have been fished in the surface film or semi-submerged.

Ronalds was among the first to demonstrate the importance of refraction to fishermen.

Scrope. Typical late eighteenth/early nineteenth century salmon flies.
1. Kinmont Willie 2. The Lady of Mertoun 3. Toppy 4. Michael Scott
5. Meg with the Muckle Mouth 6. Meg in her Braws

Bowlker, The Art of Angling, *1839 ed (frontis). Though this is an early nineteenth century illustration, the flies are typical of the patterns used for decades beforehand.*

Stoddart. Early nineteenth century Tweed salmon flies. In the text these are simply named after the winging material, typical for flies of this era.

Jones, Guide to Norway. *The revolutionaries - some of the patterns that inspired the fashion for gaudy salmon flies, which began in the mid-nineteenth century.*

Ephemera, The Book of the Salmon Fly, *1850 (frontis). Another illustration of what was to come: Fitzgibbon's frontis depicts flies far removed from those Scrope favoured.*

Newland, The Erne *(frontis showing the Fairy Fly). Newland's work shows a fertile imagination, but nowhere is it more evident than in the frontis.*

Illustration of Blacker's method for tying a trout fly.

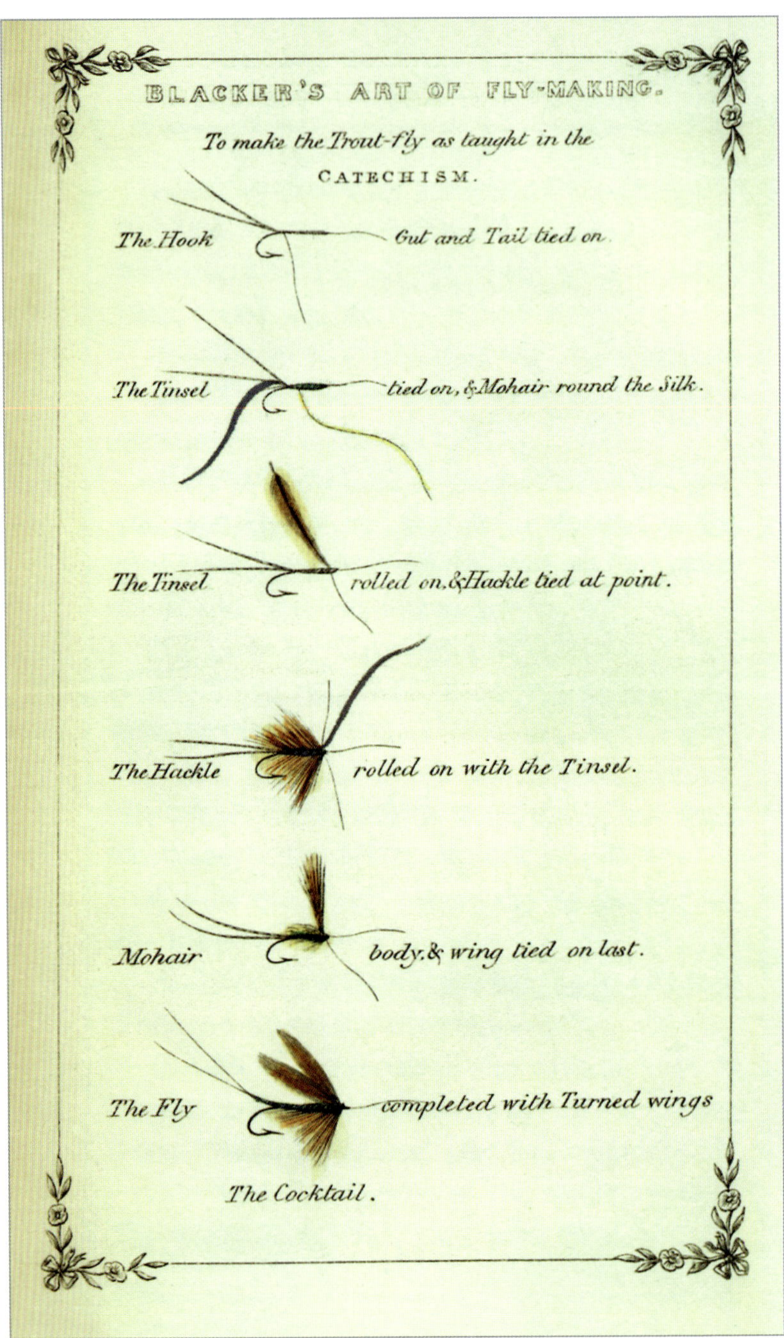

Blacker's materials - this plate shows how different nineteenth century hackles were to modern day 'genetic' ones.

Illustration of Blacker's method for tying a salmon fly.

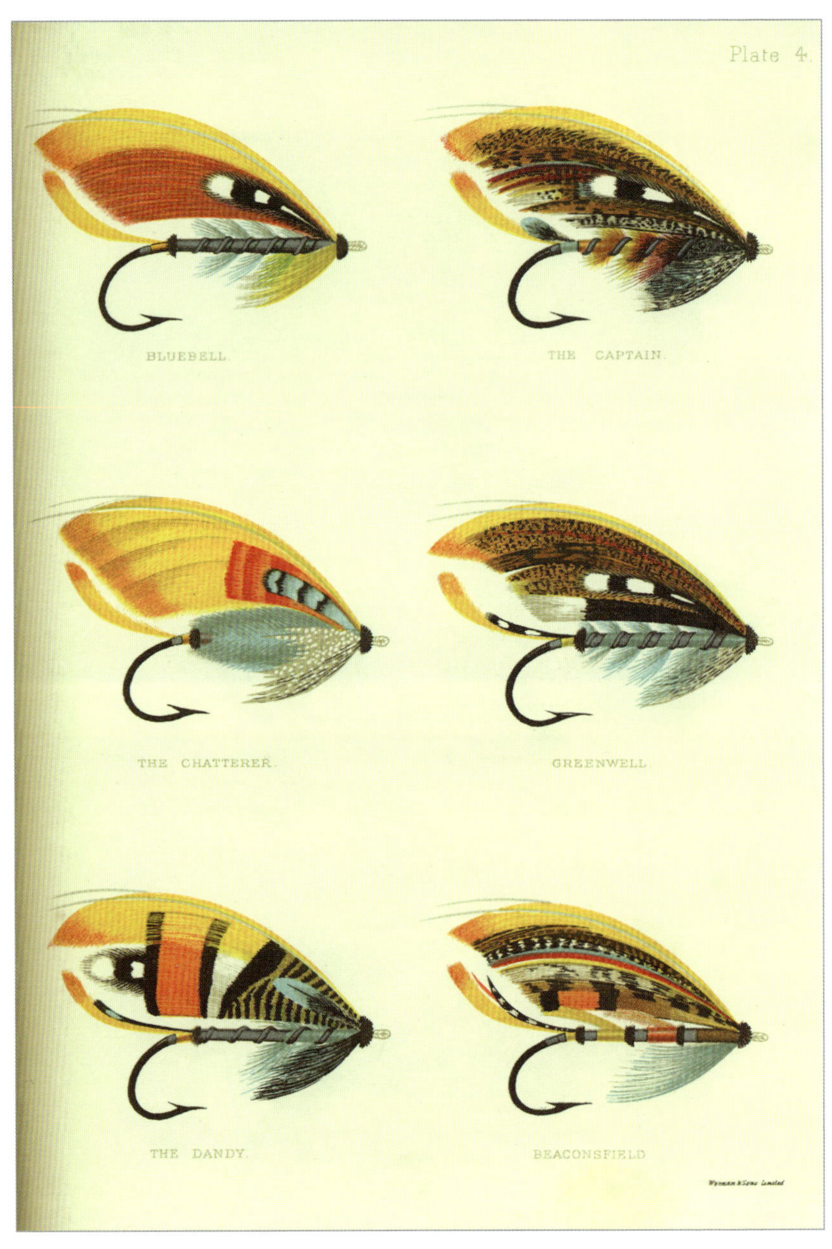

Kelson. Typical gaudy salmon flies of the late nineteenth century.

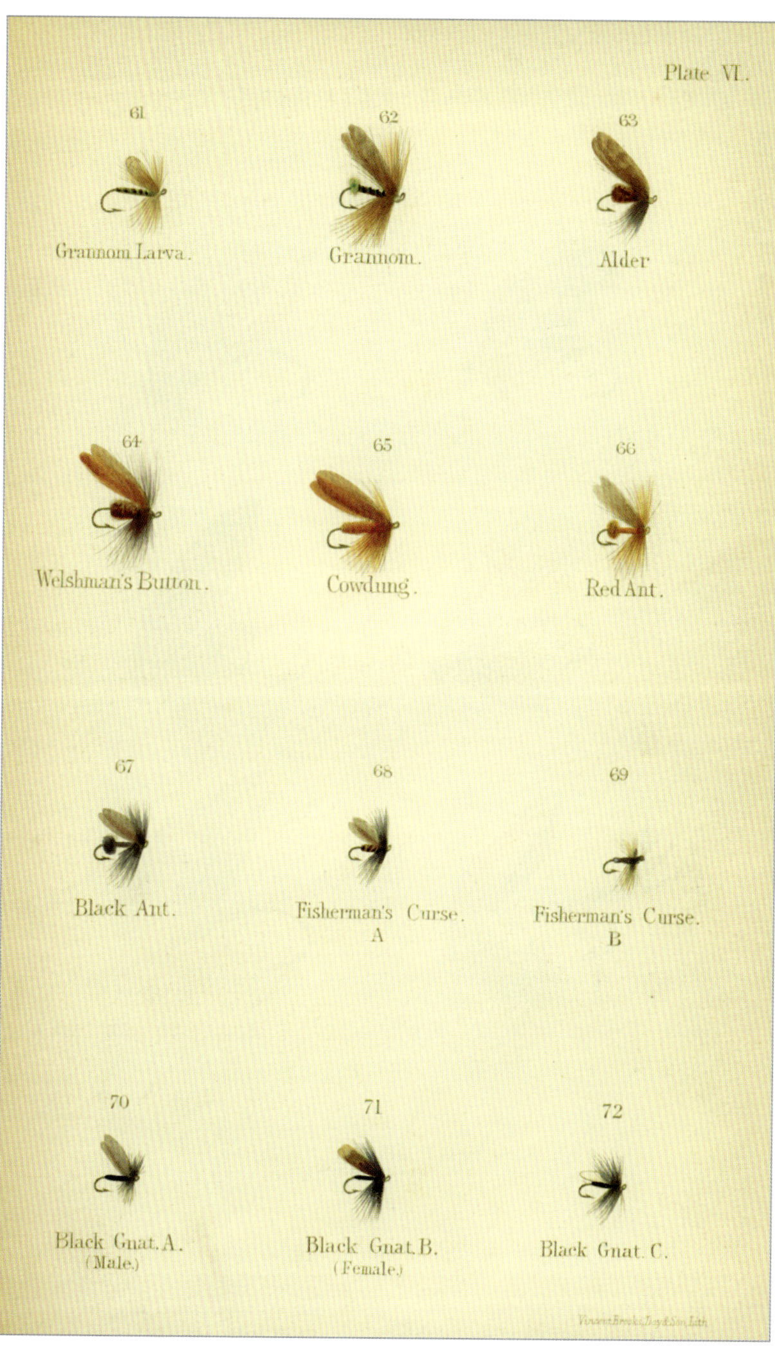

Halford, Floating Flies and How to Dress Them. *In the early years, Halford carried a surprisingly large range of terrestial patterns; including the artificial which he called the Welshman's Button and which Skues did not.*

BASS FLIES.

Made by C.F.ORVIS, Manchester, Vt.

COPYRIGHTED.

Marbury plate Y - bass flies of the late nineteenth century. The Ferguson is number 250.
The others are: 246. Bob White 247. Caddis, cork body
248. Epting 249. Gov. Alvord 251. De Gem

Skues, Minor Tactics of the Chalk Stream *(frontis). Skues' initial selection of flies shows patterns that had more in common with emergers than nymphs - 'damp flies' if you like.*

A typical spike foot reel. These are rarely found in good condition, but this one shows the typical features of this once popular reel type.

Clamp foot reels were more common than spiked reels and this one shows the wide drum and narrow spindle characteristic of reels of this period. The clamp would have had a leather circlet sewn inside to protect the handle of the rod. The small lever locks the drum.

An early narrow drum reel loaded with horsehair line. This one has a curved arm which the line must have fouled on a fairly regular basis.

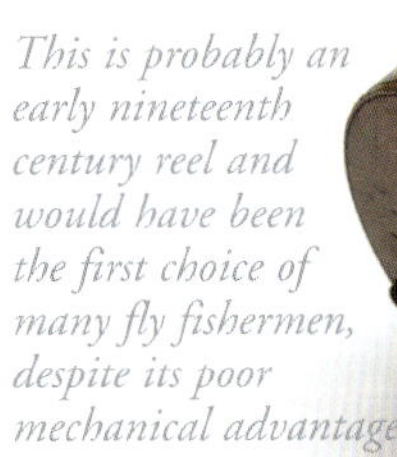

This is probably an early nineteenth century reel and would have been the first choice of many fly fishermen, despite its poor mechanical advantage.

A Chevalier, Bowness & Bowness reel made at 230 The Strand, London. This is a typical late nineteenth century trout reel.

A top of the range Jones folding handle salmon reel, built in the 1850s in Jermyn Street, London and designed to kill big fish in Norway.

The interesting thing about the North Country Spiders is that they seem to have little in common with Stewart's patterns beyond the name and indeed they represent a quite separate line of development. North Country Spiders are sparsely dressed, with as little as a single turn of soft hackle and they are designed to be fished upstream, with the fly just subsurface and as much of the line held out of the water as possible. Quite what trout take them for is open to question, but the style is so versatile that depending on how they are fished, the flies can represent spinners, still-born duns, or even nymphs. The method is one of the triumphs of wet-fly development, and it is odd that it has never been popular outside England's northern counties. It certainly works well enough elsewhere; perhaps one of the problems is that it isn't an easy technique to master.

According to Pritt, a man who clearly understood the value of the nymph at a time when many fishermen were ignorant of its value, north country school fishermen had abandoned the winged wet fly almost completely by 1860. The men who led this new way of thinking shouldn't be underestimated, because their achievement was to realise that trout find it easy to take stillborn duns which have been crunched around in the turbulent conditions of freestone rivers, and they had the courage to break away from the mainstream and design radical and new patterns to take advantage of their theories:

> It is now conceded that a fly dressed hacklewise is generally to be preferred to a winged imitation. The reasons for this are not far to seek and are satisfactory. It is far more difficult to imitate a perfect insect and to afterwards impart to it a semblance of life in or on the water, than it is to produce something which is sufficiently near a resemblance of an imperfectly developed insect, struggling to attain the surface of the stream. Trout undoubtedly take a hackled fly for the insect just rising from the pupa in a half-drowned state; and the opening and closing of the fibres of the feathers give it an appearance of vitality, which even the most dextrous fly-fisher will fail to impart to the winged imitation.[57]

Pritt's target was the traditional winged wet fly, and in his quiet way, he dealt it a heavy blow. He was one of the first anglers to question the fundamental premise of the design of the traditional fly; pointing out the inconsistencies that had been staring fishermen in the face since the days of the *Treatyse*. He stood out as a beacon of reason in the disputes that were to follow.

In the years leading up to the turn of the century, a stand-off developed between the northern English and Scottish anglers on one side and the southern chalk stream fishermen on the other. The failure of each side to grasp the problems which the other faced lead to decades of bickering. Many books of the era include a triumphal passage in which a group of northern (or southern) visitors were trounced by the application of the 'proper' technique. I find it absolutely fascinating that there was so little cross-over of skills, since the upstream Spider works perfectly well outside its accepted northern range. The reason may well be that by the time the north country technique was properly established, no southern angler in his right mind would have tried it; the penalty for such heresy being a black-balling by his enraged fellow club members. Northern anglers did try the dry fly, but as Pritt pointed out, it is an unrewarding pastime on rivers where the trout are not free-rising.

Meanwhile, American wet flies had followed their own path, departing from the straight and narrow of the sombre British tradition in order to develop into the more brightly coloured patterns chronicled by Charles Orvis, A. Nelson Cheney and Mary Orvis Marbury.[58] The 'Orvis' books are striking for their early use of lush chromolithography, and while the hundred and twenty-seven flies pictured by Charles Orvis and Nelson Cheney were probably the first colour lithographs that any fisherman ever got to see, the book which captured the American wet-fly tradition at its peak was Charles' daughter's *Favorite Flies*. Mary ran the Orvis company's fly tying department and she was inspired to set pen to paper when she realised how little standardisation there was among fly patterns – she once commented that a well-known bass fly called the 'Ferguson' was thought of in some quarters as any fly with a yellow and green hackle. Ironically, the 'Ferguson' that Mary listed is different to the one given by her father in his book printed nine years before, but we know which of them is right, because Mary had a letter from Major Ferguson authenticating the pattern he sent her as the 'true and only Ferguson'. This set Mary thinking and it wasn't long before she and her father had compiled a questionnaire which was sent out to anyone they thought had sufficient knowledge to help. The letter asked recipients for their favourite flies, their dressings, histories and when, how and where they were supposed to be used. The answers were compiled and keyed to colour plates in a book which was still in print sixty years later, such was its popularity.

An interesting story hangs on the plates from Mary's book, as the original flies from which they were produced still survive, in the American Museum of Fly Fishing in Vermont. According to John Betts, some of the plates were very nearly lost in the mid 1960s, when he was

Flies from the Marbury plates

asked to clean out the attic in the old Orvis factory building. John rescued some old plates and hooks from the junk which had accumulated over many decades and asked if he could take them home with him. Dick Finlay, the manager, couldn't see a problem, but before John went home, Dick changed his mind over the plates and took them back inside. A few years later, John's house suffered a disastrous flood which filled his basement with icy water for several days and when he finally got it pumped out, the hooks were a rusted mass of useless metal. As John says, if he had been allowed to keep the Marbury plates, they would have suffered the same fate, and he has felt a connection to the flies ever since.[59] The rediscovery of the flies led indirectly to the creation of the American Museum, because when Hermann Kessler saw them, he told Leigh Perkins that there should be a museum to keep them in.

At this point the winged wet fly quite simply got stuck. In Britain it had nowhere to go, boxed in as it was by developments to the north and south. The spider pattern failed to gain acceptance outside its original range, while the dry-fly purists built their own temples in the clouds. In America, a similar situation prevailed. The next stage in the evolution of the wet fly would be triggered by a better understanding of the part nymphs and emergers played in the life-cycle of the *Ephemeroptera* and in the trout's diet. But for the time being, there was stagnation.

New patterns of traditional wet fly continued to appear (incredibly, they still do) but the traditional winged fly had had its day, and any remaining improvements were purely cosmetic. There were no more significant advances until Skues' brilliant insights brought us the nymph. In turn, Skues' flies inspired several decades of innovation, led in Britain by Frank Sawyer and Oliver Kite.

Across the Atlantic, the vast majority of Americans remained faithful to the wet fly in a period which saw an explosion of new patterns chronicled by Mary Orvis Marbury. These flies, and the new confidence of American fishers to innovate, were the product of an unparalleled boom in sporting periodicals, outfitters and fishing and hunting clubs, involving many thousands of fishermen. Later writers often see Theodore Gordon as the cause of the change, rather than as a part of it. With the exception of the development of the nymph, the creative history of the twentieth century trout fly is an American story - and it was driven, not by Gordon, but by the introduction of a fish - the brown trout.

Salmon Flies

The late nineteenth century saw a development that had a far-reaching effect on the salmon fly, but it came from an unexpected quarter: the railway. The first track was laid in Britain in 1825,[60] and it was so successful that by 1870 Britain had thirteen thousand five hundred miles of railway. The 'permanent way' revolutionised access to Scotland, and anglers of moderate means found that they could travel north for the first time. The railway companies were quick to exploit the potential, and in 1872 the first 'angler's concession tickets' appeared, allowing club fishermen to travel at reduced rates, a development which had a dramatic effect on the popularity of fishing. Between 1870 and 1880 fishing clubs sprang up all over the country.

The importance of the effect the railway had on salmon fishing can't be overstated. Salmon were no longer the preserve of the very rich or of the fortunate local angler. With increasing numbers of fishermen heading for Scotland, the demand for new patterns of fly sky-rocketed and the dealers all over the country were only too happy to oblige. This put the traditional salmon flies which had been developed for use on their rivers of origin under attack. Many local anglers understandably saw the increasingly popular gaudy salmon fly as an Irish interloper, which displaced perfectly good local patterns. To a large extent they were right and it is regrettable that the patterns which were popular in the early nineteenth century were lost to a very great extent, buried under an avalanche of new flies. So, during the middle years of the nineteenth century the strong links which had existed between patterns and their rivers of origin began to be lost, although there were tyers who still paid lip-service to the tradition many decades later.

Stoddart's Tweed salmon flies

Before 1850, anglers like William Scrope were content to fish with a mere handful of flies all of which had strong local associations. After 1850 the sheer choice of patterns made it difficult to justify the link – not that it prevented writers like Francis from quoting selections of flies 'for the River Garry', and 'for the River Ness', and so forth. The new flies had a truly international flavour, and they appealed mightily to the Victorian psyche. Fishermen took them abroad and slew huge fish in Norway with them; so why shackle them to a tiny spate river of the west coast of Scotland? Yet there was a residual conviction, which still persists, that patterns of salmon flies were likely to be more successful if they were developed for specific rivers, on the grounds that local fish 'understood' them better. The idea of a Tweed fish being taken on a Garry fly just didn't suit every angler's sense of justice and aesthetics. The result was a deal of mental gymnastics as fishermen attempted to rationalise the reasons for the success of patterns. Again and again, patterns were published with minor tweaks which were credited with their success when used 'away from home', George Kelson being one of the worst offenders. These years were the heyday of the gaudy salmon fly and literally thousands of different patterns were invented.

The two outstanding salmon fly tyers of this period are Jones and Traherne. Jones was a tackle dealer who had a business at 111 Jermyn Street, London, in the heart of the city's most fashionable area. He sold high quality rods and reels to the leisured classes, and chose Frederic Tolfrey, a young journalist, to write a book which promoted Norway, the favourite destination of Jones' customers, but a place to which neither Jones, nor Tolfrey had ever been.[61] The *Guide* illustrates Jones' outstandingly beautiful flies in a wonderful series of hand-coloured plates which must have made them just walk off his shelves. Just compare one of Taylor's salmon fly dressings from 1800 with the Jones equivalent:

Taylor – (Unnamed fly)

> . . . the wings, the mottled feather of a peacock's wing, intermixed with that of any fine plain dusky red; the mixture for the body, the light brown hair or fur of a bear next to the skin, sable fur, and gold-coloured mohair, gold twist, a large black cock's hackle, and a red one a little larger; and for the head, a bit of deep red mohair.

Jones – The Assassin

Tail – Golden pheasant, guinea-hen, and blue macaw.
Tip – Gold twist, blue silk, scarlet silk, and ostrich.
Body – Lower half, dark blue, and upper half, claret pig's wool.
Ribbed – Gold tinsel.
Legs – Dark claret hackle.
Throat – Jay's hackle.
Wing – (Mixed) mallard, teal, bustard, black cockatoo, guinea-hen, golden tippet, and golden topping over all.
Horns – Blue macaw.
Head – Black.

In the space of a mere fifty years the salmon fly had been transformed from a workmanlike object into a jewel - and there was more to come.

John Traherne was a very different proposition to Jones. He was born in 1826, the eldest son of a landed family and inherited his father's estate in 1859. Much of his life was spent in the army, from 1845, when he obtained a commission as Ensign in the 39th (Dorset) Regiment of Foot and he reached the rank of Major, retiring in 1865. In fitting with his background, he did not neglect his social obligations and served as a Justice of the Peace, Deputy Lieutenant for his county and was High Sheriff in 1863. Though a self-effacing man, he was an experienced salmon fisherman, catching his first fish in 1850, which put him at the forefront of the new fashion. After that, the Major seems to have fished just about every river in the UK, Ireland and Norway. He was very accomplished, making a world record cast of forty-five yards and one inch in 1884 and he exhibited a case of flies at the Great International Fisheries Exhibition of 1883. It was probably this case of flies that drew George Kelson's attention and despite the fact that they were an unlikely pair, they became life-long friends. Kelson began his 1884 *Fishing Gazette* series 'On the Description of Salmon Flies', with eighteen of Traherne's patterns, an action which catapulted his friend to fame.

Major Traherne

Kelson had good reason to lionise his friend. Traherne had a rare aesthetic sense and from the 'Emerald Gem', a riot of green and blue macaw, with a filigree of golden pheasant topping as wing, to the 'Chatterer' (a pattern which I have always regarded as the definitive gaudy fly, since depending on size it requires fifty or more blue chatterer feathers to form its body), his patterns were masterpieces. They must have been incredibly expensive to tie even then, and I wonder how many people actually dared to fish them. This is the dressing for the Lapwing:

TAG. - Silver twist and green silk the same shade as the green feathers from the macaw.
TAIL. - Topping.
BUTT. - Black herl.
BODY. - In four equal sections, the first three butted with herl. No. 1 division, silver tinsel, with canary toucan above and below. No. 2, topping coloured floss silk, ribbed with fine oval tinsel, and the ordinary toucan above and below. No. 3, orange silk, ribbed likewise, with red crow above and below. No.4, red claret silk, ribbed again as before.
THROAT. - Five or six red crow and jay feather.
WINGS. - Ten enamelled thrush.
CHEEKS. - Summer duck and jungle cock, two toppings over.
HORNS. - Amherst pheasant.
HEAD. - Black herl.

More than anything else, these flies are a celebration of the materials and artistry of the salmon fly and although they are no longer used, it remains a technical challenge for even the most accomplished fly dresser to tie them well, because of the difficulty of achieving a balance between the ephemeral beauty of each pattern and the daunting amount of materials needed to tie them. They have never been equalled since.

Traherne and his generation added the final touches to the fully dressed salmon fly – probably unaware of the enduring tradition they would leave when they were gone. The popularity of salmon fishing absolutely boomed in the third quarter of the century and dealers had to struggle hard to service the demand. With so many newcomers needing direction, it was an era of instant experts and everyone and his dog seemed to be inventing new killer flies. By the 1890s, a vast selection of patterns was available, and the well-equipped salmon fisherman's fly-box was an absolute riot of colour. The selection of materials in use was quite breathtaking: tying silks, floss silks, seal's fur, pig's wool and mohair, chenilles of various kinds, and tinsels; then the hackles: white, yellowish-white, white furnace, white and other shades of coch-y-bonddhu, black, blue dun, blue furnace, red furnace, cuckoo and kneecap;[62] feathers: golden pheasant, blue and yellow macaw, scarlet macaw, blue and red macaw, toucan, Indian crow, jungle cock, green parrot, chatterer, bustard, florican bustard, guinea-fowl, mallard, teal, pintail, widgeon, summer duck, jay, scarlet ibis, turkey, swan, peacock and ostrich.

Flies were tied to exploit every possible combination of exotic material. There was a fly for every conceivable circumstance, and several flies for circumstances which were not conceivable - for example the Elsie, which George Kelson described with breathtaking chutzpah as 'a special pattern for fish lying behind upright rocks and large boulders.' By now, tying techniques were far more sophisticated than anything that had been tried even thirty years earlier. The new patterns took the technical challenge of fly tying on to a new plane, since the process of cramming so many materials into a small space mercilessly exposed the slightest technical incompetence on the part of the tyer. Compare this fragment of Kelson's instruction with Blacker or Bainbridge and it is quite clear how far tying skills had come on:

> Prepare the floss as for the tag. Release tying-silk, unwind two turns of it, and put in 'catch.' Lay the proper end of the floss in the place of the unwound turns. Release tying-silk and, in making the two turns again, bind over floss. Make off. Now, with the right fore-finger and thumb take hold of the floss beyond the shank, and smoothing all twist out of it as before, pass it into left 'catch'. Put the right fingers under the shank, take hold of the floss, and begin winding diagonally tailwards; pass floss after each diagonal coil into left 'catch', and stroke and wind alternately in increasingly wider coils up to the butt; then continue headwards, as already described for the tag, taking yet more care to stroke and smooth whilst winding on coils in decreasing closeness. These are not diagonal coils; the silk is to be worked as nearly as possible straight over the shank.[63]

By now, the vice had become generally accepted, and by the turn of the century there were four types available. The Tacklemaker's vice was a simple clamp, the jaws closed by a screw mechanism. The Halford offered another screw-adjustable mechanism, but it could be adjusted for height. The Hawksley was angled, unlike the others, which had vertical uprights and its jaws resembled a pair of sprung pliers, which were closed by hand and locked with a sliding collar; it worked well for small hooks, although its jaws gripped larger calibre salmon irons poorly. The American Thompson was the greatest of the bunch and set the pattern for the development of the modern vice, many of which are close copies of the original design.

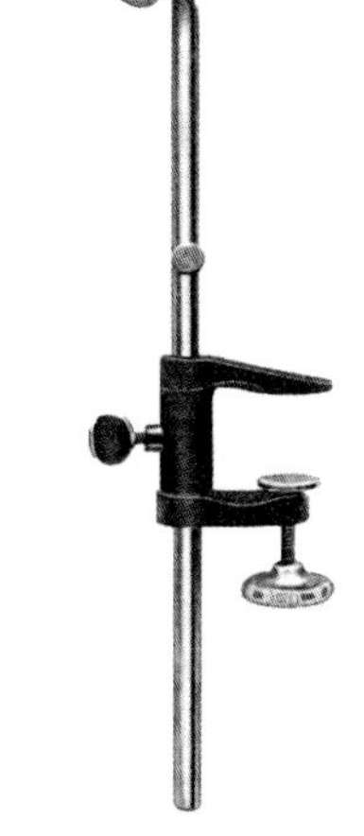

The Thompson vice

At the turn of the century, the complexity of the salmon fly was at its zenith. Some idea of the hold that the gaudy fly had over salmon fishermen's minds can be found in a quote from Kelson himself:

> Is it not notorious that in several of our rivers the fish have been educated to persistently snub old patterns in favour of the new? And is it indeed not an achievement to present to the fish a fly that he then and there prefers to your rival's – to have yourself made the attraction so strong, as to establish, more or less permanently, a decided taste in the fish, so that he refuses other flies, to wait for yours![64]

This is pure baloney, but the pretentious Kelson was typical of many salmon fishers in his uncritical worship of what he imagined as the perfection of salmon fly design. The complex beauty of patterns such as Traherne's turned Kelson's head and as a result he was completely obsessed with utter trivia, such as the tag; which he pompously venerated as 'a tribute to nature'.

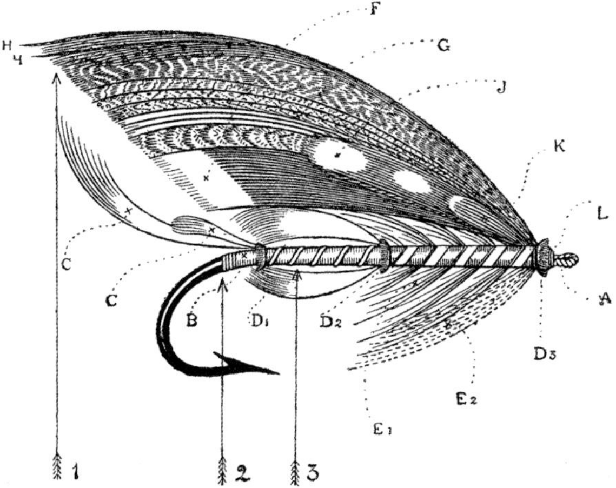

Parts of a Jock Scott salmon fly

Kelson wasn't alone in his romantic conclusions. These were the days of tying competitions, 'analytical diagrams' of salmon flies, which divided and subdivided the fly into dozens of constituent parts. It was also the heyday of the specialist fly tyer, a peculiar type whose influence on the development of the gaudy salmon fly can scarcely be underestimated.

James Wright of Sprouston, Roxboroughshire, was typical of the breed. Born in 1829, Wright's parents died in the cholera epidemic of 1846, leaving him in sole charge of the younger members of his family. His father had tied a few flies and the young James set out to teach himself how to tie his own, little realising that he was taking the first step into an occupation which would make him world famous. Aware of the limits of his father's talent, Wright begged flies from Brandling Gosforth, one of the earliest fly fishers on the Tweed, and patiently took them apart, in order to discover how other professionals assembled their creations. He learnt so much that it wasn't long before he was an acknowledged expert in tying salmon flies with plain wings, but he went on to greater things and collected numerous awards at the International Exhibitions of 1860 and 1883. Wright tied for many famous anglers, and he either created or was the first to reproduce many famous patterns, including the Greenwell's Glory and the Black Doctor. One of Wright's peculiarities was that he never had a shop as such and never advertised, carrying on his business by word of mouth. He died in 1902.

The combination of all these circumstances meant that the 1890s marked the zenith of the gaudy salmon fly's evolution, but they were also marked by the first signs of dissent. Sir Herbert Maxwell was quick to point out that:

> The popular theory encourages the extraordinary delusion that every river requires its peculiar combination of silk, wool, tinsel and feathers to take the salmon which frequent it. Thus we have Tweed flies, Tay flies, Spey flies, Usk flies, Shannon flies, none of which it is orthodox to use on any stream except that from which it derived its origin.[65]

In spite of the cult of salmon fly dressing, a debate was growing about the need for endless legions of specialised flies, fuelled perhaps by a backlash against the high prices charged for individual flies. Maxwell's final comment on the matter was a conclusion that the colour and materials of a fly mattered little to the fish, while the size and movement were all important. It is probable that few anglers paid much attention to him, for Maxwell's judgement was years ahead of its time, but the days of the gaudy fly were nearly over and the fall from grace, when it came, would be as quick as it was unexpected.

The
Dry Fly

The annual 'Mayfly Mess' held at the Royal Hotel, Winchester. Taken around 1880, the picture shows typical 'long rod' anglers, with some almost certainly fishing live naturals. Courtesy of the Flyfishers' Club.

CHAPTER SIX

The Dry Fly

Early Development

IN THE 1850s, the members of the Houghton Club, the most prestigious fly fishing club in England, could be found at the river side dressed in elegant topcoats and tall black hats, solemnly fishing downstream using long double-handed rods. When the mayfly was up, their menservants scoured the banks for live insects, which were imprisoned in zinc boxes before being transfixed on hooks attached to the end of blow-lines, which the fishers allowed to sail out before them in the gentle Hampshire wind, as their fathers had, and doubtless their fathers too. When conditions were too wild and blustery even for the blow-line, the members were inclined to resort to minnow fishing, another age-old pursuit which did not raise a single aristocratic eyebrow. As those influential men sat down to dinner in Stockbridge, to discuss the great fish and great fortunes which they had lost and won, it must have seemed to them that nothing would ever change. Yet, by the end of the century, the double-handed trout rods, the blow-line and the minnow were all anachronisms and the upstream dry fly reigned supreme, a transformation unparalleled in the history of the sport and one which owed its origins as much to social changes as to any science.

The origins of dry-fly fishing as we understand it lie in the mid-nineteenth century, but at the risk of repeating myself, the attraction of

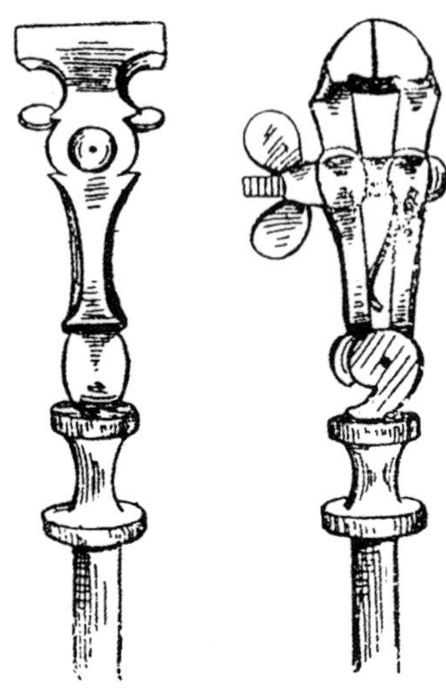

Halford's vice

a floating fly has been known from time immemorial. Even in Roman times, flies did not sink immediately and the tackle and short-line techniques our ancestors used ensured that their flies fished on or very near the surface. We can assume that our forebears were just as observant as we are and this is backed up by the evidence, all of which shows that they knew that their best chance of taking a fish was just after they had made a cast, when the fly floated best. If you want any documentary proof of this, I suggest turning to page 1144 of Blaine's *Rural Sports*, where the author makes the unequivocal statement, 'In every case, buoyancy is an essential requisite in fly-dressing.' Let me reassure you that although Blaine was a talented fisherman, he was no rocket scientist and he had certainly never heard of the dry fly, because it was yet to be invented. Nonetheless he could say with absolute certainty that:

> Even the flies which are blown on the water seldom sink; those whose habits carry them there float in security on the surface, by an admirable provision of bubbles under their feet. A fly under the water is therefore an unnatural occurrence, and accidental only; whereas ten thousand pass down the surface of the stream in a summer's day.

It's a charming thought, those little bubbles springing into place just in time to stop *Ephemeroptera* from getting their feet wet, but even if Delabere P. Blaine was unaware of surface tension, he knew exactly how flies should best be fished.

We'll pause just for a moment here, because it is important to separate the use of floating flies from the dry-fly method, a choice of terms which has caused much confusion over the years and doubtless will continue to do so in the future. These are my definitions and I am sure that many people will disagree with them, but please remember them if only because they will help make some kind of sense out of the chaos which follows:

> A FLOATING FLY is a fly which is fished with any part of the fly out of the water for most or all of its drift. Floating flies can be fished semi-submerged or downstream and methods used to encourage floating include techniques like dapping and the blow-line, although many floating flies are fished conventionally from a short rod (i.e. one less than nine foot six inches long).

> A DRY-FLY is a fly which is fished on an upstream cast and which sits with the majority of the fly above the surface of the water.

Of course, we have bastardised the term nowadays and I have heard the phrase 'dry fly' being used to describe just about any method of fishing you can think of; but in the late nineteenth and early twentieth centuries, it referred to the specific method described above. The development of that technique and the strictness with which the definition would eventually be applied by a small but influential group of fishermen on the English chalk streams is the subject of this chapter.

It is one of the great ironies of fly fishing that no one, as far as I can tell, ever set out consciously to develop the dry fly that Halford knew and codified. Instead, fishing a 'dry fly' became possible only after anglers who wanted to fish a floating fly on a silk line and gut leader managed to solve a number of difficult problems which beset them. In a sense, the history of the dry fly is the better understood as the history of the solution of those problems and that is how I intend to present it.

The general convention follows Hills' reckoning[1] that the floating fly was evolved in the middle of the nineteenth century, but this is quite wrong. As I have stated with wearying frequency, there is abundant evidence that anglers knew it was possible to catch fish on floating patterns from the moment the first fly was cast on the water. This stands to reason, given that some of the materials our forebears used for tying flies were remarkably water-repellent; namely pig's wool and bear's hair, both of which are naturally buoyant, as Barker pointed out in 1651:

> Now of late I have found that hogs wooll of several colours makes good bodies, & the wooll of a red heifer makes a good body, and beares wooll makes a good body: there are many good furres that make good bodies: and now I work much of hogs wooll, for I finde it floateth best and procureth the best sport.[2]

When I began the research which led to this book being written, I initially shared Hills' viewpoint, but the more I read, the more I realised that we are hindered by the way we refract the development of the dry fly through the lens of our own experience. The trap into which many historians have fallen into is to think of historical fly fishing techniques within the modern definitions of 'wet' and 'dry' fly fishing, a line of reasoning which is particularly unhelpful. The truth is that before the invention of silk lines, deeply fished wet flies were virtually unknown and anglers fished their flies on or in the surface layer of the water; Charles Cotton and many generations of anglers after him would rarely have fished a fly more than a few inches deep. Too many authors have been seduced by Hills' and Halford's writing and in my own view it is probable that floating patterns have been fished since the first time a fly was cast.

The evidence for this stance is fairly overwhelming. Aside from the materials used in their patterns, the list of early authors who mention the floating fly is far too long to ignore. We have heard Blaine's view, but what about Chetham, who wrote: 'Flies they take most at top of the Water, or sometimes within 2 or 3 inches of it . . .'? And then there is George Scotcher, who knew exactly how to fish a floating Black Gnat pattern in 1810:

> . . . I sometimes tie it on to a fine glass coloured round hair, and of course the other part of my bottom single hair, which falls excessively light and will lie on the water, and the fly is frequently taken, but without very much practice and care you are very apt to snap it off in throwing.[3]

I could go on. All of which serves to show that floating flies were in common use in the seventeenth century, but how about this 1590 quote?

> The darke drake Fly (in August) is good, the body is made of blacke wooll, and lapped about with blacke silke, his winges are made of the maile of the black drake, with a blacke head. Thus are they made vpon the hooke, lapt about with some corke like each Fly afore mentioned.[4]

If all of this isn't about a fly which floats, I don't know what is, and if we add the Spanish patterns described by Juan de Bergara in 1624, then we have a list of references to fishing on or in the surface film of the water which is simply too long to be ignored.

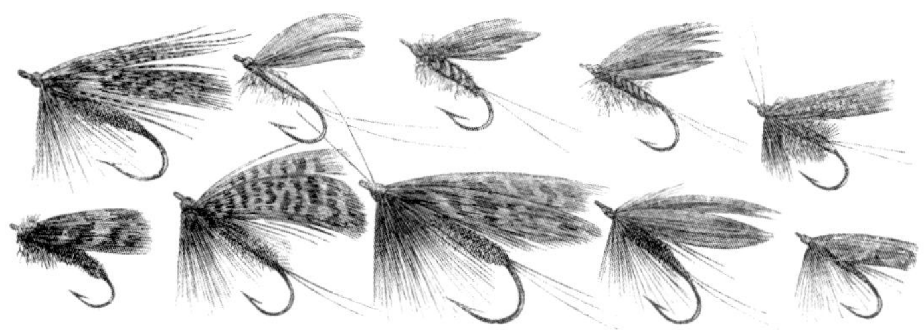

Early flies

The final metamorphosis of the floating fly into the dry fly occurred during the second quarter of the nineteenth century, when anglers began to run into difficulties caused by their adoption of 'modern' tackle. If you read books written during this period, you will find that the authors offer all kinds of advice about how to get out of trouble. In 1838 Shipley's book says:

> Let your flies float gently down the water, working them gradually towards you, and making a fresh cast every two or three yards you fish. We distinctly recommend frequent casting. A fish generally takes the fly immediately it has touched the water – provided it always be delicately and lightly flung – and the quick repetition of casting whisks the water out of your flies and line, and consequently keeps them drier and lighter than if they were left to float a longer time in the water.[5]

Three years later, Pulman said much the same:

> Now, it is impossible to make a soaked artificial fly swim upon the water as the natural flies do, so that, when cast by the angler to a fish thus occupied, it most commonly escapes his notice, engaged as he is with 'things above', by sinking in the water beneath him. This is plain, because if a wet and heavy fly be exchanged for a dry and light one, and passed in artist-like style over the feeding fish, it will, partly from the simple circumstance of its buoyancy, be taken, in nine cases out of ten, as greedily as the living insect itself. We admit, however, that to ensure this, imitation of the predominant species, at least as regards colour and size, is required; opining that if the dry-fly be widely different in these respects, the fish will be surprised and startled at the novelty presented, and suspend feeding until the appearance of its known and familiar prey.[6]

These two quotes repay careful reading. What Shipley and Pulman are actually doing is telling their audience how to cope with a new problem which they and all their contemporaries faced – waterlogging.

By the middle of the nineteenth century, waterlogging of flies and lines had become a major problem for two reasons; the upstream cast and the increasingly widespread adoption of silk fly lines. The possibilities of the upstream cast had been brought to popular attention in a very successful book written by William Stewart, although as I have written elsewhere, he did not invent it. Upstream fishing is also mentioned in the Houghton club diary by Richard Penn in 1829, and the same author gives a good description in his book, *Maxims and Hints for Anglers*.[7] However, upstream casts were nothing new in the nineteenth century and Venables had understood the basic principles two hundred years before:

> And here I meet with two different opinions and practices, some will always cast their fly and bait up the water, and so they say nothing occurs to the fish's sight but the line; others fish down the river and so suppose, the rod and line being long, the quantity of water takes away, or at least lessens the fish's sight; but others affirm, that the rod and line, and perhaps yourself, are seen also.[8]

This inspired piece of thinking was actually the product of a faulty understanding of the ocular anatomy of the trout; it stood to reason that if people couldn't see backwards, neither could fish. The supposition may well have been incorrect, but it had the desired result, because anglers who fished upstream presented their flies in the most natural manner possible and increased the number of takes they triggered. Incidentally, Venables wasn't the only writer of his day who was aware of the arguments for upstream fishing. John Worlidge[9] advised the fly fisher to wade upstream if the water was shallow and the bottom was good and made the acute observation that the fisher should, 'cast your Fly against the Stream, and the Trout that lies upon the Fin in such strong Currents, and discerns you not, being behind him, presently takes your bait.'

But although Venables and his contemporaries could fish upstream, they usually chose to fish downstream or across and downstream unless the wind made it impossible to do so; a state of affairs which is borne out by studies of 'traditional' anglers who still use fixed lines today. The reason for this can be better understood if you ever try fishing upstream with a line that is fixed to the rod tip. The only way to stay in contact with the fly is steadily to raise the rod as the fly approaches you – making it progressively more difficult to hook a fish as the rod nears the vertical. Venables could fish a floating fly, but the relatively short fixed line he used made it difficult to do so properly.

By the nineteenth century, upstream fishing was a practical proposition, although it was still much more difficult than casting a fly the other way. The changes that made this possible were advances in rods and lines, particularly the development of the tapered silk line, which when combined with a stiff-actioned rod, allowed anglers to cast into the wind. Fishermen could now make long casts upstream and they could also stay 'in touch' with the fly without too much difficulty by shortening line; but they faced an intractable problem; their lines sank.

Plaited silk lines appeared in the second quarter of the nineteenth century, but it wasn't until the late 1850s that the dressed tapered silk fly line – a casting line that was distinct from the running line – appeared.[10] Dressed tapered silk lines gave anglers a degree of control over the fly of which they had previously only been able to dream and they understandably became popular very quickly. Ultimately they would be available in three different tapers: level, which was cheap, but had the disadvantage of poor delivery; single taper, which allowed a better presentation; and double taper, which took advantage of the fact that most fishermen couldn't aerialise more than half the line and meant that a line could be reversed when one end wore out. This introduced a new problem, which was that while anglers could cast a fly a good way upstream, getting a long, drag-free drift was very difficult. Neither their lines nor their flies were designed to float for long, and something needed to be done to prevent them sinking. Clearly, some lateral thinking was going to be needed. The solution to this problem was to develop and extend the use of the false cast.

The False Cast

It is probable that false casting has been known since fly fishing began, since it stands to reason that any angler who saw he was going to miss his mark with his first cast could have whipped the fly back and made a second before the fly was wetted. For all that, you will have to look hard to find a good description of the false cast written before 1847. The reason for this otherwise glaring omission from the angling repertoire is that there probably wasn't much reason for anyone to describe it. Casting remained a simple affair as long as the line stayed fixed to the top of the rod, and it didn't take a genius to work out how to do it. But by the nineteenth century, casting was the focus of much more attention, chiefly because of the problems of managing a running line, and false casting attracted particular interest, because it had new purpose: drying the line and the fly.

The history of the false cast has been painstakingly dissected by other authors and I apologise in advance for going through it yet again. I do, however, have a new point to make, because most of my predecessors have looked at the false cast from the twentieth century perspective of drying the fly and extending line, when in fact its purpose has changed quite profoundly across the centuries.

A definition might help here:

> A FALSE CAST is a cast made where the fly touches the water on neither the forward nor the back cast.

Originally, the false cast (though no one ever bothered to dignify it with a name) was used simply to reposition the fly on the water, and this technique must have been known since fly fishing began. Once tapered, running silk fly lines became popular, the false cast undoubtedly found a new use, that of drying the line, and possibly of extending it to a limited extent.

We can actually chart this uncertain progress in the literature: Fitzgibbon gave a very hesitant account of what might have been a false cast in his 1850 book, but it sounds as if he hadn't tried it himself, and he certainly didn't connect it with the idea of drying the fly. Only a year later, Pulman described false casting clearly for the first time,[11] but although this is generally held to be the first description of a false cast used to dry a fly, his text makes it quite clear that he had just changed a waterlogged fly for a dry one. What Pulman was actually describing was a false cast for the purpose of clearing water from a waterlogged line, rather than for drying the fly. It simply didn't seem to have occurred to him that vigorous false casting might be used to dry a fly, and if the idea hadn't occurred to Pulman, it probably hadn't occurred to anyone else either.

But the idea of using the false cast to dry the fly didn't take long to take root. It is only conjecture, but I would imagine that the penny dropped when fishermen noticed that false casting to dry the line dried their flies too. Needless to say, it took a bit of experimentation before anglers got the hang of this new application of an old technique. The first time false casting is described for the purpose of drying a fly is in the 1853 edition of Stoddart's *The Angler's Companion* (it is interesting to note that he didn't mention the method at all in his first edition in 1847). Here is Stoddart's description, in which the false cast is described for the first time for the sole purpose of drying the fly:

> Under such circumstances, therefore – that is, where the fly fisher has to deal with subtle trout, in clear, glassy streams – it is not an unusual practice, on recovering the line, and before recasting, to describe a figure of eight, twice or thrice successively, in the air with the fly-cast, in order to relieve the plumage of the hooks of the moisture imbibed. Upon this practice, or 'dodge' as some might choose to term it, a good deal of stress is laid by the fishers of certain rivers both in England and Wales. I may mention, however, that, in the adoption of it, only one fly-hook is generally used; a light single-handed rod is necessary, and the line should be of extreme fineness, and neatly tapered off.[12]

Though we haven't the slightest clue who first came up with this useful idea, it clearly wasn't Stoddart. Strangely enough, we may know where it was discovered, by virtue of a piece in the issue of *The Field* dated December 17th, 1853. In an article by-lined 'The Hampshire Fly Fisher' the writer says with some feeling: 'On the other hand, as far as fly fishing is concerned, fishing upstream, unless you are trying the Carshalton dodge and fishing with a dry-fly, is very awkward.'

It is a shame that 'The Hampshire Fly Fisher' wasn't a bit more precise with his use of English, because the 'Carshalton dodge' could refer either to false casting or to dry-fly fishing itself. Certainly, within a few years, this new method of swishing a fly back and forth in the air in order to dry it had become known as 'spreading'. The technique ultimately led to the development of stiffer rods with pliant tops that could generate the line speed necessary to perform the manoeuvre and it had a far-reaching effect on the design of dry-fly rods. In those pioneering days, some thought held that it was necessary to 'crack' the fly at the end of every false cast in order to dry it properly, a method known as 'flicking'. I'm sure you have already worked out that the major problem with this technique was that it weakened the gut just in front of the hook, with the result that the fly eventually broke off on a back cast, or worse still, snapped off on the strike. The sheer bother of drying a fly every time it sank (which was pretty quickly) encouraged anglers to keep false casting to a minimum, except in conditions where the trout were large and couldn't be caught any other way - but it worked when all other methods failed.

Early Dry Flies

If you had wandered along the banks of the river Test in 1870, you would have found fewer than half the fishermen using a dry fly.[13] Many of the anglers you passed would have been fishing downstream with two large wet flies and not only that, if the wind was right, you would have seen a few dapping a live insect on a blow-line. No doubt you would have been puzzled about this, but if from your present day perspective you have trouble understanding why dry-fly fishing was unpopular before the 1890s, pause and think about the equipment at the angler's disposal. Although shorter rods were becoming more common, the fly fisherman you saw in 1870 would in many cases have been using extremely soft-actioned, double-handed fourteen foot rods. If you had retrieved an errant back-cast from the clutches of a passing hedge, you would have found that the flies were whipped on to gut, with dubbed bodies, with the result that though they did float, they didn't do so for very long.

So given the sort of tackle that was in common use at the time, it isn't surprising that many fished wet flies downstream, or the natural mayfly when it was in season. If you had walked the banks fifty years earlier, you would have found the majority of the fishermen using natural mayfly on a blow-line, although a few innovators would have been trying the artificial. You would have been impressed at how well they were doing; not only Colonel Peter Hawker but also the Reverend Durnford fished a downstream wet fly and Hawker, a great character even in his day, recorded some startling catches. He fished from horseback on at least one occasion[14] - try doing that on the Test nowadays and see how far you get. It may be interesting to know that the high country lakes of the American west were sometimes fished from horses in the late twentieth century.

F. M. Halford landing a trout

It is difficult to fix the date upon which the dry flies which we would recognise were first fished, since the change was more of a metamorphosis than a single, clearly identifiable step. A review of the patterns used in the middle years of the nineteenth century shows that there was a gradual adaptation of the old flies, which were modified and tied with hackles that accentuated their floating capabilities. An unspoken agreement drove this process: no longer was it sufficient for patterns to fish in the surface – they had to fish right on top of the surface.

Despite all the evidence that we have for an evolutionary process, one man can be identified as an early pioneer of the dry fly, a tackle dealer called James Ogden. Ogden claimed that the first time that he used the method was in 1839. This story has been challenged; J. W. Hills gives a much later date, stating that Ogden introduced the dry fly on the Derbyshire Wye in 1865, 'with such success that the owner of the water prohibited the blow-line.'[15] The consequences of the local ban may explain why Ogden kept quiet about the dry fly for so long, since the other fishermen on his beat of the Wye were so incensed that they attacked him and drove him off the water! He may have deemed it wiser to lie low for a bit. But when he did get around to setting pen to paper, the Cheltenham tackle dealer left the reader in no doubt about the importance of his discovery:

> Some forty years ago, when I introduced my floating flies, the love of angling was increasing at the rate of ten to one from when I was a lad. I always found the more a stream was whipped over, the more wary and shy the fish became; and I always made it a rule never to leave a good rising fish while he was feeding. I have tried every dodge, and often every fly in my book. By changing my end fly (not intending to do so) I have occasionally made a cast with a dry fly. In those days it was said this would scare a rising trout and cause him to leave off when feeding. On the other hand, I found while my fly was still on the surface, without a ripple [i.e. drag], it has tempted the fish to seize it, after I have been throwing a sunk fly over him, in vain, scores of times. These observations were the cause of my introducing floating flies. I found it advisable to use one fly only with a shorter casting line.[16]

Ogden comes across as a bit of an upstart, which may have put Hills' hackles up, but there is no doubt that he was a very perceptive man; for example, his comment on drag is one of the first anyone thought to make. The drag-free float is a cornerstone of the dry-fly technique and it is one of the features which distinguishes the dry-fly method from

Ogden's mayflies from Aldham. (Pictures courtesy of David Beazley)

the older floating fly technique; this alone gives weight to his account. My own belief is that despite Hills' scepticism, there are many reasons for thinking that Ogden was telling the truth. On the fourth page of his book, he gives the first instructions for tying a modern dry-fly hackle, advising that it should be wound 'well on the edge' – this is precisely the style we use today for building a collar. But for me, the deciding factor in favour of his claim to fame has to be the inclusion of two of his Mayfly patterns in Aldham's peculiar volume, *A quaint treatise on 'Flees and the art a artyficiall flee making*, which was published in 1876. The pair of detached bodied Mayflies which Ogden tied for Aldham are like nothing else ever seen before: they are very definitely dry flies and they are tied on eyed hooks. Remember these flies, because the style will surface again.

It wasn't long before it was possible to buy the new style of floating fly in the shops. David Foster sold upright split-winged floating flies as early as 1854 and published a series of patterns in 1882. Foster's patterns look very modern, with stiff cock's hackles and very upright split rolled wings, but if you look closely, you will see that all his flies are tied to gut, which was to prove a fatal weakness in their design.

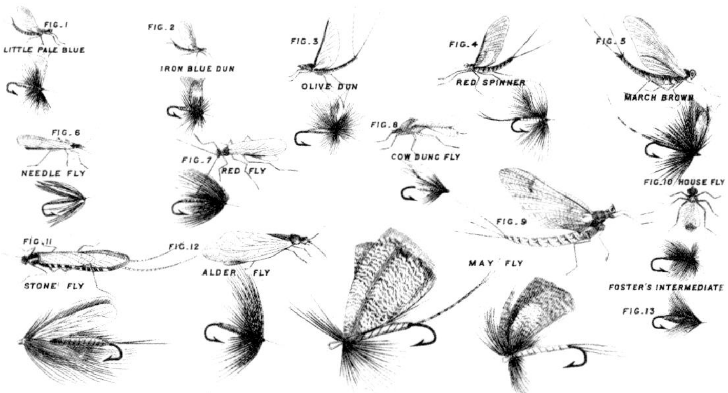

Foster's 1882 patterns

Taking everything I have said so far into account, it is probably safe to assume that the dry fly first saw use in the 1850s at the very latest and that by the late 1880s the method was well established, although it was by no means universally practised. Use of the technique was patchy and it varied from river to river and even from beat to beat. So, for example, Francis Francis said that the first use on the Itchen was in 1857, while Halford found dry-fly fishermen on the Wandle in 1868,[17] both of which tally with Pennell and confirm Francis' opinion that the dry fly was in widespread use on southern streams by 1867.

There are grounds for believing that the dry fly was only widely adopted on the Hampshire chalk streams relatively late on. Halford records that 'perhaps half - maybe fewer - had any idea of dry fly fishing' on the stretch of the Test which he fished in the early 1870s. The first time William Lunn, perhaps the most famous river keeper of all time, saw a fish taken on the dry fly was in 1883, on the Tillingbourne. Lunn told J.W. Hills that he didn't hear of a fish being taken on the Test until as late as 1888 – thirty-four years after Foster's patterns had first gone on sale, but I suspect that for once his memory was incorrect. Nonetheless, the Houghton Club members didn't universally adopt the dry fly until as late as 1893.[18]

These are, however, just dates, and the first detailed description of the dry-fly method I can find was made by H. Cholmondeley-Pennell in 1870, under the unambiguous title *Fishing with the Dry-Fly*:

> The object of the dry-fly is evident from its name – it is made to float on the water like the natural insect ... The peculiarities of the construction of the fly to enable it to fulfil this rôle, are first its wings, which generally consist of the whole tops of feathers (mallard, generally), set nearly back to back, and pointing upwards and outwards; and secondly, its body, which is composed almost entirely of materials unabsorbent of water, such as mohair and hackles.
>
> The method of using the dry-fly on the Stour and a few other rivers, where its use is best understood, is very peculiar. A large fish, say, is known to inhabit some particular hole or eddy. The spot is watched by the angler until he sees the fish rising, and then the fly is cast to fall a foot or so above him, and allowed to float (dry) passively over him. On the fly becoming wet, which happens after every cast, it is dried by being rapidly thrown to and fro, or 'spread' in the air, when it is ready for another cast; but this is seldom made until the rise of the fish is seen, or his haunt known. Some fishermen who use the dry-fly consider it is not properly dried without a little crack or 'flick' taking place at the end of the spread; but this 'flick' though doubtless very

> artistic, often whips off the fly. A stiff rod with a tolerably pliant top is best for the purpose. The dry-fly being presented to the fish in the same way as the natural fly, is most killing when the particular natural fly imitated (which is commonly the May-fly) is on the water. Smaller flies are made, but it is found difficult in practice to 'float' them; and, indeed, the whole process is cumbersome, and is only worth practising on rivers where the fish are very large and wary, or cannot be taken in any other way.[19]

The fact that it was Pennell who wrote the lines above is more than a little ironic, given that he was a dedicated three-pattern wet fly man, but it is significant because he was in a good position to know what was new in the fishing world. Not only had he edited the *Fisherman's Magazine and Review*, but he was the Inspector of Fisheries, a job which took him all over the British Isles. Pennell might have been opinionated, but he didn't miss much and his account bears a close read. First of all, he locates his early dry-fly fishermen on the Kentish Stour, in the south-east of England. This is surprising indeed. The Stour is nowhere near Hampshire, the county with which the dry-fly method is traditionally associated, though it is not that far from the Wandle, which we know to be a cradle of the dry-fly technique. But the most noteworthy thing about Pennell's account is that he describes paired, upright quill-slip wings, tied with the convex surfaces of the feather together, an attribute which is usually credited to Marryat, and that with the exception of greasing the line, it describes many of the features we associate with the Halfordian dry-fly method, right down to the desirability of only casting to rising fish.

Pennell's comment about it being difficult to fish smaller flies dry cuts to the very heart of the problems with the new technique, and it is the key which differentiates post-Halfordian dry flies from the earlier patterns, tied in Ogden's era. In his last paragraph, Pennell identifies exactly why the dry fly took so long to catch on – it was very hard to fish it. In fact it seems quite likely that early dry-fly fishers largely confined themselves to the use of patterns imitating *Ephemera danica* and *E. vulgata* and the reason there was such a patchy uptake of the method to begin with was in all probability because it was only rewarding at times and places where there was a good hatch of these large flies.

Small dry flies were hard to fish for numerous reasons. The first was that they would not 'cock' correctly. 'Cocking' was a very important concept to dry-fly fishermen, and the word is bandied about endlessly in books of the period, so perhaps it is worthwhile taking a bit of time to understand what it meant to them. At its most basic and almost certainly as Halford understood it, a cocked fly was one that landed the right way up, with its wings pointing at the sky. However, it gradually came to mean more than that, and books on dry-fly fishing written in the early, and even the late twentieth century, continually refer to flies standing on 'tiptoe'. Authors out did each other in increasing flights of hyperbole until the 1940s, when Taverner and Moore gave the following definition:

> A fly is said to cock in dry-fly fishing when it sits perkily upon the points of the hackle and rides the surface very high. In other words, the points of the hackle have but slightly penetrated the elastic skin of the water.[20]

As a counsel of perfection, this is all very well, but it is easy to establish that even the bushiest dry flies very rarely ride on their hackle points, and the vast majority just settle into the water and lie with their bodies awash and the lower hackle points submerged. At least one modern authority has pointed this out,[21] and you can confirm it independently by a few minutes' observation of a dry fly floating in the bath. Strange though it may seem, the upstream dry-fly school became so fascinated with the idea of fishing a fly balanced upon its hackle points that they failed to see the evidence on the water in front of them. It was only one of a series of observational errors that was to dog them.

A Halford mayfly (top) and an early nineteenth century mayfly

During your walk along the river bank, you would have noticed that however rarely modern dry flies float on their tiptoes, nineteenth century ones almost never did. You would have seen them landing on their sides, or even upside down and a glance at the drawings above will show you why. There was a world of a difference between early nineteenth century designs and the 'Halfordian' patterns which largely overcame the problem. But the chief difficulty was that the offending flies were most often tied to gut, which made their bodies bulky and positively encouraged them to sink. To add insult to injury, flies were extremely difficult to store, due to the bulk of the gut, which had a nasty habit of rotting during the winter. All these problems were exaggerated where small flies were concerned, because their size denied them the natural buoyancy to resist the drag of the gut.

H.S. Hall's up-eyed hooks first went on the market in 1879, and they were an instant success, in marked contrast to Hewett Wheatley's failure to establish similar hooks thirty years previously. As we know, eyed hooks had been around for millennia and it seems strange that fishermen waited until 1879 before they adopted the invention, but there were several reasons why earlier inventors failed to establish their designs. The first was that the knots necessary to tie small hooks on to fine gut took time to evolve and wouldn't appear until the 1880s. Second, Hall's marketing techniques were impeccable and above all, his product arrived at exactly the moment it was needed; just when the dry-fly men were casting around to find a solution to help them float their smaller patterns. It probably isn't surprising that Halford became Hall's greatest apologist:

> Flies dressed on eyed-hooks float much better and with less drying than those constructed on the old system. I am quite prepared to find some controversy raised on the point, and hence would urge those who dissent from this well-considered opinion to remember that in the case of the hook lashed to the gut by the waxed silk, there is in the body the additional weight of the gut itself, and, certainly, far more silk and wax, owing to the foundation of the body being increased in thickness by the substance of the gut. This increase is even more than appears at the first glance, seeing that the augmentation in the diameter of the body produces more than thrice that augmentation in the circumference or quantity of silk and wax used in binding it.[22]

I'm sure that some of you will be way ahead of me by now and are wondering why we revere Halford as the champion of the dry fly and not H. S. Hall. After all, he did tie dry flies down to a modern size 17 on his new hooks and many of his dressings appeared in the *Fishing Gazette* before they were published as a series in 1885.[23] Perhaps Hall's attention was diverted by all the energy he was putting into selling his new range of hooks, but he fell into the same trap that Louis Rhead would later do in America and he published a series of flies which were not coupled to clearly identified naturals. Many of his patterns were tied with detached bodies in a style which was heavily derivative of Ogden (see page 282 for Ogden's flies) and which simply does not work for small patterns, because they do not float at all well. In fact, after making a comparison, the cynic might suggest that all Hall did was to take Ogden's list of flies, drop the real old-timers and update the patterns slightly. But the real reason why Hall did not succeed is that a high proportion of his patterns were fancy flies that didn't imitate any particular insect at all. In the post-Ronalds era, this simply wasn't good enough.

Hall's Jenny Spinner, Black Gnat and The Intermediate from Fishing, *Salmon and Trout, Cholmondeley-Pennell (1885)*

The stage was set – but for two things. Despite the vast improvements made in floating fly design during the 1880s, it wasn't until the floating qualities of flies and lines were improved that dry-fly fishing as we know it could fully develop. One of the most important discoveries made by the dry-fly pioneers was that a paraffin-soaked fly could be kept afloat for much longer than an untreated one. American readers will know paraffin as kerosene and it is said that this happy innovation was made by a relative of Colonel Peter Hawker's, who was generous enough to confide the knowledge to a Mr Thomas Andrews.[24] Dewar, a contemporary of Halford's, described Andrews as a 'pisciculturist', and it is too much of a coincidence to imagine that this wasn't the same Andrews whose hatchery Halford visited at Guildford in 1888 and who is pictured in *An Angler's Autobiography*.

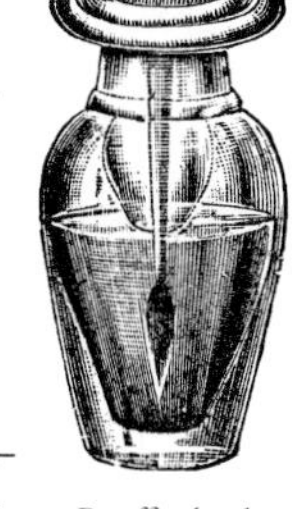

Paraffin bottle

According to Hills, the first time a Houghton club member used paraffin was in 1895, the implication being that this was pioneering stuff, but Halford said that fishermen on the upper Test knew of this valuable trick years before it became more widely known. This is quite likely to be correct and as evidence for Halford's testimony, we can quote Hi-Regan, who recalled his introduction to dry-fly fishing in 1857:

> In the 'Mutiny year' paraffin oil was little known, but 'Pegg' made many raids on the bottle of 'Burmese oil' which I used for my guns. This was the 'thinnest' oil then known, and he used it to steep fly materials before tying. These he dried, and although he lost some material by discolouration, he preserved enough for his purposes. Not thinking dry-fly fishing worth pursuing, I took no pains to acquire the niceties of it, and must store away with other regrettable indiscretions of my youth, my neglect in not learning the secret of making feathers

> 'waterproof' (Pegg's word). In this connection, may not the popularity of coot's, mallard's, teal's, and starling's feathers be accounted for? They are all birds which have oil glands for lubricating their plumage. Rail's feathers also resist moisture, to enable the bird to comfortably traverse the meadows.[25]

Paraffin was brushed on to flies and it was particularly helpful where small, less buoyant flies were concerned. It wasn't an ideal solution, because it took time for the 'slick' of excess flotant to disperse, and this made quick changes of pattern slightly difficult, but it was far and away the easiest way of getting a fly to float. The other and much trickier problem was that paraffin accentuated the colour of the majority of furs used for bodies. While this baffled anglers for a short while, it was soon overcome and there was a period when it was common to tie dry flies with quill, horsehair and celluloid, materials whose colours were not altered by paraffin and which had the added advantage of not absorbing water.

Some parties thought brushing petroleum derivatives on flies was a bit unsporting and there was much speculation that trout didn't like the flavour of natural paraffin, with the result that a period of experimentation with deodorised paraffin followed, but the fish didn't seem to mind and it was abandoned. A rather tongue-in-cheek Hills recorded some of the arguments against the material in *River Keeper*:

> Deep were the doubts expressed and gravely were heads shaken over this dangerous novelty. Would not paraffin prevent the fish from taking? Would it not put them permanently off the feed? Would it not foul the water and poison the fish? And, if none of these disasters happened, would not the cooked trout smell and taste abominably?[26]

Another popular method of treating a fly so that it would float was to dissolve Vaseline in petrol; the artificial was dipped in the solution, and the petrol left to evaporate, leaving the fly coated in the gel.

Paraffin seemed to get anglers thinking. If flies could be made to float, why not the line? Fishermen were keen to extend the drifts of their flies and much cogitation went into solving this problem. It does seem bizarre that there was such a long delay before silk lines were treated to float, but in reality it only took a few decades after the dry-fly saga began for the discovery to be made. To begin with, the accepted material for treating fly lines was deer's fat, and Hardys sold tins of red stag's fat for many years, but there was considerable experimentation and one popular solution was to rub the line down with

Vaseline and beeswax. After the First World War, Vaseline came under suspicion of rotting the line, but by then the tackle suppliers had come to the rescue and in the 1930s the most generally used flotant was Mucilin, a liquid form of which was later made available for treating flies. That didn't stop the lateral thinkers: in extremis, common mutton suet was used and Carter Platts[27] had a rather peculiar acquaintance who used nothing but raw bacon fat. He can't have had many friends in mid-summer. John Betts tells me that he has used beef, mutton and bacon fat in his time and that while none of them are a good solution, all of them work.

Frederic Halford

It is more or less customary to credit Halford with the invention of the upstream dry fly, but he didn't and never claimed to have done so; he merely refined the methods and became the high priest of the art. The other fisherman to whom he owed (as do we all) a huge debt, was G. S. Marryat, and H. S. Hall must have served as an inspiration to him. There were many more involved: E. J. Power, Dr T. Sanctuary; and various professionals including Holland, Hammond, Currell and Chalkley. This group took the floating fly, improved on it and produced the dry fly that we use today.

Since it is becoming impossible to keep Halford out of this story any more, I had better walk him out of the wings and introduce him properly. On April 28th 1879, came a chance encounter which changed the entire course of fly fishing history: Frederic Halford dropped into John Hammond's fishing shop in Winchester to buy some flies. There was another angler in the shop and although Halford may not have known him by sight, he would have known him by name, because the other fisherman already had a formidable reputation as a dry-fly man. Halford wrote very little about the event, but it must have made a deep impression upon him, even allowing for the fact that he couldn't have had any idea of what would follow. It is easy to imagine the pair standing before the counter, Halford shyly extending his hand, and the expression on his face when the other was introduced as George Selwyn Marryat. Later, Halford wrote that he was much impressed with Marryat's personality and even went so far as to admit that he was loath to leave the shop.

It is hard to think of any other encounter which has had more influence on the subsequent course of fly fishing, with the exception perhaps of Izaac Walton's meeting with Charles Cotton. Between them,

Halford and Marryat would change the face of dry-fly fishing out of recognition, developing patterns that catapulted it into the modern age. Fortunately, they were both in the prime of their lives, perhaps at the peak of their intellectual and fly fishing skills. At the time, Halford was thirty-five years old and Marryat only a few years older.

Marryat is a shadowy figure, and it is unfortunate that we know little about him beyond anecdote and a few references by Halford. He was presumably born in 1840 or 1841, since he won a scholarship to Winchester in 1854. After a period abroad with the army, he returned to England in 1870 and quickly built up a reputation as a skilled dry-fly fisherman. After Marryat met Halford in Hammond's, the two quickly became firm friends; a friendship which changed Halford's life. In 1880, Halford took rooms at Houghton Mill, where the pair did everything they could to set out as much as possible about the theory and practice of dry-fly fishing.

Houghton Mill

Halford wrote that the motivation for the development of the series of dry flies to which he subsequently devoted his life was the many discussions he had had with Marryat about the lack of uniformity among the patterns sold in the shops:

> Not only did the sizes, the shapes and the colours vary among different fly-dressers, but the same fly-tyer would make considerable variation in his flies, and at times a dozen delivered by the

> same man as the same fly would contain several varieties. The necessity of systematising our artificial flies in this way impressed itself very strongly upon us, and eventually I decided to publish a work on the methods of dressing the flies, with a considerable number of patterns described and illustrated in colours.[28]

Halford's first work, *Floating Flies and How to Dress Them*, was published in 1886. In it, Halford tells the reader that he drew heavily on Marryat's natural talent and experience and he never made any secret of the fact that he wanted Marryat to be joint author, but the latter, ever keen on avoiding the limelight, declined. The extent of Marryat's influence on *Floating Flies* can only be guessed at, but it must have been immense, given that Halford had comparatively little experience of fly-tying techniques - and, ironically, of fishing the Mayfly - at that stage. Indeed, in those early days, the majority of what Halford knew about fly tying was learned from Marryat. Their collaboration seemed set to last for many years, but sadly, Marryat died during an epidemic on 14th February 1896, and he is buried in Salisbury cathedral. Many regard him as the most skilled dry-fly fisherman that has ever lived.

Great though the blow of his friend's death was, Halford pushed on with what had become his life's work. He continued to refine his ideas, and his final selection, comprising thirty-three flies, was published fourteen years later in *Modern Development of the Dry-fly*. The thirty-three are a stunning achievement, because, with the exception of six large patterns which imitate the larger mayflies, there is a clearly identified pattern for every common smaller mayfly, with three sedges, the black gnat and the brown ant thrown in for good measure. Look at the flies carefully and compare them with Hall's series and the weaknesses of the earlier series are immediately apparent. Yes, Hall catered for the smaller mayflies, but he offers nothing like the same range as Halford and his spinner patterns only differ from the duns in name, whereas Halford's are dressed with dropped wings, just like the naturals. But the key difference lies in the style of tying. Halford's flies (think Marryat too) are tied with a dense hackle and supporting tails, whereas Hall's are hopelessly unbalanced, and given the sophistication of artwork in the late nineteenth century, he could hardly blame the illustrator.

It was characteristic of Hall that he didn't take being upstaged by Halford at all kindly and he wrote to Halford in no uncertain terms about it. It must have been a shock to Halford to receive the letter from his old friend and he devoted an entire chapter in *Modern Development of the Dry Fly* to answering his criticism.[29] The excerpts from Hall's letter do not make edifying reading and some of his bleatings are frankly pathetic. Halford's innately benign character shows when he responds politely to no-hopers like, 'I must confess that, except with regard to the spinners, I do not see anything very different from what I have used already.'

There was no slackening of progress and when his financial circumstances allowed him to retire in 1889 at the age of forty-five, Halford became obsessed with obtaining an exact match to the colour of the insects he was imitating, with the result that he spent many thousands of hours comparing his artificials to preserved naturals. To this end, *Modern Development* included an extremely useful colour key, derived from the colour chart popularised by the Royal Horticultural Society in 1905.[30]

I have often been asked what Halford really did for fly fishermen. After all, he didn't invent the dry fly, and he didn't even invent the dry-fly method. What he did do was to devise a brilliant series of patterns which allowed his peers to fish imitative small dry flies right through the season and to enjoy their sport even in the dog days of August. Nobody else could offer that, especially not H. S. Hall.

Just before I break out into song over Halford's achievements, it is worth standing back and identifying what he did do. Despite the great care he took over his work, some of it was conceptually flawed. He came in for a great deal of criticism later on over the details of his 'exact imitation', since he viewed his artificials from above, resting on a white dish, rather than from below, in the position from which the trout saw them. In addition, there is little doubt that the preservative altered the colours of his flies and thus the colours of the artificials, though Halford hotly denied the charge. It is ironic that the problem which really did dog him, despite the carefully executed and beautifully coloured drawings in his books, is that retailers frequently tied such poor imitations of his patterns that they might as well have called them by another name. But these are minor criticisms and there is no doubt that when they were properly tied, Halford's flies worked, because the collection was the mainstay of a generation of fishermen and its influence lives on into our own fly boxes, more than a century later.

Of course, there was more to Halford than just a set of patterns. He attempted to do something that no one had ever dared to do before and devised a set of rules which defined his favoured method of fly fishing. In 1886, Halford's definition of dry-fly fishing was:

> ... presenting to the rising fish the best possible imitation of the insect on which he is feeding in its natural position.

PLATE VI

IRON BLUE DUNS AND SPINNERS

No. 18
IRON BLUE DUN
MALE

No. 19
IRON BLUE DUN
FEMALE

No. 20
IRON BLUE SPINNER
MALE

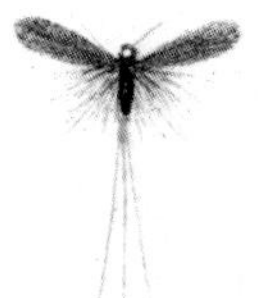

No. 21
IRON BLUE SPINNER
FEMALE

FLIES DRESSED BY C. FARLOW & CO., LTD., LONDON.
(10 CHARLES STREET, ST. JAMES'S SQUARE, S.W., AND 191 STRAND, W.C.)

Flies from Halford's final series

Which he broke down to five conditions:

> 1. Finding a fish feeding on winged insects.
> 2. Presenting to him a good imitation of the natural insect both as to size and colour.
> 3. Presenting it to him in its natural position, floating and 'cocked.'
> 4. Putting it lightly on the water so that it floats accurately over him without drag.
> 5. That the four previous points should have been fulfilled before the fish has caught sight of the angler and his rod.

One might think that Halford's five points define a narrow enough church, but others split upstream dry-fly fishing down even further, into the purist and ultra-purist schools. Ultra-purists wouldn't cast to anything except a rising fish, which meant that they could spend much of a day completely occupied by the skilled task of doing nothing but sit in watchful expectation. The impetuous purists would occasionally 'try to tempt a fish into position' by casting over a trout that wasn't rising, but which looked as if it might. That anyone could be bothered to make such a fine distinction gives an insight into the narrow minds of some of the men who fished the chalk streams in those days. Even Halford was dubious about the motives of the ultra-purists:

> Some dry-fly fishermen are such purists that they will not under any circumstances whatever make a single cast except over a rising fish, and prefer to remain idle the entire day rather than attempt to persuade the wary inhabitants of the stream to rise at an artificial fly, unless they have previously seen a natural one taken in the same position. Although respecting their scruples, this is, in my humble opinion, riding the hobby to death, and I for one am a strong advocate for floating a cocked fly over a likely place, even if no movement of a feeding fish has ever been seen there.[31]

Such narrow distinctions were to prove a recipe for trouble in later years, but in 1886, the storm clouds hadn't begun to gather. The upstream, dry-fly only school hadn't consolidated its grip on the chalk streams, and there was a wide range of methods in use. Indeed, only the year before, Marston published a far-sighted essay on dry-fly fishing in the *Fishing Gazette* which recommended fishing a dry fly both up and downstream, a tactic which Halford was happy to endorse at the time. It was early days for the new technique and the concept of the upstream dry fly was still novel enough that Halford found it necessary to describe how to dry a fly by false-casting and he even felt he needed to make the case for the single-handed dry-fly rod.

It is hard to overstate how great Halford's influence was. His name became almost synonymous with chalk stream fishing and his innovations didn't go unnoticed abroad. It was Halford's work that inspired M. Albert Petit to write the book which re-introduced and popularised fly fishing in France.[32] As we shall see later, Halford was also an important influence on American fly tying; by 1888 *Floating Flies and How to Dress Them* could be purchased for twelve dollars from *Forest and Stream* and his flies were available from William Mills of New York in the same year. American fishers were slow to adopt the dry fly until after the First World War, although three books and numerous articles were published on the subject prior to 1914.

In view of the criticism which would later be heaped upon Halford, it is worthwhile reviewing his position on other styles of fishing. It is convenient to picture him as an irritable old didact, and many writers do, but in fact he was an extremely genial character and his more extreme views were seldom expressed and crystallised very gradually in his old age. He could still (reluctantly) see the case for the downstream dry fly as late as 1913:

> There are occasionally places where upstream fishing is barely possible, and at times, too, the force of the wind is so great that even with a downwind finish and a cast of only $2^1/_2$ yards in length it is almost impossible to place a fly accurately into the teeth of the gale. Then it is permissible to fish downstream or partly across and partly down even with the floating fly.[33]

It will surprise some readers to discover that in his early books, Halford actually defended wet-fly fishing on chalk streams, but he tolerated this method of fishing less and less as he grew older. By 1913 he had decided that wet-fly fishing was a breach of chalk-stream ethics, a decision which was very likely influenced by the publication of Skues' *Minor Tactics of the Chalk Stream and Kindred Studies*:

> I will at once freely admit that upstream wet-fly fishing is not so harmful on a chalk-stream as the same method practised downstream. But in my view the continual flogging and the continual movement of the angler making his way along the bank, too often in full view of the trout, are, however, very nearly as destructive of the confidence of the fish as downstream fishing. Then, too, the distance covered by the persistent flogger

> is so great that the limits of any ordinary length of private water will be covered many times in an ordinary day's fishing. The excuse which is sometimes advanced to palliate the breach of etiquette committed in using the sunk fly on a dry-fly stream is that the aim of a fly fisherman is to kill fish with a fly whether wet or dry – surely this should not be so on water preserved entirely for the dry-fly.[34]

This was the beginning of a long drawn-out battle of wills between Halford and Skues, which was all the more extraordinary for the obliquity with which each man pursued his arguments. It takes a hard search to find any evidence of direct attacks by one master on the other, and when they do occur, they are mainly attacks made by Skues upon Halford. However, there is no doubt that the collision of the pair's philosophies took its toll on Halford, and it manifested itself in a slow shift of his position away from tolerance of the wet fly.

Every time I read Halford, I am struck by how much he enjoyed fishing a dry fly (at which he was a master) and how little he liked other methods. This dislike would be rationalised into disapproval, and finally downright opposition to the methods which he had tolerated and even enjoyed as a younger man. Perhaps this was a symptom of the growing inflexibility that affects the human mind with advancing age, although to be fair it was an attitude that was already prevalent on the chalk streams in the 1890s.

In 1913, Halford put his cards on the table and began to compare the upstream dry-fly rule to the St Andrew's 'Etiquette of Golf':

> If a member of a golf club is unsportsman-like, or possibly only careless, and habitually commits the grave indiscretion of disregarding the etiquette of the game, he will find difficulty in persuading his fellow-members to make a friendly match with him. I would suggest that the ethics of the dry-fly on a fishery where dry-fly only is permitted should be regarded in the same light.[35]

The key to Halford's thinking was expressed in the final sentence of the quote above: dry fly where only dry fly is permitted. It is very important to realise that Halford didn't object to wet-fly fishing per se. On the other hand, Halford and many others regarded the wet fly as a dangerous method on chalk streams, where he was convinced that it could be used to make large bags of under-sized fish, but Halford had no objection to its use elsewhere:

> In the hands of a past-master it [wet-fly fishing] is a most scientific and, under favourable conditions, a very deadly method of fishing.[36]

Curiously enough, although he didn't fish a wet fly himself, Halford was something of an authority on nymphs and he spent many hours studying them hatching in aquaria and in the river. Halford described the 'bulge' rise that trout make when they take nymphs just under the surface at some length, but for all his patiently acquired knowledge and experiments, he never made the leap of imagination that Skues did. This failure to connect observation with practice is uncannily similar to the story of Ronalds and I often wonder why it was that two such great men should have failed to have appreciated the evidence before their own eyes.

Other than his dislike of fishing a wet fly, I find it hard to understand why Halford didn't discover the secret of nymph fishing, because it was easily within his power to do so. Perhaps the reason was the experiments he carried out with Marryat in the early days of their friendship; experiments which by Halford's admission went disastrously wrong:

> We killed a few fish with them [the nymph patterns], but discontinued their use for two reasons. The first, that in our opinion they were essentially wet-flies, and the use of them on waters reserved for the dry-fly only, constituted a breach of the ethics of the dry-fly. The second, which may possibly be a more cogent reason in the minds of many modern anglers, was that wherever and whenever we used them we found that the number of fish hooked and lost was out of all proportion to the total bag, and that the fish rapidly became shy and unapproachable.[37]

In my experience, this a fairly accurate description of nymph fishing, although the failure must have been a surprise to Marryat, accustomed as he was to cleaning up with a dry fly. The effect it had on Halford was much more profound; perhaps because his carefully ordered view of the world forced him to construct an explanation for their lack of success, he rationalised that it wasn't possible to catch a fish using an artificial nymph.

> Some readers may inquire why the dun in the nympha state should not be imitated, and, as remarked in the previous chapter, it is my opinion that the difficulty does not lie in dressing an artificial grub fairly representing the dun nymph, but imparting to that imitation the motion and direction taken by the natural insect at that stage of its existence.[38]

This statement is extraordinary not only because it disregards the very similar problem presented by moving dry flies, but also because it ignores the fact that vision isn't the trout's keenest sense; something which had been known for sixty years even in Halford's day.

Halford was an acute observer, but in the final analysis he was a decidedly vertical thinker. In addition, once he had drawn a wrong conclusion he seldom seemed to change his mind and so it was in this case. When he had made the error, Halford compounded it by classing the upstream nymph with the downstream wet fly; a prejudice which ultimately exposed him to the severest criticism. But for all that, Halford did a great service to angling; he put dry-fly fishing on a firm footing that stood it in good stead for the future, and above all he achieved what so many of us would love to do, retired early and spent all his days in pursuit of the sport he loved best.

Dissenters

In 1912, a landmark article was published.[39] Sir Henry Cunynghame made the first description of a dry fly as seen by a fish swimming below the surface. For the first time, anglers knew how a fly actually appeared to a fish, an understanding which would ultimately have a profound effect on fly design. Within a year, Dr Francis Ward, drawing on work conducted in a specially dug observation pond, had published two articles in *The Field*, describing experiments he had conducted with trout and salmon flies, giving an illustration of how an angler looked when seen from under water.

In a book published the previous year, Ward had drawn attention to the way a fish saw a fly:

> I would mention in passing, that the most gaudy fly seen against the surface of the water merely appears a grey iridescent silhouette, and for this reason I do not think that the colour of the fly matters if the size be right for the condition of the water and the fly be fished so as to suggest life.[40]

There was considerable correspondence, and controversy soon followed. As Hills pointed out much later, the fact that the dry fly was fished because it made it easier to catch trout had been forgotten by the majority of its devotees:

> Modern writers have got into the curious trick of thinking the opposite. They talk as though it made the catching of trout

Ward's observation pond

> harder, and was meant to do so. They write as though it were introduced to protect the trout from any except the skilled. From this comes the strange inversion that the sunk fly is easier than the dry. It ought to be forbidden, they say, because any fool can kill with it.[41]

Reason, however, became an early casualty in the argument which raged on until the outbreak of war diverted men's minds on to other things. Into this maelstrom walked Dr James Mottram, blissfully unaware that he was destined to become cannon-fodder in a dispute which was to rage on until shortly before the Second World War.

An enquiring man, who was inspired by Ward's writing to bring his scientific training to the subject, Mottram advocated a new method of fly design, which concentrated upon buoyancy, silhouette and transparency, rather than upon the exact imitation of colour.[42] The doctor's dressings certainly were different; he omitted dubbing on parts of the body where the natural was transparent, tied flies which imitated fish fry, and designed buzzer patterns which were buoyed by small pieces of cork (though the idea of using cork in fly bodies wasn't new; Hi-Regan gave a pattern for a cork-bodied fly in 1886, and cork had been advocated several centuries before.) Mottram's book was influential, but his downfall was that he included a chapter on nymph fishing which irritated Skues. The latter wrote rather caustically:

> I am aware that a book called 'Fly Fishing: Some New Arts and Mysteries' (Dr. J. C. Mottram) has set out an interesting method of nymph fishing. I do not wish to be understood as disparaging his flies or his methods in any way, as I have never tried them. In theory they seem to me to have the defects of rigidity, density and dullness of colouring, and a tendency to fall heavily when cast, by reason of absence of hackle.[43]

This probably qualifies as the most intolerant statement Skues ever made, and quite apart from the fact that he really couldn't expect to have it both ways, it does make me wonder what he would have thought of something as completely heretical as Sawyer's Pheasant Tail nymphs. Anyway, lacking either Skues' charisma or support, Mottram was an easy target for his dry-fly colleagues. The pressure told, and in the end he sold out and became a dry-fly man, but in the process he played a key part in the evolution of modern flies.

In 1924, J.W. Dunne published a book which struck another blow at Halford. Dunne had become fascinated with the idea of translucency in fly bodies and he designed a series of flies tied on white-painted hooks with different coloured silks which were cleverly blended to make tertiary colours. Dunne started thinking when he bought a set of Halford's flies and found that they didn't bear any resemblance to the insects he saw:

> But to tell the truth, I was more than a little puzzled at the number of Test flies which were not included in the Halford series. Every day, and all day long, these neglected insects were hatching out in hosts. They were all duns, sober–looking duns with almost colourless legs and setæ, with wings varying from crinkled pewter to the tint of Sheffield plate worn thin, and with plain, monochromatic bodies varying from the palest honey to the darkest amber. I could only conclude that these flies were peculiar to the Longparish part of the Test, and that for the beautiful, barred olives, and for the cream-striped pale wateries, one must journey down-stream, Stockbridge way.[44]

Sadly, Dunne's patterns are no use at all to us now, mostly because he chose to use a system of specially numbered artificial tying silks which are no longer available. Until then, most dry flies had been tied in a range of silk specially developed for fly tying and marketed by Pearsall, under the 'Gossamer' brand, which were first marketed in 1885. However, the Dunne patterns are very interesting, because almost every aspect of his patterns is expressed with a number. His flies were a bold attempt to solve the problem of translucency, but they had several drawbacks. The special silk (known as cellulite) was terribly fragile, and one trout could ruin a fly. Worse still, the artificials, which looked incredibly lifelike when back-lit by the sun, lost all their translucency the moment a cloud passed over. Nonetheless, the patterns enjoyed modest success and flies tied to Dunne's recipe were available from Hardys as recently as 1966.

These new developments stirred the water enough to set fishermen thinking again and the post-Halford consensus began to break up. In 1931, E. W. Harding extended Ward's work greatly. His patient work viewing naturals and artificials with a water tank agreed with Ward's experiments twenty years previously:

> The general conclusions which may be legitimately drawn from these observations and from the light pattern theory show that its shape is of primary and its colour is of secondary importance until the fly is in the central area of the window... It is not often that an 'exact imitation', if such a thing is possible, is essential, even if the fish delays his rise to inspect the fly somewhere in the centre of his window.

In itself this was hardly new, but Harding's observations were made with an experienced fly fisherman's eye and they drove a coach and horses through the exact imitation school's theory:

> They appear to assume that the trout habitually takes the floating fly after seeing it in his window and that, therefore, he sees it against a bright light. Thence, on the analogy of human vision, they argue that he must see it as a dark silhouette devoid of colour. It would appear, on the contrary, that as often as not the trout rises to the light pattern of the floating fly before ever it reaches his window.
>
> But when the trout obviously does inspect the fly in his window, it must be remembered that his eye almost certainly magnifies largely and that, therefore, he can distinguish colour much more clearly than might be supposed. If the reader will look through a fairly strong magnifying glass at a fly against strong daylight, he will be able to distinguish its colours quite clearly, though probably unable to do so with the naked eye. When looking directly into strong sunlight, the trout probably does see only a dark silhouette, but he does not always, or even often, have to take his food in these circumstances.[45]

Harding's book was a monumental work, set against the standards of the day and it still is. It was the best attempt to date at a scientifically-based fly-fishing book and in many respects little has been done to improve on it since, except to repeat his experiments with better quality photographs. For example, he draws attention to the way the wings of a natural fly are first seen as a pale detached shadow, which only unites with the body as the fly approaches, an important point which has had the indignity of being presented as a new fact by later authors.

Even Harding's work was partly derivative. Although the dry-fly debate was essentially an English argument, it seems to me quite likely that Harding's work was based, at least in part, on Hewitt's *Secrets of the Salmon*, published in 1922. Hewitt published an extensive series of photographs of flies – both wet and dry – taken from beneath the water, using similar apparatus to Ward.

This talk of Hewitt gives us a good excuse to look across the Atlantic. Until the last years of the nineteenth century, the refinement of the dry fly was an English story, chiefly because brown trout were an Old World creature, but it wasn't long before man's urge to improve on the way nature orders things led to experiments in transplantation and although none of the people involved can have suspected it, these peregrinations were to have a profound effect on the subsequent development of the dry fly. For twenty years it seemed that the oceans were criss-crossed with the wakes of ships playing an epic game of backgammon with our trout populations and so few records were kept that it is hard to keep track of what went where, save to say that the genetic pool became irretrievably mixed up. Sea trout eggs were exported to Australia as early as 1866; brook charr were sent to England in 1869 and New Zealand in 1877; rainbows arrived in New Zealand in 1881 and England in 1884; but perhaps the most significant planting occurred in 1883, when a German steamship called the Werra docked at the New York waterfront. It was an unremarkable landing apart from one item on the ship's manifest: eighty thousand brown trout eggs lying on cool moss-lined trays.

The Werra shipment was the result of Fred Mather's attendance at the International Fisheries Exposition held at Berlin in 1880, where he met Baron Friedrich von Behr, the president of the German Fisheries Society. Mather was invited to fish on the Baron's water near Baden-Baden in the Black Forest and it dawned on him that the shy brown trout he found there were ideally situated to withstand the growing fishing pressure in the environs of cities like New York and Philadelphia. The other attribute of the brown trout that endeared them to Mather was their ability to cope with water temperatures above seventy-five degrees, which convinced him that they might do well in the rivers of the eastern watersheds, where the water was slowly warming as a result of the devastating clear-felling that had followed the American civil war. The problem Mather was trying to resolve was the impending loss of the cold-water-loving brook trout which had been the cornerstone of American fly fishing until then.

The browns were planted without any ceremony in several Eastern rivers, in some cases without any record whatsoever being made. Two more shipments followed, one from Sir Ramsey Gibson Maitland's Loch Leven hatchery in Scotland, the other from the Hampshire chalk streams. For some reason, the original Werra planting has sunk deeply into folk consciousness despite the fact that the German shipment formed the minority of the original plantings.

Mather was right; the browns did extraordinarily well, and good sized fish began to be caught on the Brodheads from 1889. The problem with the interlopers was that they were much fussier about their choice of fly than the brook trout had ever been and they could be damned hard to catch, so it wasn't long before they had attracted the derogatory name of 'German trout', an appellation which did not stand them in good stead in the war years which followed. In particular, the tendency of brown trout to settle down to feeding on a particular natural when there was a much wider selection on the menu was a sore trial to fishermen who were used to the more catholic tastes of brookies and rainbows.

The brown trout were not universally liked, but there were a few fishermen who persisted in trying to develop better methods of catching them, and one of them was a slight Pennsylvanian, by the name of Theodore Gordon. Gordon has been described as America's Walton and Cotton rolled into one, a title which I am sure he would have refused with a deprecating wince and a nervous pull at one of the hand-rolled cigarettes that played such havoc with his health. As Paul Schullery points out, the problem with Gordon is that so much mystique has built up around him that it is impossible to see the man clearly any more, so dense is the myth. Nevertheless, there are some facts about Gordon that we can be sure of. He was born in Pittsburgh in 1854, of well-to-do parents, both of whom hailed from New York.[46] The Pittsburgh winters did Gordon's chest no favours and he missed much schooling, emerging as a moody and withdrawn adolescent, but sometime after the end of the civil war he got into fishing on a serious scale and took himself off to the Catskills to find a bit of space and solitude. The problem of catching browns set Gordon thinking and some time around 1889 the dry fly caught his imagination as a result of reading Halford's books. The result was that he began an exchange of letters with the Englishman, which led to Halford sending a complete set of dry flies to America, a collection which still survives, by the way, in the Angler's Club of New York, to which it was willed by Gordon's friend Roy Steenrod. Finding Halford's flies wanting in their new environment, Gordon set out to develop his own patterns, but by 1905, his health was in a decline only matched by his finances and he died of tuberculosis in 1915. America's most famous fly fisherman is buried in the dingy surroundings of New York Marble Cemetery in downtown Manhattan, a curious resting place for one whose life was so closely associated with the bright waters of the Catskills.

The influence Gordon had on American fly fishing was exercised through his 'Little Talks on Fly-Fishing' in the pages of *Forest and Stream* and in the *Fishing Gazette*. However, he wrote at a time when a huge boom in recreation was transforming American fly fishing and it is inappropriate to give Gordon the credit for every advance that occurred during this period, as some authors are wont to do. For example, Gordon is often said to have broken the dedication of American fishermen to the wet fly and to have kick started an American dry-fly tradition which concentrated on fishing the water rather than casting to individual rising fish: this is not so. What Gordon did do was to design a series of imitations, based on his studies of North American duns and spinners, which were subtle and impressionistic enough that their influence can still be seen in the products of American tyers today.

John Harrington Keene, a British emigrant to America in 1885 probably did as much as any other angler to introduce the dry fly to the USA through his book *Fly Fishing and Fly Making* and his articles in the *American Field* and the *American Angler.*

The successful introduction of the brown trout put an end to the era of glorious wet flies which Mary Orvis Marbury's book chronicled, but it was the selectivity of this new fish which catalysed the American dry-fly tradition. It is ironic that classic flies like the Quill Gordon and Roy Steenrod's Hendrikson were designed to tempt the palate of this notoriously fickle immigrant, rather than the native brook trout.[47]

The Twentieth Century

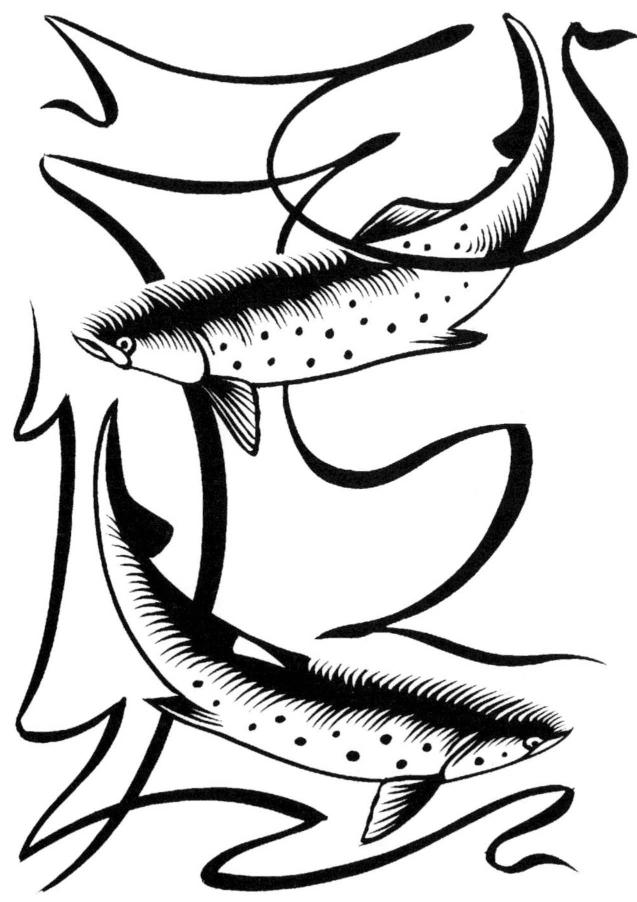

Frederic Halford and William Senior, circa 1900. Courtesy of the Flyfishers' Club.

CHAPTER SEVEN

The Twentieth Century

THE twentieth century is harder to assess in historical terms than you might think, chiefly because it is only recently past and time has yet to pass its judgement. In view of this, I have dealt with the last few decades in general terms, on the basis that it is hard to tell what is important and what is not. For example, fly fishing had contracted to a very small base by the 1970s and it is much too early to know whether the massive increase in popularity in fly fishing which started in the 1980s is a lasting trend or not. The same applies to a wide variety of new techniques which have appeared lately, from float tubing to epoxy flies. Some will prosper, some will fade into obscurity and in the end only time will tell.

Rods

At the beginning of the twentieth century, many fishermen felt that little more could be done to improve on the quality of the rods they used and this was reflected in confident articles published in the wide range of magazines available. Needless to say, there was still a lot of room for progress, but anglers had good reason to be self-assured, because the manufacturers who supplied them were at the peak of their resourcefulness. The 'hollow-built' rod is a good example of this inventiveness, a design which relies on having part of the pith of each bamboo spline pared away, reducing mass and allowing larger diameter rods to be built for any given weight. While it was attractive in theory, hollow-building was notoriously difficult to get right in practice and no one really got the hang of it until the early thirties. Edwin Powell took out a patent for a hollow rod in 1933, while Lew Stoner built a rod for Winston which had a U-shaped groove cut from the apex of each spline in the same year. Stoner's method maximised the glued area on the rod while keeping the weight as low as possible and Dick Miller used such a rod to cast one hundred and eighty-three feet in a tournament in 1938, a stunning distance even by today's standards.[1] In 1959 Hardys produced an improved hollow design using more modern glues and their Hollolight and Hollokona designs were used to break many European casting distance records.

Early Hardy Bros. rod advert

But I'm getting far ahead of myself. In 1900, a state-of the art trout fly rod was single handed, built of hexagonal split cane and generally between nine foot six inches and eleven foot long. Most salmon rods remained in the sixteen to eighteen foot range and there was an almost infinite selection of actions available, in split cane or the heavier greenheart. Trout rod weights had fallen to the extent that they were measured in ounces, but salmon rods were still heavy; the seventeen foot nine inch Hardy 'Champion' weighing 2lb 8oz, while the 'Hi-Regan' sixteen footer came in at a hefty 2lb 3½ oz.

Greenheart might have been the darling of British fishermen, but it couldn't hold its place against high-quality cane rods and from 1900 onwards it began to be relegated to making second quality trout rods. This transition of allegiance was very gradual and the 'old' materials persisted for much longer than many people think. For example, Hardys sold 'third quality' wood rods, constructed of hickory, lance-wood and split-cane bamboo until 1925. The firm produced hickory rods until 1939, and incredibly, Hardys greenheart rods didn't go out of production until 1952, the material having done sterling service for nearly seventy years. That was by no means the last gasp for the material, because Orvis made a very small number of 5¼oz greenheart trout rods in the late seventies and the well known US historian and writer Paul Schullery tells me that they are very pleasant to fish with.

The Ferrule Versus the Splice

Given that the Americans had cracked the design of strong, lightweight ferrules, you might assume that the splice would have rolled over and done the decent thing, but far from it. As it turned out, the splice had its heyday quite late in its career; during the nineteenth and early twentieth centuries. By the beginning of the twentieth century, the splice should have been dead, but the natural conservatism of many anglers combined to ensure that it wasn't. The influential 'Jock Scott' was still recommending the splice over the ferrule as late as the 1950s,[2] and spliced rods could still be bought from Sharpe ten years later, though they were well out of the mainstream - by 1960 the splice was an anachronism's anachronism. In a last rage against the dying of the light, the champions of spliced rods maintained that they were lighter, had better actions and were the only rods that cast 'true', but their words fell on deaf ears. Ferrules were easier and very few fishermen could see any virtue in laboriously whipping a splice together when the sections could just be pushed together and held in place by suction.

By now, every angler was likely to own several reels, which brought up a new problem of matching a series of reels to a single rod. In response, reel seats began to standardise, a good example being the 'Universal' reel seat invented by Dr Emil Weeger, a design which was introduced by Hardys in 1883. The Universal had two wedge-shaped holders, the lower one fixed to take one end of the reel foot, the other a loose ring that pushed down to secure the reel. By 1913, a further refinement had been made and Hardy released their patent 'screw winch fitting'. This new reel seat hid the one side of the reel mount in a recess in the cork at the bottom of the cork handle and trapped the other end of the reel foot under a locking ring. This was a great idea and a century of ingenuity has done nothing to improve on it, so with minor modifications this type of reel seat is still in widespread use today.

Cork was now in widespread use as a covering for handles and it quickly became the hallmark of a modern rod. Prior to the 1880s, butts were made either by machining a swelling into the material, or less frequently, by wrapping it with materials like pig skin. By 1910, the use of cork was almost universal and the material hasn't been bettered yet, although some cheaper modern rods use synthetic materials.

That irascible old Irishman, James O'Gorman, would have been deliriously happy with the advancements in rod rings. The old drop ring which swung loose, fastened to the rod by a hoop set parallel to the line of the rod, had gone out of fashion by the beginning of the twentieth century. Snake and bridge rings were the rule on better rods; tip rings were lined with agate on quality rods, and made of tempered steel on second quality rods. Modern advances in tip rings would make a study in themselves, but most of the changes have been cosmetic rather than functional. American rods in the early years of the century often had a tip ring which was set almost in the plane of the rod, rather than being tipped down at nearer ninety degrees to the shank as is favoured these days. This feature can be seen on many early Leonards. Later Leonards used agate-lined rings fixed at a greater angle to the blank, and Hardys adopted the same style, bracing the ring with two German silver struts. Agate was dropped after the Second World War and most modern rods feature variants of the 'perfection guide' – a pear-shaped ring, often set at an angle nearer to forty-five degrees to the blank, so do fashions change. Running guides have been through a similar metamorphosis. The ring and keeper style which was popular during the nineteenth century went out of favour very quickly after

1900, chiefly because the swinging rings collapsed during a vigorous cast and trapped the line, killing any shoot. They were replaced for a very short period around the turn of the century with small 'tunnel guides' which were formed from a double twist of wire, but these were quickly toppled by the all-conquering snake guide, which appeared on English rods from about 1900. For reasons which escape me, if you hold an American rod with the tip facing away from you, the snake guides open to the left, while English guides open to the right. No doubt there is some deep Freudian significance to this.

Advances in casting technique meant that extra large bridge rings soon began to be fitted, to facilitate the shooting of line, and as far as trout rods were concerned, with the exception of the type of material used and a other few minor details, every single feature of modern rod fittings had been incorporated by 1930.

Salmon Rods

By the end of the First War, the consensus on salmon rods which had held so solidly for three hundred years was about to be broken. The key personality behind this trend was A.H.E. Wood, a deep thinker who revolutionised salmon fishing by inventing the 'greased-line' technique in the early 1930s.[3] Wood was a great bear of a man and a very interesting personality - he was an all-round athlete, an authority on bee-keeping, and is remembered as the creator of a renowned rock garden. In addition, he was a distinguished engineer and in his time was a director not only of BSA, but also of Daimler.

A.H.E. Wood. He is on the right in the picture, which was taken in 1923, and comes from Greased Line Fishing for Salmon, *by 'Jock Scott'.*

Wood developed a system which not only allowed summer fishing for salmon, but which encouraged the use of shorter rods and it transformed the face of salmon fishing. Hardys manufactured a series of similar split-cane rods carrying his name, but the rods weighed between $12^1/_4$ and $13^1/_2$ ounces, which may explain their lack of popularity with mere mortals who lacked Wood's terrific physique. While Wood fished with single-handed twelve foot rods, his less muscular friends and readers took to using stiff trout rods nine or ten feet in length. The old consensus was cracked, and once people had tried the new technique, it didn't take long for the new ideas to take over. A floating line didn't require a long, strong rod to lift it and the days of salmon fishing as a weight-lifter's sport were numbered.

Once the use of a long double-handed rod was called into question, everything changed. Nine feet was the target to beat, and it didn't take long to fall. Ten years after Wood's experiments, Lee Wulff took the issue to its logical extreme. Wulff fired a broadside at convention; the first of many gauntlets he threw down:

> How light can a rod be and still be adequate to handle a large salmon? There used to be agreement that a certain minimum length or weight of rod was essential for properly handling these large and powerful fish. Little by little the acceptable length of the rod has come down. As a pioneer in the use of extra light tackle for salmon, by 1940 I had come down to a 7-foot 2-and-a-half ounce fly rod, and since then have rarely used anything heavier. In 1943, in order to demonstrate to the most confirmed doubter, I eliminated the rod entirely from my tackle. Casting some 30-odd feet by hand, I hooked a 10-pound salmon and played it by holding the reel in my right hand, reeling with my left, until I could finally reach down and tail it with my own hand, ten minutes later.[4]

The arguments that Wulff put forward were so persuasive that the 'long' rod vanished from North American fishing within a decade. The short rod became the trade-mark of the American fly fisherman, and for a time anglers got so carried away that rods shrank to vestigial sizes. If salmon rods shrank, trout rods almost disappeared. Arnold Gingrich[5] fished for a time with a Phantom rod – a four and a quarter foot split-cane trout rod weighing one ounce, which was manufactured by Hardys.

For a long time, double-handed salmon rods were virtually eliminated from the United States, and only recently have they begun to make a comeback, as a Spey-casting craze sweeps America. Isn't it strange how fashions ebb and flow? The changeover seemed to occur in about 1994; before then I had to sneak about if I fished anywhere in North America with a long rod, for fear of being lectured on post-imperialist fly fishing culture; nowadays a small, curious queue forms at my side.

Glass and Carbon Fibre

The design and fittings of fly rods were pretty much agreed and so the next revolution was one of technology rather than technique. It didn't go smoothly. In the late thirties a few rod makers were seduced yet again by the possibilities of tubular steel as Carter Platts confirms in 1938:

> During the last few years a movement has been afoot to introduce the tubular steel rod to the British angler. It has already established itself in America, and, after handling both fly and bait-casting rods of this type, I am convinced that the steel trout rod is the rod of the future. The supercilious angler's sneer that he preferred to do his trout fishing otherwise than with nine feet of gas-pipe is as vacuous as were the jeers with which the unbeliever greeted the introduction of steel shafts for golf clubs, now popular the world over.[6]

With the delicious luxury of perfect hindsight, we sympathise. Steel was just a diversion and much better materials were on the way. After an experiment by Dr Arthur Howald in 1944, the first fibreglass rods were produced by the Shakespeare company in 1946. Howald's patent caused quite a few problems for the rest of the industry, because it prevented any other supplier from making rods from spirally wrapped longitudinal fibres; everyone else had to make their blanks from woven cloth and the results were noticeably inferior. By the time the patent had expired, carbon fibre had come along and so many anglers never had the chance to try a really good glass rod. Nevertheless, glass fibre was an easy material to work with and by 1949 several American tackle manufacturers were using it. There were many different types of lay-up: Howald's rods were built of fibreglass laid up over a wooden core; Shakespeare's Wonder rods were solid; but hollow designs subsequently appeared, produced by Conolon, who developed the technique of winding the glass cloth over a steel mandrel, which was extracted after the resin cured. John Betts tells me that Shakespeare's balsa-wood cored rods were the very best they ever made and came close to cane in terms of 'cell' structure. The current Hexagraph range of fly rods uses a variation of the same system, with graphite strips glued to a polyurethane foam centre and from personal experience I can say that these are the most wonderful rods to use, as long as you don't demand a quick action.

Fibreglass didn't come a moment too late for US anglers, because the post-war communist regime in China, no friend of America, had enforced an embargo on the export of Tonkin cane. By 1948 the embargo was biting deep and the majority of US companies gave up the production of split-cane rods over the next decade, with the result that cane rods vanished from American catalogues in short order. Those manufacturers that managed to carry on did so by importing from third parties, usually in Europe, which were not so badly affected by the embargo.

At least to begin with, fibreglass rods were expensive, and it took a while for tackle makers to work out successful tapers, all of which restricted their popularity; the result was that split cane rods could be found in European tackle catalogues right into the 1960s, by which time the American market was completely dominated by glass. Tradition had a hand here and many manufacturers had enormous investments bound up in split cane, so fibreglass upset the apple cart good and proper. The biggest challenge the new material brought was that it could be mass produced, threatening the carefully-established position of the major suppliers of split-cane rods, who relied on highly-paid skilled workforces, whose knowledge had been hard-won over many years of apprenticeship. In addition, anyone could get hold of good quality fibreglass, while high-grade bamboo sources were jealously protected. All of a sudden it seemed possible that any new start-up could check the tapers on another supplier's best rods and build a cheap and effective competitor. As it turned out, the established manufacturers' fears were largely unjustified, but a measure of the new material's popularity was that by 1978 almost ninety-seven per cent of all rods made in America were built from glass.[7]

In such a time of change, it was inevitable that there was a certain amount of subterfuge. Hardys' first fibreglass rod wasn't built until the early fifties, and there is an interesting story about its production, told here by James Leighton Hardy:

> The introduction of this new material disturbed Hardys greatly; so much so that they devised a strategy of building bad rods on the supposition that the angling public would assume that if Hardys could not build a decent rod out of glass fibre, it could not be a suitable rod-building material. They marketed their first hollow glass fibre rods under the Palaglas name which were made from blanks imported from Germany. The directors were so worried about the potential ruination of the split-bamboo market that they specifically forbade me to use glass fibre rods during the 1957 and 1958 World Casting Championships.

> This put me at something of a disadvantage with those of my competitors who were using this lighter and more suitable material.[8]

As a rearguard action, the tactic was doomed to failure and Hardys eventually gave in with good grace, beginning the production of fibreglass rods in earnest during the 1960s. One of their more important innovations was the introduction of Jon Tarantino's patented spigot ferrule during this period. Despite the enormous upset it caused, fibreglass enjoyed a relatively brief ascendancy, for in the late 1960s the Royal Aircraft Establishment at Farnborough discovered an exciting new material which they called carbon fibre, which they thought might have many uses - including rod building. Some material was sent to Hardys, who were much more enthusiastic and they made their first production carbon fibre rod in 1976.[9]

Hardys' first carbon fibre rod

Hardys' production of carbon fibre rods was greatly helped by their co-operation with Richard Walker, a well-known all-round fisherman who had worked at the Royal Aircraft Establishment during the war. Walker appreciated just how great the advantages of carbon fibre over any other rod building material were, not least its greater stiffness and much lower weight. The material was enthusiastically adopted, and it didn't need much selling. Rod weights plunged, reaching the point where line weight became a major consideration in rod handling. Today a typical modern fifteen foot carbon fibre rod weighs around the one pound mark, and a nine-foot rod three and a half ounces. A table given by John Ashley Cooper makes a useful comparison:[10]

Rod length	*Greenheart*	*Split cane (spliced)*	*Fibreglass*	*Carbon graphite*
16 ft			30oz	
15 ft	35oz	28oz	25oz	13½oz
14 ft	30oz	23oz	21oz	11½oz
13 ft	24½oz	18½oz	17oz	10oz
12 ft	19oz	14½oz	13oz	9oz

If anyone is wondering why there was such a sudden switch to carbon fibre, and why fibreglass didn't replace split cane overnight in Europe, the answer lies in the table. Although glass rods have many redeeming qualities, they weigh more or less the same as their split cane equivalents, and they offer the fisherman few advantages other than price. Carbon fibre, on the other hand, is nearly half the weight of either split cane or glass.

Once the technical problems of using the new material had been solved, carbon fibre rods entered mass production and neither of the older materials could offer any contest. Cane was swept away by the mid 1980s, although it is making something of a comeback on aesthetic grounds. Personally, I do not fish with split cane very much: while it has been said that you can't make a Stradivarius out of carbon fibre, it is possible to make a magic wand.

Reels

The early years of the twentieth century also saw the appearance of modern reel designs. Metallurgists had solved most of the problems that had dogged early aluminium alloys and so manufacturers were free to experiment. A lot of tweaking of designs went on. For example, in 1910, Farlow released the Patented Still-Handle Reel, which resembled the Patent Lever in all respects except that the handle didn't revolve when line was stripped from the drum. In the same year, Farlow marketed the Cooper Multiplying Reel, which had a handle which extended beyond the frame for winding, but which tucked in during casting, and in 1915 they produced the Heyworth, which had a silent check.

Sadly, the Depression and the Second World War took their toll on the reel industry as much as they did on society at large. The years from 1930 to 1950 marked a low water mark in modern reel development, with few innovations, and a general tendency of suppliers to mark time. Many of the reels produced during this period were of worse quality than those manufactured fifty years earlier. The sixties boom economies fuelled the recovery of the tackle suppliers, but their ranks had been dramatically thinned, and many of the old names were gone forever.

One small piece of the jigsaw puzzle of modern reel design was still missing. It had occurred to many experts that a reel should have:

> . . . plenty of capacity to hold the bulky line plus about one hundred yards of strong backing, it should be as light as possible. An exposed rim for braking when playing fish is a very

> desirable feature, but care must be taken to avoid damage to the rim and the intrusion of sand beneath it, either of which can cause the reel to lock.[11]

Exposed rims were nothing new in the seventies; Nottingham reels had worked on this principle since the mid-nineteenth century. But, for reasons which escape me, by the third quarter of the twentieth century, the exposed rim wasn't *de rigeur* on fly-reels in the same way as an adjustable check. It was the feature that completed the design of the modern reel: a large diameter narrow drum, with variable drag, a wide spindle, line guard and an exposed rim. For some reason, despite the enormous popularity of fly fishing magazines and the appearance of numerous articles calling for change, the penny didn't drop, and anglers continued to buy badly designed reels. In the end it took another twenty-five years before the majority of tackle manufacturers heard the call. We still haven't quite reached nirvana where reels are concerned, although I notice that in the last two years there has been a considerable improvement in manufacturer's ranges. Looking at my collection of modern reels, it is surprising how few of them accommodate all of the features on this hard-learnt list.

There have been a number of developments since the 1970s, but these have only been refinements. Spools are easily interchangeable thanks to quick releases, powerful disc drag mechanisms appeared in the 1980s (and are becoming a fad, featuring upon the smallest trout reels) and the highest quality reels are machine cut from 'bar-stock' aerospace quality aluminium, making them, in theory at least, indestructible.

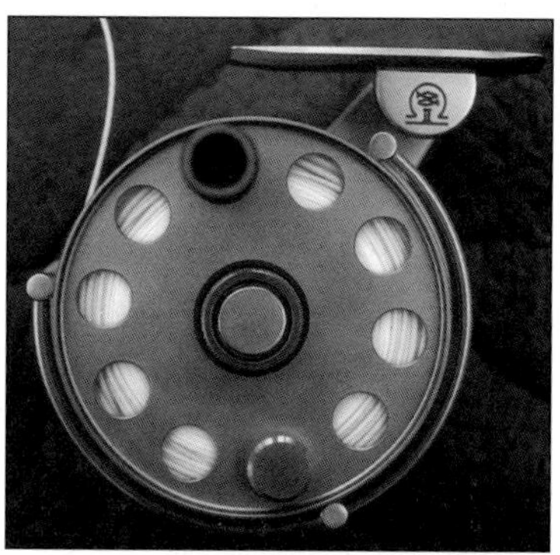

Ari't Hart fly reel

The new millennium seems to have ushered in a renaissance of design, almost equalling that of the turn of the last century. Part of the reason for this has been the easy availability of computer numerically controlled (CNC) lathes which, with careful programming, can be used to cut solid aluminium billets, known as bar stock, into complex shapes.

Prior to the introduction of the CNC lathe, reels were made by the cumbersome process of die casting. Two systems were used. Pressure die casting was the most common, but reels produced that way had an inferior finish to the ones made using the more sophisticated gravity die casting technique. Gravity die cast reels are typified by those made by Hardys in the late twentieth century; reels of complex shape with low porosity, good surface finish and high resistance to corrosion.

The trouble with die casting of any description is that mass production eventually leads to deterioration of the castings, with the result that filing and filling of castings becomes necessary. The other problem is that making the 'chills' into which the molten metal is poured is a highly skilled process, and much trial and error is required to arrive at the correct arrangement of vent holes to allow smooth filling and gas escape. By comparison, setting up a CNC lathe is a relatively trivial task. The situation is analogous to the challenge that glass fibre offered to split cane, and it isn't difficult to see which process is going to win. Today, the manufacture of quality reels in small quantities is a commercial prospect and so many reel manufacturers have set up in the last few years that the director of one long established tackle manufacturer told me recently that 'any fool can make a reel.' Perhaps any fool can, but it takes experience and talent to design a great reel; qualities which, I might add, not all of the well-established suppliers seem to have acquired.

While many of the products of the bar stock era are overpriced gizmos, built for folk with more money than sense, that isn't to say that there aren't some real jewels out there, like Ari't Hart's stunningly functional designs. Developers have finally been freed from the straightjacket of the die casting system, with the result that it is much more common for reels to conform to the fisherman's ideal, rather than the limitations of a particular production technique. It will take a few years for the market to settle down, but hopefully the increased competition will encourage the big names to knuckle down and design quality reels at a decent price.

One of the fascinating things about the proliferation of reel manufacturers in recent years is the way some of the newcomers have been inspired by the past. The last twenty years have seen a surge of nostalgia, and it is interesting to see the designs appearing that imitate classics of a century ago. Vom Hofe reels have qualified for particular attention, and Hardys' have recently launched a reproduction of the Cascapedia reel. We have come a long way since Barker's unfathomable illustration.

Cascapedia reel

Hook Scales

If the problem of establishing a common reference scale for hook sizes taxed many good minds in the past; it still continues to do so. Various methods of hook measurement can be used; the overall length, the length of the straight part of the shank and width of the gape, to name but three. All have their strengths and weaknesses, which relate to the different proportions each manufacturer gives to their hooks. In particular, the ratio between width of gape and length of shank varies widely between different lines. Overall length is the easiest measurement, but the different dimensions of the bend of a Limerick and say a Sneck bend would result in two hooks with very different lengths of shank being classed as the same size. When eyed hooks appeared, another variable had to be taken into account, as eye size could make a major difference to the length of a small hook.

Most modern systems have usually concentrated on standardising the length of the shank, but even this isn't fool-proof. Shank length is a difficult measurement to make on a hog-backed or sedge hook, and differences in

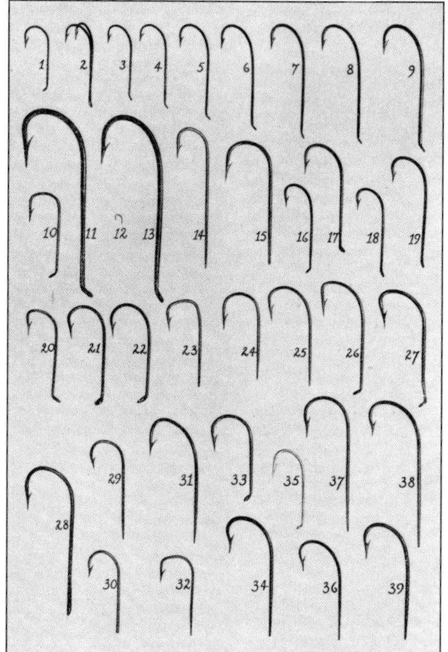

Taverner hook bends

1. Hamilton deep-gape (No. 7). (Hardy.) 2. Low-water double (No.9). (Hardy.) 3-9. Low-water singles (Date: 1930). (Nos. 10 to 4). (Hardy.) 10. Dry-fly, square-bend sneck (No. 6). 11. Ideal (No. 4/0). (Haynes.) 12. The smallest roach hook made. (Allcock.) 13. Oval wire (No. 4/0). (Hardy.) 14. Kirby bend for lures (No. 4). (Hardy.) 15. Salmon bait-hook (No. 1/0). (Hardy.) 16. Summer hook, down-eyed (7/8"). (Farlow.) 17. Summer hook, up-eyed (No. 4). (Forrest.) 18-19. Rational series, Dr Pryce Tannatt (Nos. 1" and 3/16"). 20. Forged snecky Limerick (No. 4). (Allcock: 1619.) 21. Model Perfect, kirbed, down-eyed (No. 4). (Allcock: 4991.) 22. Model Perfect, straight, down-eyed (No. 4). (Allcock: 4991S.) 23. Kendal sneck, tapered (No. 4). (Allcock: 195.) 24. Carlisle round-bent (No. 4). (Allcock: 262.) 25. Sproat, hollow point (No. 4). (Allcock: 777.) 26. Limerick, hollow point, down-eyed (No. 4). (Allcock: 1810.) 27. Cholmondeley-Pennell Limmerick (No. 3), returned eye, upturned shank. 28. Cholmondeley-Pennell Kendal, returned, straight and brazed eye. (Date: ? 1875.) 29. Kendal tapered. (Date: 1870.) 30. Kendal tapered, superfine, blued. (Date: 1870.) 31. Hollow point Limerick tapered. (Date: 1880.) 32. Sneck, square-bent. (Date: 1870.) 33. Cholmondeley-Pennell, short-shank, round-bent, down-eyed. (Date:1880.) 34. O'Shaughnessy Limerick. 35. Silver hook (No. 5). (Alexander Martin.) 36. Limerick, forged. (Date: 1880.) 37. Adlington, of Dublin, round-bent (No. 4). (Date: 1870.) 38. Kelson, forged. (Allcock:1901.) 39. Dublin Limerick, tapered.

bend and eye diameter can conspire to make a small hook appear larger than its official size. Then again, no single system can easily take account of hooks which are classified differently by custom, for example long-shank trout hooks, which take their size from the gape of the hook, rather than the length of the shank. Consider the extension of the current system of measurement to account for sizes below size 16, and we are only marginally in advance of the chaos of the nineteenth century. To make matters worse, if such a thing is possible, there is another numbering system for hooks in widespread use. This system refers to shank length, and is expressed as 1X, 2X, 3X, and so on to 6X, long or short. A hook classified as 1X long therefore has a shank which is as long as the shank of the next largest size of hook up. Under this nomenclature, a size 6 hook, 2X long has a shank length equivalent to that manufacturer's standard size 4 hook. No wonder there is a certain amount of confusion.

As long as different makers continue to produce different patterns of hook, we are unlikely to see any improvement. Unfortunately, the ideal hook, as described by George Selwyn Marryat, is unlikely ever to see the light of day:

> . . . the temper of an angel and the penetration of a prophet; fine enough to be invisible, and strong enough to kill a bull in a ten-acre field.[12]

To which we might add, '. . . and described on a scale inscribed on tablets of stone by the hand of God,' but one suspects that such a desirable and reasonable thing is unlikely to see the light of day during our lifetimes.

When it is borne in mind that some of the scales, particularly Redditch, were extended by different manufacturers without consultation, the table will give the reader some idea of the chaos that prevailed. Until the 'new Redditch' scale (which we use today)began to be adopted between the First and Second World Wars, the size of a particular hook was anybody's guess. Nowadays, the uncertainty is less, but it still remains, with similarly numbered hooks from different manufacturers varying by as much as two sizes.

Various well-intentioned individuals attempted to clear up the uncertainty by producing one universal hook scale, but almost without exception this had the opposite effect to the one they intended. The fate of the attempts to propose umbrella systems for hook scales would make an interesting study of itself, given that they have always fallen by the wayside. For example, Cholmondeley-Pennell brought out a

Comparative scale of hook sizes

Hook scales	*Sizes (small to large)*
Carlisle	12 or small midge, 11 or middle midge, 10 or large midge, 9 or small fly, 8 or middle fly, 7 or large fly, 6 or small cod-bait, 5 or middle cod-bait, 4 or large cod-bait, 3 or small worm, 2 or middle worm, 1 or large worm, small grilse, middle grilse, large grilse, small salmon, middle salmon, large salmon
Redditch'new'	18,17,16,15,14,13,12,11,10,9,8,7,6,5,4,3,2,1,0,2/0,3/0,4/0,5/0, 6/0,7/0, 8/0, 9/0, 10/0 *(good illustration page 464 of Kelson)*
Redditch 'old'	13,12,11,10,9,8,7,6,5,4,3,2,1
Redditch (1830)	12,11,10,9,8,7,6,5,4,3,2,1,0,00
Adlington†	00,0,1,2,3,4,5,6,7,8,9,10,11,12,13,14,15,16,17,18,19,20
Kendal (1830)	000,00,0,1,2,3,4,5,6,7,8,9,10,11,1213,14,15 *(partial illustration in Bickerdyke)*
Pennell	000,00,0,1,2,3,4,5,6,7,8,9,10,11,12,13,14,15,16,17,18,19
H. S. Hall series	000,00,0,1,2,3,4,5,6,7,8,9,10 *(Taverner illustrates in* Trout Fishing*)*
Sell	(Trout) 8,7,6,5,4,3,2,1 (Grilse) 4,3,2,1 (Salmon) 6,5,4,3,2,1
Philips	Midge, fe, f, ff, fff, C, CC, B, BB, 9, 8, 7, 6, 5, 4 *(Ephemera illustrates)*
O'Shaughnessy	(Trout) 9,8,7,6,5,4,3,2,1 (Grilse) 4,3,2,1 (Salmon) 6,5,4,3,2,1
Limerick 'rational' scale	000,00,0,1,2,3,4, 4fi, 5, $5^1/_2$, 6, 7, 8, 9, 10, 11, $11^1/_2$, 12, 13, $13^1/_2$, 14, $14^1/_2$, 15, 16, 17, 18, $18^1/_2$, 19, 20, 21 *(Maxwell illustrates)*
Cholmondeley-Pennell	000, 00, 0, 1, 2, 3, 4, 5, 6, 7, 8, 9, 10, 11, 12, 13, 14, 15, 16, 17, 18, 19

† Also Hutchinsons. This was the scale generally used for round-bend hooks.

successful series of eyed hooks in the late 1880s and his scale was used until the beginning of the Second World War. Pennell attempted to take a patent out on his hooks, but couldn't do so and had to settle for trade-marking them.

A few years later Pryce-Tannatt made a brave attempt to develop a unified system of salmon hooks, the product being marketed for a time by Forrest of Kelso.[13] The hooks were blind and were divided into four sub-groups, A, B, C and D. Group A were large long-shanked 'Dee' style irons running from three inch down to two inch. Groups B and C differed in that the B hooks were long-shanked light irons and the C hooks were short-shanked heavy irons. Sizes in B and C ran from two inch down to one and a quarter. Sizes in groups A, B and C decreased in quarter inch increments, but sizes in group D decreased by one eighth of an inch. The D series consisted of four sets of hooks, two different types of single and two different types of double hook. Only in the D series did any of the hooks have eyes.

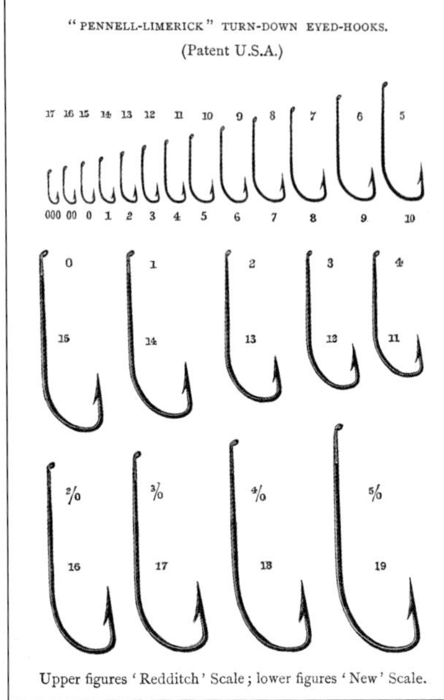

Pennell-Limerick hooks

Pryce-Tannatt's system never proved popular, probably because no one apart from the inventor could understand it, but also because if it had been adopted, every other hook-maker would have had to completely retool. The scale, like so many others, only worked for hooks which had a specific shape. For this reason it is highly unlikely that any system of hook measurement which gives an exact size and does not vary from supplier to supplier will ever be adopted.

Cholmondeley-Pennell deserves the last word. The totally unexpected result of his attempt to rationalise hook sizing was that for many decades, dry-fly hook sizes were given on his scale, known as the 'new' scale, while wet-fly hook sizes were given on the 'old' Redditch scale. In the midst of the complete confusion that resulted, the tackle industry quietly got on with their business, comforted perhaps by a booming trade in patent devices for converting one scale to the other. In 1905 Pennell wrote feelingly:

> I wish that I had never evolved the 'New Scale'. No doubt the invention was to try to make things theoretically more perfect, but in practice I doubt if the result has been anything but an unmitigated nuisance to myself and everybody else who has to deal with it, especially the hook makers.

Despite its inventor's later reservations, the new scale was popular and it was only after the end of the Second World War that the practice of referring to hooks as '00' and '000' began to die out. The Redditch scale reasserted itself, and things are quiet at the moment, but I am absolutely certain that we haven't seen the end of the quest for the perfect hook scale.

Conversion scale for trout hook sizes [14]

Redditch ('old' scale)	6	7	8	9	10	11	12	13	14	15	16	17	18
Pennell ('new' scale)	9	8	7	6	5	4	3	2	1	0	00	000	0000
Kendal	8	7	6	5	4	3	2	1	0	00	000	N/A	N/A
Model Perfect	4	5	7	8	10	13	14	15	16	18	19	20	21

Sizes run from large to small

Doubles, Trebles and Quadruples

The double salmon hook can be considered to be a reasonably mature invention, given that the Swiss used them during the Bronze Age, but it seems that the invention didn't travel well, as the first mention of a double salmon hook in the English literature was as late as 1590.[15] One of the earliest illustrations of a fly tied on a double hook is in Rennie's *Alphabet of Angling*, published in 1833. The woodcut shows an artificial dragonfly which would be better suited to the top of a ladies' hat than the end of a fly line; the bouffant creation pictured almost certainly is a salmon or a pike pattern.

Early double hooks were whipped together, but later versions were made by braising the metal. In his quest to bring rationality to the world of hooks, Cholmondeley-Pennell designed and marketed a series of doubles in the 1880s, by which time the idea wasn't regarded as dangerously novel any more and after that double hooks became increasingly popular for salmon fishing. There were some interesting variations on the theme of the double hook, not least Messrs D and W.H. Foster's 'Invisible Double Hook', which had the two points set at one hundred and eighty degrees to each other, rather than ninety degrees as is more common today.[16]

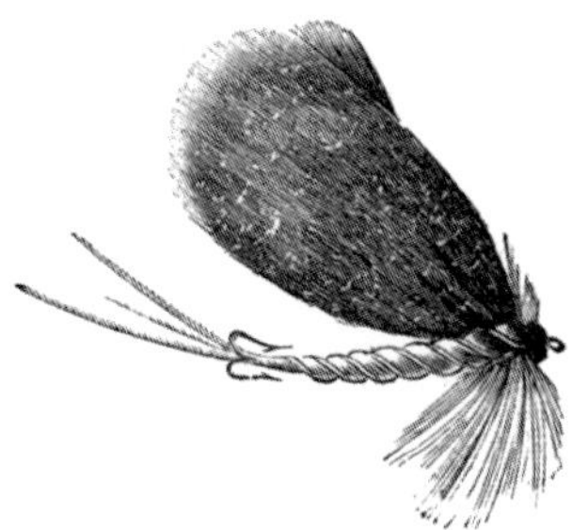

Mayfly on Foster double hook

Treble hooks share the chequered history of their cousins. There is an ancient eyed quad hook in the British Museum and it is possible that treble and quadruple hooks have been made for a thousand years. The records indicate that their use for fly fishing is much more recent and they were mainly used in larger sizes for live and dead baiting until the twentieth century. It isn't too hard to understand why, because in the late nineteenth century the trebles that were being used for spinning were a source of much complaint. Hooks frequently broke as a result of damage done to the temper during the brazing procedure and if they couldn't get this right a hundred years ago, I doubt that they did much better in ancient times. The trouble was caused by the selection of wire that was too fine and which became brittle during the manufacturing process. It wasn't until after the Second World War that trebles came into widespread use for fly fishing, as it was only then that it became possible to manufacture reliable hooks in the small sizes required.

We have dozens of different shapes, types and sizes of hooks now and it isn't a recent phenomenon. There is something about the naïve simplicity of a hook which provokes inventors to experiment and they have been at it for many years. Henry P. Wells[17] in 1885 gives an interesting illustration of a hook he describes as 'The Barbless'. True enough, the hook doesn't have a barb, but the drawing shows a tongue that descends from the shaft at an acute angle, just touching the point exactly at the place where the barb would have been struck. Wells seemed to be pretty taken with the design, telling the reader that it '. . . is quite prompt to engage, requires less force than any other to embed it, and, as to holding power, is so dead sure that to my mind it is almost unsportsmanlike to use it.' It vanished into obscurity along with dozens of other clever innovations. But there will be more like it.

Floating Lines for Salmon

The twentieth century has seen a revolution in fishing techniques, with new frontiers opened and many old methods improved out of recognition, or totally discarded. In some respects, salmon fishing has benefited more than any other discipline from this climate of invention. Inevitably, powerful personalities have been the drivers of change. If any man after George Kelson can be said to have altered the course of the way we fish for salmon, it is A.H.E. Wood, to whom I have already briefly alluded. Until Wood's discovery of the greased line in the early twentieth century, salmon fishing finished, to all intents and purposes, at the end of spring, with a brief revival in the cold and cloudy days of autumn. The impact that Wood's ideas had on salmon fishing is difficult to comprehend now, but at the time they were little less than revolutionary. After Wood, summer fishing became not only possible, but profitable and even the experts were a little awed. No less an authority than Eric Taverner said that with Wood's discovery: 'A new world is spread before one's eyes.'

In practical terms, the history of salmon fishing is relatively short, as it wasn't a popular activity before the middle of the nineteenth century. Its rise in popularity coincided with the adoption of tapered silk lines and gut leaders, which allowed longer casts to be made. Before 1800, salmon fishers were a small and select bunch of comparative oddballs like Franck who wrote very little about the technique they used. So prior to Wood, to all intents and purposes, all that salmon anglers knew was fishing with sinking lines. Their lines might have floated for a while at the beginning of the day, but the silk rapidly absorbed water and sank like a modern intermediate and once the line was soaked, the fly couldn't be fished at the surface except in fast streams. Wood changed a century of tradition by using ordinary oil-dressed double-taper lines, dressed with Hardys' 'Ceroléne' grease, imported from India and a single, level gut cast. His flies stayed near the surface and he went to great lengths to ensure that they did so.

Until Wood appeared on the scene, it seems that very few salmon fishers had devoted much thought to the way the fly 'swam'. That was set to change. Wood took mending to the extreme, as part of a system of fly fishing which presented the fly to the fish 'sidling past him and floating downstream' like a dead leaf.

The 'greased line' method is much misunderstood and I have heard the term applied to almost every type of salmon fishing involving a floating line. The key to Wood's method was presentation: any pull on the fly by the action of the stream on the line was seen as undesirable and he mended the cast obsessively to achieve the effect. He used the line to 'float' and control the fly, suspending it just beneath the surface of the water and controlling its path so that it swam downstream free of the slightest pull, fished in a natural manner; wobbling, rising and falling with the play of the eddies exactly as would an insect, or a little fish which was in trouble.

The idea had come to him in 1903, when he was fishing for salmon held up at an eel-weir. Having fished the pool at length and failed to take any fish, Wood sat down to think. While he was sitting, he saw several fish rise to take white moths from the surface:

> As luck would have it, I happened to have with me a white Moth trout fly; this I tied on the cast and sat on the plank-bridge over the weir. Then, holding the gut in my hand, I dibbled the fly over them. After some minutes, one of the salmon became curious enough to rise up to examine the fly, but at the last moment thought better of it; this I believe was due to its attention being distracted by my feet, which were dangling over the plank, barely six feet away from the water. I changed my position, knelt on the bridge and let down the fly. This time the fish came more boldly at the fly and it was followed by others; but I had pricked several before I realised that, because I was kneeling directly above them, I was, in striking, pulling the hook straight out of their mouths. So I changed my tactics, and, by letting go of the cast at the right moment, succeeded in dropping the fly actually into the open mouth of the next fish that came to it. I then picked up my rod, ran off the bridge, and made all haste downstream. All this time the line and cast were slack and floating down; yet when I tightened on the fish, I found it had hooked itself. By the use of this trick I landed six fish, lost others and pricked more than I care to say, all in a few hours. After that experience, I discovered myself fishing on the surface or as near it as I was able. The final advance came, when I started using a greased line to assist in keeping the fly in the right position, and thus I evolved out of a simple experiment what has become a most interesting mode of salmon angling, the greased line method.[18]

I have always wondered why the lesson Wood drew from his 'experiment' was that the line should float, not that salmon can be taken on a floating fly, but nonetheless, that is the assumption that he made. In fact, Wood did advocate fishing a floating fly in low-water conditions in summer, but only after the greased-line technique had failed. If he had taken one more step, he would have been able to claim greased-line fishing and the dry-fly method as his own, but perhaps one revolutionary idea is enough for anyone.

Wood fished the greased line by preference, even in spring, and he only turned to the sunk line when his own method had failed. His 'system' became very sophisticated and he took account of the effect of temperature on salmon taking, used it to decide on hook size, and also described the effect of air that is colder than the water in putting salmon off the take. And in passing, Wood also sounded the death knell for the gaudy salmon fly, with particular finality. In the process of his development of greased-line fishing, Wood realised that the old, heavy patterns of fly, so suitable when fished deep, were hindering his technique. So, according to 'Jock Scott':

> As his experience grew, Mr. Wood insisted more and more strongly upon the importance of cutting down the dressing of flies for use in low water and beneath a strong sun. His summer flies consisted of an almost bare hook and two or three hairs of hackle; therefore the 'Blueshanks' and 'Redshanks' were the logical outcome of this tendency.[19]

Wood's summer patterns grew sparse to the point where any further reductions would have made them disappear; which in a sense they did. The 'Blueshanks' and the 'Redshanks' took the ultimate step and they were just bare hooks, with the shank painted the appropriate colour. They were a far cry from anything Blacker would have recognised, but they caught fish; lots of fish.

Many fishermen find it hard to understand why Wood is so important in the history of salmon fishing. After all, few if any people fish with his greased-line method anymore. What was important was that he taught us that salmon could be caught on or near the surface, using a floating line. It was the mass conversion to the floating line which made modern salmon fishing and in particular, dry-fly fishing for salmon, possible.

Nylon

Undrawn gut had become almost impossible to find by the beginning of the Second World War, by which time most gut was being imported from Spain. Needless to say, there were many attempts to find a solution for this pressing problem, and the trade was so desperate that a project aimed at growing silkworms in the US was funded, although it came to nothing. Many efforts were made to find a substitute and in 1909 or 1910, a material called 'Japanese Gut' or 'Gut Substitute' made an appearance. There were various brand names for the material, including 'Telerana Nova', 'Padrona', 'Jagut', and 'Subgut'. The raw material for Japanese Gut was silk; this was twisted into a thread of the required thickness and boiled in a mixture of animal glue and an extract of seaweed. The end-product was chemically dried and polished, but the results were unpredictable to say the least and it had few fans. The great strengths of gut substitute were that it was strong, inexpensive and was available in lengths of up to one hundred yards, but like gut, it required soaking before use.

In the days of man-made, rot-proof, low memory, low maintenance lines, it is easy to forget what a trial the care of equipment was to the early fishermen. Drawn gut was sized using the 'X' system, which when originally conceived, ran from 0X, the largest size, to 8X, which was the smallest. The origin of the system is interesting in itself, because it is about two hundred and fifty years old and, as many readers will be surprised to hear, is based on an international system used for sizing the wire used to make watch parts. When gut first began to be drawn, by sharpening the end of the strand and pulling it through the bored centre of a jewel, the manufacturers found they needed a common measurement system and after casting around without much success, they settled on the watchmakers' old favourite. The X system was perfectly adequate for gut, but in the metric age it is gradually falling into disuse, because the very wide variation in diameter of nylon leaders means that measurements frequently fall outside the range of the old scale.

The biggest problem with gut was that in the sizes below 4X it had a breaking strain of less than a pound, which was a serious problem for dry-fly fishermen, who needed fine but strong tippets to outwit educated fish. This inspired a certain amount of skulduggery. It is very difficult to tell the difference between one fine piece of gut and another by eye alone, and some retailers and even suppliers took advantage of the fact that few anglers carried micrometers with them to cheat by marketing 3X gut as 4X and so forth, with the aim of embellishing their reputation for selling 'strong' gut. The result was endless confusion, which was well covered in the angling periodicals of the day, and although I give a table of gut specifications (opposite) it has to be accepted as an approximation.

Just to show how much we take nylon for granted, I include a column in the table showing breaking strains for a modern fluorocarbon leader material to allow comparison with gut of similar diameter. As you can see, fluorocarbon is roughly four times as strong for any given diameter, and that is before knots are taken into account. Every knot weakens a leader and while we take single-piece, extruded, nine foot leaders for granted, our grandfathers would have built a similar set-up with at least six knots.

Japanese gut ceased to be available to the Allied countries on December 7th 1941, with the attack on Pearl Harbour. By 1944 or 1945 other gut substitutes had become available from French and Spanish suppliers, but they were swept aside by an extraordinary new material – nylon. Nylon was patented by Dupont in 1938, and for many years

Silkworm gut specifications [20]

Description	*Gauge*	*Metric*	*Imperial*	*Test (pounds)*	*Fluoro-carbon (pounds)*
	8X	0.075	0.003	0.18	1
	7X	0.10	0.004	0.3	2
	6X	0.125	0.005	0.5	3
	5X	0.15	0.006	0.8	4
	4X	0.175	0.007	1.2	4.75
	3X	0.20	0.008	1.6	6
Refinucha	2X	0.225	0.009	1.8	8
Refina	1X	0.25	0.010	2.2	10
Fina	0X	0.275	0.011	2.8	12
Regular	10/5 (01X)	0.30	0.012	3.2	13.5
Padron 2nd	9/5 (02X)	0.325	0.013	3.5	15
Padron 1st	8/5 (03X)	0.35	0.014	4.5	
Padron 1st	7/5 (04X)	0.375	0.015	7.0	
Marana 2nd	6/5 (05X)	0.40	0.016	8.7	
Marana 2nd	5/5 (06X)	0.425	0.017	10.2	
Marana 1st	4/5 (07X)	0.45	0.018	12.5	
Marana 1st	3/5 (08X)	0.475	0.019	15.2	
Marana 1st	2/5 (09X)	0.50	0.020	19.0	
Imperial	1/5 (010X)	0.525	0.021	23.5	
Hebra	0/5 (011X)	0.55	0.022	25+	

1X and 2X gut was often drawn, depending on the availability and cost of Refina and Refinucha.

was made under licence in the UK by ICI. For obvious reasons, fishermen knew little about it until after the conflict had finished, but it soon became the subject of intense interest.

Immediately post war, two types of nylon line were manufactured; monofilament and braided. Braided nylon became hugely popular with spin fishermen using the ubiquitous new fibreglass rods. Early monofilament, although much cheaper than gut, wasn't anywhere near as popular - for good reason. Different products suffered variously from memory, lack of stiffness, a tendency to spring or cut through at the knots, and excessive elasticity. The other trouble with early nylon leaders was that they often kinked or broke unexpectedly during casting. This list of deficiencies is enough to make anyone wonder how on earth the new material gained such a loyal following, but compared to gut, nylon required virtually no care and it could be manufactured in truly enormous lengths.

Some of the problems experienced in the early days stemmed from fishermen's lack of understanding of nylon's properties, but others were the result of variable quality of the product and it took time before manufacturers got the hang of producing reliable line. The tribulations of fishing with nylon, and the fact that gut was so much more reliable, especially in the finer gauges, meant that gut soldiered on for a few more years, with a few die-hards using it well into the 1960s. Nowadays, gut is only a memory, and I wonder if it is even made anymore. All my enquiries have failed to find a source of supply.

Synthetic Fly Lines

By 1945, it was rare to find an angler who fly fished with anything other than a silk line, and a reasonably standard system of designating fly line diameters and hence weights, had been settled upon. The most commonly used system designated size by letters, running from AAA to K, although the numbers one to thirteen were also used. The official measurement system is shown below:

Diameters of silk fly lines in inches

AAA	AA	A	B	C	D	E	F	G	H	I
0.070	0.065	0.060	0.055	0.050	0.045	0.040	0.035	0.030	0.025	0.022

However the system wasn't that standardised and there were marked variations between manufacturers, all of which made choosing a line something of a lottery. The problem is superbly illustrated in the next table, adapted from *A Trout and Salmon Fisherman for Seventy-five Years*, by E. R. Hewitt, published in 1948. Based on Hewitt's measurements, a 'Halford' D line as measured is the equivalent of an E on the table above.

Size	C	D	E	F	G	H
Imperial	0.050	0.043	0.038	0.032	0.028	0.025
Intrinsic	0.057	0.049	0.042	0.038	0.033	0.029
Halford	0.050	0.040	0.038	0.033	0.031	0.029

To show how non-standard measurements were, Eric Taverner gave yet another table in *The Angler's Weekend Book*, which disagrees with all the figures above, classing the Halford line as a B!

A	B	C	D	E	F	G	H	I	J	K
0.045	0.04	0.0375	0.0335	0.0296	0.0256	0.022	0.0197	0.0167	0.01575	0.013

Much worse things happened, and it isn't surprising that absolute confusion reigned at times. The Hardy catalogue of 1900 has an hilarious entry, which was prompted by the particularly non-standard sizing of the company's 'Kelson' lines. In a well-meaning attempt to clear up any confusion which the particularly non-standard Hardy line sizing system might have caused in the angler's mind, the editor of the catalogue resorted to the following, straight-faced explanation:

> . . . the No. 2 being equal to the No. 4, 3 equal to 3, 4 equal to 2 and 5 equal to 1 in illustrations. No 6 being a size finer.

Hardys were not the only ones to have trouble describing their products with this classification. The system had complete indigestion when it came to dealing with tapered lines, which by loose consensus were described by combining several letters together, leading to the unwieldy nomenclature shown in the table below:

Conversion table for silk lines to AFTMA (approximate)

Silk	AFTMA	Silk	AFTMA
IGI	DT3	IGJ	WF3
HFH	DT4	HFG	WF4
HEH	DT5	HEG	WF5
HDH	DT6	HDG	WF6
HCH	DT7	HCF	WF7
GBG	DT8	GBF	WF8
GAG	DT9	GAF	WF9
GAAG	DT10	GAAF	WF10
GAAAG	DT11	GAAAF	WF11
GAAAAG	DT12	GAAAAF	WF12

Under this system, the 'Corona' lines, sold by Hardy and made by Cumberland, measured as follows in 1965:[21]

1965	*Corona*	*Description*	*Max. thickness*	*Rating*	*AFTMA*	*Length*
Trout	No. 1	Ex fine	0.032	IGI	4	30 yards
	No. 2	Fine	0.038	HEH	5	30 yards
	No. 3	Medium	0.044	GDG	6	30 yards
	No. 4	Heavy	0.052	FCF	7	30 yards
	No. 5	Ex. Heavy	0.056	GBG	8	30 yards
Salmon	No. 6	Ex. Fine	0.048	FCF	8	40 yards
	No. 8	Medium	0.056	EBE	9	40 yards
	No. 10	Heavy	0.064	DAAD	10	40 yards
	No. 12	Ex. Heavy	0.072	DAAAD	11	40 yards

However, if one searches through enough Hardy catalogues, Corona lines with very different tapers and numbering systems can be found. In the 1937 catalogue, the numbering system is reversed, with the heavier lines having the higher numbers. No doubt this accounts for the confusion which traditionally surrounds Corona line sizes.[22]

1937	*Corona*	*Description*	*Points*	*Max. thickness*	*Rating*	*Length*
Trout		Ex fine	0.21	0.030	IEI	35 yards
		Fine	0.22	0.034	IDI	35 yards
		Medium	0.023	0.040	ICI	35 yards
		Heavy	0.024	0.048	IBI	35 yards
Salmon	No. 1		0.048	0.080		42 yards
	No. 2		0.048	0.072	CAAAC	42 yards
	No. 3		0.044	0.068	DAAAD	42 yards
	No. 4		0.044	0.064	DAAD	42 yards
	No. 4½		0.040	0.061	EAE	42 yards
	No. 5		0.036	0.056	FBF	42 yards
	No. 5½		0.034	0.053	FCF	42 yards
	No. 6		0.032	0.050	GCG	42 yards

You would think that all these different systems would have caused chaos and they did to some extent, but fishermen had a very different attitude to lines before PVC made it possible to knock out one identical product after another. While we are obsessed with the AFTMA rating nowadays, it was very difficult to build silk lines to an exact specification, and within limits, the diameter of a silk fly line wasn't considered to be too critical. Lines were matched to rods by trial and error and on the whole the quality of the line finish was more important than overall measurements.

Nylon cored fly lines first appeared during the thirties and it was immediately apparent that the new material had many advantages, not least the fact that it was much more elastic than silk and didn't rot. The problem was that to begin with the technology couldn't come up with a finish whose elasticity matched that of the line and the one thing these early synthetic lines all shared was a short life: sooner or later the constant stretching of the nylon shattered its outer, protective layer. Fortunately, in 1949 another new material, polyvinyl chloride, became available, and the first workable nylon fly line appeared. As a product, it was far from perfect, but it was so clearly superior to silk that it sounded the death knell of the old material.

It took time to get the new lines right. The first ones were made with hollow nylon cores and the taper was produced by varying the amount of nylon fibre in the core, but water seeped into the cores, with the result that the lines sank. Then, in 1954, Scientific Anglers patented a technique for applying a variable thickness of PVC coating to a level braided core, a process which allowed tapered lines to be produced relatively cheaply on level nylon cores. The taper of these AirCel lines could be controlled very precisely and it wasn't long before the invention of a method of altering the specific gravity of the PVC coating (and hence its buoyancy) gave the product greater flexibility than anyone had imagined in their wildest dreams. The WetCel series of lines was an early result of this discovery.

The potential of PVC lines was further exploited by Scientific Anglers when they marketed a sink-tip line which used higher specific gravity plastic for the tip of the line. This type of adaptability quickly made PVC the dominant technology; and it encouraged an era of experimentation with tapers that shows no sign of abating at the time of writing.

Against the ferocity of this onslaught, silk simply couldn't hope to survive. It put up a strong rearguard action and the life of silk lines was extended by various dodges, including the use of Bakelite varnish, but the days of the old material were numbered. Now it is hard to find a silk fly line in good order, but I notice that one or two specialist suppliers have sprung up in the last couple of years, if you are prepared to pay royal sums of money for their products.

As PVC replaced silk, the unsatisfactory classification system used for fly lines broke down completely. The old system was designed for one material with a relatively fixed density, but silk and PVC have radically different densities. So, for example, a C silk is roughly equivalent to a D AirCel line, but once Scientific Anglers discovered how to vary the density of PVC, the system could no longer cope at all. When a silk line was replaced by a sinking line like a WetCel, which letter to go for was anybody's guess.

An urgent solution to the problem was needed and it came from the American Fishing Tackle Manufacturers Association, who proposed a new classification based on the weight of the first thirty feet of fly line, excluding the parallel tip section. I think it is fair to say that a system like AFTMA could probably only have evolved in America, where the tackle suppliers weren't hidebound by stuffy tradition. This new system worked well for lines of different densities, even down to the inclusion of a helpful terminology which described the taper in broad terms. The code as currently used is given as a four or five character alphanumeric: L for a level line (rarely seen nowadays); ST for single taper; DT for double-taper; and WF for weight-forward; the line weight is next; and finally a letter indicates whether the line floats (F), sinks (S) or is a sink-tip (FS). Using this terminology DT8F is a double taper eight weight floater. Once again, conservatism meant that fishermen and the trade didn't take to the AFTMA numbering system immediately, with the result that for a long while products were randomly identified by one system or the other and occasionally both, an unsatisfactory situation which continued until the end of the 1960s.

American Fishing Tackle Manufacturers Association line weight codes

Code	*Weight (grains)*	*Tolerance (grains)*
1	60	54-66
2	80	74-86
3	100	94-106
4	120	114-126
5	140	134-146
6	160	152-168
7	185	177-193
8	210	202-218
9	240	230-280
10	280	270-290
11	330	318-342
12	380	368-392

The radical change in the materials from which fly lines were made was paralleled by an increasing interest in tapers. Silk lines were available in three formats: level; single; and double taper; but the advent of PVC lines meant that much more sophisticated tapers were possible. Ironically, the great leaps in the understanding of multiple tapers had been made by tournament casters using sections of level silk fly line, which they spliced together to make custom outfits for distance casting. I say ironic, because the finish on a silk line breaks down very rapidly with extreme double-haul techniques, and they must have trashed lines as if they were going out of fashion. Much of the development took place on the Pacific coast of America and was undertaken by steelhead fishers like Peter Schwab, who needed to punch out heroically long casts.This new concentration on distance bore fruit very quickly and in 1938, Marvin Hedge stunned an international tournament using a custom-built weight-forward line and his newly developed double-haul. By the time Dick Miller pulled off a cast of one hundred and seventy-nine feet, weight-forward lines and double-hauling had become standard practice. All modern compound taper fly lines owe a debt of gratitude to these early experimenters.

All the major planks of fly-fishing practice were now in place. Although a plethora of books have been written in the last few years, the majority have been consolidations of work that has gone before. The fly fisher no longer carries one reel, one fly line, and a few spare gut casts. He or she carries a floater, an intermediate, a sink-tip and several sinkers, in a bewildering combination of tapers: weight-forward; shooting heads; density-compensated lines; low-stretch cores; the list is endless. George Kelson would have been proud of us.

Dry Flies for Salmon

British fishermen stayed loyal to traditional 'fully-dressed' patterns of fly, dressing them more lightly as the floating line demanded. Most, but not quite all, because Courtney Williams records that Mr Percy Laming of Alresford, Hampshire, used a greased line with a large floating March Brown to fish for salmon on the Scottish Dee in 1897. Sadly, I have never been able to discover any more about him, and whatever the nature of Mr Laming's experiments may have been, his dry flies didn't catch on and the challenge of salmon fly development passed to America.

Having taken to fly fishing for salmon relatively late, the Americans used derivatives of British patterns until the turn of the nineteenth century. Fifty years of experience was enough to convince them that something different was needed and there are hints that American fisherman were catching salmon on floating (or at any rate, just awash) flies as early as 1883. Like so many developments in fly fishing, the idea of using a dry fly for salmon passed through many hands before it was brought to final perfection. The first serious experiments seem to have been made some time before 1903, when Theodore Gordon tied dry flies for salmon and a friend of his caught fish with them on the Restigouche.[23]

Gordon's experiments seem to have ended there and it was left to Colonel Ambrose Monell, Edward Hewitt and George LaBranche to continue the development of the dry fly for salmon.[24] These three knew each other well and they swapped ideas and techniques to such an extent that it is difficult to say where the credit lies for any particular advance. In general, Hewitt was the most inventive. Monell didn't write anything, but La Branche credits him as the originator of much of their work.

George Michel Lucien La Branche was a well-to-do young stockbroker when he killed his first salmon on Monell's water on the Upsalquitch in New Brunswick. He had used a dry fly at Monell's suggestion:

> I needed but little urging to make the trip and, when I stepped into the river to make my first cast, my only thought was the manner of handling the vigorous runs and leaps I anticipated that the fish would make. Naturally, I was disappointed when my well-laid plans could not be put into execution. The fly was cast well enough apparently to rise a fish, but, applying trout-stream knowledge to my fishing, and striking as I would have done if trout fishing, I promptly jerked the fly away from four fish that rose (or perhaps it was one fish that rose four times) without even pricking a fish. After being soundly berated by my mentor, I did not strike when the next rise came, but let the fish set the hook – and was fast.[25]

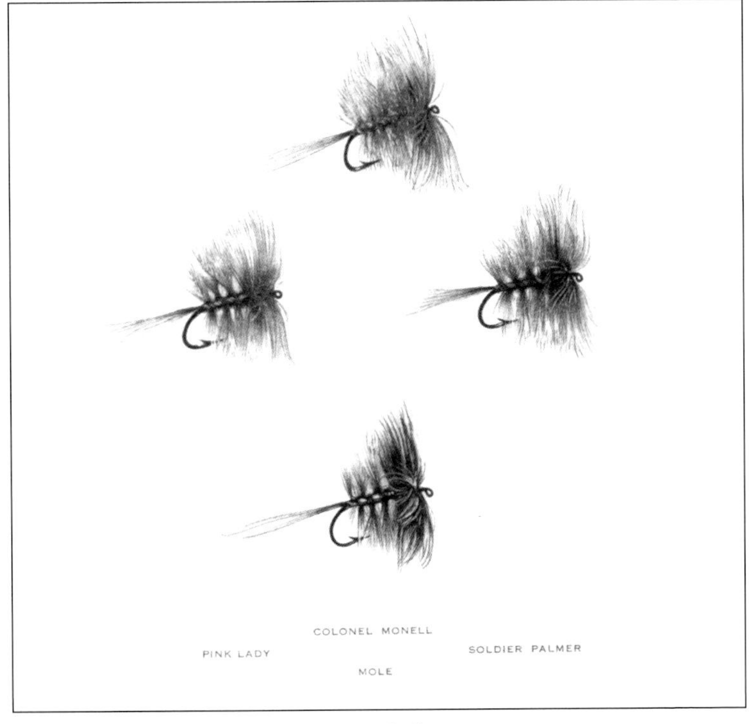

La Branche flies

Although La Branche eventually proved that salmon would take just about any kind of dry fly – he wrote of catching fish on size 14 Pale Evening Duns – the situation seemed to demand specialised patterns and he went to the trouble of developing a unique series of palmer hackled flies for the purpose. The patterns rode high on their hackle points and were so bushy that they were compared unflatteringly to bottle brushes.

There was a good deal of interest in Monell, Hewitt and La Branche's work on both sides of the Atlantic; at one stage Westley Richards advertised the patterns at eight shillings and sixpence the dozen in 1926, but fishing the dry fly for salmon didn't become popular until the 1930s, when Lee Wulff revisited the whole problem of floating flies for salmon and indulged in some major design work. On Labor Day 1930, Wulff decided to imitate a large grey upwinged fly that was hatching in great quantities. He set out to tie a fly with a larger and bulkier body than the natural, so that it would float better and be relatively long lasting. The result was the Gray Wulff, a pattern which was so successful that it encouraged the inventor to develop the White Wulff and the Royal Wulff. The three patterns became highly popular with salmon fishermen, and formed the mainstay of many fishermen's dry-fly boxes until new patterns like the Bomber displaced them. The range of dry flies for salmon has been greatly extended in recent years, with the addition of deer hair patterns which float like corks; and new techniques such as the riffling hitch continue to emerge.

The dry-fly method works well for salmon in the US, Canada, Iceland and Russia, but it seems to be best for relatively high densities of fresh-run fish in clear water when water temperatures are over sixty degrees Fahrenheit, which may explain why it is not so uniformly successful in Northern Europe.

The Kelson Controversy

The rise of the gaudy salmon fly is an excellent example of the mass hysteria which grips fly fishing from time to time. When the gaudy fly craze was at its height the columns of fishing periodicals were filled with impassioned arguments about the precise dressing of flies, as if the fish took any notice of the number of toppings, or the colour of the horns, or the number of turns in the tag of a fly. Nowadays these earnest letters are difficult to read with a straight face, but at the time their authors were deadly serious and reputations hung in the balance. George Kelson was self-appointed high priest of the salmon fisher's art, perhaps in unconscious imitation of Frederic Halford, but most likely because of an almost infinite capacity for self-promotion, which finally led to his undoing. The controversy over a long-forgotten fly known as the Inky Boy, is an excellent example of how triumph can turn to tragedy. The subject is dealt with very well by Geoffrey Bucknall in his book *To Meet the First March Brown*, but it bears repetition here.

Kelson led a colourful life. His son once summed him up with the immortal words, 'If people behaved that way nowadays they would be locked up!' It only takes a brief perusal of the *Fishing Gazette* to realise that there was no shortage of people who would have done exactly that, had the opportunity arisen. Despite his flamboyant nature, Kelson was a fine athlete, shot, swimmer and raconteur. He captained the Kent XI for some years and also won medals as a steeplechaser, but his greatest love was fishing and in between trips on which he caught at least three thousand salmon, he entered and won several casting tournaments and served as the angling editor of *Land and Water*. Unfortunately, a quirk of his personality meant that he wasn't above claiming other people's salmon fly patterns for himself or his friends, and for a long while he got away with it because when he was wrong, he was authoritatively wrong. Quite simply, there was no one with sufficient stature prepared to take him on.

The Inky Boy was a wonder fly invented by Kelson himself, but many of his readers found it was totally useless and wrote to tell him so, in an exchange of letters which can be found in the 1908 *Fishing Gazette*. Kelson solemnly asked for samples and then made much of the fact that the unsuccessful patterns all differed in some way from the dressing he specified. With a final flourish, he derided the failed readers' patterns as unsuitable for catching anything but common chub. Here is the dressing:

Tag: silver twist and two turns of crimson Berlin wool
Tail: a topping, a point of the tippet imitation of the Querula Cruenta and a narrow strip of Summer Duck
Butt: black herl
Body: thick black horsehair, closely coiled
Hackle: from the centre of body of Tourocou crest
Throat: a buttercup yellow furnace hackle
Wings: Golden Pheasant tippet in strands, unbarred Mandarin drake, a right and left hand claret strand of Tourocou, two narrow strips of Summer Duck, a suspicion of gallena and a topping

Kelson might have got away with it had not R.B. Marston, the editor of the *Gazette*, made the mild observation that there was no reason why a slight variation from the original dressing should cause fish to refuse the fly. Kelson's reply was magisterial:

> . . . what in the name of Fortune can be the reason for throwing cold water on the infinitely more important measure of being careful and accurate in a fly for use when the most difficult conditions prevail?

Marston's response was to print a cartoon which showed a grateful Inky Boy bursting into tears, under the caption 'I hope I am correctly dressed at last!' This provoked a hurt reply from Reginald Kelson, defending his (by now invalid) father's reputation. Marston's vicious riposte was:

> His [i.e Kelson's] book is supposed to give us the history of certain salmon flies. I say that some of these he claimed to have invented or named were neither invented nor named by him . . .
>
> Kelson claimed he was the inventor of making salmon flies with mixed wings. Salmon flies with mixed wings were made before he was even heard or thought of . . .

In a cold-blooded attack which leaves a sour taste in the mouth, and doesn't give the slightest doubt about how far he was prepared to go, Marston went on to dissect Kelson's claims step by step, finishing with an extraordinary article in which he listed Kelson's assertions in a column on the left and rebutted them in merciless detail on the right. The editor finished with a slightly weary: 'Shall we cry quits, K?' but there was no need because his adversary, more than seventy years old and in ill-health, was already finished. Neither of the protagonists gained much from the exchange, but Kelson's credibility was shattered, and so was the myth of the gaudy salmon fly.

Hair Wing Flies

The way was cleared for a new line of thinking and it duly emerged. The fully dressed salmon fly began its fall from grace after the First World War, to be replaced by hair winged patterns, which were far easier to tie and just as effective. The exact parentage of the hair wing or bucktail is obscure, although it is usually accepted that it originated in North America during the late nineteenth century.

Bucktail flies were probably first used for bass fishing in the late 1880s or the early 1890s and these may have been the inspiration for the new patterns. This is not an easy story to disentangle and as Joseph Bates has pointed out, some of the early tyers publicised their work so little that others who had made the same discovery rather later on were sure that they were the inventors.[26]

The inventor of the hair wing is conventionally taken to be Carter H. Harrison, who tied a hair-wing pattern for trout and fished it while staying on an Idaho ranch belonging to the Chicago lawyer Alfred Trude in 1901. Fable has overtaken this story, not least because Trude successfully prosecuted Patrick Prendergast, the man who murdered Harrison's father, and saw him hanged in 1893, but here is an account of how the fly came to be tied:

> The fly was first tied in jest on a muskie hook, a wing of hair from a red spaniel, and red worsted from a cabin rug. It looked so good, however, that it was later tied with a fox squirrel wing, red yarn body ribbed with flat silver and a red rooster hackle, no tail.[27]

The Trude worked well and it was progressively refined by Bill Beaty, Cliff Wyatt and Dan Bailey, who introduced a dry version. Colonel Lewis S. Thompson further adapted the fly and used it for salmon on the Restigouche, probably in 1928, or maybe even a few years after that.

While the first Trude was tied as a joke, its successors were not and while the motivation behind this radical departure from the feather wing tradition is unknown, it isn't hard to guess. Many of the materials used for tying 'standard' fly patterns were getting hard to find in Europe, never mind America, and the temptation to experiment with local materials which were abundant and cheap would have been impossible to resist.

The Trude may not have been the first bucktail, because there are a number of other claimants. In 1888, Charles Orvis wrote in *Forest and Stream* about the use of a fly made by cutting narrow strips of hairy deer skin, which were wrapped about the hook and tied in at one end. He commented that the Indians made the patterns to perfection, using different colours and lengths of hair. Orvis' report is supported by William Bartram, a naturalist, who recounts his friend's fishing for large-mouth bass (or possibly bowfins) in the Carolinas during the 1760s:

> Two people are in a little canoe, one sitting in the stern to steer, and the other near the bow, having a rod ten or twelve feet in length, to one end of which is tied a strong line, about twenty

> inches in length, to which is fastened three large hooks, back to back. These are fixed very securely, and covered with the white hair of a deer's tail, shreds of a red garter, and some parti-coloured feathers, all of which form a tuft, or tassel, nearly as large as one's fist, and entirely cover and conceal the hooks; this is called a bob.[28]

It stretches credulity to call this a fly, but you can see where the frontiersmen might have got their ideas from.

No less a tyer than Theodore Gordon had experimented with a hair-wing pattern as early as 1880, a date confirmed by Roy Steenrod.[29] His intention was to tie a better pike fly, but he found accidentally that the pattern would catch other game fish, including salmon and striped bass.

> Some years ago we tied some flies on an entirely different principle, our notion being to turn out something that would have real life and movement and resemble a small bright fish in colouring. If you could see one of these large flies played, salmon-fly fashion, by a series of short jerks of the rod top, and notice how the long fibres expand and contract, how the jungle fowl feathers (in a line with the hook) open and shut, you would see at once that it must be very attractive to any large game fish.[30]

Gordon's Bumble Puppy pattern wasn't exactly simple. The full dressing for it is: Tag – Silver and red silk. Tail – Scarlet ibis, two mated feathers, back to back and quite straight on hook. Butt – Red or yellow chenille; have tried black ostrich. Body – white silk chenille, ribbed flat silver tinsel (must be bright), body full, not thin. Hackle – Badger, large long, and lots of it. Wings – Double or single, according to size of hook; strips of white swan or goose, over white hair from deer, white bear, or goat. Sides – Jungle fowl, low. Shoulder hackle – Over wing, a good widgeon feather as long as or longer than the badger. Head – Red or yellow chenille, or black, plain varnished.

To confuse matters even further, in 1892 an angler called W. F. Burrell wrote that he was using '…Coachman and Deer-hair flies; the latter are tied from deer's hair when it is 'in the red'. . .,'[31] and to cap it all the idea of the hair wing may not even have originated in North America, because at least one Scottish angler was using hair-wing flies as early as 1850:

> An old angler I met on Tweedside over sixty years ago showed me some of his flies. The under wings were composed of about eighteen hairs from the heel or fetlock of a carthorse, dyed red, blue, or yellow - the effect is certainly charming.[32]

If I add that yet another early adopter of animal hair wrote in the *Fishing Gazette* in 1878 about tying saltwater flies using white hair from a goat's beard,[33] you will see that you can take your pick as to who first thought of the method. My own view is that fishermen have probably experimented with hair wings for much longer than we think and that it is more than possible that the technique was copied from native North Americans. Perhaps the truth is that like so many discoveries, hair-winged flies were invented by many people at many different times, without any of them realising what an important step they had taken. Remember that in those days, people didn't place articles in fishing magazines the moment it occurred to them to make a minor variation to an existing pattern so that they could call it their own, so it can be tricky working out when exactly a thing got itself invented.

Whatever the origins of the hair wing may be, a tyer called Ralph Corey popularised a down-wing dry fly called a Corey Calftail in Lower Michigan just after the First World War and by 1929, upright divided hair-winged dry flies were being fished on the Beaverkill and the Ausable, at which point it does become possible to begin to reliably trace some kind of genealogy of hair wings.

Despite the confusion about who may have invented it, there is no doubt that the major development of the hair-wing salmon fly was undertaken in the 1920s and 1930s on the north-east coast of North America. The fully-dressed wet fly was widely used in America at the time and a group of fly tyers began experimenting with simplifications of conventional patterns. They worked so well that it wasn't long before they abandoned the use of feathers in the wing and started to tie with local materials such as bear, squirrel, wood chuck and deer. The success of these patterns elbowed out the traditional British salmon flies, and led to a new and innovative school of North American fly tyers, which isn't showing many signs of slowing up.

The pioneering spirit of the age was summed up by Lee Wulff, who recalled how his friends began to tie salmon flies with animal hair wings:

> In Corner Brook, near Newfoundland's Humber, I fished long ago with Ted Bugden and Max Rabbits. Ted was an experienced and excellent fisherman, and Max was new at the sport. I taught them both how flies were made. Max was especially adept with his fingers and almost immediately started turning out professional-looking flies. Ted's flies were quickly but sturdily

> made. He soon ran through his gift materials and fell back on coloured yarns and some coarse bristles from a moose's hide. His flies lacked finish, but they did catch fish, more fish, as it happened, than did Max's careful copies.
>
> Flies with wings of bucktail, squirrel hair, moose hair, caribou and elk hair are quite effective for salmon. Hair flies can never have the svelte look of precision so essential to the conventional salmon fly. The hair, being stiffer, doesn't arrange itself with the neatness of feathers. Because of the thickness of the hair fibres at the butt ends, the heads of hair flies can never be as trim and neat as those of feathered construction. The success of the hair flies is a fair indication that these details are not necessarily important to a salmon.[34]

It was a sign of the growing American dominance in the field that hair-winged patterns made the transfer back across the Atlantic very quickly, chiefly because they were at least as effective and very much cheaper than traditional dressings. Although the process took a long time to complete, due to a decided reluctance by British anglers to change, the hair wing had become a significant influence on British patterns by the 1960s, by which time many patterns had been adapted to allow hair-wing ties and by the 1980s very few traditional flies were to be seen on either side of the Atlantic.

With the acceptance of the new materials came a new mood in European fly tying. In the 1950s Richard Waddington invented his eponymous hook, which mounted the first challenge to the heavy single irons that had been the standard for spring fishing. The Waddington was successful, but it was very ungainly and it was difficult to vary the weight of the lure in order to control the depth at which it fished. Now I think about it, ungainly is an understatement; the larger Waddingtons could be incredibly dangerous to fish, especially when Spey casting in a contrary wind, and they weren't adopted very widely because within a very short space of time, an improved mousetrap appeared - the tube fly.

Like the hair wing, the origins of the tube fly are uncertain. We know that North American native people tied lures for salmon on quills as long ago as the nineteenth century, but the idea seems to have entered mainstream salmon fly fishing during the 1940s and most sources credit the Scots with the invention. As ever, the stories conflict. One version says that the tube fly was created in about 1945 by a fly dresser called Winnie Morawski, who worked for the tackle firm of Charles Playfair and Co. at Aberdeen. To begin with, Winnie tied traditional salmon patterns on an unusual base made from the hollowed out sections of turkey quills, with the treble strung inside the quill. Then a doctor called William Michie called at the shop, and he suggested that Winnie used sections of surgical tubing as a substitute for the quill. Later development resulted in the wing being dressed in a collar right around the tube, perhaps inspired by the Waddington, and the treble was left outside the tube, so that the fly could 'escape' up the line when a fish took.

Another version says that during the 1940s an Edinburgh surgeon was so struck by the possibilities of surgical drain tubing that he took some home with him and tied some dark stoat's hair on to it, before attaching a treble and creating the Stoat's Tail. Tube flies are very popular as I write and are fished on plastic, aluminium and brass tubes of varying length, depending on the depth at which the angler wishes the fly to fish.

There is an interesting postscript to the Kelson controversy and the development of the hair-wing salmon fly. Fishermen took a long while to give up their affection for the fully-dressed 'gaudy' fly, and it could be found in quite ordinary tackle shops right into the late 70s and even early 80s. As it became harder to find fully-dressed flies, collectors have moved in and a substantial market in 'specimen-tying' has begun to emerge. This market is currently in full swing, with newly-tied flies changing hands for five hundred pounds or more and antique flies realising incredible prices. The result has been a revival of traditional salmon fly-tying, particularly in America and new patterns are being devised. The leaders of this school include Schmookler, Alcott and Sawada. Some of their patterns are fishable, but many are not, being too fragile to be risked at the end of a fly-line, or even (God forbid!) in a salmon's mouth. A tyer called Steve Fernandez has taken the 'salmon fly as art' one stage further and many of his flies not only have extreme shapes, but are no longer tied on hooks. Whether they 'count' as salmon flies any more is a matter of debate – but then there were those who said the same of young Mr Blacker's creations.

Trout Flies

The legacy of the dry-fly fishermen is an obsession with high-quality hackle, which became an increasingly scarce commodity between 1875 and 1970. Fortunately, biology came to the rescue. In 1866, Gregor Mendel, a neurotic Moravian monk, botanist and plant experimenter, discovered the basic principles of heredity at the Augustinian monastery of Brno. His work wasn't widely accepted until 1900, sixteen years after his death, but it ultimately came to the rescue of fly tyers, because the pressure on the supply of good quality hackles had become unsustainable by the last quarter of the nineteenth century. By 1900, farmyards could no longer satisfy the market, and hackles obtained from butchers' shops or poultry markets had become the main source of fly tying materials. As demand began steadily to outstrip supply, it became clear that the commercial production of English hackles wasn't a viable proposition. Dealers began to import capes from as far afield as India and China, but the random nature of poultry breeding meant that the supply of the rarer colours of hackles was always inadequate. The stage was set for the development of selective breeding.

Game cock

Mendel's challenge was taken up in the earlier years of the twentieth century by Dr William Baigent (1864-1935) of Northallerton, North Yorkshire. Baigent selectively bred Old English Gamecocks for forty years, crossing them with Andalusians to add blue to the range of hackle colour he maintained. Although he wrote occasionally for the *Fishing Gazette*, Baigent didn't keep any notes and unfortunately he died while working on a manuscript. His work was published posthumously during the Second World War, though only about fifty copies were circulated, but other members of a small British group who continued selectively breeding birds for specific hackle colour, included Thomas Hughes, John Henderson, John Evans and Frank Elder, who died in 1977.

Back-crosses to Old English Gamecocks were a major part of these early breeders' strategy. Their efforts would ultimately make possible the commercial production of 'genetic' capes for fly tying materials. These men have received little recognition; but for their patience the face of fly fishing might be very different today and the dry flies we know would be extremely expensive to tie.

Despite this new interest in the production of hackles for fly fishing, the shortage of quality poultry hackles became increasingly acute in the years between 1880 and 1950. The commercial breeders who took up the gauntlet thrown down by Baigent were for the most part in America, and it is still in that country that most of the modern

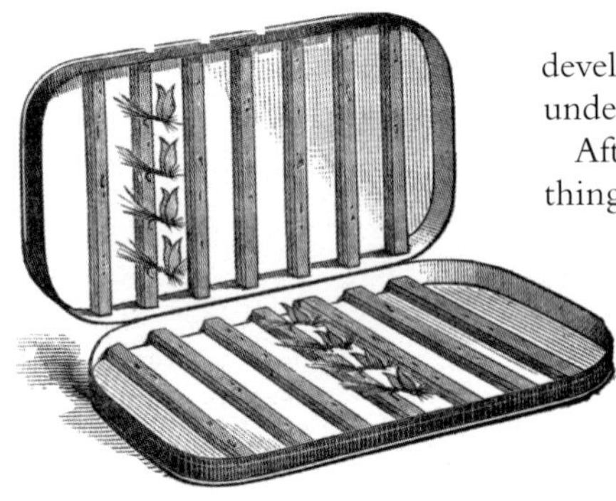
Trout fly box

development of genetic hackle is being undertaken.

After the First World War, many things changed for ever, not least the way dry flies were fished. This is generally presented as a split which opened between American and British fly tyers in the early years of the century, though the schism was quite slow and difficult to see at the time. Much of the experimentation which underlies the modern American tradition was carried out by the Catskill school of fly tying; a group which included such legendary characters as Roy Steenrod, Edward Hewitt, Herman Christian, Reuben Cross, William Chandler, the Dettes, the Darbees and Art Flick. But the spur to an explosion of American fly tying creativity which shows little sign of subsiding today was the publication in 1935 of Preston Jennings' unassuming little volume: *A Book of Trout Flies*. Although his work did not cover the entire US, Jennings is the counterpart to Britain's Alfred Ronalds, and his work laid the foundations for a keen interest in angling entomology that still persists; one which underlies much of the development of American imitative patterns today. Jennings was a meticulous character who actively involved biologists in the identification of insects which he and his friends collected, and he used the knowledge he had gained to weed out the 'legacy patterns' which had dogged American fly fishing up to that point.

Another development which had a profound effect on fly tying world-wide was the fall of the Halford school. Halford had reigned dominant in British dry-fly fishing in the years spanning the end of the nineteenth century, but in retrospect his hegemony was relatively brief and perhaps it is surprising that it held sway as long as it did in times of such great change.

The reason for the decline in popularity of Halford's patterns in England isn't so hard to establish. The flies stood or fell on the acceptance that they were exact imitations, but a growing number of fishermen began to question what the word 'exact' meant. The key question was: were the flies exact from the trout's viewpoint, or from the fisherman's? In the 1890s, exact imitation had come to mean the closest possible imitation of the shape and colour of the natural insect,

G.E.M. Skues

as seen by the fisherman. As a philosophy, it had its strengths, but it only went part of the way towards providing the answer. By the 1930s, as the result of the work of Ward, Hewitt, Harding and others, exact imitation had come to mean something entirely different and anglers had a different idea of how patterns should look to the fish. It was this growing realisation that was the undoing of Halford.

The patterns Halford so painstakingly crafted over half a lifetime are rarely used nowadays. As we saw in the preceding chapter, the flies and the philosophy behind them began to go into eclipse within a few years of Halford's death in 1914, overtaken by new ideas. Almost every part of Halford's carefully assembled philosophy has yielded under attack; the last bastion to crumble being the habit of winging dry flies, which became steadily less popular after the early seventies. Despite this Halford is and will remain one of the giants of fly fishing, one of the very few men who has had the status to cast his shadow down the years to our own time.

We have already met George Edward Mackenzie Skues, the young lawyer who was instrumental in the fall of the dry-fly school. Skues was born abroad in 1858, his father being surgeon to the Newfoundland Companies. His family returned to England when Skues was three, but his father's job meant frequent moves until Skues won a scholarship to Winchester in 1872. His first attempt at fly fishing was made that year using an eleven foot rod, a silk and horsehair line and a Wickham's Fancy. By his own admission, Skues wasn't very good to begin with and it was a long time before he caught his first trout. He had his first day on the Itchen in 1887, a day which began a love affair with the chalk streams which ended for him in 1949, though his upstream nymph technique lives on.

We remember Skues as the inventor of nymph fishing, but at this point I should put in a plea for John Younger, the shoemaker of Kelso, whose extraordinarily acute observation led him to perform what must have been some of the first experiments with the method as long ago as the 1830s. For all that the majority of nineteenth century anglers believed that duns fell on the surface from above, the existence of nymphs had been known for centuries. John Taverner gave an excellent description of them in his wonderfully titled *Certaine Experiments Concerning Fishe and Fruite*, published in 1600, and Ronalds mentioned them in *The Fly-Fisher's Entomology*, but this knowledge made little impact because the iron tradition of the downstream winged wet fly left little space for patterns which specifically imitated nymphs.

When Skues began to conduct his experiments, chalk stream anglers were baffled by the conundrum of 'bulging' fish, a phenomenon which we now know to be caused by trout taking nymphs just under the surface and leaving a humped rise-form. There were endless solutions for this irritating, but all too common problem. Tricks of the trade included using a brightly-coloured pattern, and a fancy fly or a dry Gold-ribbed hare's ear were other common standbys, but it was widely assumed that bulging fish were uncatchable. A friend of Halford's, writing under the peculiar nom-de-plume of 'Ballygunge'[35] summed up the general feeling by saying of bulging trout that, 'you might as well chuck your hat at them' as try a fly.

In the end, unable to solve the problem, the dry-fly brigade simply rationalised it away. It didn't dawn on them that there might be other methods beyond the upstream dry fly and the downstream wet fly and they drew instead the collective and mistaken conclusion that it was unsporting to fish a wet fly in any shape or form.

> Some anglers entertain a theory that 'bulging' fish may be attracted by an ordinary sunk artificial with its wings cut off, which is held to give it a resemblance to the nympha. But in practice the theory does not work out, for even if you could exactly imitate the nympha, you could not impart to it the necessary movement in the water. Keep to the Dry Fly, or leave the 'bulging' trout alone.[36]

Human nature being what it is, I find it easy to understand why the dry-fly men made the mistake they did. The irony is that they erred because although they never fished subsurface patterns, they couldn't see beyond the winged wet-fly tradition and made the mistake of lumping the nymph together with it - and in making the error they set their faces against the use of wet flies in any shape or form. I used to wonder what it was that set Skues' fertile mind thinking about nymph fishing, until I had the chance to watch Milorad Stanisic fishing with traditional fixed-line rig on a small river in the Stara Planina region of Serbia, not far from the village of Dojkinca. Mile has never used a reel, and although he has substituted glass fibre for hazel and nylon for horsehair, his method is identical to the one his ancestors knew: the rod tip is held high so that the fly never sinks more than a few inches deep and the fish take with classic nymphing rises. As I have related elsewhere, Skues saw this technique, or something very like it, in Bosnia in 1897, thirteen years before he wrote *Minor Tactics of the Chalk Stream*, the book which brought him immortality. Although Skues never connected his Bosnian experience with his 'discovery' of nymph fishing, it is difficult to imagine that it didn't make as powerful an impression upon him as it did on me. It is tempting to believe that Skues, the sophisticated English lawyer, subconsciously re-learnt a lesson on his Bosnian trip that every angler who was proficient with a short hazel rod and fixed line had always known; that more fish take just under the surface than ever do upon it. If so, he must have kept that observation at the back of his mind for nearly eleven years while he fished a dry fly and studied Halford's books.

Skues wasn't in thrall to any tradition, but in the face of the consensus facing him he realised that he had to tread gently:

> In dealing with this subject, I am conscious that I start with a weight of opinion against me among the fishermen of the chalk streams. I have known some of them say in a shocked tone, "But that is wet-fly!" as if it were some high crime and misdemeanour to use a wet fly upon a chalk stream.[37]

To begin with, Skues fished with variants of Scottish patterns, drawing from Webster's extraordinary book, *The Angler and the Loop Rod.* Subsequently he switched to a wet Tup's Indispensible. Skues probably chose this fly because he knew Austin, its inventor, and he was party to the secret of the complete dressing, but sadly he doesn't mention how he persuaded a ram to part with hair from its testicles. Later Skues experimented with other patterns ranging from a Greenwell's Glory to the Black Gnat, but for a long while he was loath to abandon conventional flies. The breakthrough that made him famous came in July 1908:

> I caught an Itchen fish one afternoon, and on examining his mouth I found a dark olive nymph. My fly-dressing materials were with me, and I found I had a seal's fur which, with a small admixture of bear's hair, dark brown and woolly, from close to the skin, enabled me to reproduce exactly the colours of the natural insect. I dressed the imitation with short, soft, dark blue whisks, body of the mixed dubbing tied with well-waxed bright yellow silk, and bunched at the shoulder to suggest wing-cases, the lower part of the body being ribbed with fine gold wire. Two turns of a very short, dark rusty dun hackle completed the imitation, much to my satisfaction.
>
> Apparently it was no less agreeable to the trout, for, beginning to fish next morning at ten o'clock, I found six fish rising in a shallow. I began with a small Red Sedge, as no dun was yet on the water, and missed several of them. Then, putting up a Pope's Green Nondescript, I again missed three fish in succession. I then bethought myself of my nymph, and, knotting it on, in a few minutes I had five of the six fish, and had lost the other.[38]

Skues was convinced enough to abandon modifications of traditional patterns and it wasn't long before he was tying his own dressing of Alder Fly larvae, caddis pupa and fresh-water shrimp. These flies were among the first true imitations of emergers and marked the beginnings of the move away from the traditional winged wet fly. Incidentally, Skues thought the caddis pattern was so effective that he declared it unsporting and kept it a secret.[39]

Skues' discovery of how to control the depth at which the upstream nymph was fished was another important milestone in the development of nymph fishing. He took notice of a discovery by his brother that if the leader was soaked in paraffin down to within a few inches of the nymph, the fly could be fished just under the surface with deadly effect. With the much later discovery of the deeply fished nymph in the fifties by Sawyer and others, the circle would be almost complete.

Skues' method of tying nymphs

When Skues next published on the subject of nymphs in 1921, he knew he had a great deal of support and no longer felt the need to tread carefully, so he took on the Halford school directly. By now, Skues had reinforced his theories by spending some time in Dr Ward's pioneering underground observation chamber, which was let into the side of a pond. Skues writes about this episode almost as if it left him in awe: he was very struck by the effect of the 'window', and the area of total internal reflection which surrounded it. He studied a dry mayfly pattern in the observation chamber, observing that the gut was not very noticeable; and a wet one, commenting that the gut stood out like a sore thumb. A new Halford spinner pattern was pronounced useless, with typical Skuesian scorn. But the thing which impressed Skues most of all was the appearance of a floating mayfly, when it appeared in the window:

> In the rainbow semi-circle of light above the observer's head in the pond, the whole artificial May fly became not only visible, but extraordinarily and brilliantly so. The wings seemed coated with a spun-glass brilliance which was particularly attractive.[40]

I have always wondered what kind of dry flies Skues might have designed after the day he spent sitting in that chamber, but I suppose it would have been out of character for him to deviate from the path he had chosen. But in making his trip to see Ward, Skues became part of the great tradition of scientific fly development which began with Rennie and Ronalds and which found its modern roots in Ward's underwater observations of natural flies. The effects of the scientific tradition can be seen in modern flies, which can be broadly split into two categories. On the one hand we have impressionistic artificials which (as far as we can judge) look life-like to the trout, although to our eyes some of these patterns may not resemble insects at all. Another cycle of development has led to the ultra-realistic school of flies seen today, some of which resemble their subjects so closely that it is difficult to tell one from the other. Marinaro's 'thorax' patterns,[41] Swisher and Richards' 'No-Hackle' series [42] and most recently Professor L.T. Threadgold's 'footprint' flies[43] are all excellent examples of impressionist school patterns; while the ultra-realistic school can claim Bill Blades, Bob Mead, George Grant, Bill Logan, Ted Niemeyer and many others.

It is important to realise just how divergent these schools of fly tying are, since to some extent they inherit the spiritual legacy of patterns tied by the colourists and the formalists in the last century, although they start from a much more modern viewpoint. Given the diametrically opposed philosophies of those two groups, I am intrigued that there hasn't been an almighty argument between the impressionists and the ultra-realists, but maybe it is a good sign - perhaps fly fishermen are getting more tolerant of each other these days. An indication of that tolerance can be seen in a third class of fly that inhabits our boxes; winged wet patterns which are only a short step removed from their nineteenth century forebears. The presence of flies like the Butcher and the Peter Ross may not owe much to science or impressionism, but it speaks of a healthy respect for tradition, and my own view is that we are none the worse for having the shade of Alfred Ronalds at our sides. Ronalds would be quite at home with my loch fly box although I sometimes wonder whether he would think my palmers, flies that hark back to the seventeenth century, set a bad example.

The years prior to the Second World War saw a resurgence of dry-fly purism, and Skues and his supporters came under heavy and sustained attack. On February 10th 1938, an extraordinary event occurred when the committee of the Flyfishers' Club called a debate on the subject of nymph fishing in chalk streams. The audience read like an honour-roll of fly fishing. Skues, Mottram, and Hills attended, and the event was opened by Dr Walshe, who made a great speech in defence of the dry fly. Skues responded, quoting selectively from Halford in order to undermine the dry-fly purists' case and to bolster his own. Hills showed great character by backing Skues. Mottram objected to nymph fishing using Halford's argument that it caught too many under-sized fish, and a variety of others opposed the technique because they feared a mass reversion to traditional wet-fly techniques. The remainder of the arguments were generally of poor quality, but despite the array of talent in the dry-fly corner, the only serious opposition to Skues was mounted by Sir Joseph Hall, in a closely reasoned argument which questioned Skues' somewhat partisan quoting of Halford. Ultimately, the field was left to Skues, who must have reflected that it was an odd thing for all this anger to be vented on the ethics of fishing a tiny fly under water, when the world stood at the gates of Armageddon.

As time has passed, memories have dimmed, but the ferocity of the Flyfishers' debate is still remembered. William Stephens, who edited Sawyer, found it necessary to defend the nymph as late as 1958,[44] and one still hears northern English wet-fly fishermen muttering darkly into their pints about interfering southern dry-fly fishermen. In reality, the dispute doesn't merit the iconic status it has acquired, and it never did. Only a few of the more narrow-minded ultra-purists were silly enough to imagine that the chalk stream rules could be applied universally. On the other hand, the selective quoting of Halford used by the nymph and wet-fly men in support of their case has only served to perpetuate the argument. The myth that the giant of the dry-fly school was against all wet-fly fishing, regardless of circumstance or location, is still widely believed today and one of the aims of this book is to destroy that myth and set Frederic Halford in perspective. The argument, like the protagonists in the great debate, should be allowed to rest in peace. Their only fault was that some of them forgot that fly fishing is a pastime, not a religion, and that is the kind of mistake that anyone could make.

Streamers

I make no apologies for introducing streamers at this point because I see them as the bridge between traditional trout flies and saltwater flies, even if that is not what their originators intended. Like bucktails, streamers have their roots in the 1880s, though the mists of time are pretty thick and it isn't really possible to do more than to guess at their origins. In *Streamers and Bucktails*, Joe Bates quotes a letter written to him by Harvey Donaldson, a firearms expert from New York. Donaldson told him how he and an aptly named companion, Leonard F. Fish, modified some bucktails in 1898:

> The cook had been cleaning some chickens, so we tried tying some feathers on top of the bucktails. This didn't work, so I eventually tied four feathers (two of them on each side, back to back) on a bare hook. That really worked! We used the flies *only* in fast water.[45]

Other than Donaldson, the development of streamer patterns seem to have mostly taken place in the state of Maine. Bates relates how the disconcertingly named Alonzo Stickney Bacon, a guide on the Grand Lake Stream tied streamers for *ouananiche* (landlocked salmon):

> Alonzo was in his canoe, fishing with artificial flies. He could not get a rise. He was seated on a cushion filled with hen's feathers. There was a hole in the cushion and a long white feather protruded. Alonzo plucked the feather from the cushion; tied it to a hook, and used it as a lure. The ouananiche took it with avidity. Other fishermen copied the lure.[46]

Inevitably, streamers didn't stay true to their simple beginnings and the original Maine flies which bore the generic name of 'Rooster's

Regret' were soon transformed into a riot of attractive patterns. The group of tyers who managed this transformation included Herbert L. Welch, Gardner Percy, Bert Quimby, Emile Letourneau and Fred Fowler and they produced patterns like the Black Ghost, Ligget's Special, the Supervisor and the Bolshevik. But the tyer who really made the streamer her own property was Carrie Stevens of Upper Dam House. Carrie was sent a streamer by Shang Wheeler and it inspired her to tie three flies for him, flies that were the forerunners of a spectacular collection known as the Rangeley's Favourites. She tied dozens of different variations, including flies like the Gray Ghost, Green Beauty, Water Witch and the Greyhound, which she sold to customers as far abroad as New Zealand. After her, it was difficult for anyone to consider tying a dull streamer ever again.[47]

Saltwater Fishing in America

One of the first American anglers to pursue saltwater fish with a fly was A. W. Dimmock. He is best known for his work, *The Book of the Tarpon*, which was published in 1911, but he wrote about the subject as early as 1908, in an article titled 'Salt-Water Fly Fishing', which appeared in the magazine *Country Life in America*. Dimmock's style is ever so slightly ponderous, although he rescues it with the occasional sally, like this one: 'My latest theory is that the best time to catch fish is when they bite, but that view is subject to change.' Perhaps his style isn't really an issue, because in the true spirit of early saltwater anglers, Dimmock was prepared to catch anything that swam, and he fished for Spanish mackerel, skipjack, tarpon, channel bass, lady-fish, sheepshead, mullet, crevally and redfish. He nonchalantly recommended 'old flies that had been chewed up by salmon and eaten by moths,' fished on a very stiff eight-ounce fly rod, using a multiplier loaded with at least a hundred yards of line; radically light gear compared with his British

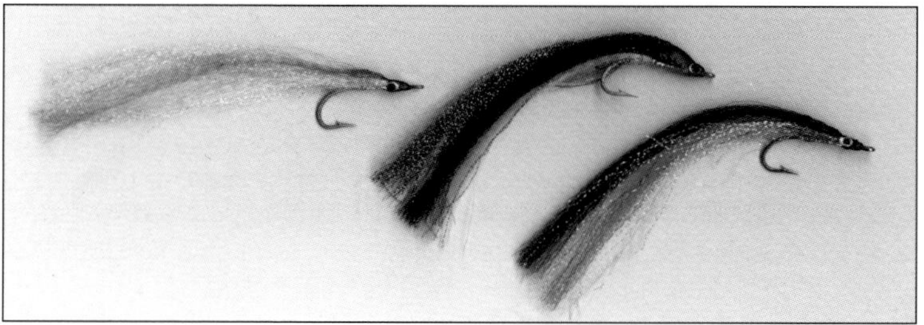

Typical saltwater flies

counterparts, and with the exception of the flies, recognisably modern.

These days, saltwater flies are a breed apart from their freshwater cousins, generally counterfeiting bait fish, and with some notable exceptions, tending to sturdy impressionism rather than exact imitation. The progenitors of modern American patterns evolved in the twenties, when Loving began tying flies for striped bass in Chesapeake Bay. Abercrombie and Fitch sold tarpon flies devised by Howard Bonbright during that period, although it wasn't until the mid-fifties that the sport really began to take off. Favourite flies in those days included tarpon patterns with splayed wings and split brass bead heads, including Homer Rhode's bonefish and snook flies and Harold Gibbs' striper bucktail, which first saw the light of day in the early forties but is still fished today. Rhode, incidentally, took bonefish and permit on a fly as long ago as 1930, which will surprise many readers, and it is interesting to recall that saltwater fly fishing for Pacific salmon was about as popular as it ever was going to be by the mid-thirties. It might have become more popular still had not the Second World War intervened.

After the war, Joe Brooks became a leading figure in saltwater fly fishing, and in the process he did a great deal to popularise the sport. Brooks started wetting lines in the sea during the twenties, and he caught a bonefish on the fly in 1946, while he was fishing with a guide called Jimmy Albright. The pair were lionised overnight, and Albright's Frankee-Belle bonefish pattern has never had any cause to look back since. Brookes wasn't the first to take a bonefish on a fly, and there is and probably always will be a great deal of controversy about who did. J. P. McFerran of Louisville, Kentucky is one claimant, and he is recorded as having caught a bonefish in the Florida keys as long ago as 1891.[48] Holmes Allen of Miami accidentally landed one while fly fishing for snapper in 1924, and Colonel L. S. Thompson caught several bonefish as a by-catch while fly fishing for baby tarpon in 1926 (he used a size six Royal Coachman by the way, proving that you can't keep a good fly down.) Deciding who tied the first fly specifically intended to outwit bonefish is harder, but the honour is generally given to Captain Bill Smith, who whipped a long hackle from an Islamadora chicken on to a hook, and used it to catch a bone in 1939.

The really phenomenal growth in saltwater fly fishing occurred during the seventies and eighties, when some well known fishing personalities made it an almost personal crusade to bring the new frontier to anglers' attention and this is probably why most people think of saltwater fly fishing as such a recent phenomenon. The growth in knowledge and tackle related to the sport during this period was absolutely phenomenal and it is probably fair to say that ninety-five per cent of what we know about saltwater fly fishing has been discovered in the last thirty years. In many ways, saltwater fishermen represent the leading edge of fly fishing in general, although this is partly because development in other branches of the sport is either very slow or completely stalled.

Saltwater patterns have been consistently innovative, not least because of the harsh environment they have to endure and their names roll out of the imagination and off the tongue, like the classic 'Lefty's Deceiver', a baitfish pattern invented by Lefty Kreh in the early sixties, and Bob Nauheim's Crazy Charlie, which was designed in the late 1970s. Development has moved at a breathtaking pace ever since. Even in the short history that saltwater fly fishing has managed to accumulate, marked regional differences have appeared in saltwater patterns. Flies from the north Atlantic and Pacific coasts of America tend to resemble freshwater streamers or bucktails, while their southern counterparts have a unique style, involving chenille bodies, bucktail or saddle hackle wings, and contrasting hackle collars. The emphasis is on brightness, and new materials; the one thing which can consistently be said of saltwater fly fishing is that it is exceptionally innovative.

Bonefish aren't the only creature which swims in the salt, and the sixties marked a diversification into new fields. After several years of experimentation, Dr Webster Robinson succeeded in landing the first Pacific sailfish on a fly, using a home-made styrofoam popper tied on a 7/0 hook to take a seventy-four and a half pound fish. The first Atlantic sailfish was landed two years later. With that capture, fly fishermen realised that everything was possible and there are very few species the saltwater crew aren't hunting down right now.

Modern Flies

These days the sheer volume of fishing publications is almost indigestible and scarcely a week passes without one 'expert' or another claiming to have found a new Holy Grail. However, it is possible to identify several different strands of development, though all of them are extensions of old ideas:

1. The use of new materials, particularly synthetics.
2. Further development of the nymph.
3. Artificials which fish in the surface film.
4. Dry artificials which duplicate the pattern made by the dun in the mirror, rather than 'exactly imitating' the fly (upside-down flies, no-hackle duns, parachute duns, funnel duns)

5. 'Impressionist' flies.
6. Micro-patterns.

A key part of the modern development of the fly has been the use of a much wider range of materials, including artificial substitutes for natural materials. This revolution has been led from both sides of the Atlantic, and a wide range of artificial materials are now in use, ranging from foam, through epoxy, to plastic winging materials. In the course of this experimentation, developments have disseminated across fly-tying disciplines to an extent that has never happened before, with saltwater techniques affecting stillwater angling and both influencing fly fishing in rivers.

I have listed the developments which I think have been innovative, but unfortunately the majority of the new flies we see are the sad products of collusion between competing magazines anxious to fill pages and what amounts to a new profession of author/developers, many of whom are motivated to churn out endless new patterns for financial gain. In my opinion, ninety-nine per cent of the new patterns we see are completely superfluous and they do fly fishing a disservice by confusing beginners and obscuring real innovation. I know this is a particularly harsh view and I am sure it won't win me many friends, but I recently asked the editor of one of the magazines in question how many patterns he actually used and his reply was six. Feel free to draw your own conclusions, but I don't think that many of the thousands of patterns we see released every year will still find places in boxes even twenty years from now.

This scramble to put patterns on pages has had some unexpected side-effects and we keep reinventing stuff. While I don't think twentieth century fishermen are any more inclined to plagiarism than their ancestors, there is no doubt that we have been remarkably keen to revive old patterns in new guises. To give a few examples, parachute duns were first marketed in the thirties by Alexander Martin of Glasgow, but have experienced a strong revival in recent years; as have patterns incorporating glass or metal beads at the head, which actually seem to have been an invention of central European fly fishers in the very early twentieth century. Strike indicators, far from being the last word in modern nymph fishing, were discussed in some detail by Stewart, a hundred and fifty years ago; upside down flies were first discussed by Venables, more than three hundred years ago; and 'reversed' flies, with the hackle and wings at the bend of the hook, were known as long ago as 1808.

Woven bodied flies, another 'modern' fad, also have a longer history than most people would credit. Bill Beaty, one of Montana's first professional fly-tyers, claimed to have invented them, but Franz Pott of Missoula, Montana seems to have been first out with a patent - in 1925 - which goes to show that patent patterns aren't that new, either. Even the line tray has a longer pedigree than one would expect, given that it was first mentioned by the tireless Mr Geen in 1902. I don't mean to belittle what people are trying to do nowadays, but just to add a note of caution; not everything under the sun is new!

Needless to say, we don't have all the answers. Despite all our technological prowess, some of the questions are taking forever to answer. For example, take the question of colour. Leaving aside the argument between the formalists and the colourists, Sir Herbert Maxwell proved long ago that he could catch trout using blue or even scarlet mayflies,[49] but on the other hand, fish rarely seem to take the natural Pale Watery dun, which is almost identical in size and shape to the Iron Blue – only differing in the subtleties of its overall coloration. It is a sobering thought that in some respects we are no nearer to a solution to the problem of colour than our ancestors were a hundred and fifty years ago. Finding the right track is proving as hard as it always did. Skues once described flies as coming from the 'Impressionist, Cubist, Futurist, Post-Impressionist, Pre-Raphaelite and Caricature' schools and seventy years on, we don't know which school, if any, is the right one.

The problem is that while we do have some very successful patterns, it is hardly possible to work backwards and establish what makes them so attractive to fish. That isn't to say that there isn't some room for the aggressive deconstruction of a few artificials to find out which bits of them are so crucial to their success, but fly tyers are reluctant to take the hatchet to their own, or even other people's, creations, and on past experience the process is highly unlikely to give us the whole answer. Take the problem posed by patterns which look like exact imitations, but which aren't – I'm talking of the Adams and the dry Pheasant Tail here. To us, these flies don't represent any particular insect, the way say a March Brown does. Instead they are impostors cleverly cast in the mould of the traditional dry fly and it is quite clear that the trout don't give a damn whether they can identify them or not. To the fish, the flies are food – to us they are a puzzle. Is it possible to find an answer?

Sixty years ago, Harding said, 'Unless we know how the trout sees the real fly, we shall miss, as likely as not, the essential features which our imitation should contain'.[50] As the twentieth century draws to a close, we are hardly any closer than he was to finding the solution and the answer, if it is ever found, may have to wait for another generation.

My hope is that that generation will not make the mistake of disregarding the lessons of history. Sir Isaac Newton, a contemporary of Walton's and one of the defining figures of the scientific revolution of the seventeenth century, was generous enough to acknowledge his debts to his forebears in a letter to his fellow physicist Robert Hooke with the immortal words, 'If I have seen further it is by standing on the shoulders of giants.' The real triumph of angling literature and art across the centuries is that authors have not been afraid to build upon the work of others. In the age of carbon fibre and bar-stock reels, where last year's product is old hat, and last century's is completely forgotten, it is rather pleasing to find that this tradition has survived, and so we can trace the scientific legacy of Alfred Ronalds through Edward Ringwood Hewitt, and Colonel Harding to Vincent Marinaro, all the way to John Goddard and Brian Clarke. These are the giants whose shoulders the next generation of anglers will stand upon. Who knows how far they will see?

* * *

Which leaves me the author's privilege of the last word. Behind me lies at least two thousand years of fly fishing history and I hope that I have done the subject justice. Ahead of me – who knows how long there is? There are so many threats to fly fishing and the human race in general that I would rather not think about them all; which perhaps, is one of the reasons why I go fishing in the first place. So I would like to end this story where I began it; in Macedonia. That troubled land has known the boots of many armies, the horror of civil wars, good times and bad, feast and famine; but somehow in the late eighties, with the carbon rod perfected and bar-stock reels rolling off the production lines in their thousands at several hundred dollars a pop, Mr Pendzerkovski,[51] a man who had learnt the lessons of history pretty thoroughly, thought it proper to go fishing with a hazel rod cut from the bank, ten feet of monofilament and two flies, one of which may or may not have dated back to Roman times. Now he was a very successful fisherman.

Bibliography

Publication dates indicate the edition used for reference, not necessarily the date of first publication.

Aldam, *A quaint treatise on 'Flees and the art 'a artyficiall flee making*, 1876

Anon, *Fly-Fishing in Salt and Fresh Water*, 1851

Arundo, *Practical Fly Fishing*, 1849

Ashley Cooper, *The Great Salmon Rivers of Scotland*, Gollancz, London, 1980

Bailey, *The Angler's Instructor*, 1857

Bainbridge, *The Fly Fisher's Guide*, 1816

Barker, *Barker's Delight or The Art of Angling*, 1651

Bates, *Streamers and Bucktails*, 1979

Belton, *The Angler in Ireland*, 1834

Berners, *The Treatise of fishing with an Angle*, Medlar Press edition, 1999

Best, *A Concise Treatise on the Art of Angling*, 1786

Bickerdyke, *The Book of the All-Round Angler*, 1922

Blacker, *The Art of Fly-making*, 1855

Bowlker, *The Art of Angling*, 1746

Brookes, *The Art of Angling now Improved with Additions and Formed into a Dictionary*, 1766

Brown, *American Angler's Guide*, 1845

Bucknall, *To Meet the First March Brown*, Swan Hill Press, Shrewsbury, 1994

Carrere, *La pesca de la trucha con mosca artificial*, 1934

Carter Platts, *Modern Trout Fishing*, A&C Black, London, 1938

Chetham, *The Angler's Vade Mecum*, 1681

Cholmondeley-Pennell, *The Modern Practical Angler*, 1870

Cholmondeley-Pennell (ed), *Fishing, The Badminton Library of Sports & Pastimes*, 1885

Cholmondeley-Pennell, *Modern Improvements in Fishing Tackle*, 1887

Chitty, *The Illustrated Fly-Fisher's Text-Book*, 1845

Cole, *The Young Angler's Pocket Companion, or a New and Complete Treatise on the Art of Angling*, 1795

Cutcliffe, *Trout Fishing in Rapid Streams*, 1863

Daniel, *Rural Sports*, 1807

Dennys ed. Lawson, *Secrets of Angling*, 1690

Dewar, *The Art of Fly Making*, 1855

Dewar, *The Book of the Dry Fly*, 1897

Dunne, *Sunshine and the Dry Fly*, 1924

Edmonds and Lee, *Brook and River Trouting*, published by the authors, Bradford, 1916

Fitzgibbon (ed), *A True Treatise on the Art of Fly Fishing, Trolling etc.,* 1838

Fitzgibbon, *A Handbook of Angling*, 1847

Fitzgibbon, *The Book of the Salmon*, 1850

Fortin, *Les Ruses Innocentes* , 1660

Foster, *The Scientific Angler*, 1882

Francis, *A Book on Angling*, 1867

Franck, *Northern Memoirs*, 1694

Gingrich, *The Joy of Trout*, Crown Publishers Inc., New York, 1973

Goodspeed, *Angling in America*, Houghton Mifflin Company, Boston, 1939

Hale, *How to Tie Salmon Flies*, 1892

Halford, *Floating Flies and How to Dress Them*, 1886

Halford, *Dry-Fly Fishing in Theory and Practice*, 1889

Halford, *An Angler's Autobiography*, Vinton & Co. Ltd., London, 1903

Halford, *Modern Development of the Dry Fly*, George Routledge, London 1910

Halford, *The Dry Fly Man's Handbook*, George Routledge, London, 1913

Harding, *The Fly Fisher and the Trout's Point of View*, Seeley Service & Co., 1931
Hardy, *Salmon Fishing*, Country Life, London, 1907
Hardy, *The House the Hardy Brothers Built*, Fly Fishers' Classic Library, Bovey Tracey, 1998
Harris, *An Angler's Entomology*, Collins, London,1952
Henshall, *The Book of the Black Bass*, Stewart Kidd Co., Cincinnati, 1923
Hewitt, *A Trout and Salmon Fisherman for Seventy-five Years*, Scribner's, New York,1948
Hills, *A History of Fly Fishing for Trout*, Philip Allan,1921
Hills, *A Summer on the Test*, Philip Allan,1930
Hills, *River Keeper*, Geoffrey Bles, London, 1934
Hi-Regan, *How and Where to Fish in Ireland*, Sampson Low, Marston & Company Ltd, London, 1906
Hoffmann, *Fishers' Craft and Lettered Art*, University of Toronto Press, 1997
Horie, *Jissen Tenkara Technique* (Practical Tenkara Technique), Yama-Kei Co., Ltd., Japan, 1997
Howlett, *The Angler's Sure Guide*, 1706
Hurum, *A History of the Fish Hook*, Adam & Charles Black, London 1976
Ishigaki, *Kagaku suru kebari tsuri Tenkara* (Scientific Fly fishing Tenkara), Kosaido Co. Ltd, Japan, 1992
Jacob, *The Compleat Sportsman*, 1718
Jones, *Guide to Norway and the salmon fisher's pocket companion*, 1848
Kelson, *The Salmon Fly*, 1895
Kumagai, *Yamazuri no Rondeau* (Rondeau of Fishing in the mountain stream), Yama-Kei Co., Ltd., Japan, 1985
LaBranche, *The Salmon and the Dry Fly*, Scribner's, New York,1924
Lawson, *The Secrets of Angling, by J. D. Esquire. Augmented with many proved experiments*, 1620
Leeson and Schollmeyer, *The Fly Tier's Benchside Reference*, Frank Amato Publications, Portland, Oregon, 1998
Mackintosh, *The Driffield Angler*, 1806
Malone, *Irish Trout and Salmon Flies*, Colin Smythe Ltd, Gerrards Cross, 1984
Markham, *County Contentments*, c. 1612
Markham, *The Pleasures of Princes*, 1614
Marston, *Walton and the Earlier Fishing Writers*, Elliott Stock, London,1903
Mascall, *A Booke of Fishing with Hooke and Line*, 1590
Mayer, *Sport with Gun and Rod in American Waters*, 1883
McDonald, *The Complete Fly Fisherman*, Scribner's, New York,1947
McDonald, *The Origins of Angling*, Doubleday, New York,1963
Maxwell, *Salmon and Sea-Trout*, 1898
Mottram, *Fly Fishing, Some New Arts and Mysteries*, The Field & Queen Ltd, London, 1915
Newberry, *Beni Hasan*, 1893
Norris, *The American Angler's Book*, 1864
Ogden, *Ogden on Fly Tying*, 1879
Orvis & Cheney, *Fishing with the Fly*, 1883
Orvis Marbury, *Favorite Flies and their Histories*, 1892
O'Gorman, *The Practice of Angling Particularly as Regards Ireland*, 1855
Peard, *A Year of Liberty*, 1867
Penn, *Maxims and Hints for Anglers*, 1833
Pequegnot, *French Fishing Flies*, Nick Lyons Books, New York, 1987
Petit, *La Truite de Rivière*, 1897
Pritt, *North Country Flies*, 1886
Pryce-Tannatt, *How to Dress Salmon Flies*, A & C Black, London,1914
Pulman, *Vade Mecum of Fly-Fishing*, 1841, 1846, 1851
Pulman, *The Book of the Axe*, 1854
Radcliffe, *Fishing From the Earliest Times*, Murray, London,1921
Raimondi, *Le Caccie delle Fierre*,1621
Reguart, *Diccionario Historico de las artes de pesca nacionales*, 1795
Rennie, *Alphabet of Angling*, 1833
Righyni, *Advanced Salmon Fishing*, Macdonald General Books, London, 1973

Ronalds, *The Fly-Fisher's Entomology*, 1836
Salter, *The Angler's True Guide Being a Complete Practical Treatise on Angling*, 1808
Samuel (attrib) *The Arte of Angling*, 1577
Saunders, *The Compleat Fisherman*, 1724
Sawyer, *Nymphs and the Trout*, Stanley Paul, 1958
Schullery, *American Fly Fishing: A History*, Nick Lyons Books, New York,1987
Schwiebert, *Trout,* André Deutsch, New York,1979
Scotcher, *The Fly Fisher's Legacy*, Honey Dun Press, London,1974
Scotcher's Notes, The Honey Dun Press, London, 1975
Scott, *Game Fishing Records,* Witherby, London, 1936
Scott, *Greased Line Fishing for Salmon*, Witherby, London,1933
Scott, *Fine and Far Off*, Seeley Service, London,1952
Scrope, *Days and Nights of Salmon Fishing*, 1843
Skues, *Minor Tactics of the Chalk Stream and Kindred Studies*, A & C Black Ltd, London, 1910
Skues, *The Way of a Trout with a Fly*, A & C Black Ltd, London, 1921
Skues, *Side-lines, Side-lights & Reflections*, Seeley Service & Co., London,1932
Skues, *Nymph Fishing for Chalk Stream Trout*, A&C Black Ltd, London, 1939
Stewart, *The Practical Angler*, 1857
Stoddart, *The Angler's Companion to the Rivers and Lochs of Scotland*, 1847
Snart, *Practical Observations on Angling in the River Trent*, 1801
Swisher and Richards, *Selective Trout*, Crown Publishers Inc., New York, 1971
Taverner, *Certaine Experiments Concerning Fishe and Fruite*, 1600
Taverner, *Salmon Fishing,* Seeley Service & Co., London, 1931
Taverner, *Trout Fishing from all Angles*, Seeley Service and Co., London, 1933
Taylor, *Angling in All its Branches*, 1800
Tenorio, *La aviceptologia, o manual completo de caza y pesca*, 1843
Theakston, *List of Angling Flies*, 1862
The Angler's Weekend Book, Seeley Service and Co., London, 1946
Threadgold, *Dry Flies, an Improved Method of Tying*, Swan Hill Press, Shrewsbury, 1998
Tolfrey, *Jones's Guide to Norway,* 1848
Turner, *Fishing Tackle, A Collector's Guide*, Ward Lock, London,1989
Turton, *The Angler's Manual*, 1836
Valverde, *Manual de Pescador*,1879
Venables, *The Experience'd Angler, or Angler Improved*, 1662
Vukovic,T., Ivanovic,B., *Slatkovodne ribe Jugoslavije*, Beograd,1971
Waddington, *Fly Fishing for Salmon*, Faber & Faber, London, 1951
Wade, *Rod Fishing in Clear Waters*, 1860
Walton, *The Complete Angler,* 1676
Walton, (ed. Hawkins), *The Complete Angler*, 1760
Walton, (ed. Edward Jesse,) *The Complete Angler*, 1867
Ward, *Marvels of Fish Life*, Cassell, London,1911
Webster, *The Angler and the Loop Rod*, Blackwood, London 1885
Wells, *The Contemplative Angler*, 1842
Wells, *Fly–rods and Fly–tackle*, 1885.
Williams, *Angling Diversions,* Herbert Jenkins, London, 1945
Williams, *Trout Flies, a Discussion and Dictionary*, A& C Black, London, 1932
Williamson, *The Complete Angler's Vade Mecum*, 1808
Woolley, *Modern Trout Fly Dressing*, Fishing Gazette, London, 1932
Worlidge, *Systema Agriculturae*, 1675
Wulff, *The Atlantic Salmon*, Barnes, New York,1983
Yamamoto, *Nisi-Nihon no Yamazuri* (Mountain Fishing in West Japan), Tsurinotomosha Co., Ltd, Japan, 1973
Younger, *River Angling for Salmon and Trout*, 1864

Notes to Chapters

Foreword

1 Published by John Murray, London. A second edition with a most valuable bibliography was published in 1926.
2 Published by the University of Toronto Press, Canada.
3 Published by Philip Allan & Co., London.
4 Reprographic replica (1998) reprinted from Speculum 60/4.

Introduction and Beginnings

1 Incidentally, if this is the case, and you are wondering if someone who wrote in such an outmoded style could ever have enjoyed life, I did.
2 Epigrams V, 18, probably written in about AD 90.
3 *Fishing From the Earliest Times*, Radcliffe (1921) p152.
4 Translation as given by Radcliffe, *Fishing From The Earliest Times* p187.
5 Hammond, *The Location of the Trout River Astræus*, Greek, Roman and Byzantine Studies 32.6, p. 173f.
6 *Slatkovodne ribe Jugoslavije*, Vukovic, T., Ivanovic, B. (1971)
7 *Fishing From The Earliest Times*, Radcliffe (1921) p191.
8 *Fishing From The Earliest Times*, Radcliffe (1921) p190
9 *Fishing from The Earliest Times*, Radcliffe (1921) p191
10 *The American Fly Fisher*, vol 22, no. 4, Fall 1996.
11 Letter, Dr Goran Grubic, 19th February 2000. I received the letter just as this book was in its final edit.
12 *A History of Fly Fishing for Trout*, Hills (1921)
13 *Feudal Society*, Bloch, (1965), vol 1 p109.
14 Best accessed in *Aelfric's Colloquy*, ed. G. N. Garmonsway (3d ed. rev. Exeter, 1978)
15 *Iron mining in medieval Serbia and Bosnia*, Simic (The Institute for Mining, Belgrade, 1988)
16 Letter, Dr Goran Grubic, 24th March, 2000
17 The oldest known book on Japanese fly fishing, '*Kei Jaku Seki Tsui* dates to 1678.
18 *Kagaku suru kebari tsuri Tenkara* (Scientific Fly fishing Tenkara) Hisao Ishigaki, Kosaido Co. Ltd. (1992)
19 *Yamazuri no Rondeau* (Rondeau of Fishing in the mountain streams), Eizaburou Kumagai, (Yama-Kei Publishers Co., Ltd. 1985)
20 *Jissen Tenkara Technique* (Practical Tenkara Technique), Keigu Horie, (Yama-Kei Publishers Co., Ltd. 1997)
21 *Nishi-Nihon no Yamazuri* (Mountain Fishing in West Japan,) Soseki Yamamoto (Tsurinotomosha Co., Ltd 1973)
22 'Fishing for Sport in Medieval Europe: New Evidence', Richard Hoffmann, *Speculum* (1985) also The Treatise on Angling in the *Boke of St. Albans* (1496) Background, Context and Text of The treatyse of fysshynge with an Angle. (Scripta: mediaeval and Renaissance Texts and Studies, 1.) Brussels: Scripta, Vrijheidslaan 17 – published under the auspices of the Universitaire Faculteiten St.-Aloysius (UFSAL), W.L. Braekman 1980.
23 Translation given in *Fishers' Craft and Lettered Art*, Hoffmann, University of Toronto Press (1997) p 147. The original manuscript is Tegernsee Fishing Advice, München, Bayerische Staatsbibliothek, Cgm 8137, fols. 97r-109v.

24 Unfortunately, the meaning of the word stingel is unclear. It may mean a feather, the tail or abdomen of the fly, the shaft of the feather, or less plausibly, a hackle from the neck of a chicken.
25 Again, the best source is Richard Hoffmann's *Fishers' Craft and Lettered Art*.
26 Rawlinson C 506, Bodleian library.
27 'publishing, history of' *Encyclopædia Britannica Online*. www.eb.co.uk: 195/bol/topic? eu=117358&sctn=15
28 There are numerous editions of the *Treatyse of Fishing with an Angle*, but good sources for most readers are John McDonald's *Origins of Angling*, (1963) p66, and The Medlar Press facsimile edition (1999).
29 *The Field*, January 1898. See also *Side-lines, Side-lights & Reflections*, Skues (1932) p188.
30 *French Fishing Flies*, Jean-Paul Pequegnot, Nick Lyons Books (1987) p.17.
31 Fishing 'Alla Valsesiana.' *The American Fly Fisher*, volume 5, no. 3 pp10-11, and also Fly Fishing in Valsesia, Italy: An Ancient Technique. The American Fly Fisher, volume 24, no. 2, pp2-5. The existence of this ancient technique is in marked contrast to the general perception that fly fishing in Italy began in the late 1940s, as an English import.
32 Personal communication, Tino Corderas I Pol.
33 *Fishing Rivers of Serbia*, Markovic (1962)
34 Letter, Dr Goran Grubic (see note 11)
35 *Life and Ways of Catching Freshwater Fish*, Sabaneev (1970)
36 Letter, Dr Goran Grubic (see note 11)
37 *Fishing From The Earliest Times*, Radcliffe (1921) p313
38 L.C.R. Cameron, *Rod, Pole & Perch* (London: Martin Hopkinson, 1928), pp.157-58. Macedonia's most famous son Alexander the Great, 'Lord of Asia', used the shipyards at Amphipolis (previously called Nineways) to help to build his navy. He who held the city controlled the waterway into the Strymon Valley and the outlet of trade from the Balkans and the Danube Valley.
39 'Iron mining in medieval Serbia and Bosnia', *Simic* (The Institute for Mining, Belgrade, 1988)
40 McDonald, *Origins of Angling* (1963) p51.
41 *Secrets of Angling*, Dennys ed. Lawson (c.1653)
42 *The Origins of Angling*, McDonald, Doubleday (1963) plate opposite p 114.
43 Which were, of course, invented much later, appearing in *Fly Fishing Strategy*, Winchester Press (1976)
44 *A Booke of Fishing with Hooke and Line*, Mascall (1590)
45 *The Pleasures of Princes*, Markham (1614) p.24.
46 *The Art of Angling*, Bowlker (c. 1746) p.57.
47 *A Concise Treatise on the Art of Angling*, Best, 2nd edition (1789) p.99 et seq.
48 *A History of Fly Fishing for Trout*, Hills, Philip Alan and Co. (1921) p21.
49 *Side-lines, Side-lights & Reflections*, Skues (1932) p50.
50 Made by doubling the loop round on the hook.
51 McDonald, *Origins of Angling* (1963) p52.
52 Crewel, a thin worsted yarn used for tapestry and embroidery
53 This and the next quote are from *The Secrets of Angling by J.D. Esq, Augmented with Many Approved Experiments by W. Lauson*, reprinted for Robert Liphook (1811) p19 -20. This is a reprint of the 1623 edition.
54 Again, see Hoffmann's *Fishers' Craft and Lettered Art* for an excellent translation and interpretation.
55 Probably the purple heron.
56 *Tetrastes bonasie*, a central European grouse.
57 The Evidence for Early European Angling III, *The American Fly Fisher*, Volume 21, No 2, p8. Hoffmann.

58 *Fishing From The Earliest Times*, Radcliffe (1921) p311.
59 *Angler on a Wintry Lake*. See O. Siren's *History of Early Chinese Painting* (1933). The original is in the Tokyo museum.
60 Needham Science and Civilisation in China: Volume IV: *Mechanical Engineering*.
61 The Earliest Fishing Reel: A New Perspective, *The American Fly Fisher*, Vol 23, No. 3., Fred Buller.
62 *Origins of Angling*, McDonald (1963) p50
63 *Beni Hasan*, Part I, Plate 29, P.E. Newberry (1893).
64 *Natural History*, xxi. 66
65 *Origins of Angling*, McDonald (1963) p47

The Seventeenth Century

1 *The Experience'd Angler, or Angling Improved*, Venables (1662)
2 *The Angler's Vade Mecum*, Chetham (2nd ed. 1689) pp3-4
3 *The Art of Angling*, Barker (1659) p3.
4 *The Complete Angler*, Walton (1676) pp258-9
5 *The Experience'd Angler or Angling Improved*, Venables (1662) pp4-5
6 *Alphabet of Angling*, Rennie (1833) p68
7 *Alphabet of Angling*, Rennie (1833) pp69-70
8 *The Experience'd Angler, or Angling Improved*, Venables (1662) p99.
9 *The Compleat Angler*, part II, Cotton (1676) pp35-37
10 *The Book of the Axe*, 3rd edition Pulman (1854) p124
11 *The Angler's Vade Mecum*, Chetham, 2nd edition (1689) p10
12 *The Compleat Angler*, part II, Cotton (1676) p35
13 *The Compleat Sportsman*, Jacob (1718) pp126 - 128
14 'El Manuscrito de Astorga', Bergara (1624). The most widely available modern translation is by Preben Torp Jacobsen, 1984. For the quote, see p67.
15 *The Art of Angling*, Barker (1659) pp 44-46
16 *The Compleat Angler*, part II, Cotton (1676) p 58. He paraphrases Venables, who had made the same point earlier.
17 *Certaine Experiments Concerning Fish and Fruite*, Taverner (1600). I used a modern reprint published by Sherrat and Hughes for the Salmon and Trout Association, 1928 p 9.
18 *The Experience'd Angler*, Venables (1662) pp 23 - 24
19 *The Experience'd Angler*, Venables (1662) p 25
20 *The Experience'd Angler*, Venables, (1668) p29.
21 Tail, or in colloquial English, back side.
22 The pile of velvet.
23 Fine worsted.
24 *List of Angling Flies*, Theakson (1862)
25 Hair-link.
26 *The Complete Angler*, part II, Cotton (1676) pp 38 - 41
27 *The Complete Angler*, part II, Cotton (1676) pp 43 - 44
28 *The Art of Angling*, Barker (1659) p25
29 *The Art of Angling*, Barker (1659) p26
30 *Les Ruses Innocentes*, Fortin (1660) Figure 26. For a detailed account of this, see Fred Buller's article in *The American Fly Fisher*, Vol. 25, No. 3, pp8-12.
31 29th September, the feast of St Michael.
32 Best accessed in the version given in *The Origins of Angling*, McDonald (1963) p 56.
33 *Barker's Delight or The Art of Angling*, Barker (1659) p 26
34 Short pieces of silk; the remnants of longer threads.
35 Mohair.
36 *Northern Memoirs*, Franck (written in 1658, published 1694). Most easily found in the Edinburgh, Constable and Co reprint (1821) p178
37 *Northern Memoirs*, Franck (1694). In 1821 reprint pp 301-303
38 *Dictionary of National Biography*, Oxford University Press (1927)

39 *Angling in America,* Goodspeed, (1939) p17
40 *The Experience'd Angler,* Venables (1662) p39
41 *The Art of Angling,* Brookes (1766) p161

The Eighteenth Century

1 See *The History of Cockfighting,* Scott (ND)
2 *Angler's Vade Mecum,* Chetham (2nd ed 1689) p189
3 *The New Shorter Oxford English Dictionary,* Clarendon Press, Oxford
4 Brookes, *The Art of Angling now Improved with Additions and Formed into a Dictionary,* 1766, p 94.
5 *The Driffield Angler,* Mackintosh (1806) p122
6 *Ogden on Fly Tying,* Ogden (1879) p16
7 I am grateful to Alejandro Viñuales and to Tino Corderas i Pol for the information they gave me on this topic.
8 *The Art of Angling,* Bowlker (c. 1746) pp56-57
9 In my third edition of Hawkins these follow on from p303.
10 *A Concise Treatise on the Art of Angling,* Thomas Best (1787)
11 *The Complete Angler,* Walton (ed. Hawkins) 1775 p115. This note varies in location between editions, but it is in the long footnote about materials needed for fly tying towards the middle of chapter five of part 1. Thanks are due to Ken Cameron for drawing this to my attention.
12 *Pesca de la trucha con mosca artificial: Tecnicas modernas de la mosca ahogada,* Carrere (1963) (Fishing the trout with artificial flies: Modern wet fly techniques). The 1934 edition of this book lacks the Peña patterns.
13 Translation by myself and Tino Corderas i Pol.
14 *A Concise Treatise on the Art of Angling,* Thomas Best (2nd ed. 1789) p85
15 *Northern Memoirs,* Franck (written in 1658, published 1694). Most easily found in the Edinburgh, Constable and Co reprint (1821) p307
16 *List of Angling Flies &c,* Theakston (1862) p113
17 *American Fly Fishing, a History,* Schullery (1987) p23. If you want to know more about the history of American fly fishing, you can do no better than to read this book.
18 *The Anglers Sure Guide,* Howlett (1706) p67
19 *Fishing Tackle, A Collector's Guide,* Turner, 1989
20 *The True Art of Angling,* Ustonson (1770)
21 *Concise Treatise on the Art of Angling,* Best (1787) p63
22 *A Concise Treatise on the Art of Angling,* Best (1786) p64.
23 Flyfisher's Club collection, 69 Brook St., London
24 *Angling Diversions,* Courtney Williams, Herbert Jenkins, p153 (ND).
25 *Les Ruses Innocentes,* Fortin (1660)
26 *The Complete Angler,* Walton and Cotton, ed. Hawkins (1760).
27 *Rod, Pole & Perch,* Cameron (1928) pp154-155
28 *The Art of Angling,* Bowlker c. 1746 p79
29 *The Compleat Sportsman,* compiled by Mr T. Fairfax (1758) p147.
30 *The Art of Angling,* Charles Bowlker (1774) pp96-97
31 *Angling in All its Branches,* Taylor (1800) p248
32 *Angling in All its Branches,* Taylor (1800) pp249–250. This was first brought to my attention by Ken Cameron.
33 *An Angler's Entomology,* Harris (1952) plate 32
34 *Irish Trout and Salmon Flies,* Malone (1984) p3
35 *The Angler in Ireland,* published anonymously by Belton (1834) Vol. 1 p36
36 *The Experience'd Angler, or Angling Improved,* Venables (1662) p17-18

37 *The Book of the All-Round Angler*, 1889, Bickerdyke
38 *The Driffield Angler*, Mackintosh (c.1806) pp64-65.
39 *The Journal of A.J. Lane*, Lane (1843) p67. Medlar Press edition (1995)
40 *A Book on Angling*, Francis (1867) p115

The Early Nineteenth Century

1 *My Life as an Angler*, Henderson, 1879 p101
2 *The Oxford English Dictionary* gives the first date for this usage as c. 1730. The first use relating to a sportsman's attendant was made in 1848.
3 *A Book on Angling*, Francis (1867) p274.
4 *The Fly-fisher's Guide*, Bainbridge (1816) p18
5 'The Split Bamboo rod', by William Mitchell, in *Sport with Gun and Rod in American Woods and Waters*, edited by Alfred Mayer (1883) p601.
6 *The Practice of Angling Particularly as Regards Ireland* (1845) Vol I, p5
7 *The Angler's Companion to the Rivers and Lochs of Scotland*, Stoddart, 1853, p37
8 *Practical Fly Fishing*, 'Arundo' (1849)
9 *The Driffield Angler*, Mackintosh (1806) p110
10 *The Illustrated Fly-Fisher's Text-Book*, Chitty (1845) p30
11 *The Angler in Ireland*, Belton (1834) Vol I, p259
12 *How and Where to Fish in Ireland*, Hi-Regan (1886) p1
13 Named after a Mr Sproat.
14 *The Scientific Angler*, Foster (1882) p276
15 *The Illustrated Fly Fisher's Text-Book*, Chitty, (1845) p220
16 *The Angler in Ireland*, Belton (1834) p35-37
17 *The Illustrated Fly Fisher's Text Book*, Chitty (1845) p44-45
18 Possibly osmunde.
19 *A Year of Liberty*, Peard (1867)
20 *The Driffield Angler*, Mackintosh (1806) p174
21 Mackintosh made mention of 150 yard 'woven' lines in *The Driffield Angler* (1806) p 115
22 *The Fly Fisher's Guide*, Bainbridge (1816) p21-22
23 *The Practice of Angling, Particularly as Regards Ireland*, O'Gorman (1845) Vol 1. p25.
24 *A Book on Angling*, Francis (1867) p280
25 *Fishing From the Earliest Times*, Radcliffe (1921)
26 *The Compleat Fisherman*, Saunders (1724). Nb. that Kelson attributes the first importing of silkworm gut to William Hay, MP for Sleaford.
27 *The Book of the Salmon*, Fitzgibbon, 1850 p19
28 *The Angler's Companion to the Rivers and Lochs of Scotland*, Stoddart (2nd edition 1853) p26
29 *The Practice of Angling*, O'Gorman (1855) p40
30 *The Angler's Companion to the Rivers and Lochs of Scotland*, Stoddart (2nd ed 1853) p56
31 In a second edition of Chetham's *Angler's Vade Mecum* (1689).
32 *The Angler's Sure Guide* (1706) p13
33 *The Fly Fisher's Guide*, Bainbridge (1816) p34
34 *The Art of Angling now Improved with Additions and Formed into a Dictionary*, Brookes (1766) p96
35 *The Fly Fisher's Guide*, Bainbridge (1816) p36
36 *The Practice of Angling Particularly as Regards Ireland* (1845) p19
37 This section is summarised from David Beazley's excellent article: 'Fishing Reels, A History' *Journal of the Flyfisher's Club*, Summer 1997, Volume 76, No. 284.
38 *The Angler's Companion to the Rivers and Lochs of Scotland*, Stoddart (1853 2nd ed.) pp31-32
39 Anyone who wishes to know more about the history of fly fishing in America would do well to read Paul Schullery's excellent book, *American Fly Fishing: A History*, 1987
40 An alloy of copper, zinc and nickel, which is also known as Nickel silver.

41 *The Book of the Black Bass*, Henshall ('new' edition, 1923) p223
42 Patented in 1856 by John Bailey.
43 'Fly Lines and Lineage', Betts, *Fly Tyer*, Winter 1999
44 *A True Treatise on the Art of Fly Fishing*, Trolling etc., edited by Fitzgibbon (1838) p102
45 *Fishing From the Earliest Times*, Radcliffe, 1921 p191
46 *The Art of Angling now Improved with Additions and Formed into a Dictionary*, Brookes (1766) p117
47 *Rural Sports*, Blaine (1840)
48 *Fly-Fishing in Salt and Fresh Water*, (1851)
49 *The Illustrated Fly-Fisher's Textbook*, Chitty (1845)
50 *A Book on Angling*, Francis (1867) p403
51 *The Art of Fly Making*, Blacker (1855) p106
52 *River Angling for Salmon and Trout*, Younger, (1864) p62
53 *The Angler's Companion to the Rivers and Lochs of Scotland*, Stoddart (2nd ed. 1853) p168

The Late Nineteenth Century

1 *A Book on Angling*, Francis (1867) p274
2 In Britain 'a deal' is a plank nine inches wide, not more than three inches thick and at least six feet long. Norway deal was cut from the spruce *Abies excelsa*.
3 *A Book on Angling*, Francis (1867) p279
4 *The Practical Angler*, Stewart (1857) p50
5 *The Modern Practical Angler*, Cholmondeley-Pennell (1870) p83
6 *The Modern Practical Angler*, Cholmondeley-Pennell (1870) p51
7 *Halcyon; or Rod fishing with Fly, Minnow and Worm*, Wade (1861) p45
8 *A Book on Angling*, Francis (1867) p122
9 *American Angler's Guide*, Brown (1845)
10 *The book of Tchouang-Tseu*. Also see the *History of T'Chou and T'au* Book 7, chapter 71 (currently housed in the National Museum of Paris).
11 *Salmon Fishing*, Hardy (1907) p42
12 in *Practical Observations on Angling in the River Trent*, Snart (1801) p86
13 *A Handbook of Angling*, Fitzgibbon (1847) p278
14 *A Handbook of Angling*, Fitzgibbon (1847) p282
15 *Angling Diversions*, (not dated, but published in 1945) p74
16 'The Split Bamboo Rod', *Sport with a Gun and Rod in American Woods and Waters*, edited by Alfred Mayer (1883) p597
17 The Split Bamboo Rod, *Sport with a Gun and Rod in American Woods and Waters*, edited by Alfred Mayer (1883) p598
18 *A History of Fly Fishing for Trout*, Hills (1921) p93
19 Much of the history of early split cane in America is derived from *The Book of the Black Bass*, Henshall (1923) pp156-174. Note that Henshall added a great deal of material on this subject in editio subsequent to the first, following a fairly brisk correspondence in various magazines, including *The American Angler* and *Scribber's Magazine*, October 1876 p744. Mitchell, who wrote a piece in *The American Angler* disputing the dates of Phillippe's rods, later retracted his version, and wrote to Henshall to say so - you can find this on page 160 of the 1923 edition of Henshall.
20 *The Field*, May 3rd, 1873.
21 *Canoeing in the Wilderness*, Thoreau
22 Much of this section is derived from *Trout,* Schwiebert (1978) p932 onwards
23 'Salmon Fishing' by A.G. Wilkinson in *Sport with Gun and Rod in American Woods and Waters*, edited by Alfred Mayer (1883) p409
24 *The House the Hardy Brothers Built*, James Leighton Hardy, Fly Fisher's Classic Library (1998) p96
25 *Salmon and Sea-Trout,* Maxwell (1898) p33
26 *The Book of the Dry Fly*, Dewar (1897) p119

27 *Fishing Gazette*, 31st May 1884 et seq.
28 I am indebted for much of the H. S. Hall saga to David Beazley and his excellent 'The Saga of the Snecky-Limerick', *The Flyfishers Journal*, Summer 1995 pp19-22 and Winter 1995 pp34-37
29 *Fishing (Salmon and Trout)*, The Badminton Library of Sports and Pastimes, ed. Cholmondeley-Pennell (1885) p31
30 *Salmon Fishing*, The Lonsdale Library, ed. Taverner (1931) p115
31 *Angling Diversions*, Courtney Williams, Herbert Jenkins p184.
32 *The Art of Angling*, Bowlker (c. 1746)
33 *The Complete Angler*, ed. Edward Jesse (1867)
34 *The Angler's Manual*, Turton (1836)
35 *The Contemplative Angler and Practical Angler*, Wells (1842)
36 *The Art of Angling now Improved with Additions and Formed into a Dictionary*, Brookes (1766; 1st ed.1740)
37 *The Fly Fisher's Guide*, Bainbridge (1816)
38 *The Complete Angler's Vade Mecum*, Williamson (1808)
39 *Rural Sports*, Daniel (1807). Many of the plates are dated 1801.
40 *Scotcher Notes*, The Honey Dun Press (1974) p9
41 *Trout Fishing From All Angles*, Taverner (1933) p203
42 'Sea Fly-Fishing', *Fishing Gazette*, (May 31st, 1878) p258.
43 'An Evening's Fly-Fishing in the Sea', *Fishing Gazette* (May 3rd 1878) p205.
44 *The Complete Angler's Vade Mecum*, Williamson (1808) p273
45 *The Book of the Salmon*, Fitzgibbon (1850) p20, and *A Handbook of Angling* (1847) p11 et seq
46 *The Book of the Salmon*, Fitzgibbon (1850) p 32-33.
47 *A True Treatise on the Art of Fly-Fishing*, Shipley (1838) p77
48 Knotted horsehair lines can still be bought from Carla Dalberto, Frazione Balangera, 13019 Varallo (Vercelli), Italy.
49 *The Illustrated Fly-Fisher's Text-Book*, Chitty (1845) p12
50 *Game Fish Records*, Scott (1936) p67
51 I am indebted to John Betts for his help with this section.
52 *A True Treatise on the Art of Fly Fishing*, Shipley (1838) p68
53 *Salmon and Sea-Trout*, Maxwell (1898) pp37-38
54 *The Angler's Companion to the Rivers and Lochs of Scotland*, Stoddart (2nd ed. 1853) p60
55 *The Practical Angler*, Stewart (1857) p66
56 It was published in 1807 as a *List of Wharfedale Flies*, with additional flies by J.W. Sagar added. Sagar's list dates from 1790.
57 *North Country Flies*, Pritt (1886) p19
58 *Fishing with the Fly*, Orvis and Cheney (1883) and *Favorite Flies and their Histories*, Mary Orvis Marbury (1892)
59 This story is much better told by John in 'American Classics,' *Fly Tyer*, August 1997 pp36–37. If you read this footnote, you should join the American Museum of Fly Fishing.
60 'Rocket' Encyclopædia Britannica Online. www.eb.co.uk:195/bol/topic?idxref=528934
61 *Jones's Guide to Norway*, Tolfrey (1848)
62 The reverse of coch-y-bonddhu i.e. red where cock-y-bonddhu is black etc.
63 *The Salmon Fly*, Kelson (1895) p76
64 *The Salmon Fly*, Kelson (1895) p15
65 *Salmon and Sea-Trout*, Maxwell (1898) p114

The Dry Fly

1 *A Summer on the Test*, Hills (1930) p24
2 *Barker's Delight or The Art of Angling*, Barker (1651) p10
3 *The Fly Fisher's Legacy*, Scotcher (c. 1810) p21. Most easily found in the Honey Dun Press edition (1974) p 21.
4 *A Booke of Fishing with Hooke & Line*, Mascall (1590) p18.

5 *A True Treatise on the Art of Fly-Fishing*, Trolling etc., Shipley, edited by, and probably written by, Fitzgibbon (1838) p78.
6 *Vade Mecum of Fly Fishing*, Pulman (1841) p49
7 *Maxims and Hints for Anglers*, Penn (1833)
8 *The Experience'd Angler, or Angler Improved* (1662) Venables p99.
9 *Systema Agriculturae* Worlidge (1675) p257
10 *The Angler's Instructor*, Bailey (1857) p23.
11 *Vade Mecum of Fly-Fishing*, Pulman, 3rd ed. Published in 1851, see p132. The previous edition says: '... if a wet and heavy fly be exchanged for a dry and light one, and passed in artist-like style over the feeding fish, it will, partly from the simple circumstances of its buoyancy, be taken, in nine cases out of ten, as greedily as the living insect itself.'
12 *The Angler's Companion to the Rivers and Lochs of Scotland*, Stoddart (1853) p80-81
13 *A Summer on the Test*, Hills (1924) p26
14 *The Diary of Colonel Peter Hawker* 1802-1853, Greenhill Books (1988) p94
15 *River Keeper*, Hills (1934) p17
16 *Ogden on Fly Tying*, Ogden (1879) p31
17 *A History of Fly Fishing for Trout*, Hills (1921) p129
18 *River Keeper*, Hills (1934) pp14-15
19 *The Modern Practical Angler*, Cholmondeley-Pennell (1870) pp96-97
20 *The Angler's Week-End Book*, Taverner and Moore (1946) p366
21 *The Fly Tier's Benchside Reference*, Leeson and Schollmeyer, Frank Amato Publications (1998) p66
22 *Floating Flies and How to Dress Them*, Halford (1886) p2.
23 *Fishing, Salmon and Trout*, Cholmondeley-Pennell (1885) pp362-379
24 *The Book of the Dry-fly*, Dewar (1897) p138
25 *How and Where to Fish in Ireland*, Hi-Regan (1906) footnote p24
26 *River Keeper*, Hills (1934) p16
27 *Modern Trout Fishing*, Carter Platts (1938) p72
28 *An Angler's Autobiography*, Halford (1903) p105
29 *Modern Development of the Dry Fly*, Halford (1910) pp87–97.
30 *Repertoire de Couleurs pour aider à la détermination des couleurs des Fleurs, des Feuillages et des Fruits,* la Société Française des Chrysanthémistes et René Oberthür, avec la collaboration principale de Henri Dauthenay et celle de MM. Julien Mouillefert, C. Harman Payne, Max Leichtlin, N Severi et Miguel Cortés.
31 *Dry-Fly Fishing in Theory and Practice*, Halford (1889) p42.
32 *La Truite de Rivière*, Petit (1897). The French school evolved between the late 1920s and the fifties.
33 *The Dry-Fly Man's Handbook*, Halford (1913) pp62-63. He elabo rates on the problem of drag when fishing downstream on p116.
34 *The Dry-Fly Man's Handbook*, Halford (1913) p75
35 *The Dry-Fly Man's Handbook*, Halford (1913) p76
36 *The Dry-Fly Man's Handbook*, Halford (1913) p68
37 *The Dry-Fly Man's Handbook*, Halford (1913) pp126-127
38 *Dry-Fly Fishing in Theory and Practice*, Halford (1889) p122
39 *Fishing Gazette*, April 27th 1912.
40 *Marvels of Fish Life*, Ward (1911) p28
41 *A Summer on the Test*, Hills (Philip Allan and Co. 1930) p23
42 *Fly Fishing Some New Arts and Mysteries*, Mottram (1915) p121 et seq.
43 *The Way of a Trout with a Fly*, Skues (1921) p85.
44 *Sunshine and the Dry-fly* (1924) p2
45 *The Fly Fisher and the Trout's Point of View*, Harding (1931) p78-79
46 *The Complete Fly Fisherman*, McDonald (1947) is a good place to start if you want to learn more about Theodore Gordon.

47 *Trout*, Schweibert (1979) pp364–367

The Twentieth Century

1 *Trout*, Schwiebert (Andre Deutsch 1979) p984.
2 *Fine and Far Off*, Scott (1952) p45
3 *Greased Line Fishing for Salmon*, Scott (1935)
4 *The Atlantic Salmon*, Wulff (2nd ed. 1983) p41
5 *The Joy of Trout*, Gingrich (1973) p15
6 *Modern Trout Fishing*, W. Carter Platts (1938) p10
7 *Trout*, Schwiebert (André Deutsch 1978) p1131. This book has a very good chapter on twentieth century fly rods, on which much of this section depends.
8 *The House the Hardy Brothers Built*, James Leighton Hardy, Flyfisher's Classic Library (1998) p113
9 *Trout*, Schwiebert (André Deutsch 1978) p1135
10 *The Great Salmon Rivers of Scotland*, Ashley Cooper, Gollancz (1980) p152
11 *Advanced Salmon Fishing*, Righyni, Macdonald General Books (1973) p71
12 *Angling Diversions*, Courtney Williams, Herbert Jenkins p97
13 *How to Dress Salmon Flies*, Pryce-Tannatt (1914)
14 *Trout Flies, A Discussion and a Dictionary*, Courtney Williams, A&C Black (1932) p65.
15 *A Booke of fishing with Hooke & Line*, Mascall (1590)
16 *Modern Improvements in Fishing Tackle*, Cholmondeley-Pennell (1887)
17 *Fly–rods and Fly–tackle*, Wells, 1885.
18 *Greased Line Fishing for Salmon*, Scott (1935) pp69-70
19 *Greased Line Fishing for Salmon* (1935) p107
20 Adapted from *Trout*, Schweibert (Andre Deutsch, 1979) vol 1, p798
21 Figures from 1965 *Hardy catalogue*, courtesy of Mr J. L. Hardy
22 Figures from 1937 *Hardy catalogue*, courtesy of Mr J. L. Hardy
23 *Fishing Gazette*, April 25th, 1903
24 *The Salmon and the Dry Fly*, La Branche (1924)
25 *The Salmon and the Dry Fly*, La Branche (1924) p2.
26 *Streamers and Bucktails*, Bates (1979) p22
27 Quoted from *Streamers and Bucktails*, Bates (1979) p22. The original text is from *Montana Trout Flies*, which was privately printed by George Grant, p194.
28 *Travels Through North Carolina and South Carolina*, Bartram (1791), but best accessed in *American Fly Fishing, a History*, Schullery (1987) p 20.
29 *Streamers and Bucktails*, Bates (1979) p21
30 From letters, Jan 24th 1903 and April 25th 1903.
31 *Favorite Flies and their Histories*, Marbury, 1892 p499. 'In the red' refers to the summer coat of the deer.
32 *Fishing Gazette* 22nd February 1913 (J. H. Willey)
33 'Sea Fly-Fishing', *Fishing Gazette* May 31st, 1878, p258.
34 *The Atlantic Salmon*, Wulff (2nd ed. 1983) p66
35 *Fishing Gazette*, March 13th, 1909.
36 *The Book of the Dry Fly*, Dewar (1897) p90
37 *Minor Tactics of the Chalk Stream*, Skues (1910) p126
38 *Minor Tactics of the Chalk Stream*, Skues (1910) p32
39 *Minor Tactics of the Chalk Stream*, Skues (1910) p35
40 *The Way of a Trout with a Fly*, Skues (1921) p40
41 *A Modern Dry-Fly Code*, Marinaro (1950)
42 *Selective Trout*, Swisher and Richards (1971)
43 *Dry Flies, an Improved Method of Tying*, Threadgold (1998)
44 *Nymphs and the Trout*, Frank Sawyer. Stanley Paul (1958)
45 *Streamers and Bucktails*, Bates (1979) p24
46 *Streamers and Bucktails*, Bates (1979) p24

47 Carrie Stevens: A Family History, Hilyard, *The American Fly Fisher*, Vol 26, No. 1, pp6-14.

48 *Where, When and How to Catch Fish on the East Coast of Florida*, 1902

49 *The Field*, June 19th, 1897. Also see pp129-136 of *Salmon and Sea Trout*, Maxwell (1898)

50 *The Fly Fisher & the Trout's Point of View*, Harding (1931) p144

51 If you missed Mr Pendzerkovski, you had better go back to Chapter One.

Index